CW00553438

CROOKED TALK

CROOKED TALK

Five Hundred Years of the Language of Crime

Jonathon Green

BOOKS

Published by Random House Books 2011

2 4 6 8 10 9 7 5 3 1

Copyright © Jonathon Green 2011

Jonathon Green has asserted his right under the Copyright, Designs
and Patents Act, 1988, to be identified as the author of this work

First published in Great Britain in 2011 by
Random House Books
Random House, 20 Vauxhall Bridge Road,
London SW1V 2SA

www.randomhouse.co.uk

Addresses for companies within The Random House Group Limited
can be found at: www.randomhouse.co.uk/offices.htm

The Random House Group Limited Reg. No. 954009

A CIP catalogue record for this book
is available from the British Library

ISBN 9781847946287

The Random House Group Limited supports The Forest Stewardship Council® (FSC®),
the leading international forest certification organisation. All our titles that are printed
on Greenpeace approved FSC® certified paper carry the FSC® logo.
Our paper procurement policy can be found at:
www.randomhouse.co.uk/environment

Text design by Dinah Drazin

Typeset by Palimpsest Book Production Ltd, Falkirk, Stirlingshire

Printed and bound in Great Britain by Clays Ltd, St Ives plc

Contents

INTRODUCTION

Slang is half a millennium old at least. It has been collected for that long. But it has, at least as recorded, one origin: in the beginning was crime. Or more properly cant, the jargon, the 'occupational' slang of the wandering beggars of 16th-century England. It was this jargon which even gave its name to the beggarly brotherhood: 'the canting crew'. Whether, as sometimes suggested, there really was a hardcore Elizabethan underworld, with hierarchies of villain and a secretive, task-specific vocabulary, remains a subject of debate. But the words were collected and they remain, however tiny a role they play today, at the very heart of generations of slang dictionaries.

And criminal language has remained. It has changed of course; the *upright man* or the *dimber-damber* of the 16th century have long gone, but the *top face* and the *don dada* of the 21st fulfil the same roles as the bosses of their world. No-one would recognise *Mort Wapapace* today, but the *flatbacker*, one of her successors in the oldest profession, is simply her modern incarnation.

The essence of all forms of slang is secrecy, the deliberate masking of what one does by the terms in which one discusses it. Alongside such vital tools as *wheels* and *shooters* it is a commodity in which criminals have always invested heavily. It has evolved – one has to keep at least one step ahead of the authorities – but the world it represents – violence, theft, prisons, trials, informers, policemen or prostitution – remains constant. Some words are surprisingly long-lived: *pig* for policeman dates to the 18th century, *cop* to the 19th. And as new areas of crime have appeared, for instance drug dealing, which simply did not exist prior to the early 20th century (since recreational drugs were still legal before the First World War), so has slang embraced them with speed and fluency. In a rough count of slang terms in my own database (some 110,000 in all), the label 'drugs' has been affixed to 4,000 of them. And 'crime', in one shape or form, to around 5,000 more. Prison alone racks up a respectable 1,800.

Today, of course, the vocabulary of crime is much more accessible. Like the rest of slang, it is subject to far wider forms of representation than were its earlier uses. That said, the very secrecy of criminal language has always given it an allure. It is not only the modern tabloid press who like to showcase their knowledge thereof. And a spicing of criminal terms will always give added flavour to a book, a play or to a movie or TV script. The playwright Thomas Dekker knew that in 1600, the sporting journalist Pierce Egan two centuries on, and so, too, do many novelists and script-writers today.

Like the poor, the criminal are always with us, and so is their language. It is perhaps, at least from the lexicographical point of view, the one undeniable upside of what they do. At a risk of dismaying the authorities, let's keep it coming.

Chapter 1

SWINDLERS, CONMEN AND FRAUDS

The thing that hath been, it is that which shall be; and that which is done is that which shall be done: and there is no new thing under the sun.

Ecclesiastes, I: 9

IN THE BEGINNING: 16TH-CENTURY SWINDLES

In 1591 the playwright Robert Greene, whose own raffish life ensured that the information he collected was far from merely theoretical, published *A Notable Discovery of Coosnage*, one of a number of what were known as coney-catching pamphlets, a *coney* being in standard English a rabbit and in cant the gullible target of any of a large variety of swindles, frauds and confidence tricks. Greene set out the primary occupations of late 16th-century criminals thus:

> *High-law* robbing by the highway side; *Sacking-law* lechery; *Cheating law* play at false dice; *Crossbiting law* cozenage by whores; *Cony-catching law* cozenage by cards; *Versing law* cozenage by false gold; *Barnard's law* a drunken cozenage by cards.

We can disregard the first three: *high law* can be found at The Highwayman (in VIOLENT CRIME, page 114), while *sacking law* and *cheating law* simply pertain to prostitution and gambling. Let us consider the remainder, the founding fathers, as it were, of every con trick and rip-off that has followed.

The word crossbite, in existence until the 19th century, is based on standard English's *cross*, i.e. double-cross (thus the 19th-century **crossman**, a swindler), and *bite*, to take advantage of or to deceive. The essence of the trick, indeed the underlying psychology that lies behind every form of confidence game, is the idea of 'the biter bit', i.e. the ensnaring of a gullible victim who thinks that there is nothing untoward going on or indeed very often who thinks that he is getting something for nothing. Of course, the victim of the **crossbiting law** (in cant *law* denotes some form of criminal speciality, a precursor of the similarly defined *game*; in this case, the ancestor of the modern *Murphy game*) had no illusions that payment would be required: he was, after all, hiring a prostitute, but he would not have expected the 'extras' that would be demanded. The basic trick was simple: the customer and prostitute retire to a bedroom, they commence activities, the door bursts open and there is the **crossbiter**, posing as a 'brother' or 'husband', and the threats and demands follow (see Criminal Practices in Brothels, page 218). **Crossbiting** could also refer to cheating by cards or dice (especially when the victim is a cheat himself), while **crossbite** could mean both an act of trickery and a cheat or swindler (as could the **crossbiting cully**).

In a similar way, **coney-catching**, present until the 19th century, could also work as a generic, and even the **coney-catching law** appears to be no more than subjecting a victim to any successful confidence trick. Greene's first pamphlet was called simply *The Art of Conny-Catching* (1591) and a year later, posing shamelessly as 'Cuthbert Conycatcher' and savaging 'this R.G.' for giving away trade secrets, he offered *The Defence of Conny-Catching*. As noted, a **coney** (**cony** or **conny**) was a rabbit in standard English, and various animals, birds and fish have been found to mean 'sucker'. Aside from the unfortunate coney himself, the participants were the **setter** (from the species of hunting dog, who 'sets up' game), the **verser** (from standard English *verse*, to pour out the voice, i.e. his deceiving patter; he would often claim to be a friend of one of the sucker's friends) and the **barnacle** who plays the 'helpful passer-by', keen to help the victim ensnare himself even further (the term is based on the 14th-century standard word *barnacle*, a type of pincer used to restrain recalcitrant horses, and the under-lying image is of 'clinging on'). The money gained was the **purchase**, although it cost the team nothing.

Animals and Birds in Swindling

There have been many avian fools, from the *gull* to the *goose*, in standard English. In the 16th to 18th centuries, a **gull-groper** swindled such a gull, based on either *gull*, a young, unfledged bird, or *gull*, to swallow, in this case a dubious story. Later on, in the 18th and 19th centuries, a **goose shearer** 'sheared' or plucked a foolish *goose*. The late 16th and early 17th centuries saw the **bat-fowler** (from standard English *bat-fowl*, to go fowling at night by dazzling the bird with a light then knocking it down – with a bat) indulge in **bat-fowling**. **Shark** was first recorded before 1600 to mean a conman and is still in use today, e.g. *pool shark*. From this era, the **rook** is another term for swindler that has survived. He took his name from the allegedly larcenous character of the bird; and lent it for use as a verb meaning to swindle as well. It is possible that the racecourse swindler the **blackleg** or **blackshanks** of the late 18th to early 20th centuries was a pun on cant's rook, as this bird does have black legs. Alternate sources offer another pun, on the equally black-legged **game-cock**, or a nod to the black boots such swindlers wore. Blackleg, while used extensively in its day, did not survive the First World War other than, of course, in the context of strike-breaking.

The **versing law**, based on substitution, played on the victim's greed, showing him pieces of counterfeit gold and hinting at ways in which he might benefit his own pocket by procuring them. The **verser**, again, was the one who 'told the tale', while the **cousin**, the victim, plays both on *country cousin* (i.e. gullible) and standard English *cozen*, to cheat. The **suffier** (possibly from Netherlands High German *suff*, drink) posed as a drunk, gullible himself, who is put forward by the verser as someone the cousin can exploit. He is mistaken and goes home poorer; but perhaps wiser too.

In **barnard's law** we encounter our cast of verser and cousin once more, accompanied by the **taker**, who picks up the gullible victim, typically the usual country visitor, and the **barnard** (from standard English *berner*, one who waits with a relay of hounds to intercept a hunted animal), who plays a seemingly foolish drunk, against whom the verser sets the cousin's greed. The scam works through the verser first tricking the cousin with marked cards, then 'generously' offering to teach him the trick, and then suggesting that he in turn trick the drunken barnard. Another loss for the naïve cousin, and if he gets suspicious then the **rutter** (probably from standard English *router*, a robber, a ruffian), who has been lounging by the tavern door, causes some form of disturbance while the rest of the team slip away.

Abraham's Shams

In the late 19th century, **abram** or **abraham work** meant general trickery, while **abram** or **abraham suit** (from standard English *suit*, a petition) meant working as a writer of begging letters, the pursuit of many small-time confidence tricksters of the period. Since such figures invariably pleaded poverty, the use of *abram* or *abraham* can be linked back to the 17th-century cant *abram*, *abram-man* or *abraham-man* (a wandering beggar), and adopting tattered clothing and posing as a madman was an imposture known as *shamming abram*.

The First Scam was a Sham

Sham, now standard English, was cant for a specific trick or hoax from the late 17th century until it joined the mainstream in the 19th century. It was based on the standard words *shame* or *shamed*, and is explained by the lawyer and writer Roger North in *Examen* (1740): 'The word Sham is true Cant of the Newmarket Breed. It is contracted of ashamed. The native Signification is a Town Lady of Diversion, in Country Maid's Cloaths, who to make good her Disguise, pretends to be so sham'd! Thence it became proverbial, when a maimed Lover was laid up, or looked meager, to say he had met with a Sham'. The 18th-century villain could **cut a sham** or **put someone upon the sham**.

THE SWINDLER AT WORK

Swindlers in the 16th and 17th Centuries

Robert Greene's *dramatis personae* were not the only early conmen at large. The **retriever** played the same role as the verser above, actually engaging in the game of chance through which the victim was defrauded. With insouciant xenophobia **Greek**, which already meant both incomprehensible language and any dubious individual, could also mean a sharper or swindler. The victim was roundly mocked in some cant names for swindlers, such as **fool-monger**, one who 'trades in' the credulity of fools, **fool-taker**, a dice- or card-sharp and thus **fool-taking**, the swindling of fellow-gamblers, and **fool trap**, a term which in the 19th century was also used to mean the vagina or the high-class prostitute for whom it was her stock-in-trade. The word **foy** was an abbreviation of **foist**, a card-sharp or cheat, while **shifter** and the later (19th-century) **shifting cove** came from standard English *shift*, to employ underhand methods, and beyond that *shift*, an expedient, a means to an end. The **shark-shift** doubled up on the villainy, combining with the term **shark** for a conman. The **fater** lasted until the early 19th century and came from the French *faiteur*, a maker; he was placed in 'the Second (old) Rank of the Canting Crew' by the lexicographer known only as B.E. (Gent.[leman]) in his *New Dictionary of the Canting Crew* (*c.*1698); as well as a cheat or impostor he might be a fraudulent fortune-teller.

Other Animal and Bird Suckers

calf   16th century to present day
calf-lolly   17th century
codshead   16th to 19th centuries
coney   late 16th to 19th centuries
gudgeon   late 18th century
jay   19th century to present day, America
monkey   1920s, America
pigeon   16th century to present day
woodcock   16th to 18th centuries

Swindlers in the 18th Century

Bilk, at least as a verb, remains current, although it is now standard English. It comes from the jargon of cribbage, and is linked to the standard word *balk*, to hinder. At first, in the late 17th century, bilk was a name for the trick; a century later it became a term for the trickster himself and the **bilker** was one who habitually cheats, especially in refusing to pay a bill such as a cabman's fare. The **bilking house** or **bilking crib** in early 20th-century America and Australia was a brothel where clients were robbed, while back in England, to *bilk the schoolmaster* was to gain knowledge without paying for it, i.e. the experience that supposedly comes with just living one's life.

The **duffer** is another survivor, but only in Australia's **cattle-duffer**, a cattle-thief. He was first noted in England in 1747 as a salesman of smuggled goods. His 'shop' was most likely found in a yard near St Clement's Church in the Strand and his stock was actually cheap, mass-produced items, sold at a substantial mark-up, and he exploited that common target, the provincial who was up in London. *Bluffer* too lives on as a consummate liar, but as a swindler in the late 18th century it was short-lived. Present from at least 1709 as a term for a swindler, *operator* remains among the survivors, although again with slightly different meanings – a ruthless manipulator and a major criminal. A *crimp* meant a swindler from the mid-18th century until well into the 20th century, but it was a more general extension of the late 17th century's *play crimp*, to effect betting swindles on the turf. The origins for this are vague: the *Oxford English Dictionary* mentions an early, generally negative use 'of doubtful meaning'; the *crimps* who pressed unwilling unfortunates into the Royal Navy came later.

In 1785 Francis Grose defined a *mace* as 'a rogue assuming the character of a gentleman, or opulent tradesman, who under that appearance defrauds workmen, by borrowing a watch, or other piece of goods till one [that] he bespeaks is done [i.e. swindled].' Known equally as a *mace-cove* or *macing cove*, *mace-gloak*, *macer* or *maceman*, his gentlemanly pose and his plausible 'line' set him among crime's elite groups. The word is rooted in the older early 18th-century phrase *on the mace*, living as a swindler, and later (in the 19th century) living on credit (though this perhaps was no more than a euphemism). Therefore, *strike the mace* meant to persuade a shopkeeper to sell one goods on credit, although one has no intention of ever making that credit good; it could also apply when the target was a friend. To mace was to swindle, thus to *mace the rattler* from the late 19th century into the 20th meant to travel by train without buying a ticket. Ultimately, the etymology for mace remains unproven, but there may be a link to the mid-18th-century *mason*, one who procures goods on credit with no intention of paying for them. Far more obvious was the contemporary and still-current *sharp*, a shortening of cant's earlier *sharper* and based on the standard English verb *sharp*.

Swindlers in the Victorian Era

In the 19th century confidence trickery joined the party (at least linguistically as many tricks were the same swindles of old), and the modern cheating vocabulary, some of it effectively standard English today, began to expand.

Fiddle, Diddle and Chisel

Fiddle began as a standard term meaning to swindle; it was based on the implication that the **fiddler**, who in turn had begun life as no more than a ne'er-do-well in the 1770s and would not become a fully fledged conman for 80 years, could make people 'dance to his tune'. **Fiddle** meant swindler or card-sharp, as well as the swindle itself, a sense that is still in use today. The fraudster was **on/at the fiddle** from the 1910s onwards, while fiddling has come to mean many things in the 20th century, including begging, cheating one's expenses and, in the 1960s, working as a petty thief.

The **diddler** (from a figurative use of standard English *diddle*, to jerk from side to side, to quiver) sounds like a fiddler, but its synonyms – **Jeremy Diddler**, **Jerry My Diddler** – betray its origins: the cheating 'Jeremy Diddler', a character in James Kenney's farce *Raising the Wind* (1803). The word has lasted, nonetheless, as has **diddle**, which means both a swindle and (more commonly) to swindle. (To **raise the wind** was slang for obtaining a loan.)

Chisel began life as a verb and while its roots remain obscure, its first appearance was in a Scottish lexicon of 1808, there spelt *chizzel*. The *Oxford English Dictionary* places it alongside the tool and thus implies some kinship based on 'cutting away'. The **chisel** started life as the swindler in the mid-19th century and became the swindle itself from the 1930s onwards. Despite these British origins, **chiseler** for a swindler developed in America in the 1910s, although its usage spread abroad, while being **on the chisel**, meaning cheating, only featured in the United States in the 1950s. A swindler was also a **chizzer** or **chiz** in England in the mid-20th century, and the latter also worked as a verb and a noun, as most notably expressed by the peerless Nigel Molesworth in Geoffrey Willans's *Down with Skool!*: 'A chiz is a swiz or swindle as any fule kno'.

Gouge, Spiel, Bunco and Others

The standard word *gouger* denotes one who gouges out another's eye in a fight; to *gouge*, still standard English, is to cheat, and 19th-century American cant used **gouge** or **gouge game** for a swindle or confidence trick; the **gouger** is the swindler.

Another term coined in the mid-19th century (originally in America) and still popular today is **gyp** (**gip** or **jip**). It was and remains quite consciously derogatory, since it comes from *gypsy* and, as such, is an ethnic slur. Its initial incarnation was as a thief, but the image of trickery ran parallel. As well as the conman it has also meant the con trick, and often describes someone who has reneged on their debts. The 20th century has seen a number of compounds: **gyp joint**, anywhere, especially a club or bar, where the unwary will be swindled; **gyp artist**, a swindler, and his female partner the **gyp moll**; **gyp racket** is the world of swindling, while **get the gyp** means to be swindled. The **gypper** or **gipper** was used in America from the 1920s onwards to mean a swindler.

Playing Games

It was invariably fixed, and there was never the slightest doubt as to the winner, nevertheless the most common term for confidence trickery was **game**. It was something that the swindler had to **play**, while the conman also **played** [the victim] **for a sucker** or **dummy** or some other form of dupe. The performance of a major con, which involved long preparation and an authentic (if elaborately faked) 'backdrop' was also known as a **play**. Particular games were devised, such as the **drop game** (see page 22).

The term **mag**, referring to confidence trickery, was linked to slang's *mug*, the mouth or face, and the mag referred to the verbal side of swindling. Thus to **chuck a mag** was to work as a confidence trickster, while to ***tip the mag*** meant to talk duplicitously and fool a gullible victim. The word also provided the occupation of being ***on the mag***, and the verb *mag*, to cheat, especially through insincere talk.

Based on the German *spielen*, to play, cant's initial use of ***spiel*** meant to gamble in the mid-19th century. Thereafter spiel meant to talk, to patter and thence to shoot a line. The ***spieler***, still in existence today, could mean a swindler, a fraud, a card-sharp or a crooked gambler, as well as the place where one went to play. Swindling was ***speelering*** or more commonly ***spieling***, also used for gambling or card-sharping. Like a number of German/Yiddish words, e.g. *shicker*, drunk, it has been picked up in Australia, where one also finds the backslang ***eelerspee*** and its extension ***eeler-spieler*** in the 20th century.

Backslang

Backslang was a costermongers' creation of the 1830s, and used widely in London markets. The vocabulary ran to around 130 terms. Although it could be adapted to any word, e.g. *nammow*, a woman, or *esclop*, a policeman, it was especially found for sums of money, e.g. *yenep*, a penny, *flatch*, a halfpenny and *yennork*, a crown (five shillings or 25 pence).

If the spieler tends to stay to the east of the Atlantic, the world of ***bunco*** or ***bunko*** lives strictly to its west, from its late 19th-century origins to the present day. The term, based on Spanish *banca*, a card-game similar to monte, referred both to the swindler and the swindle, specifically a dishonest 'game of chance'. It could also be used as a verb. In more general terms, it has expanded beyond crime in the 20th century to mean any form of deceit, flattery or empty nonsense. Among its compounds are ***bunco artist*** or ***bunko boy***, a confidence trickster, and ***bunco game*** or ***bunk game***, a generic for swindling and confidence trickery but also specifically a 'fixed' gambling game.

The conman can also be a **bunco man**, **banco man** or **bunk man**.

These terms have become common, but the crime journalist Herbert Asbury noted in *The Gangs of Chicago* (1940) that 'the true bunko man specialised in playing banco, sometimes called bunko, which was an adaptation of the old English game of eight-dice cloth', while the conman ran any old swindle. Members of the **bunco squad** or **bunko people** form a special police squad devoted to combating confidence tricksters, while the **bunco steerer** is that member of the gang whose task is to entrap or 'steer' the victim into the current.

The Faker, Lumberer, File and Others
On the whole the conman's names are as random as the disguises he might choose to adopt. In the late 19th and 20th centuries, the **faker** and **fakir** were indeed far from 'genuine' but both were based on cant *fake*, to make, even if the second is surely underpinned by the counterfeit oriental gurus (standard English *fakir*, from Arabic *faqīr*, a 'poor man') who populated carnivals and medicine shows in the States.

Lumber and Its Uses

Outside the world of confidence trickery, but still within the criminal underworld, **lumber** had many uses. As a noun in the mid-18th century it could mean stolen goods or a place to store them, indeed anywhere frequented by villains in the late 18th to mid-19th centuries. In the 18th and mid-19th centuries, such a place was also known as a **lumber house** or **lumber ken** and its landlord was the **lumber cove**. In the 1930s to 1980s, however, a **lumber gaff** was the flat from which a prostitute worked.

Other *lumberers* have included a prostitute or pimp who specialised in robbing her/his clients, and an Australian traffic cop in the 1960s.

The **lumberer** began his career in the mid-19th century as a pawnbroker and graduated in the late 19th-century to a swindling tipster and thence to any form of swindler. The term was based on cant's **lumber**, which meant to 'chat up' a stranger, especially with the intention of robbing them, in the mid-19th and 20th centuries. Lumber offered a number of underworld uses but all came from the 17th-century standard term *Lombard*, a bank, a money-changer's or money-lender's office, or a pawnshop (itself derived from the Lombards, or natives of Lombardy, who were celebrated medieval bankers).

The *file* (also ***old file upon the town***) was an experienced fraudster or confidence trickster in the early 19th century (for its etymology see Pickpockets, page 54). At the same time, the **snide** or **snyde** meant a generally fake or deceptive person, as well as a confidence trickster. It has been linked to two German words: *aufschneiden*, to boast, to brag, to show off, and *schneide*, to cut, e.g. counterfeit coins. The **beat** 'beat' the rules of society from the mid-19th century, as did the **beater** in the 1930s onwards as both a swindler and one who refuses to pay their debts, although the latter at least might have been linked to slang's less positive **deadbeat**, another who reneges on their debts.

Descendants of the taker from the 16th-century barnard's law included the **take-in** from the late 18th, 19th and early 20th centuries, and the **take-down** from the late 19th century onwards (mainly in Australia). Both could mean the swindle and the swindler. Australia also saw **lurkman** from the mid-19th century onwards, meaning a general confidence trickster who pursued various lurks or crimes. Australia and the United States used the **nipper** (from *nip*, to steal) at the turn of the 19th/20th centuries.

Modern Swindlers

Perhaps the most substantial of the 20th century's usages – which on the whole are again quite random – are cant's variations on the standard word *wide*. It has been in figurative use since the 16th century, meaning going astray, deviating from the proper course (of life or of action) and as such an abbreviation of the standard phrase *wide of the mark.* By the mid-19th century **wide** had been recruited into slang to mean 'sharp' and immoral and the image was now less that of missing some moral mark but of being 'wide-awake' to life's opportunities, legal or more likely otherwise. The synonymous **wide-o** or **wide-oh** appeared in the 1920s. *Half-wide* meant reasonably intelligent, aware of what goes on – and thus, in certain contexts, corruptible – from the 19th century onwards, while **wideness** from the late 19th century was a synonym for perspicacity or intelligence and later (2000s) for audacity. The ultimate example, however, is **wide-boy**, a coinage from the 1930s describing a type whose philosophy was summed up in the title of British novelist Robert Westerby's *Wide Boys Never Work* (1937). His peers the **wide man**, **wide chump** and **wide con** were more short-lived, appearing first as a swindler and then briefly as a professional thief in the 1950s. To **come wide** meant to get the better of, to **put someone wide** was to inform, to 'put in the picture', and those who epitomised wideness in their cunning were **as wide as . . .** whatever was the best-known local thoroughfare, e.g. Regent Street or Broadway.

Another conman celebrated in a book title is the **grifter**, any variety of non-violent criminal living primarily on his or her wits in America in the 1910s to the present. The book in question is Jim Thompson's *The Grifters* (1963). **Grift**, any crime that depends not upon violence or coercion but on 'lightness of touch and quickness of wit' (David Maurer, *The Big Con*, 1940), is a variation of **graft**, which in standard English means hard work but in slang refers to corruption, especially in the context of a politician or policeman. The **grafter** is another a swindler, often working within a fair, carnival or mock-auction, and he first appeared in the late 19th century. **Scam** appeared in the 1940s, from the standard word *scheme*, and is one of those slang words that are so much in use nowadays that they have become colloquial at the very least, if not completely standard English. Its derivatives for a swindler, however, remain slang: **scamster**, **scam artist** and **scamhead**.

A number of 20th-century terms are based quite simply on the image of 'who does whom'. Thus in America there was the **cleaner** in the 1920s, from *clean out*, to render impoverished, and the **clipper** in the 1940s–1960s, from *clip*, to steal; while in Britain in the 1930s

Regional Variety: the World of Australian Swindlers

Australian swindlers
carl rosa   1960s to present (rhyming slang for a poser, thus a fraudster; ultimately from the popular Carl Rosa Operatic Society, founded in London in 1875)
rorter/wroughter   1920s to present (either from the Yiddish *rorität*, anything, or from rhyming slang *rorty* = naughty)
sooner   1930s (someone who would 'sooner [i.e. "soon as"] do one thing as another', in this case work honestly)
strong man   1930s to present (someone who 'pushes through' or 'breaks down' one's resistance)

Australian swindles
lash   1920s to present (originally meant violence)
ready/ready-up   1900s to present (also as a verb, all based on the idea of readying or preparing the victim)
roughie   1930s to present (usually in the phrase **put a roughie over**, from *rough deal* or *rough luck*)
twine   1960s (from the verb *twine*, to pass counterfeit coins)

Australian verbs meaning to swindle
balance   1910s–50s
on the never   late 19th century (working a con trick in which the victim will 'never' get his money)
pull someone's leg   1920s (a more villainous use of the usual meaning, to tease)
slip up   late 19th century to 1900s
touch   late 19th century (often as **touch for**, elsewhere found in the context of a loan)

was the **reamer**, from standard's *ream*, to stretch, to tear in pieces, and the **swizzler**, still in use today and from standard English *swindle*. The power of a good 'line' is evoked in the **salesman** (from America in the 1920s), the **soft song man** (America and South Africa in the 1920s–1960s) and the **slick** (1940s to the present day in Britain), from the standard word *slick*, smooth, plausible, glib. **Shuckman** featured in the 1960s, and it derived from standard English *shuck*, a husk, and thus, figuratively, nonsense. Its most common derivatives are primarily American: **put the shuck on** has meant to trick or to fool verbally from the 1970s onwards, while **drop shuck** meant to take advantage of a victim or fool in the 1940s. Perhaps the best-known use is the mostly black-American phrase **shuck and jive** (elided as **shive**), meaning to act deceptively, to confuse.

SPECIALISTS AND THEIR CONS

Confidence tricksters often opted for a single speciality: the idea presumably being that practice made perfect.

Gold, Silver and Hard Cash

The Trimmer
In the late 16th and 17th centuries, the **trimmer** worked a substitution scam, whereby relatively worthless silver, known as **white wool** (*white* being a cant generic for silver, while *red* was used for gold), was substituted in place of proffered gold. The gold pieces used to entrap the victim were known as **Jason's fleece**, playing on the Greek myth in which Jason stole the Golden Fleece and on the standard verb *fleece*, to strip someone of their money or possessions.

The Gold Brick Game
The 19th century saw the **gold brick game**, and thus the verb **gold-brick**, to swindle (and slang's *goldbrick*, an idler). It was originated in 1880 by Reed C. Waddell (*c.*1860–95), a high-stakes gambler whose funds were running low. A Waddell 'gold brick', the first one of which he sold for $4,000, was in fact a triple-gold-plated lump

of lead, with 'official' markings chiselled into its surface and a small chunk of real gold embedded in it – which could be removed and taken to an assayer's office if the victim required reassurance. Waddell never sold a brick for less than $3,500 and made an estimated quarter of a million dollars from the scam in five years.

Hard Cash

The lob, buzzer and burner all pursued hard cash. In the 18th century, the **lob** referenced the standard term *lob*, a country bumpkin: the conman posed as such and used his apparent stupidity to fool shopkeepers by asking for change for a high-value coin and then switching coins to make a profit. In the 19th century, the **buzzer** used sleight of hand and some hidden wax to fool a shopkeeper into parting with a gold sovereign. The American **burner** had a less than subtle technique: a story was told – sometimes no more complex than asking for some change for a banknote – that resulted in the production of the victim's wallet; the burner then snatched it and ran off.

Paper Money

It may or may not be a testimony to the increased literacy of the 19th century that confidence tricks involving writing were on the increase. A certain amount of patter might be involved, but the basis of cheque fraud, the manipulation of bank accounts and various other paper-based schemes required, if nothing else, the ability to sign one's name. (For specific terms for counterfeit money and forgery rackets, see Forgery and Counterfeiting, page 41.)

Passing Paper

Paper has meant any form of money order, IOU, promissory note or financial document other than actual cash since the 1770s and money itself, usually notes, from a decade later. It was first used to mean specifically counterfeit notes in mid-19th century London, and America's 20th-century **paper pusher** passed them. Most terms are found in the 20th century, including **bad paper, bad dough** or **hot paper** for any form of fraudulent document, counterfeit money or similar written or printed frauds. In America, to **hang paper** is to pass bad cheques, money orders or fake notes, and gives the **paper hanger** or **paper layer**, one who habitually passes over such imposters. However, Edwin Sutherland claims in *The Professional Thief* (1937) that these were terms used only by amateurs, never by professional thieves. Either way they, and the synonymous verbs **lay paper**, **sling paper**, **pass paper** and **burn paper**, remain popular, as does **paper-hanging**, passing bad cheques. Other American 20th-century uses of this form of paper include **bouncing paper**, bad cheques (playing on the mainstream slang *bounce a cheque*), and **orphan paper**, counterfeit money. To be **bad-papered** means to get an IOU that will not be paid by the debtor.

From Cheques to Credit Cards
The first use of the term kite, taken from the toy and ultimately from the bird, is in the phrase to **fly a kite** or **fly the kite**, which from 1805 meant to obtain credit against bills, whether or not the 'paper' is valid or fraudulent and whether or not an account exists in the banks on which the drawing is made. **Kite** meant a promissory note and slightly later a cheque, while as to pass a bad cheque it is recorded from *c*.1840. The image in all uses is 'something that flies away'. The activity was **kite-flying**, the fraudster a **kite-flyer**. The 20th-century uses tend to focus on cheques, whether forged, stolen or unbacked and otherwise known as **dodgy kites**. The fraudulent cheque specialist was the **kiter**, **kite-man** or **kite-merchant** (1920s to present) and when such 'merchants' combined into a gang in the 1930s and 1940s they became a **kite-mob**, descending on a variety of banks and brandishing newly stolen cheque-books. **Kite-fishing** in the early 20th century was stealing mail containing bank cheques from homes and offices.

The bad cheque, fraudulent monetary draft or counterfeit banknote was not invariably a kite; by 1890 it was a **stumer**, a word that while rejoicing in a variety of spellings (from *shtoomer* to *stewmer*) has no hard-and-fast origin. It may come from Yiddish *shtoom*, silent (about the cheque's invalidity), or the northeast dialect *stumor*, a 'difficult person to handle'. In America, more recent terms have been the *stiff* in the 1950s, ultimately from slang *stiff*, a corpse, thus the cheque is 'dead'; the *map* in the 1920s to 1960s; and the *Jew cheque*, from the 1980s onwards, which – in unremitting anti-Semitic stereotyping – refers to any form of cheque that is obtained through fraud, e.g. on Social Security.

Also in America, a *note shaver* was a promoter of bogus financial companies, while a *note layer* was a short-change swindler in the 1940s (the laying down and picking up of notes was designed to confuse the shopkeeper). In the 16th and 17th centuries a specific scam was *ferreting*, a trick that involved the offering of spurious credit and the subsequent profitable dunning of the victim who has taken it. It comes from slang's *ferret*, a tradesman who entices the young and naïve to spend money on credit, then promptly duns them for his bill. Bringing it right up to date, the 21st-century *cracker* also uses credit to his advantage: his speciality is employing fake or stolen credit cards for bogus online purchases, while to *work on the plastic* (current from the 1970s) is to use stolen credit cards for a variety of frauds and swindles.

Counterfeit Notes
In the 19th century the *boodler* appeared in Australia and America, specialising in passing counterfeit notes; the name comes from *boodle,* which first meant a crowd of people, similar to *caboodle,* and went on to mean counterfeit money and thereafter money that has been acquired illegally or through corruption. Its source is either the Dutch *boedel*, household effects, and thus one's personal estate, or Scots *bodle*, a small coin worth two Scottish pence – originally worth one-sixth of an English one and as such deemed worthless. To this day, a boodle also refers to a wad of money used in an elaborate confidence trick: packaged like a bundle of bank-wrapped notes, it actually comprised a large note on top and bottom, and $1 bills in the middle. Many similar concoctions existed (see box), often replacing the lump of low-denomination bills with counterfeit bills or even paper.

Fake American Bankrolls

boodle	Michigan roll
California bankroll	Minnesota bankroll
Chicago bankroll	Missouri bankroll
Kansas City roll	mitch
Michigan	Texas roll
Michigan bankroll	

Counterfeit money also lay at the base of the American **green goods game** (or **racket, swindle, business**), common in the late 19th to mid-20th centuries, in which the goods were green dollar bills, albeit fake ones. The con epitomised the utility of playing on human greed: the sucker would be convinced (and rarely needed much convincing) that it was possible to buy 'real' money, vastly below par, which had allegedly been printed off a plate stolen from the government mint. At the peak of the scam the country was overrun with flyers offering the chance to make such purchases and the suckers queued up to cash in. They might be shown some actual greenbacks by an itinerant **green goods man** but at the crucial moment these were substituted for fakes; alternatively they simply sent in their payment, and received duds in return. And who would report their own highly illicit attempt to buy counterfeit dollars?

A similar sleight of hand was involved in **the wipe**, recorded in America in the first half of the 20th century. It was based on persuading the victim that money, which is first secreted in a hand-kerchief (known as a *wipe*), can by some 'magic' be raised to higher denomination. (Similar swindles in 1940s America include **the ducats**, which used marked cards (*ducats*); and **the rocks**, using fake diamonds.)

Dropping Things

Of the longest-lived con trick was that which in the mid-19th century was generalised as the **drop game**. Schele de Vere set it out in *Americanisms* (1872): 'A man walking before [the victim, usually an out-of-towner in the big city], pretends to find a well-filled pocket-book, and either offers it to him, minus a certain sum for immediate need, for advertising, with the expectation of a liberal reward, or, with more cynicism, downright suggests a division of spoils. In either case his greed is justly punished by finding himself the owner of a roll of counterfeit bills, and out of pocket for the sum of good money.' It was just the latest version of an old trick, the earliest examples of which were known as **gold-dropping** in the 17th century, as performed by the **gold-dropper**, **money-dropper** or simply the **dropper**. He would drop something supposedly valuable in the path of a potential victim, who is either lured into a game of supposed chance, where the victim is introduced to some of the sharper's friends, who propose a game of cards or dice, or alternatively persuaded to buy the 'valuable', with the conman claiming that although they should, by rights, share the profits, he will sell his share and let the victim have the whole benefit. A later development in the late 18th and 19th centuries was known as **ring dropping**, which used counterfeit 'gold' rings; the conman was the **ring-dropper** or **ring faller**. The technique is still widely used.

In the late 18th to 19th centuries, *fawney* (*fawny* or *forney*) meant a ring (from the Irish *fáin(n)e*, a ring), and the **fawney-rig** (also *fawney-drop*, *fawney-dropping* or *fawney-rigging*) was just another name for ring-dropping. The trick was practised by the **fawney-dropper** and was also known as **fawney-bouncing** (from slang's *bounce*, to lie), in which variation the justification for the sale is a supposed wager, which the seller can win only by selling the ring to the victim. To **flash a fawney** was to wear a counterfeit ring and to **go upon the fawney** was to perform any form of fraud involving bogus jewellery. In America, into the 20th century, the *fawney-man* dispensed with the 'tale' and simply sold bogus jewellery, often from a *fawney-shop*, where fake or cheap jewellery was sold. With all that in mind, slang lexicographer Eric Partridge suggested, and the *Oxford*

English Dictionary seems to agree, that the word *phoney*, hitherto etymologically debatable, was a direct descendant of fawney.

Perhaps the most bizarre version of the old faithful was **glim-dropping** – from *glim*, an eye – popular in the 1940s and 1950s in America. The trickster allegedly drops an artificial eye in a shop. He offers a reward if it is found. The merchant cannot do so, but a second conman arrives, and 'fortuitously' finds the missing *peeper*. He then says he will claim the reward, at which point the merchant, loath to miss a chance of cashing in, buys it from him so he can claim the reward himself. There is no reward.

Selling Things

The **jack in the box** was a confidence trickster doubling as a street pedlar in the late 17th and early 18th centuries, the trick figuratively 'popping up' from his box of goods just like the toy. Posing as an 'honest' pedlar also underpins the mush-faker and the spunk-faker. The **mush-faker** (or **mush-fakir, mush-rigger, mushroom-faker** and **mush toper feeker**) of the 19th and early 20th centuries advertised himself as a mender or seller of umbrellas, from slang's *mush*, an umbrella (based on its 'mushroom' shape), plus either: *fake*, to make (ultimately from Latin *facio*); *rig*, to fool; or Romany *tober*, the road. The respectable job was a cover for more fraudulent pursuits. In America in the 1940s, the **mush** was itself a form of con game, as played at a baseball park and presumably only working on a rainy day. In it, the trickster poses as a bookmaker, takes bets then raises an umbrella and vanishes as fast as possible among all the other raised umbrellas. America's 19th-century **spunk-faker** supposedly sold matches (*spunks*) but, once more, an outwardly respectable if impoverished profession was likely to be hiding less reputable, and usually fraudulent, pursuits.

In the UK, in the mid-19th century to the present day, the **knocker game**, otherwise known as working **on the knocker** or **on the knock**, involved touring houses, ostensibly to buy or sell goods, but specifically to trick or bully people into selling heirlooms, antiques and the like for minimal prices. Such operators would also peddle **knocker gear**, low-value goods that are used as a pretext for gaining an introduction to a householder, who will then be defrauded.

The mock auction, whereby the naïve are geed up by implausibly generous 'free gifts' and then encouraged to put up disproportionate amounts of money for virtually worthless goods, is to be seen in many modern marketplaces. Such auctions were held in the 19th century by the **touzery** or **towzery gang**, possibly rooted in standard English *touse*, to pull about or abuse. In America the scam was known as **Peter Funkism**, and **Peter Funk** (or **Peter Funker**) was defined by the lexicographer Schele de Vere in his *Americanisms* (1872) as 'the person who aids in getting up so-called mock auctions, sales held for the sole benefit of inexperienced countrymen, at which more or less worthless articles, imitation jewelry, watches of gilt copper and the like, are offered; where unwary purchasers are forced to take a large quantity while they only bid for a very small portion.' Peter Funk did not of course exist, his was simply a generic German/Dutch proper name and as such seen as implying greater trustworthiness than those of the more recent immigrants such as the Jews, Italians and middle-European *Bohunks*.

Spinning a Yarn

To *gag* was slang for talk and the **gagger** told convincing 'sob-stories', or even posed as a deaf-mute, in the late 18th and early 19th centuries. **Gagging** involved persuading a stranger that one was an old, if forgotten friend – and asking for a loan. A **low gagger** told fraudulent tales of supposed suffering at sea, typically at the hands of the pirates of the Barbary Coast. Such techniques were hardly new: among the 16th century's mendicant villains were a number of supposed sufferers. These included the **dommerar**, who feigned dumbness, claiming to have been a victim of the un-Christian Turk who, on capturing him during a sea voyage, had torn out his tongue for denying Mohammed. The **counterfeit crank**, who faked sickness, especially epilepsy, was backed up by convincingly horrific sores and wounds that had been created by the application of various herbs. His 19th-century descendant was the **scaldrum dodge**, deliberately burning the body with a mixture of acids and gunpowder in order to simulate scars and wounds intended to soften hearts.

Swindles, Tricks and Fraud: a Selection

Archbishop Laud   1950s–60s (= fraud; based on William
 Laud (1573–1645), Archbishop of Canterbury. However,
 the term only appears in Robin Cook's *The Crust on its
 Uppers* (1962) and may be a nonce-use, i.e. a one-off
 use)
bunk   1900s (a fraudulent scheme, derived from original
 use for nonsense)
canoevre   early 19th century (perhaps linked to standard
 English *manoeuvre*)
cobweb rig   late 18th to early 19th centuries (a
 particularly well-wrought and complex scam)
fetch   mid-16th to early 19th centuries (from standard
 English *fetching* or conjuring up a tale)
f.p.   20th century to present (stands for false pretences,
 thus fraud)
lark rig   late 18th century (presumably performed in the
 guise of a 'bit of a lark', i.e. horseplay)
old moody   1930s to present (also **moody** meaning
 illegal or illicit; rhyming slang based on *Moody
 and Sankey* = hankypanky, or trickery; ultimately
 from Dwight Lyman Moody (1837–99) and Ivo
 David Sankey (1840–1908), a pair of American
 evangelists)
plant   late 18th century to present (wherein the villain
 plants false information)
the queer   mid-18th to mid-19th centuries (a noun use
 from cant's all-purpose negative adjective)
rip-off   1970s to present (much beloved of the hippies
 and now at least colloquial if not standard)

The 17th century's **feager** or **feaker of loges**, literally a 'maker of words' (from slang's *fake*, to make or do, plus Greek *logos*, a word), was a beggar who backed up his fraudulent tales with purpose-written fake documents. The **dudder** or **dudsman** of the 18th and early 19th centuries was another criminal beggar, often dressed in the typically nautical *duds*, i.e. clothes, who wandered the country selling goods that they claimed fraudulently had been smuggled.

Anything for a few pence: the **nuxyelper** of the mid-19th century faked a fit in order to gain money from bystanders; the word combined the medical Latin *nux vomica*, the vomit-inducing fruit from which strychnine is produced, and standard English's *yelp*. The **queer plunger** of the late 18th and early 19th centuries threw himself into a river and was promptly 'rescued' by a gang of associates; they would then pursue the authorities, claiming a reward for their 'act of kindness'. Appearing from the 1900s onwards, the **flopper** pretended to have slipped on a shop floor or been knocked down by a slow-moving automobile; they then claimed damages, usually offering to take a quick cash payment rather than go to an insurance company; thus the **flop game** or **flop racket** meant performing such frauds. In America it also meant a beggar who pretends to be crippled, from the 1910s onwards. In the late 18th to early 19th centuries, the **carrier-pigeon** focused his fraudulent intentions on lottery office-keepers, while the **mosker** targeted pawnbrokers in the late 19th to mid-20th centuries. Mosker comes from *moskeneer*, to pawn, based on Hebrew *mashkon*, a pledge, whence *mishken*, to pawn.

Long Cons

To **wire** had meant to swindle from about 1850, but in the late 19th and first half of the 20th centuries the swindle known as **the wire** and the operations of America's **wire-tapper** epitomised the type of confidence trick known as the **big store**, described by the American expert in criminal vocabulary David Maurer in 1940 as:

an establishment against which big-con men play their victims. For the wire and the pay-off [both based on horse race betting], it is set up like a poolroom which takes race bets. For the rag [based on share dealing], it is set up to resemble a broker's office. Stores are set up with a careful attention to detail which makes them seem bona fide. After each play, the store is taken down and all equipment stored away.

Such a **long con** can take months of planning and engages a number of people in its working. For example, in the wire the swindler convinces a victim that he can intercept the wire that brings racecourse results to betting shops and by briefly postponing the passing on of the information on a race can make it possible to lay down sure-fire bets – since one actually knows the result – and thus cheat the bookmakers. As illustrated in the movie *The Sting* (1973) – which took Maurer's book *The Big Con* as its guide – this entails the creation of an authentic backdrop (known as the **frame**; to 'build the set' was to **frame the gaff**), the employment of a cast of extras, some faked-up technological wizardry and anything else necessary to convince the sucker that the establishment is a genuine one.

The Sting

In the 20th century and beyond, a **sting** is any form of robbery, but particularly a complex fraud planned well in advance. It was based on the verb sting which meant to cheat from the early 19th century. To **put the sting on** appeared in America in the 1940s and is still in use, meaning to cheat, to swindle, to defraud. Briefly in the early 20th century in America, the **stingaree** was a swindle based on short-changing a cashier. The term also gives the punning 20th-century American phrase **put the bee/B on**, to swindle, to hoax, to victimise; the bee has a 'sting', although 'b' is also the initial letter of **bite**, which has meant to cheat or deceive since the 1580s.

Bookmakers and Lawyers

The world of bookmaking created its own subset of terms. Honest
or not, the profession traditionally lacks the best of images, and the
word *shicer* (also *shiser*, *shyser* etc.) had also meant a prostitute, a
criminal, an idler and a defaulter on debts before it came to mean
a dishonest bookie in the early 20th century. Its origins are most
likely an extended use of the German *Scheisse*, shit, but as the overlap
of spellings suggest it may also come from slang's *shyster* (also *shice*,
shise or *shuyster*), a dishonest lawyer. This too has been linked to
German, in this case *Scheisser*, shitter, although less distasteful (but
perhaps less pertinent) is an alternative: the Dutch *scheidsman* or
schiedsreichter, an arbitrator. Whatever the origin, both bookies and
lawyers lack respect. As the *New York Herald* explained on 6 August
1874 the city's courts:

> are steadily haunted by a host of vultures, who are known as 'shysters'
> but who profess to be called lawyers. With a few honorable excep-
> tions these men are entirely without education or decency, and many
> of them cannot tell a volume of Parker's Criminal Law from a Greek
> Testament.

It was one of these whose name suggests yet another alternative
etymology: one Scheuster (pronounced 'shyster'), whose courtroom
antics so infuriated Justice Osborne of the city's Essex Market Court
that he began talking of 'scheuster' practices.

THE ACT OF SWINDLING

Swindling has been so widespread that it has spawned a rich vocabulary of words that ultimately simply mean 'to swindle'. What follows
are the key words, some of which have gone through subtle shifts
of meaning over time.

16th- and 17th-century Swindling Words

Cog, among the most widely used of 16th-century terms for deception, is frustrating. At least as regards etymology: the *Oxford English Dictionary* makes no comment as to its origin, does not label it as slang or even colloquial but admits to it being a 'ruffian's term'. As such, and in its uses, many of which exist until the 19th century, it must have been cant. It began as a term for cheating at dice, meaning to use any form of illicit sleight of hand, specifically to make a surreptitious change of a crooked dice for a legitimate one (or vice versa) during a game. Further senses followed as the 16th century proceeded: to palm off fraudulently, to put out or distribute falsely; to deceive or to cheat out of; thus one might *cog a dinner*, to cheat someone out of a dinner and thence in the 17th century onwards, to cheat at cards, or in any other manner. A final 17th- and 18th-century sense was to flatter, to wheedle and to wheedle someone out of (something). In all senses, the parallel noun implying the act was *cogging*. A *cog-foist* was a cheat and to *cog forth* was to control the fall of dice by sleight of hand.

To *nick* also began in the world of gambling in the mid-16th century, meaning to win at dice or cards, usually by cheating; by the late 17th century it had gained the sense of swindling. Its origins were in Romany and were underpinned by the standard verb *nick*, to catch, to seize, to take advantage of an opportunity; itself a figurative use of standard *nick*, to mark, i.e. for oneself. *Prig* (perhaps linked figuratively to standard English *prick*, to skewer) initially meant to steal, evolving into a synonym for confidence trickery in the mid-18th century. *Skelder*, a distorted pronunciation of the Dutch *skellum*, a rogue or a pestilence, meant, in the late 16th and 17th centuries, to work as a professional beggar, especially when posing as a wounded or discharged soldier, and concurrently and into the 18th century, to swindle or defraud; thus *skeldering*, begging or swindling.

From the 17th century onwards, *sell*, usually fairly 'honest' in its meaning, became, when used with a person as its object, to deceive or swindle someone, especially to take someone in by promoting something, e.g. a company or a coal-mine. In the 19th to early 20th centuries, sell could also be a noun meaning a trick or deception, or a swindler.

Words for Swindling: a Selection

the C/cee   20th century, America (stands for confidence
trickery)

humbugging   mid-18th century to present (a specific use
of the standard English term)

padding   late 17th century (perhaps from standard
English *pad*, to stuff (with nonsense), or from cant
pad, the road and thus the conversation that
accompanies walking alongside the sucker)

rinky dink/rinky-do   20th century to present, America
(usually as **give someone the rinky dink**)

sharping or **the sharping lay**   late 17th to early 20th
centuries (based on the duplicitous slang *sharp* or
sharper)

shaving   17th to 19th centuries (from the earlier slang
verb *shave*, to defraud or rob)

The 18th Century

Do, a word that slang has adopted for various forms of sex and
violence, has also meant to swindle since the mid-18th century, often
in the form **done**, cheated. That period offered little new vocabulary
but it gave extra spins to another couple of words, more usually
found in alternative contexts. To **queer**, more usually found meaning
to spoil or put out of order, and occasionally to ridicule, was now
added to the swindling lexis as a verb; just as to **play the queer**
meant to hoodwink. The word *slang*, while old as a form of language,
had not been recorded to mean this until 1756 (in William Toldervy's
History of the Two Orphans: 'Thomas Throw had been upon the
town, knew the slang well'). However, it appears in the 1740s as both
a noun meaning nonsense and a verb meaning to cheat, to swindle
or to defraud; thus **slanging**, cheating or swindling, and the phrase

there's slanging dues concerned, i.e. one has been cheated. The first such example was set down in the records of the Ordinary [i.e. Chaplain] of Newgate's regular *Account of the Malefactors executed at Tyburn* for the 'hanging day' of 18 March 1741: 'The next exploit Jenny went upon was, *Slanging the Gentry Mort rumly with a sham Kinchin* (that is, Cutting well the Woman big with Child).' Cutting here does not mean a deadly assault – it was only her purse that suffered. 'Jenny' was Jenny Diver (real name Mary Young) and one of contemporary London's most notorious pickpockets. She was *turned off* on Tyburn's gallows in 1641 alongside sixteen men and three other women.

The 19th Century

To *ramp* in standard English means to act in a threatening manner; in cant its initial use in the early 19th century was to rob with violence, and one could thus be *done for a ramp*, convicted of a violent crime. The sense of swindling grew in parallel and lasted throughout that century. At the same time, a *ramper* meant both a prisoner who initiates a new convict by robbing them of their possessions and also a racehorse swindler. The idea of physical violence underpins a number of 19th- and 20th-century terms for swindling, including, in late 19th-century Australia, to *lam* or *lamb*, which was linked to Old Norse *lemja*, to lame, i.e. as a result of a beating, and still means to beat up although the sense of swindling has gone. The late 19th century's *stiffen* became *stiff* in the 20th century and both are still present today, with *stiffed* meaning swindled and *stiffing* robbery.

In America, to *honeyfugle* (*honeyfogle* or *honeyfuggle*) was common in the 19th century, meaning to swindle. The word comes from the dialect *connyfogle*, to entice by flattery, to hoodwink, or *gallyfuggle*, to deceive or trick. A similar American term, *horns-woggle*, began in criminal mouths during the same period but has since entered the mainstream and is still around today. The quasi-onomatopoeic *flim-flam* or *flim*, with its sense of speedy dexterity, again from the late 19th century onwards, meant both to practise a short-change swindle and thence to perpetrate any con trick;

while to **dinker** may have been linked to standard English *dicker*, to bargain. To **hype** or **hipe**, from the 1910s onwards, means both to swindle and to operate a short-change racket, known as **the hype** (from standard English *hyperbole*). The simplest of all, bereft of both 'man' and 'trick', is **confidence** used as a verb meaning to defraud or swindle in the late 19th to mid-20th centuries.

Less obvious is Australia's late 19th- and early 20th-century term **on the billiard slum**, and thus **give it on the billiard slum** and **go on the billiard slum**, to defraud. The image is of the game *billiards*, i.e. of a ball bouncing at various angles. The confidence trickster is similarly 'bent' or deliberately confusing the sucker by offering anything but a 'straight line'. Like **rig** or **racket**, **slum** is a catch-all term for criminal pursuit, usually modified by a descriptive noun. Sport, of a sort, is seen in the mid-19th- to early 20th-century **give someone a chalk**, from the chalking of points on a board, and in **deal off/from the bottom of the deck/pack**, originally coined in the late 19th century and still in use today, which echoes a classic method of cheating in cards. Cards are also behind America's term **euchre**, to swindle, seen in the mid-19th century to the present day, and based on the once-popular card game, although there may be a punning link to the *tricks* one must take.

The Modern Era

In the 20th century, terms and swindles abound. American terms include **hit on**, also borrowing from a less larcenous slang term for to approach sexually; to **toss (someone) around** was unequivocal and also meant to deceive or generally mistreat. To **ream** or **rim** are both based on standard English *ream*, to stretch, to tear in pieces. Slang's sexual use of *ream*, to penetrate anally, came slightly later but may be an extra ingredient of the swindling one. The idea of 'fucking someone over' or just 'fucking' them gives another American term, **yentz**, which meant to have sexual intercourse as well as to swindle or to make someone the victim of any form of deception; such trickery is **yentzing**. It comes from Yiddish *yenzter*, synonymous with *fucker* but ultimately from the contrived euphemism *yents*, translated as 'that' or 'the other'. Yiddish also produced an English term, *gazump* (also *gazoomph* or *gezumph*), which meant to swindle in the first half of the 20th century; thus *gazumper*, a swindler, most probably based on Yiddish *gezumph*, to cheat or to overcharge. The term is now probably best-known in the context of greedy price-hiking within the British housing market (which has also provided the antonym *gazunder*).

To Swindle: a Selection

daisy beat   1950s to present (rhyming slang = cheat)

flap a jay   late 19th century to present (to trick a gullible person)

flimp   1910s–50s (from the western Flemish *flimpe*, to hit in the face)

granny   mid-19th century (the idea of deception comes from the wolf's disguise in the story of 'Little Red Riding Hood')

green   late 19th century (to render someone gullible, based on the standard English *green*, naïve)

have someone in   1940s to present (the swindling version of the older and more mainstream *have someone on*, to tease)

lace   1970s, America (from standard English *lace*, to set upon with a whip)

skin or *skin out (of)*   mid-19th century to present

skin the lamb   mid–late 19th century (also played on standard English *fleece* and meant to swindle or blackmail)

snip   18th and 20th centuries (based on a figurative snip of the scissors that cuts away one's money)

stun   mid-19th century (usually in the phrase to *stun out of*, to defraud)

w   1910s (abbreviation of *welch*, meaning to renege on a deal or debt)

THE VICTIM

'It's a good flat that's never down,' said the 18th century's conmen, a maxim that 'translated' as 'only the most naïve of dupes won't eventually realise what's going on' (using the slang *down*, meaning aware). The maxim reminded the swindlers to keep on their toes. Stealing from music, *flat* was the antonym of *sharp*, the swindler, and was the most common term for the sucker or victim for over a century. Appearing in the mid-18th century, it succeeded the various specific terms listed by Robert Greene in 1591 in his *A Notable Discovery of Coosnage*, including cony, conny and coney, as well as the 17th-century **bub**, an abbreviation of **bubble** that meant both the dupe, who was **bubbleable**, and the scheme in which he was ensnared, which was as insubstantial and ephemeral as the standard English *bubble* in question. (Its best-known use was in the *South Sea Bubble*, the ultimately disastrous rush of inflated stock dealing of 1720.)

Flat initially represented the peasant whose rustic simplicity rendered him automatically gullible (in time the term also defined a prostitute's customer). By the 19th century, it was a term in prolific use. The **prime flat** was the ultimate example of the type, one who really might never be *down*. The conman was a **flat-catcher** and his trade was **flat-catching**. To **strike a flat** meant to encounter a gullible victim, and to **brush up a flat** to flatter them into believing one's schemes.

Flat lasted throughout the 19th century, but the term of choice since the 1900s has been **live one**, as in the New York journalist Helen Green's *Actors' Boarding House* (1905): 'He was lining up a live one for the good old wiretapping game.' And among the longest-lived is **mark**, which has been in use since the mid-18th century; its source is standard English *mark*, to note down, i.e. as a possible victim.

Luring a Victim

Entrapment
'First catch your cony', to paraphrase the old recipe, and the swindler's first task is to identify the rabbit, or indeed pigeon,

woodcock or similar (see page 5) that he intends to dupe. This was known in the late 17th to mid-19th centuries, without the least attempt at euphemism, as **hunting** or **squirrel hunting**. And to facilitate the hunt a variety of **lime-twigs** or snares (from standard English *lime-twig*, a twig smeared with birdlime for catching birds) might be placed in his way in the 16th and 17th centuries. Things might be pushed along if one **dropped a cog**, that is, gained oneself an introduction to the target by dropping a coin where they might see it, then picking it up and starting a conversation. The **rosary man** in the 1940s played much the same game, ensnaring the victim by the fortuitous 'dropping' of a wallet. There is no obvious link to the standard English *rosary* beads, used by the Catholic faithful to help remember a specific set of prayers, other than as a play on the standard verb *tell one's heads* (to say one's prayers) and 'telling' the victim a story. In America, to assess the potential gullibility of a possible victim was to **qualify** them in the 1970s, while, in the 1940s, to place them in the position for the trick to be carried out was to **ride** them **in**. Once trapped, the victim is considered to be **right** (1980s to the present) and can be introduced to the main player, the **inside man** (known from the 1930s in America), who will take the lead role in tricking the victim.

The agent of such entrapment has gone by several names. In the late 18th and 19th centuries he was a **picker-up**, from the mid-19th century he has been an **outside man** or **outsider** in Britain, while in America a **steerer** (a term that has also been used for anyone, e.g. a cab driver, hotel doorman etc., who points someone towards the variety of self-indulgence they seek, e.g. sex, drugs, gambling) or a **roper** or **roper-in**, with its image of cowboys lassooing errant cattle. However, note American philologist Maximilian Schele de Vere in *Americanisms* (1872): 'Rope in, in the sense of gathering in, enlisting, is a bold metaphor derived from the common practice of gathering the cut hay of a meadow by means of a long rope, drawn by a horse.' The **shill**, who is found in a number of criminal endeavours, arrives once the trick is in motion; he plays an enthusiastic 'member of the public' urging the sucker to ever-greater financial commitment.

Smooth Pitches
The persuader's basic armoury consists of smooth words. From the 1930s, the swindler's specific line of persuasion might be termed a **pitch**, or in America a **scolding**, or a *razz* or **razzoo**, which comes from slang's *raspberry* (from rhyming slang: raspberry tart = fart) and more commonly suggests the derogatory 'Bronx cheer'. The late 19th century to the present day sees **spiel** for this persuasive patter and thus **spiel in**, to attract with patter, as well as **spiel**, to shoot a line, and **spieling**, persuasive talk. Mid-19th-century synonyms are the **kid** and the **patter**, which offer the image of a cheapjack extolling his wares or a conjurer using language to divert the audience's attention while his hands perform the tricks. Perhaps the most common term is the 20th century's **tale**, any form of words designed to ensnare the listener for commercial purposes. (As **the tale** in the 1940s, it was a specific con where someone is persuaded to pay the conman, posing as a bookmaker, for a lost bet that he did not ask to be made.) A **tale-pitcher** or **tale-teller** is a trickster who **tells** or **pitches the tale**. One could also **pitch the cuffer** from standard English's *cuffer*, a yarn or story; itself from *cuff*, to discuss, to tell a story.

Other Means of Persuasion
When words are insufficient the victim can be shown some form of reassuring 'proof' such as America's 1930s coinage **scenery**, which can mean both an impressive 'board of directors' or a pile of fake dividend cheques. One could even toss around some cash, some **coarse ones** or **coarse notes**, which were large-denomination dollar bills in 1930s and 1940s America. Another scheme is simply to get the victim drunk, and the wine used to perform this task was known as **shrap** from standard English *shrape*, a bait of chaff or seed laid for birds and thus any form of snare. A tried and tested stratagem, already seen in the barnard's law of the 16th century, is initially allowing the victim to win, before taking his every penny when his 'luck' changes. America has plenty of words for this form of entrapment, including to **bankroll** in the 1940s and to **cop and blow** in the 1910s–1940s, while the conman who used this method was the **convincer** in the 1940s.

The Kill

But not all flats are 'good' and some do indeed get 'down'. America sees the most varied terms for the warmth or otherwise of the sucker: he may lose interest or **chill** in the 1940s, or worse he may **heat up**, in the 1930s to the present day, and make a fuss or even call in the authorities. In the same era, the undaunted swindler will still **come hot** in America and go ahead with his plan, even when the victim makes it clear that he is aware of being duped; everything should then move smoothly towards the **kill**, a British term from the same era which represents the actual moment of bringing a confidence trick to a climax.

In the mid-20th century in America, with the con successfully attained (assuming that no-one has **ranked the joint**, i.e. blundered in any aspect of the deception, and that it has not been necessary to **scoff the flash**, consume or otherwise use up anything that is being displayed as a lure), the conman must leave and so must the victim, who must be **sewn up** or deprived of any opportunity to cause trouble. This moment of dismissal, known as the **round-up** in the 1900s, may be followed by an act of **streeting**, i.e. guiding a victim away from wherever the trick has been taking place. Meanwhile the swindler or swindlers will **cool out**, that is, sensibly avoid the victim from whom the money has been extracted and whom they hope will soon leave for his home. After that, it's just a matter of dividing up the **nut** or profits.

Chapter 2

BLACKMAILERS AND OTHERS

Our readers are not perhaps aware that there is such a term in the English language as a *Coneyacker*. Indeed we cannot wonder at their ignorance, as, until this morning, we never ourselves [. . .] had heard of or even imagined such a term. It is, we believe, solely a police term, and signifies a dealer in counterfeit money.

Commercial Advertiser (NY), 26 January 1827

BLACKMAIL

Compared to many other crimes blackmail has inspired very few slang terms. Perhaps this lack reflects the nature of the beast, shaming even those who practise it. This form of morality-based extortion has been known as to *rent*, apparently first used by Oscar Wilde and his circle to mean to obtain money by criminal means, e.g. to blackmail. *Boot polish* is black (or can be) and it can smear: it was used in the 1950s to mean blackmail, while in 1930s America *skull and crossbones*, with its black flag and implications of piratical activities, was found. Like so many other transfers of money in the criminal world the payment of blackmail is the *pay-off*, except that it is rarely paying off in full.

The first use of terms specifically for a blackmailer are 19th-century coinages: the *ghoul* attempted to blackmail a woman who is deceiving her husband, and the *socketer* took his name from the 17th-century term *socket-money* (ultimately from *socket*, the vagina), which was money paid by a man to his wife to placate her after he has been caught in an adulterous affair. By the 19th century it meant any form of hush money, and thence the blackmailing socketer's name.

The end of that century brought in the abbreviated *'mailer*, used in Australia, where you also found the *tout*, one who spies for the purpose of blackmail. The 1920s homosexual world called certain blackmailers *dirt*, an unequivocal denunciation of a man who professed homosexuality simply for the purposes of blackmailing those he encountered. Such duplicity is known as *bleeding dirt*. Contemporary America used the *roller*, a figurative extension of the term's usual meaning: one who robs drunks and other defenceless people. The best-known term remains the *shake artist* or *shakedown artist*, who since the 1930s has been an extortionist in general and a blackmailer in particular.

Shake as a verb was used from the late 19th century to mean to blackmail, while to *put the shake on* first appeared in the 1920s, and the majority of synonymous terms start with the same verb. All are 20th-century coinages, starting with *put the bee/B on* in the 1910s. The bee is a play on slang's *sting*, to extort, but also suggests the initial letter of *bite* and *put the bite on*, both verbs meaning to blackmail. Other terms have included *put the bit on* (from the standard word *bit*, the mouthpiece of a horse's bridle, used to restrain the animal); the phrase is paralleled by the 17th- to 19th-century *have a hank on* (from standard English *hank*, a restraining or curbing hold). To *squeeze* has meant to pressurise since the 18th century and used for blackmailing since the 19th century certainly; it has been succeeded by *put the squeeze on* or *give someone the squeeze*; the *squeezer* is the blackmailer. To *put the arm on* or *give someone the arm* was a 1930s coinage originally meaning to attack from behind by choking the victim with one's forearm before robbing them; since then, with *lay the arm on*, it has come to mean to pressurise with threats of violence, to extort 'protection' payments, to beg for money, and to blackmail.

To Blackmail

Many blackmail terms take the form of 'put something on someone', as, for example, to put the squeeze on; but there are exceptions:

bite
come (on) the bounce
drop the lug on
give someone the squeeze
hold up
mouse (thus *the mouse*, blackmail)
rattle
rent
shake
skin the lamb
squeeze
stick up
touch up

EXTORTION

The standard English verb *extort* is based on the Latin *extorquere*, to twist out of, and the noun *extortion* is defined literally as 'wresting or wringing (something)' from a person. Setting aside blackmail (see above), there are a number of methods of extortion, known for a century as a **hold-up** (even if no weapon is involved), and terms for those who practise them.

The earliest of such terms for the practitioner of extortion is the 17th century's **shark**, a direct reference to the never-sleeping marine predator. The 19th century added the **bull** or **bully trap**, who impersonated an official in order to extort money, and the **nailer** (from slang's *nail*, to get hold of), while the 1930s coined the **sandbag artist**, who figuratively bashes one over the head.

As evocative as anything that followed was the 17th-century verb to **bleed**, which remains as potent an image as ever. The 19th century saw to **pump**, to **pot** (a more villainous version of its parallel meaning, to outdo, to outwit or deceive), and to **put it on someone**, in which guile is as useful as actual menaces. The late 19th century added a pair of long-lasting terms: to soak and to shylock. To **soak** or **soak it to** suggests forms of extortion that are less than obviously illegal and has meant to overcharge or at least charge exorbitant prices, as much as it has to demand money with actual menaces. The more recent **clip** and **put the clip on** mean just the same. Shylock comes, of course, from Shakespeare's classically anti-Semitic character, created for his play *The Merchant of Venice* (1600). To **shylock** was technically to offer a personal loan, but was soon revised to mean to lend money at extortionate rates of interest; thus the noun form **shylocking**. The noun *shylock*, a moneylender (whether honest or, as stereotyped, otherwise), had emerged in the mid-19th century, applied by those who had found themselves 'in the hands of the Jews'.

One might **sting** someone for money by begging or borrowing it in a demanding manner; to **take/send to the cleaners** was – and still is – a phrase meaning to reduce to penury as well as to defraud, outwit and otherwise remove all of a victim's assets in a wager, by extortion or by similar legal or illegal means. The victim can be **hijacked**, **socked** (literally 'hit') and **taxed**.

FORGERY AND COUNTERFEITING

The Forger

The forger is literally a maker, and existed as such for two centuries (usually dealing in paperwork) before the term first referred to the counterfeiting of coins. The *faker*, as a term for maker, dates back to the late 17th century and came from the Latin *faceo* by way of French *faire*. Fake was used widely in slang from the 19th century onwards, to mean to make or to do, for instance to *fake one's slangs*, to cut off one's irons to escape from custody. However, the first link to forgery is **bene faker**, or **bene feaker**, which dates back to 1612 and meant literally a 'good-maker'. He was definitely a counterfeiter, initially of documents, for which he was also known as a **benfeaker of gybes** (a *gybe* being a form of pass, used by beggars to secure alms), and later of money.

The 19th century added the **bit faker**, literally 'money-maker', who was a coiner or a counterfeiter, and his profession: **bit-faking**. Bit, for a piece of money, also combined in the **bit-maker** and **bit turner-out**, and the **bit smasher**, from slang's *smash*, to counterfeit. What he made was **bit-queerems** (from slang's *queer*, bad). The forger could also be a **cobbler**, linked to standard English *cobble*, to put together or join roughly or clumsily, a 20th-century figure whose talents focused on passports, currency and stocks and bonds. The 19th century's **face-maker** stamped the monarch's face on what he created, giving the phrase to **draw the king's/queen's picture**, which, since a British banknote always carries the current monarch's head, is to create counterfeit banknotes. The short-lived verb **Fauntleroy** memorialised one Henry Fauntleroy, who was neither little nor lordly but a 40-year-old bank clerk who faked up his wealthy clients' signatures and in 1824 became the last man to be hanged for forgery in England.

However, generally, by the 19th century forgers were seen as 'writers' rather than 'makers', thus the **figure-dancer**, who specialised in altering the figures on banknotes, usually adding a zero to multiply a sum by ten. The term puns on the forger's ability to 'make figures dance' and the showbiz figure dancer who performed representations of famous historical events. Other writers included the **scribe**, the **penman** and the **scratchman** or **scratch**, and in the mid-20th century the punning **bill-poster**, i.e. a passer of bad cheques. Most defiant of etymology was the **koniacker** (also spelt variously **coneyacker**, **coniacker** etc.). This counterfeiter, flourishing between the 19th century and the 1930s, may have played on the *coney*, the sucker, although slang lexicographers John S. Farmer and W.E. Henley suggested in *Slang and Its Analogues* (1890–1904) that it was 'obviously, a play upon *coin*, money and *hack*, to mutilate'. Brandy, it seems, did not enter the picture.

Finally witness 'Abraham Newland, a New Song', a ballad of *c*.1800:

'I have heard people say that "sham Abraham" you may; But you mus'n't sham Abraham Newland.' To **sham Abraham Newland** was to forge banknotes and came from the proper name of Abraham Newland, chief cashier of the Bank of England (1778–1807). His name, synonymous with a banknote, lasted through the 19th century, and as the sporting journalist Pierce Egan noted in *The Finish to the Adventures of Tom and Jerry* (1830): 'May the tears of distress always be wiped away with the soft paper of Abraham Newland.'

Counterfeit Money and Other Objects

Queer, Snide and Sour

If the language of forgery is relatively limited, the shortfall is made up by terms for the counterfeited objects, whether coins, notes or other useful documents. For the pre-20th-century criminal the adjective *queer* was an all-purpose term that rendered all it touched 'bad' or 'untrustworthy'. Never so much as in descriptions of the counterfeiter and his art, of which the following are all examples that were used in the 18th to 19th centuries.

There was the basic **queer money** that covered all varieties. The fake money could be **queer blunt**, from slang's *blunt*, a coin (and itself based either on the French *blond*, yellow or in this case gold, or from the standard English *blunt*, referring to the edge of unmilled coins). *Cole*, i.e. coal, was part of that group of terms in which money equalled a staple of life, typically the *needful* or the modern *bread*; thus there was **queer cole**, made by a **queer-cole maker** and distributed by a **queer-cole fencer**. Based again on another slang term for money, *bit*, there was the **queer bit** and the **queer bit-maker**. **Queer ridge** came from slang's *ridge*, gold, which may have been linked to *red*, also synonymous for gold in slang. Turning to paper notes there was **queer paper**, a **queer rag** (thus the **rag trade**, the purchasing of counterfeit banknotes and the subsequent passing them off to innocent victims), **queer screens** and **queer soft**. In all cases the nouns meant counterfeit paper currency.

A **queersman** both created and distributed the counterfeits, a **queer shover** or **shover of the queer** passed them on to the gullible. To distribute such fakes was to **push/shove the queer**. Finally, since faking was not restricted to money, there were **queer tats** and **queer lambs**: specially made dice that were guaranteed to favour the cheating player. Tats had been generic for dice since the 17th century, while lamb probably came from *Fulham* or *fullam*, an earlier version of these not quite cubic cubes (itself from either *Fulham* in London, as a place of manufacture, or standard English *full*, suggesting the weighting of the dice).

Outlasting queer was **snide**, the origin of which lies either in the German *aufschneiden*, to boast, to brag or to show off, or *schneide*, to cut, i.e. the cutting of fake coins. The term appeared in America in the mid-19th century and continues to be used. It meant counterfeit money and could be used in various compounds: the **snide lurk**, the passing of counterfeit money; the **snide shop**, an agency that organises the passing of such money; the **snide pitcher** or **snide pusher**, a passer of the fakes; and the **snidesman, snideman** or **snider**, a counterfeiter. Snide itself graduated beyond forgery and came to embrace any dubious person, especially an actual conman, worthless goods which nonetheless were touted as valuable and thence anything counterfeit; in South Africa the current use denotes imitation diamonds (known earlier as *snide sparklers*), fake gold, or platinum and silver jewellery.

The late 19th century had **sour** (supposed silver coins made from pewter), **sour dough** (the pun may be coincidental) and **sour paper** (bad cheques), and the **sour-planter** whose task it was to **plant the sour**, to distribute the counterfeits.

Fake Coinage

Birmingham, the British version that is, has been stereotyped as in some way fraudulent since the 17th century. Its growing ability to mass-produce what was supposed to be the preserve of craftsmen worried observers who duly sneered. Thus a **Birmingham** or **Brummagem** was a counterfeit coin. Other terms for fake coinage include the **rap**, an 18th-century Irish term for a counterfeit halfpenny; **browns and whistlers**, counterfeit halfpence and farthings in the 19th century, which rang false when tapped; the 16th century's **slip**, and thus the phrase **nail up for a slip(s)**, to reduce (through poverty) to using counterfeit coins. In the 19th century, a **wrong 'un** was any bad coin (a **stiff 'un** was a bad note), as was a **sham** or a **duffer** (from *duff*, useless). Confusingly **dough**, usually just money, could also mean counterfeit coins in the 1940s, and to **cook dough** was to manufacture the stuff.

To Palm It Off

Terms meaning to pass bad money and, latterly, cheques and other documents have included:
do soft   mid-19th century
drop (and thus the **dropper**)   20th century
palm   18th century to present
pitch   mid-19th to early 20th centuries
plant   19th century
put off   mid-17th century to 1900s
work off   late 19th century

Fake Notes
Moving from coins to notes, in the 19th century one saw *flash* and a *flash note* for counterfeit currency; while in the mid-20th century *flash dough* was the sort of counterfeit stuff used specifically in a confidence trick. A roll of counterfeit notes was a **dummy**. Among the earliest terms for forged notes was *lil* or *lill* from the Romany *lil*, a book or paper; it was used in the mid-19th century, as was **screeve** (from *screeve*, to write) and the American **pictures** (in this case of presidents not kings and queens). The 20th century saw **funny money** or **funny paper** and **hard money** for counterfeit notes; they could also be **slither** (the speedy path through one's fingers) and **slush**. From the late 19th century **bum** was used for counterfeit: **bum dough** and **bum paper** were created by the **bum dough artist**, and the **bum checker** or **bum cheque artist** was another form of paper-hanger.

Paper has meant counterfeit banknotes since the mid-19th century and forged or useless cheques or other financial instruments since the 20th. See Paper Money (in SWINDLERS, CONMEN AND FRAUDS, page 18) for all forms of *paper-hanging* and *kite-flying* and other terms for swindles that involved passing fraudulent documents, whether counterfeit banknotes (*stumers* and *stiffs*) or otherwise. *Boodle* has also meant counterfeit money, and the late 19th-century phrase **walk the boodle** was to distribute counterfeit notes.

To Pass Bad Money

Slumming (from slang's *slum*, a trick or deception, possibly underpinned the alternative sense of a wad of notes) was the mid-19th-century term for the whole science of distributing fake money. There were terms for the generic passing of counterfeit money but the mid-19th-century **work the bulls** meant specifically to pass fake crowns. To **job out** was to distribute the counterfeit money to criminal associates and dealers, who would then bring it into general circulation. One way of doing this was the **pinching lay**, a variety of petty crimes involving cash: passing counterfeit money, stealing from shops, giving short change. Alternatively one might **ring the changes**, deceiving a shopkeeper by passing counterfeit money or substituting a worse article for a better one.

Chapter 3

STREET CRIME

And we shall caper a-heel and toeing
A Newgate hornpipe some fine day
With the mots their ogles throwing
And old Cotton humming his pray,
And the fogle hunters doing
Their morning fake in the prigging lay

W. McGinn, *The Pickpockets' Chaunt* (1829)

CUTTING PURSES AND PICKING POCKETS

Street crime is the opposite of what you might call in-your-face villainy: muggings or snatch-and-grab (**grab-and-flee** they call it in the Caribbean). Instead, it's behind your back, or down by your side or . . . anywhere that you don't notice. Now you see it and now you don't and only the **fence**, checking over the swag, has time to ponder your lost possessions.

It all started, centuries back, with cutting purses, before moving on to picking pockets. In the beginning, hanging temptingly from the belt, the purse was suspended like a small sack outside the clothing and was therefore vulnerable. Later on, the pocket was sewn inside clothing like a hidden bag, and was perfect for a criminal hand to dip into.

The word *pocket* began life in the 14th century as a synonym for a sack or bag. In their somewhat shrunken form these pockets could be attached, like the purse, to the outside of one's clothes. Not until the 16th century did they become incorporated inside one's clothes. Still, while we get the *cutpurse* ('one who steals by the method of cutting purses,' said Dr Johnson in his *Dictionary* of 1755, 'a common practice when men wore their purses at their girdles'), we do not get 'cut-pocket'. (Fans of the great modern American novelist Chester Himes, however, may recall a scene in one of his Harlem novels in which a respectable church lady, who wears her purse slung from her belt but *under* her dress within a hanging pocket, finds that her outer garment has been neatly razored away – and the pocket removed with it.) On the other hand Chaucer's *Knight's Tale* (*c*.1386) offers **pick-purse**, a seeming bridge between *cutpurse* (1362) and *pickpocket* (1592) and synonymous with the second, although it has long since vanished.

Considering these somewhat confusing origins, it is perhaps not surprising that even if the standard terms sound as though they deal with very specific criminal operations, the slang terms that they conjured up have boundaries that are somewhat ill-defined. What was good for the cutpurse could also work for the pickpocket and vice versa. In addition, some of these early words are problematical. Criminal slang – or cant, as it is technically known – didn't start getting collected until around 1535, and then not too much of it. Improved glossaries appeared as the 16th century progressed, but it's still hard to be definite about chronology.

THE CUTPURSE

For the cutpurse, it's all about the knife – the active 'cutter' – rather than the purse, which is simply and passively 'cut'. That said, Shakespeare does have **bung**, from the Frisian *pung* (purse), which he uses to mean the man who cuts the purse from its legal owner. As he puts it in *Henry IV Part II* (*c*.1597): 'Away, you cut-purse rascal! you filthy bung, away.' There's also the **cool** – a name for the man again, and one that most likely comes from the French *cul*, the buttocks, near which the purse hung.

Nevertheless, the emphasis is mostly on the tools of the trade – or, to be more specific, the knife. Even bung turns up again in the 17th-century **bung-nipper** or **bung-nibber**, literally 'purse cutter';

the ubiquitous cant verb **nip** (it also means to steal, to shoplift, to arrest, to have sexual intercourse and to cheat) borrows from the standard English *nip* – to cut or snip. Logically enough a nip was a cutpurse, as were the **nipper** and **nipping Christian**, a slightly later 17th-century compound that does not imply religiosity, but simply uses Christian as a generic word for any human being, even a criminal one.

The 16th-century standard English term *foin*, referring to a thrust with a pointed weapon, was criminalised to mean, at first, a cutpurse, and later a pickpocket. The ultimate etymology is Old French *foine* or *fouisne*, a three-pronged fish-spear. Shakespeare in *The Winter's Tale* (*c*.1610) provides **pick and cut** to describe the job-related actions of picking up or holding the purse and then cutting it. This action was often rendered simpler by the wearing of a horn sheath – the **horn-thumb** – over one's thumb. This provided a form of 'chopping board' against which the purse-string could be held tight for the knife to quickly do its job. Such sheaths gave rise in the 17th century to another term for a cutpurse: **child of the horn-thumb**. Neither the subsequent **clipper** nor the **knight of the knife** require comment, although the latter was one of many contemporary 'knights' who ennobled employments that were not quite of the aristocratic ilk that the word might suggest.

The **curtal** in the 18th century (from *curtal*, anything docked or cut short, and originally a horse's tail) was another knife wielder, but usually devoted his blade to cutting off pieces of the expensive fabrics that might hang from shop windows. Earlier, around 1560, he had been a mendicant villain who was distinguished by the short cloak he wore, similar to those of the Franciscan monks known as the Grey Friars. From shop window fabrics, he extended his enthusiasms to women's silver-threaded ('laced') or silken gowns and their jewels, and even beyond: lead was soft and curtals cut into that too, taking water-pipes, gutters and spouts. With all that on board, purses, which they also pursued, seem almost an afterthought.

Knights of the Realm

It was common to elevate an ordinary person or criminal
practising a distinctly ignoble occupation by awarding them
the chivalric honour of a knighthood. This particular irony
was found throughout the slang of the 16th to 18th centuries,
and even into the 19th and 20th centuries, although on a
more simple jocular basis.

knight of the awl   cobbler
knight of the blade   thug, wandering villain, shearer
knight of the brush   chimney sweep, artist
knight of the cleaver   butcher
knight of the elbow   card-sharp
knight of the forked order   cuckold
knight of the grammar   teacher
knight of the green cloth   gambler
knight of the gusset   pimp
knight of the napkin   waiter
knight of the needle   tailor
knight of the pad   highwayman
knight of the pencil   bookmaker
knight of the pestle   apothecary
knight of the petticoat   brothel bouncer
knight of the pigskin   jockey
knight of the pisspot   doctor
knight of the quill   author
knight of the rainbow   footman, waiter
knight of the shears   tailor
knight of the spigot   publican
knight of the spout   pawnbroker
knight of the thimble   tailor
knight of the whip   coachman
knight of the yardstick   draper

The Life of a Cutpurse

A share of the cutpurse's booty was a **snap**, and came from the standard English *snack*, which in turn was synonymous with *snatch*, a grabbed or snatched handful or mouthful. Snap was also used to refer to a hanger-on, usually an older cutpurse whose reflexes were in decline; nonetheless, he demanded a share of the profits. He was also known as a **cloyer**, either from cant's *cloy*, money or purse, or standard English *cloyne*, to act deceitfully or fraudulently. What they all shared out was **snappage** or **snappings** (the older man getting ten per cent of the take), and denying the snap his share was dangerous. As the playwright and author of 'canting' pamphlets Thomas Dekker explained in *The Belman of London* (1608): 'If the Nip deny Snappage the Cloyer forthwith Boyles [unmasks] him, that is, bewrayes [reveals] him, or seaseth on his cloake.' The booty itself was the **cargo** in the mid-18th century and later a **trick**.

THE PICKPOCKET

The merry old gentleman, placing a snuff-box in one pocket of his trousers, a note-case in the other, and a watch in his waistcoat pocket, with a guard-chain round his neck, and sticking a mock diamond pin in his shirt: buttoned his coat tight round him, and putting his spectacle-case and handkerchief in his pockets, trotted up and down the room [. . .]. He would look constantly round him, for fear of thieves, and would keep slapping all his pockets in turn, to see that he hadn't lost anything, in such a very funny and natural manner, that Oliver laughed till the tears ran down his face. [. . .] At last, the Dodger trod upon his toes, or ran upon his boot acci-dently, while Charley Bates stumbled up against him behind; and in that one moment they took from him, with the most extraordinary rapidity, snuff-box, note-case, watch-guard, chain, shirt-pin, pocket-handkerchief, even the spectacle-case.

Charles Dickens, *Oliver Twist* (1838)

If in the context of pickpocketing it seems hard to avoid some reference to *Oliver Twist*, then it is because when Dickens wrote the book this particular crime was more widespread than ever. Statistics for 1860 assess the value of pickpocketed articles at £6,200 – a sum that is now worth in excess of £4 million, using calculations based on average earnings. Dickens's fascination with pickpockets was shared by Henry Mayhew, a journalist who wrote extensively about the Victorian underclasses in the *Morning Chronicle* and then used his research to produce a groundbreaking piece of sociology, *London Labour and the London Poor* (1861–2). Dickens certainly read Mayhew, although *Oliver Twist* actually appeared three years before Mayhew got going, and it seems that Dickens gathered his material in much the same way – wandering the streets and talking to people – though Mayhew's approach was more exhaustive and scientific.

While Dickens was a novelist and Mayhew a journalist, their findings do seem consistent with one another. Both show the passage of the pickpocket from ragged street brat, who was quite possibly the child of criminals, to the more assured and better dressed teenager – the ***natty lad*** or ***kid*** of the late 18th century – who gradually improved on his way to the ranks of the very acme of pickpocket-dom, the ***swell mob***. Once pickpockets had made it this far they might have specialised – in the theatres or buses or railway stations, or even on the trains themselves, as well as some of their smarter destinations such as Ascot or Epsom at Derby-time. The swell mob earned their name both from their success and from the fact that their dress aped the ***swells*** on whom they preyed. (An alternative term for this professional pickpocket was ***man of the world***.) The ***cadger***, meanwhile, was their antithesis – the lowest rank of the profession. Both Dickens and Mayhew described the training up of these children, their instructors using equipment such as dummies sewn with bells, which rang when hands were insufficiently nimble; Fagin, that merry old gentleman of *Oliver Twist*, could have stepped out of Dickens and straight into Mayhew.

Names for Pickpockets

Picking pockets was nothing new in Dickens's and Mayhew's time. The standard English word *pickpocket* is first found in 1591 in the playwright Robert Greene's pamphlet *A Notable Discovery of Coosnage* (i.e. fraud). In the same year, his *The Second Part of Conny-Catching* offered **foist**. This, the earliest cant synonym for pickpocket, was first recorded a few years before Greene, but the word had been in use since 1545, when it had meant a dice cheat. (In fact, foist has meant a cheat both in cards and dice, and could also be a trickster.) Greene is a fascinating figure. Best known as a successful playwright, hack writer and bitter rival of Shakespeare (who later transformed Greene's prose story *Pandosto* into *The Winter's Tale*), he flirted with the underworld, writing supposedly instructive pamphlets that played unashamedly on his readers' thirst for low-life titillation. There is certainly no small admiration in the description he gives of the foist when he tells readers:

> the Foist is so nimble handed that hee exceeds the iugler [juggler] for agility, and hath his legier de maine [deftness] as perfectly: therfore an exquisite Foist must haue three properties that a good Surgion should haue, and that is an Eagles eie, a Ladies hand, and a Lyons heart: an Eagles eie to spie a purchase, to haue a quicke insight where the boong lies, and then a Lyons heart not to feare what the end will bee, and then a Ladies hand to be little and nimble, the better to diue into the pocket. These are the perfect properties of a Foist.

From Figs to Files

Another key word in this early period was **fig**, meaning to pickpocket and descended from the standard word *feague*, to overcome by trickery, to beat. Feague itself was a busy word. Not only had it morphed to fig and acquired its pickpocketing sense, but it also meant to have sexual intercourse, and – rather bizarrely – to ram a piece of ginger into a racehorse's rectum, thus enlivening, however briefly, its prowess on the track. Now it became part and parcel of that activity known as the **figging law**, first cited in Gilbert

Walker's *A Detection of the most vile and detestable use of Dice-play* (1552): 'Thus they give their own conveyance the name of cheating law; so do they other terms, as sacking law, high law, figging law, and such like.' Forty years later Robert Greene, in his *Notable Discovery of Coosnage*, laid out the personalities and practices involved:

> In Figging law. The picke pocket, a Foin; He that faceth the man, the Stale; Taking the purse, Drawing; Spying of him, Smoaking; The purse, the Bong; The monie, the Shels; The Act doing, striking.

In the early 17th century, a new word found its way into the vocabulary of pickpocketing: the ***file***. It meant an act of pickpocketing as well as the pickpocket himself and could also sometimes refer to an accomplice. Over time, it acquired more general senses: an artful, cunning or shrewd person, for example, or a man, a 'fellow'. An ***old file*** was an old and/or experienced person. The origins of the word are not entirely clear. It could be related to the French *filou*, meaning a pickpocket. On the other hand there is the standard English word *file*, which could mean a rascal as well as the metal tool used to cut through things. Just to make things more interesting, there is also an 18th-century French phrase *file doux*, to flatter or wheedle, to 'play the sleeping dog' – in other words, to lie in wait.

File generated its own family of words during the 17th to 19th centuries. The ***file-lifter*** doubled up on the basic meaning, since a ***lifter*** was a pickpocket or a thief of unattended packages. The ***file-lay*** or ***filing lay*** combined it with cant's *lay* (a criminal 'job') to mean the act or profession of pickpocketing. A female pickpocket was a ***fro file***, drawing on the German *Frau* or Dutch *vrouw*, a woman. *Cloy* or *cly* both meant a purse or the money it contained, and a ***file cloy*** (or the earlier ***foyl-cloy***) might be said to ***foyl*** *someone's **cloy***. There was also the *buttock and file*, a prostitute who doubled as a pickpocket, usually with the help of her man. Not, of course, to be confused with the *buttock and twang* (from *twang*, to steal), a prostitute who did not double as a pickpocket.

The Buzz Words

Buzz offered a variety of compounds, most of which were coined in the 19th century. Some of these were simple synonyms – the **buzzer**, the **buzman** or **buzzman** and the **buz-glouk** and **huz cove** (*gloak* and *cove* both meant man or fellow). The **buz bloak** sounds like more of the same (*bloke* has of course survived in mainstream slang), but was in fact a pickpocket who specialised in loose cash and purses, as opposed to jewellery or handkerchiefs. This nod to the particular characteristics or preferred activity of the pickpocket was found in other terms as well. The **bloke-buzzer** preferred to target male victims. The **buz-faker** was one who *faked*, i.e. made his victims drunk before robbing them (**buz-faking**, however, was any form of pickpocketing). A **buz-napper** (or **bus-napper**) was from *nap* – to steal – and described a young pickpocket, and a **buz-napper's kinchin** (literally 'pickpocket's child') was a lookout for the team. A **buz-knacker** was a trainer of young pickpockets; based on the standard English *knacker*, a harness-maker, it suggests an image of the trainer as one who taught his young charges to accept the rules of their game. His training 'school', à la Fagin's Saffron Hill lair, was the **buz-napper's academy**, where they might practise on a **buz-napper's bloke** – the dressed dummies recorded by Dickens and Mayhew. And while purse-snatching lacks the skills of pickpocketing, it did manage to steal a piece of its vocabulary: in 1950s America it too was known as **buzzing**.

Buzz Like a Bee
Writing in his autobiography *A Narrative of Street-Robberies* (1728), the street robber, transportee and informer James Dalton used another of the generic pickpocketing terms when he suggested to

A Pickpocket Chronology

Slang terms for a pickpocket have changed over the centuries, although some, like dip (which started in the 19th century), are still in use.

16th Century
foist

17th Century
Captain
conjuror
file
fork

18th Century
angler
dinger
dive
knuckle

19th Century
abstractionist
artist
bugger
cly-faker
conveyancer
conveyer
dip
eldpineer
fammer

finger-smith
grafter
gun
peninsular
snatcher
stogger
toucher
whack

20th Century
cannon
digger
frisker
grabber
greasy fingers
hooker
jostler
legshake artist
ma-liner
puller
shot
shot broad
sticksman
whiz
workman

women that 'if [...] they would put their Pockets between their Hoops and their upper Petticoats, they might defy all the Buzzes in London to haul the Cly'. Dalton himself, whose informing did not save him from his death on the gallows in 1730, is memorialised in plate 3 of the satirist Hogarth's *Harlot's Progress*, where his 'Wigg Box' can be found above the whore Moll Hackabout's bed. As for his advice, whether many women would have understood it is unknown, but the **buzz** or pickpocket and the concept of **buzzing** like a bee implies the speedy sleight of hand used by a master of the profession.

From Guns to Peninsulars
Yiddish, the Germano-Hebrew dialect of the Ashkenazi Jews, has long since played a role in slang and cant, and in the mid-19th century one would find *gonnof* (from Hebrew *gannabh*, a thief) used to mean a thief. Abbreviated as **gun** it gave another popular synonym for pickpocket, which links to the current punning term **cannon**, although the jostling of a thief who 'cannons' into a victim might also have contributed.

In general slang a *jostler* was a cheat; however in 1950s cant he could also be a pickpocket, and while the act of pickpocketing certainly involves cheating the victim out of his possessions, the word reflected the physicality involved in the crime. The quasi-assault of the victim also underpinned the late 18th- to 19th-century *dinger* (literally one who *dings*, i.e. hits hard) and **whack**. A less violent physical proximity is reflected in **squeeze-play**, a 1940s term for the act of pickpocketing, combining both the image of squeezing up to a victim and a pun on baseball jargon *squeeze-play*, 'a tactic whereby the batter bunts so that a runner at third base can attempt to reach home safely and score' (*Oxford English Dictionary*).

The most recent term, although launched in the 1920s, is another reference to movement (and movement at speed): **the whiz** (or in 1930s rhyming slang **bottle of fizz**), meaning both the occupation and the individual who does it. Again one finds a set of compounds: **whiz artist**, **whiz boy** and **whizzer** refer to the individual; **whiz mob**, **whiz gang** and **whizz mob** to the team. All might be **on the whiz(z)**.

Some names, all from around the mid-19th century, are less

obvious: the **bugger** took his name from the phrase *a bug in the head*, in this case one devoted to illegality; the **stogger** may also have derived from dialect – in this case *stog*, a stab, a thrust; the **eldpineer**, a veteran pickpocket, was perhaps some form of play on standard English *elder*; the **peninsular**, the era's name for a female pickpocket, might derive from the standard word for a projecting strip of land (i.e. she sticks out a finger for thieving).

And Finally...
Surely the most elaborate term was the **running rumbler** of the late 18th century. One of a team of pickpockets, he rolled a large grind-stone down the street and when pedestrians moved to get out of his way, the rest of the team would rob them. More direct was **hoisting**, a pickpocket technique from the same era whereby a victim was lifted bodily and held upside down so that any valuables fell out of his pockets, which would then be seized by the criminals.

Crime and Punishment

Crime, of course, is followed – one hopes – by punishment. If the modern pickpocket is caught, they may well go to prison. But this was not always so. Like the unpopular old women branded as 'witches' who were subjected to the ducking stool, the early 19th-century pickpocket was immersed in water for his or her sins. To do so was to **drake**, a pun on duck (i.e. in a pond). The rogue himself was either an **anabaptist** or, later, a **baptist**, terms based either on the Anabaptists (from Greek *anabaptismos*, to baptise over again), an early 16th-century German Protestant sect that was typified by the re-baptism of all its members, or on the Baptists, who immerse new converts in water.

The Pickpocket at Work

Dip and Dive
The actual act of picking a pocket is perhaps reflected most obviously in **dip** (still perhaps the most widely used term for the professional), meaning both the perpetrator and the act. In the 19th century, the **dip lay** and **dipping gag** were pickpocketing, and a **dipper** or **dipping-bloke** might *go on the dip*. There was even a faux-academic term for the world of pickpocketing – **dipology**. We will look more closely at the importance of the hand or fingers in the pickpocketing lexis, but a pertinent example here is the **dipping duke** (from *duke*, a hand), the 'tool' with which a pickpocket works.

From the 18th to mid-19th centuries, the noun **dive** was a popular synonym for the dip, while the verbal use, meaning to pick a pocket, lasted from the early 17th century to the mid-20th. In the 1930s **high dive** meant to pickpocket and to pick a specific pocket was to **dive into the sack**, a phrase that remained in use from the late 17th century until the early 19th.

Hands in Pockets
For obvious reasons, a number of names refer to the hands. Usually these are one's own, although the celebrated Jenny Diver, pseudonym of Mary Young, went a little further before her career ended on the Tyburn gallows in 1741. She had a pair of false arms and hands made which would be ostentatiously displayed folded demurely in her lap as she sat in church amid her rich neighbours. Her real hands, meanwhile, were busy emptying their bags.

Terms that derived from the pickpocket's primary tool could be of two sorts – those that referred directly to the hand (or a part of the hand) itself, and those that alluded to what the pickpocketing hand was busy doing. In 1970s British black use **sticksman**, however, is a bit of both: it may refer to the *sticks* (i.e. the fingers), or it may be based on the sticking of one's hand into another's pocket. America's mid-19th-century **abstractionist** alluded to the action of the hands and fingers. Based on the standard English *abstract*, to remove, it sounds as if it had escaped from a vaudeville poster. From the same period **conveyancer** or **conveyer** punned both on *convey* (again in its standard sense – to move, i.e. from the victim's pocket to one's own) and on the legal term *conveyancer*, a lawyer who arranges the movement of property from one owner to another. The early *conjuror* of the 17th century stressed the thief's dependence on sleight of hand. Far more down to earth were the *digger* (1930s–1950s), *grabber* (1920s), *hooker* (1920s; specialised in watches), *puller* (1940s), *snatcher* (late 19th century; often a young and inexperienced pickpocket who might still grab rather than slide the loot from the target), *toucher* (mid-19th century) and *frisker* (20th century). Slightly more abstract, to *run the rule over* (late 19th century) or *fan* (20th century) was the running of hands over a victim to check for a wallet or bankroll, and to *peck* was to put one's hand into a victim's pocket, likening the pickpocket to a hungry bird.

Fam itself meant a hand (seemingly rooted in standard English *fumble*) and is one of the earliest canting terms on record, available since at least 1698. In the mid-19th century its extension *fammer* meant a pickpocket, while *fam-lay* had been in use to mean the act of pickpocketing since the 18th century. The notional state of *fam-rust* implied a lack of practice: one's skills had become 'rusty'. As part of the hand, the *knuckle* also became eligible for use as a synonym for a pickpocket in the late 18th century. The basic term soon produced the variations *knuckler*, *knucker*, *knucksman*, *knuckling cove* and the *knuck* (or *nuck*), as well as the female *knucklejill* and to *go on the knuckle* – to work as a pickpocket. *Finger-smith* (combining *finger* with the suffix *-smith* meaning an adept or an expert) meant a midwife in slang and a pickpocket in cant in the 19th century. *Angler* was another term appropriated from elsewhere in slang. The original criminal angler was a thief who used a pole with a hook at one end (the angling stick) to 'fish' items from open windows, unguarded market stalls, passing carts, and so on; the pickpocketing angler of the early 18th century required only his fingers to fish for his spoils. The *fork* was again a reference to the digits: the forked fingers used to grasp an object and slide it from the pocket. It has been in use since the late 17th century, although the synonymous rhyming slang *joe rourke* doesn't appear until the 1930s. Fingers also led to the 1940s American verb *two-finger*, and the South African name for pickpocketing from the 1980s, the *two fingers*. Finally, we have the 1990s term **greasy fingers**, so called because things 'stick' to his fingers.

The role of the hand or fingers underpins some less obvious terms. Although more often used as a challenge ('put up your fists!') in tales of juvenile derring-do, to **put up the dooks**, from *duke* (the hand), meant to pickpocket. So too did **clapperclaw**, literally to 'clap with the claws', which also has violent connotations – to claw or scratch with hands and nails, to beat or thrash.

When it comes to places where pickpockets operate, there has always been a rich vocabulary of specialist words. As the notorious Jenny Diver and her wooden arms proved in the early 18th century, church was always a good place for a pickpocket to work: while the congregation were supposedly focused on more lofty things than their pockets and purses, those pockets and purses were vulnerable to the attentions of the enterprising thief. *Autem* and *kirk* are both terms for a church, and those who operated there were known as **autem-** or **anthem-divers** in the 18th century and **kirk-buzzers** in the United States in the 19th. Also in the 18th and 19th centuries, the **groaner** or **sigher**'s name reflected his less subtle approach; his exaggeratedly enthusiastic (albeit completely spurious) devotions drew the congregants' attention away from his actual, nefarious, purpose.

On Location

Crowds, of course, have always been a natural hunting-ground. Pickpockets were to be found at the **breaking up of the spell** (from *spellken*, literally a 'play-house', i.e. a theatre) – the end of the nightly performances at the Theatres Royal, London in the 19th century (at this time they were the only two legally permitted theatres). As the crowds dispersed, pickpockets moved among them. The image of 'breaking out' of an enclosure also underpinned the **breaks**, which could refer to any crowded area which offered opportunities to a pickpocket. The **brief-snatcher** targeted such areas, stealing winning tickets from members of a racecourse crowd; it was known both as **brief-snatching** and **duket-snatching** (from *ducat*, a ticket). Less specific, but in the same venue, to pickpocket at a racecourse was to **dwell in the box**. Public transport, too, provided lots of potential victims. The ***chariot-buzzer*** targeted the passengers crushed into the busy omnibuses (i.e. 'chariots') of the 19th century. A more recent version is to ***work*** or ***ride the tubs***, which in the 1920s–1940s was to work as a pickpocket on the buses or at bus-stops (an earlier meaning was somewhat more glamorous: the commission of crimes, typically card-sharping, on board trans-atlantic liners).

Away from the crowds, coatrooms and cloakrooms have also had their specialists, such as the ***cold-finger man*** of the 1940s (a reference to hanging around in chilly air conditioning?) who might ***work the bob*** by robbing jackets and coats that have been hung up while people wash their hands. The term is from rhyming slang's *bob squash* – a wash, i.e. a wash room or public convenience.

Fashion and Crime

Some criminals have specialised in certain types of victims, rather than the place in which they stole from them. Female dress in the 19th century, with its bustles and hoops and layers of underwear that kept the garment some way away from the actual body, made women perfect targets for hands that wandered for monetary rather than sexual purposes. Such hands belonged to the ***moll buzzer***, ***moll-wire***, ***dame buzzer***, ***moll buzzard*** or ***moll worker*** – all pickpockets who specialised in female victims. Allied were ***moll-buzzing***, purse- or bag-snatching, and to ***buzz a moll***, to target a woman. The practice was still common in the mid-20th century when the slang collector Hyman Goldin explained the process in his *Dictionary of American Underworld Lingo* (1950):

> The theft is accomplished in the following manner: An accomplice, known as the buzzer, accosts a victim and asks to be directed to a given place in the neighborhood. The destination is so chosen that the victim must turn her back to the carriage to point. The purse-snatcher now advances from the direction which the victim is facing and deftly seizes the purse. The victim seldom discovers her loss until the thieves have disappeared. Premature discovery requires the buzzer, feigning solicitude, to block pursuit and delay any outcry until the snatcher has escaped.

The *moll buzzer* or *moll-wire* could also be a female pickpocket and synonymous were *moll hook*, *moll-knuck*, *moll-tooler*, *molley*, *moll-tool* and *mollwhiz*. There was also *maltooling*, which referred to a female pickpocket working the omnibuses with the other *chariot-buzzers*.

The fashion that made women easy targets also lent its own terms to the criminal's vocabulary. To *bustle* was to pick pockets, and women in the late 19th century sometimes worked *the bustle* – a trick whereby a young woman asks the proposed victim of the crime for the time, then pretends to stumble against him (getting in the way as the bustle of her dress might), so that her accomplice can protest to the man while the woman effects the theft. And clothing took an even more active role in the life of the pickpocket when it hid their criminal deeds. The *benny worker* found in America in the 1920s–1940s disguised his hands under an overcoat or *benny* (itself from slang's *benjamin*, an overcoat, which emphasised the predominance of Jews in tailoring – Benjamin being a 'typical' Jewish name). *Smother*, another slang term for overcoat, gave the *smother game*, in which the overcoat again was used to hide the thief's hands.

When the generic term is pickpocket, it is unsurprising that other terms have been based on the pockets into or under which they made their way. The *fob-diver* or *fobber* of the 19th century special-ised in removing small change from the victim's fob pocket; such pickpockets were often those who had lost their skills and could no longer attempt less accessible pockets such as the breast pocket (*pit*) that the *pit-worker* targeted. And in the 20th century we find the *prat-digger*, who steals from the hip pocket. The *prat* (as in showbiz's pratfall) had meant a buttock since the 16th century: the word seems to be echoic of the buttocks hitting a hard surface. Slang adopted it to mean a hip pocket, and the theft of a wallet from this popular pickpocket's target was a *prat frisk*. To ascertain the presence of a wallet in the trouser pocket was the job of the *prat man*, while pushing someone so as to place them in the correct position for pickpocketing was known as to *prat someone in*. Such a pickpocket might also be *on the bottle*. The latter is also a reference to plucking a wallet from an unguarded hip pocket but, thanks to rhyming slang, is not immediately obvious. It derives from *bottle and glass*, which rhymes with *arse* (the buttocks), and thus means the back or hip pocket. Therefore, *on the bottle* means theft from such a back pocket. In the 1910s, we have **jerver**. The *jervis* or *jervy* was the driver of a coach, recognisable by his distinctive striped waistcoat. A waistcoat (and that garment's watch pocket) came to be known as a *jerve*, and thus the person who extricates watches from said pocket was the jerver.

Handkerchief Thieves

Few slang terms for clothing are so lovingly evoked as the apparently lowly handkerchief. Those made of cotton were of little interest, but the silk handkerchief, whether sported by the smart East End coster-monger or the West End clubman, was another story. Of all the pickpockets' targets, there was nothing quite as alluring, at least in the mid-19th century, as a large and ornate silk handkerchief. In *Oliver Twist*, our first introduction to the still-invisible Fagin is the announcement that he's 'a sortin' the wipes' and it is the naïve Oliver's inability to take sensibly to his heels, rather than stare dumbstruck as Charley Bates abstracts one of these from a gentle-man's tailcoat, that leads him to the police court.

In the 17th and 18th centuries, the catch-all cant terms for hand-kerchief were **wiper** (which could also be applied to the pickpocket who stole them) and, as in Dickens, **wipe**. A specialist such as a **wipe-drawer** or **wipe-hauler** might **draw**, **bite**, **nap** or **nim a wipe**. A century later the American underworld embraced both the term and the item itself: **the wipe** was a form of confidence trick based on persuading the victim that money could be raised to a higher denomination, for which purpose it must first be secreted in a handkerchief. It is at this point that the switch was made, and when the victim retrieved the handkerchief, it contains nothing but waste paper.

The silk handkerchief was a **sleek wipe** or a **rum wipe**, but these much desired targets had a further generic: **billy**. The term 'honours' King William IV, in whose reign (1830–37) the use of silk handker-chiefs first became widespread. Previously their popularity had been primarily in the prize-ring, where fancy handkerchiefs were an essential trademark of certain fighters, but around this time they also formed a central part of costermonger fashion. As journalist and social commentator Henry Mayhew noted in *London Labour and the London Poor* (1861–2):

> The costermonger [...] prides himself most of all upon his neckerchief and boots. Men, women, boys and girls all have a passion for these articles. The man who does not wear his silk neckerchief [...] is known to be in desperate circumstances, the implication being that it has gone to supply the morning's stock money.

Given the popularity of these handkerchiefs, and the variety of their styles, in the mid-19th century the basic billy expanded to provide a number of variations, none of which the self-respecting **billy buzman** would have wanted to overlook.

The **belcher**, **belcher fogle** or **belcher wipe** was a tribute to the prize-fighter Jim Belcher (d.1811), whose preferred adornments these were. The original belcher could refer to any spotted handkerchief, but the fashionable costermonger defined them as those with a blue background and white – or occasionally yellow – spots. Another fighter, Jack Randall 'The Nonpareil' (1794–1828), was celebrated in the **randal's man**, which was a handkerchief in his own preferred pattern of green base and white spots. Prize-fighting also provided the **blue billy**, a blue handkerchief with white spots that was both worn at and, according to John Camden Hotten's *Slang Dictionary* (1867), used during prize fights: 'Before a set to it is common to take it from the neck and tie it round the leg as a garter, or round the waist to "keep it in the wind".' The blue billy soon made its way to New York, where we find it defined in James McCabe's study of *Lights and Shadows of New York Life* (1872) as 'a strange handkerchief'.

The **blood-red fancy** was a crimson handkerchief, the **yellow fancy** had white spots on its yellow background (the simpler **yellow man** was all-yellow), and the **cream fancy** or **cream billy** had a white or cream background with a variety of patterns. The **Kent**, **Kent clout** or **Kent rag** covered any variety of coloured handkerchief, presumably as favoured in that particular county or perhaps manufactured there, while the **Spittleonian** was yellow and manufactured in Spitalfields in the East End of London. The **kingsman** or **kinsman**, presumably another reference to the monarch of the time, meant any silk handkerchief irrespective of its colour, although the term could specifically refer to a handkerchief with a green base and a yellow pattern. The rather grand sounding **kingsman of the rortiest** was a very gaudy variety. The debatable origin of *rorty*, meaning fine or splendid, is either from Yiddish *rorität*, anything choice, or from rhyming slang (= naughty).

Whatever the colour or pattern, all of these handkerchiefs were – quite literally – up for grabs. And grabbed they were, by pickpockets whose various names had close links to the valuable silken cloths they pursued. The **clouter** relates to the use of *clout* as a generic for clothing, but *clout* also meant the handkerchief itself. (In Australia and America, the use of clout meaning to steal is taken from the pickpocketing clouter.) A **queer clout** was a cheap, probably cotton, handkerchief that as such was not worth the wiper's time, unlike the silk or other high-quality material **rum clout** and **squeeze-clout**, which was also a neck cloth. On spotting one of these spoils, the thief might **top a clout** if he managed to position the handkerchief in the victim's pocket in readiness for its subsequent removal. (Although not all were accessible to pickpockets. The **kidment** was a handkerchief that was attached to the pocket from which it protruded, so that a pickpocket, however careful, would alert the handkerchief's owner when an attempt was made to remove it.)

Like clout, **fogle** meant a silk handkerchief, and as such might be targeted by a **fogle-hunter** or **-drawer**. It was most likely borrowed from the quasi-Italian languages Lingua Franca (a form of pidgin spoken in theatres and circuses) and Polari (originated among sailors and theatre people and still popular in the gay world), and presumably was based on Italian *foglia*, a leaf. There are, however, claims for the word coming from French argot *fouille*, a pocket, and, although even less likely, German *vogel*, a bird. (The latter supposedly links to the 'bird's eye' pattern of some handkerchiefs, known as *bird's eye fogles* or *bird's eye wipes*.) A further set of terms was attached to **stook**, a term for a handkerchief most likely rooted in German *Stück*, a piece of cloth. There was **stook buzzing**, the **stook buzzer** or **stook hauler**.

Finally, one encounters the seemingly geographically specific *St Giles buzzman*. Why the pickpockets of the St Giles *rookery* (a notorious criminal slum), based near Oxford Street's junction with Charing Cross and Tottenham Court Road (it vanished when New Oxford Street was cut through in 1847), should have been especially keen on stealing handkerchiefs is unknown – other than their undeniable value, of course. What seems most likely is that the St Giles prefix was simply an all-purpose term that could be appended to anything criminal.

St Giles and Friends

Several canting terms of the 18th and 19th century referenced the St Giles area of London (see above). *St Giles's breed*, *St Giles's* and *St Giles's company* all meant criminals as a class; *St Giles's carpet* was a sprinkling of sand on the street (presumably to mask spilled blood – or perhaps nothing more than an overflowing sewer); and *St Giles's Greek* meant slang or cant, *Greek* in this case being an all-purpose term for any incomprehensible language.

But as we've seen, not all handkerchiefs were valuable, and criminal language reflected this disparity in the way it described these less desirable accessories. In cant the *snotter* meant a dirty, ragged handkerchief (it came, unsurprisingly, from the standard English word for nasal mucus – snot, which itself dates from the 14th century). Snot also provided the basis of the disparaging *snottinger*, a run-of-the-mill pocket handkerchief. Nonetheless there must have been some profit in them for the less discerning thief, since the phrase *snotter-hauling* referred specifically to stealing such handkerchiefs.

The Loot: from Watches to Wallets
Other specialist terms refer to the chosen booty itself, the stuff
that was so carefully picked from the pocket (or purse or bag).
Thus the **chain man** and the **watch-maker** both took watches,
the former in the 1930s, and the latter in the mid-18th century. The
dummy-hunter or **dummee-hunter** stole wallets (*dummies*)
throughout the 19th century. A *reader* was a wallet or pocket-book
in the 18th century, so a **reader hunter** or **reader merchant** might
drawer, **nail** or **nap a reader** when he stole one. Such criminals
would be tempted by a *hanger*, a wallet protruding from a pocket
or purse, and thus ripe for removal. The 19th-century **poge-hunter**
opted for purses (*poges* or *pokes*). A *prop* (from Dutch *proppe*, a
skewer, a brooch) meant variously a scarf- or tie-pin, a woman's
brooch or a valuable piece of jewellery; all of which terms lasted
from the 19th century well into the mid-20th and the **prop-getter**
stole them all. However, the upmarket **stone getter** of the early
20th century was more selective, restricting himself to brooches,
particularly diamond ones.

The Pickpocket Team

The pickpocket tends to work in a team, and there is potentially an
individual available to cover every task: one to do the actual work
of 'dipping' or 'lifting', one to distract or jostle the victim, one to
whom the stolen goods are passed, one to cover the escaping 'lifter'
and one to look out for the police or other authorities. Occasionally
the theft might be a one-man show, in which case the usual multi-
person team is 'short'; thus in 1920s America the lone pickpocket
would **work on shorts**.

The Pickpocket Himself
However many members there are in a team, one has to extend
their hand and actually dip into a purse or pocket to remove the
prize. As opposed to generic synonyms for pickpocket, there are
some specific names for the person who actually gets the job done.
In the 20th century these have included the **worker**, the **instrument**
and the **claw**. In the mid-19th century the terms **tool** (briefly **tooler**)

and *wire* appear very much interchangeable, as seen in the criminal memoir *Leaves from the Diary of a Celebrated Burglar and Pickpocket* (1865):

> The rest of the 'stalls' [were] there waiting for the appearance of the 'wire' [. . .] they were getting uneasy at the absence of their 'tool' and began drinking, smoking and reading the morning papers.

General Assistant

In his *History of* [. . .] *the World's Most Notorious Highwaymen* (1719), Captain Alexander Smith offered the 'Thieves' Exercise', a mini-glossary of cant presented as a sort of phrasebook for thieves. A number of its terms pertain to pickpocketing, such as **Bulk the Call to the Right**, explained as 'for a fellow in a crowd to jostle a man or punch him so on the right breast, so that putting his hand up to ease himself, the bulker's comrade picks his pocket on the left side and gives the booty to another to carry off'. Another is the command **Tip the cole to Adam Tiler**, which is explained as 'to give the pickpocket-money, watch, handkerchief, or any other thing to a running comrade, that in case the taker thereof is apprehended, he may have nothing with which he is charged found upon him'. The *adam tiler* Smith mentions, still in use in America in the reduced form **adam**, continues to defeat attempts at etymology. The meaning is simple – an assistant – but why? The most likely suggestion is the combination of *Adam*, as a generic for man, and German *teile*, a share or slice, in other words a man who took a share of the profits.

Other assistants were known by terms appropriated from elsewhere in slang, such as the **hustler**, more commonly a person who lives on their wits and ingenuity, or **punter**, more usually a bettor. The **reefer** borrowed *reef*, to roll up and secure all or part of a sail, from sailing jargon (in this case the theft is secured). The hapless **scarecrow** was a disposable young assistant who could be turned over to the police in order to save the more experienced members of the team; the image behind the term might be that of making him as easily visible as a scarecrow standing in a field.

The Jostler or Distracter

Like the conjuror whose name criminal slang borrowed, the active pickpocket relies as much on misdirection as on actual sleight of hand. As we've seen, this can be done by distracting the victim's attention, but more than likely it will be somewhat less subtle: an accomplice simply shoves against the victim to force them against the actual thief.

Perhaps the best-known, and as a late 16th-century coinage certainly the oldest, term for any type of assistant is ***stall*** or ***stale*** (from standard English *stall*, a decoy bird). By the late 18th century, the stall was also a manoeuvre whereby a target was pinioned and rendered open to theft, and later to ***chuck (someone) a stall*** was when one member of the team walked in front of the victim to slow him or her down while another picked the pocket.

Other non-physical interference was created by the ***cover***, ***cover guy*** or ***cover-up man***, a confederate who screened the operations of a thief or pickpocket. Such a figure was also known as a ***gammon***, but this is a term that continues to defeat the etymologists. The most popular theory is a link to the backgammon jargon *gammon*: to defeat an opponent before they have been able to remove a single 'man' (thus inflicting a crushing defeat). However, other claims have been put forward for the simple *(play a) game* (especially as game is also itself a possible origin of backgammon), as well as a figurative use of the *gammoning*, or 'tying up' of a bowsprit or a piece of ham. Whichever the true origin, ***give gammon*** meant to stand next to a person while an accomplice picked their pocket. Along the same lines, ***shade*** meant to protect a pickpocket while they worked, just as one might shade someone from the light, and to ***smother*** was to use some form of object to obscure the victim's view while the pickpocket zeroes in.

Thereafter, it's all rough stuff. The ***bulk*** or ***bulker*** of the 17th century most likely came from the standard use of *bulk* meaning a large lump; in this case the human 'lump' pushes one around or stands in one's way (alternatively the root may lie in the obsolete 14th-century *bulk*, to beat). The term was expanded to give the duo of the ***bulk and file*** – the assistant and the expert thief: one jostled the victim while the other picked the pocket. Quite unequivocal in their physical technique were the ***bumper***, the ***bumper-up*** and the ***bump man***, as well as the ***elbow***. The antique ***shoulder-sham***, literally a 'shoulder-trick', could also refer to the individual who enacted it, as did the **push-up man**, who pushed up the arm of the victim to facilitate access to their wallet; he might be part of a **push-up mob** who specialised in this method.

Removing the Loot
Once the wire has removed his hand (and what it has obtained) from the victim's pocket, the first priority is to get rid of the booty and render himself **clean**. For this there have existed a number of helpers. Among them a 19th-century trio: the **baggage-man**, the **carrier** and **stickman** (who not only took possession of the stolen item but was also responsible for hindering any attempts by the police or public to capture another member of the team). Spell it how you wish, all variations of **lamster** come from American prison use and originally meant an escapee or fugitive; in the 1920s the word was appropriated to mean the member of a pickpocket team who escapes with the loot. The root of the word lies either in *lammas*, to depart, or slang's *lam*, to hit (and thus a pun on *beat it*, to run off). To **stand Miss Slang** came from *sling*, to throw (in this case the stolen item); it referred to an accomplice who stands to one side, ready to be passed whatever has been stolen by the **slanger**.

The Lookout
In mainstream slang *dekko* is a glance or look, coming from a blend of Hindi *dekh-nā* and Romany *dik*, both meaning to look. In 20th-century America this has led to the **decker** for the pickpocket's lookout.

THE STREET CON ARTIST: PEAS, THIMBLES, GARTERS AND OTHER TRICKS

> They'd sheared the rubes and flapped the jays, flimflammed them at the jam auctions and suckered them at three-card monte, yet [...] the rubes were jostling each other to try again [...] for the chance of being sheared, suckered, hooked, fleeced, and flimflammed one more time.
>
> Nelson Algren, 'The Last Carousel' in *Texas Stories* (1995)

Both pickpocketing and street gambling games are types of street robbery that depend on keeping the victims completely ignorant. The difference being that with pickpocketing the target is simply unaware of what is going on; but with street gambling games, the victim is in fact an eager participant in what is happening. The problem is that they haven't a clue as to what is really going on.

Prick the Garter

Prick the garter is one of the oldest popular gambling games. It is played by taking a leather strap, usually a belt but failing that any length of material: this is the 'garter'. Fold it into loops and hold the 'fold' firmly in one hand. With the other, brandish a large needle: this is the 'pin'. Offer to bet against any onlooker that they won't be able to take the pin and prick that place where the garter is folded. Let them try, see them fail, take their money. The slang lexicographer John Camden Hotten elaborated on the trick in 1859, explaining that this 'gambling and cheating game' is:

> ... generally practised by thimble riggers. It consists of a 'garter' or a piece of list [i.e. selvage or whole cloth] doubled, and then folded up tight. The bet is made upon your asserting that you can with a pin 'prick' the point at which the garter is doubled. The garter is then unfolded, and nine times out of ten you will find that you have been deceived, and that you pricked one of the false folds. The owner of the garter, I should state, holds the ends tightly with one hand.

Found wherever people gathered in the open air – typically fair-grounds, markets and racecourses – it was variously known as **prick (in) the belt, prick the girdle, pin and girdle** or **pitch the nob**. No acceptable etymology has been found for this last, although the popular term for one who ran such a game was a **nob-pitcher**. It is possibly linked to the obsolete *nob*, a knot (i.e. the folded garter), or to *nob*, slang for head, here extended to mean a target. The prick the garter form has been recorded since the 18th century, but an earlier name is 200 years older – the **fast and loose** of George Whetstone in the play *Promos & Cassandra* (1578): 'At fast or loose, with my Giptian [i.e. a gypsy], I meane to haue a cast.' Using fast in the sense of 'fixed or immovable', the phrase refers to the pin being able to fix the loop in place. In time, fast and loose (usually prefaced by *play*) entered mainstream use, first of one who was inconsistent or variable and later of one who trifled with another's affections.

Playing a Different Kind of Game

To **play at prick the garter**, it might be added, is one of a number of phrases that, in their additional meaning to have sexual intercourse, punned on popular games of chance. Others included **play at mumble-peg, at tops and bottoms, where the Jack takes Ace, at all fours, at in and in** and **at level-coil.** The last did not involve gambling but was an early form of musical chairs popularly played at Christmas, in which each player was in turn driven from their seat and replaced by another; it comes from the French *(faire) lever la cul (à quelqu'un)*, to make someone raise their buttocks, properly 'arse' – also found in Italian as *levaculo*.

Thimble Rigging

If we believe the American writer Luc Sante, in his 1991 account of New York's underclass *Low Life*, the cheating 'game' of **thimble-rig** (literally a 'thimble-trick') is one of 'the only major gambling games actually invented in the United States', and originated around 1860. However, the English writer and bookseller William Hone's *Every-day Book* had in 1825 already mentioned the same game's existence in Britain, and the term was being used figuratively a decade later. **Thimblerigger**, the man who runs the game, does appear first in America, but again somewhat earlier than Sante suggests, in 1831.

The thimble-rig was essentially the forerunner of the modern three-card trick or three-card monte (although it can still be found). The ***thimble-cove***, who ran the game, placed three thimbles in a row on a flat surface with a pea beneath one. The thimbles were then very rapidly manipulated and the punters asked to bet on which thimble now hid the pea. It was very rare that anyone – other than the cove's accomplice – managed to guess correctly.

From the mid-19th century the game was known as ***pea and thimble***. Dickens included the game and the ***pea and thimble men*** who ran it in his description of a racetrack scene in *Nicholas Nickleby* (1867):

> Here a little knot gathered round a pea and thimble table to watch the plucking of some unhappy greenhorn and there, another proprietor with his confederates in various disguises [. . .] sought by loud and noisy talk and pretended play to entrap some unwary customer, while the gentlemen confederates [. . .] betrayed their close interest in the concern by the anxious furtive glances they cast on all new comers.

Thimble, quite coincidentally, has other criminal uses. A *thimble* (or *thim*) meant a watch from the late 18th century until the 1940s, and a ***thimble-screwer*** a thief who specialised in stealing them. It may have derived from its earlier nautical use, which defined thimble as a thick ring of metal, through which a rope can be pushed; there was some similarity in shape. One who was wearing a watch was said to be ***thimbled***; but it could also mean arrested, punning on the idea of 'watch' (i.e. that carried out by the police).

Back to street gambling, across the Atlantic one could also find the ***shell game***, in which walnut shells substitute for thimbles – an alternative name was ***the nuts***. The ***shell man*** or ***shell worker*** who ran the game might ***spiel the nuts*** (the spiel refers to the distracting chatter with which he helped to cover up his manipulations). A lesser known version dating from the 1940s, substituting small boxes for the shells, was the ***block game*** (also known as ***the peeks***, as one peeks beneath the boxes). The pea or similar small object used in these and other similar American games was the ***little joker***, perhaps referring to the sharper having the last laugh on the victims.

Tricks with Three Cards

Thimble-rigging did not vanish, but the version that has evolved (based on three playing cards – one usually a queen, the others not being court cards) is much more popular and can still be found across the world. In Paris, for instance, instead of cards three rubber discs are used – all backs are the same, but one face is white while the other two are black. The principle is of course always the same: in every version the bettor must work out which is the target object, card, disc etc. The end is always the same: in no version does he or she ever succeed, other than when the **sharper** is attempting to gee up a crowd. And probably not even then; if anyone is guessing correctly and pocketing piles of notes while loudly attesting to the honesty of the game, you may assume that what you are seeing is an accomplice who will soon be giving his 'winnings' back.

The modern game has various names, the primary ones being the **three-card trick** or **three-card monte** (occasionally **molly**). The etymology of the first is self-explanatory; the second refers to the game of *monte*, a gambling game similar to faro (itself regularly fixed – yet another surefire way of losing one's money), played with a pack of 45 (sometimes 40) cards. Monte was especially popular in Spain, Central and South America and in the Spanish-influenced areas of the western United States, and in *Suckers' Progress* (1938) – his history of American gambling – Herbert Asbury (of *Gangs of New York* fame) maintains that 'Three-Card Monte was a Mexican invention, and a misnomer if ever there was one, for it had no more actual relationship to Monte than to Old Maid.'

It is possible that the idea of the three manipulated objects gave a slightly earlier name to an even earlier version of the game: **thrums**. 'The Flash Man of St Giles', a canting ballad of the 1780s, included the lyrics 'We have mill'd a precious go / And queer'd the flats at thrums.' **Queer the flats** meant to exploit the suckers; it is hard to see thrums, for which the only other known definition is threepence, meaning anything but the three-card trick.

The game could be conducted by a **charley-pitcher, three-card charlie** (using the proper name as a generic term for a man) or a **three-card (monte) man**. In Australia the **monte-man** or **monty** might run the game, or he might also be an all-purpose swindler who never picked up a card or (though in this definition he might on occasion be honest) a racecourse tipster. Stephens and O'Brien in their *Materials for a Dictionary of Australian Slang* (unpublished; collected 1900–10) defined him as a professional card or gambling swindler and offered the synonyms **spieler**, **blackleg**, **takedown**, **magsman**. Somewhat confusingly, Australians and New Zealanders commonly use monte to mean an absolute certainty and, with even greater faith, an admirable person.

A **nobbler** might also be a manipulator, although in context he was more likely to be one of the accomplices posing as an enthusiastic and egregiously successful bettor. Such an accomplice might have been a **button** or **buttoner**: a suggested etymology is the relative unimportance of buttons, but more feasible is the idea of 'buttoning up' the victim. For a button to draw in a sucker, allowing them small victories and thus increasing their confidence (and bets) prior to taking their money, was to **reload** them. In the 1940s, the accomplice was known as a **shill**, although the term (possibly abbreviating the Irish *shillelagh*, a cudgel – thus he 'cudgels' the victim into participation) was used for anyone who lured the target into any sort of crooked game (as well as into brothels, strip-clubs and other places where they were likely to come out substantially poorer). Another rank of helper was the **slide**, the member of the team who kept an eye out for police and warned the rest so that all could 'slide off' in time. (Like shill, this gave a more general term – the **slide game**, any form of confidence trick whereby the trickster takes the victim's money and vanishes.)

Aside from names based on 'three', the trick is most commonly associated with **broads**, a canting term for playing cards. *The broads* can indicate the con itself, and to **toss the broads** is to conduct the game of three-card monte (and thus to deal any card game, especially a crooked or illegal one). The **broadsman** 'officiates' at the table; his 19th-century forbears were the **broad faker**, **-pitcher**, **-spieler** or **-tosser**, who would **fake** or **work the broads**. Broads were not restricted to this specific trick: the word was commonly compounded to mean a cardsharp (such as the 19th-century **broad cove**), and the **broad-fencer** peddled lists of racing tips (known as 'correct cards') at horse races. The **broad mob** was a gang of card-sharpers and to **spread (the) broads** was to play cards, usually when cheating or running some form of swindling game: one fans out the cards across the table for the punters to make their choice.

Other terms related to the objects played with or played on: the cards and the 'table' (or other form of flat surface on which any of these tricks were played). The queen of any suit is the **lady**, and to **find the lady** gives another synonym for the game. The **sweat board**, **cloth** or **table** was the board or cloth upon which three-card monte took place; the sweat presumably was that of the losing suckers. Finally, the American **flat joint** is widely used to refer to any form of a crooked gambling game or casino, but it comes originally from fairground or carnival use, when a *flat* was a crooked or doctored 'wheel of fortune'.

Pitch and Toss

The game of pitch and toss is known in cant as **mag-flying** and has been recorded since the mid-18th century. In the modern world it is far better known as **two-up** or **swy** (from German *zwei*, two), a gambling game that might be termed Australia's alternative national (if technically illegal) sport, and which is based on betting on the fall of a pair of pre-decimal-era pennies, flipped upwards from a wooden paddle or **kip**.

The original was described a century later in the anonymous memoir *Leaves from the Diary of a Celebrated Burglar and Pickpocket* (1865):

> Mag-flying [. . .] consists in tossing or twinkling in the air two pence or half-pence. The two pence or half-pence are placed upon a small flat piece of wood [. . .] tail uppermost, and thrown up in the air with a twinkling motion, caused by the twist given to the piece of wood, at the time of parting from it; if they fall head uppermost the tosser wins whatever bet there may be on it; if tail appears he loses, if one head and one tail, he tosses over again.

The *mag* (or *meg*) was a halfpenny, and as well as mag-flying it gave **fly the mags**. The seemingly unconnected **pieman** (in the 19th century the player who shouts out 'heads' or 'tails' in the game and in the 1900s the game itself) referred specifically to the 'toss' part of its name, playing on the pieman's once common cry 'Hot pies, toss or buy! Toss or buy!'

The mag made an appearance in Arthur Morrison's then-shocking chronicle of the most poverty-stricken of the East End's many impoverished streets, *A Child of the Jago* (1896): 'Those of the High Mob were the flourishing practitioners in burglary, the mag, the mace, and the broads, with an outer fringe of such dippers – such pickpockets – as could dress well, welshers and snidesmen.' Here, however, mag meant confidence trickery or swindling in general. The language expert Michael Quinion, on his *World Wide Words* website, suggests that the swindling **magsman** or **mag** may have come from the monetary meaning, and certainly one cannot avoid the swindling element of the pitch and toss game, which would usually be fixed by double-headed halfpennies (or whatever other method). But Quinion notes a more likely link to mag as meaning the mouth, and thus the important role of smooth patter in deceiving the victim and putting over the con. Whatever the etymology, what is common is that the magsman was seen as a crook who used his intelligence, as Michael Davitt writes in *Leaves from a Prison Diary* (1885): 'The order of magsmen will comprise card-sharpers, "confidence trick" workers, begging-letter writers, bogus ministers of religion, professional noblemen, "helpless victims of the cruel world", medical quacks and various other clever rogues.' Tossing halfpennies does not seem to be part of his CV.

Chapter 4

THEFT AND ROBBERY

Rum coves that relieve us
Of chinkers and pieces
Is gin'rally lagged
Or wuss luck gets scragg'd

H. Baumann, 'A Slang Ditty' in *Londonismen* (1887)

GENERAL THIEVING

The Thief

Thief is one of the oldest terms in English; it dates back at least to the late 7th century and takes its source from a root meaning to crouch down. The clusters of terms that have been associated with the various branches of larceny are substantial in number. The thief may not have been the only member of the *family*, as the real criminal fraternity – prefiguring the fictional Corleones – called themselves from the 18th century on (two centuries later the term would become the *Johnsons*, presumably from the generic simplicity of the surname), but he seems to have been the best attested.

The first of such terms, testifying to what he might term his M.O. (i.e. *modus operandi*) today, was the **filch**. The word has no provable origin, though claims have been made for links either to Welsh *yspeilio*, to steal (with a 'common' change from 'p/sp' to 'f'), or Lowland Scottish *pilk*, to pilfer. In this case the implement seems to have created its wielder – the filch was a short pole, with some form of hook on its end, which the filch, **filcher**, and later **filching cove** used to 'fish' for objects on stalls, in the open fronts of shops, or on passing carts and the unguarded like. Filch was also found as a verb, first appearing as such in John Awdeley's *Fraternitye of Vacabondes* (*c*.1561) (devotees of criminal cant will also note *bowsing*, i.e. boozing, and as such one of the longest surviving of the words used by the professional criminals of the era):

> A Prygman [thief] goeth with a stycke in hys hand like an idle person. His propertye is to steale cloathes of the hedge [. . .] or els filch Poultry, carying them to the Alehouse, whych they call the Bowsyng In, & ther syt playing at cardes and dice, tyl that is spent which they haue so fylched.

Reference to the 'fishing' aspect of such thefts continued in the near-contemporary **angler** or **anglero**, who used a pole known as an 'angling stick'. (The angler returned in the late 19th century as a smash-and-grab thief, while the 18th-century **angling-cove** was a receiver of stolen goods, hence **angling**, receiving stolen goods; in both cases he was one who 'fishes in troubled waters'.) There was also the **hooker**, which might be expanded as the **bene hooker boy**, an expert thief (1930s America had **hooky**, but he was just a simple thief). The **comber** was from *comb*, which was another name for the hooked pole used to steal items from stalls or shop windows – as was the 16th-century **curb**, based on standard *curb*, to bend. To curb was to use the pole to steal and the **curbing law** was the 'official' term for such a theft. As Robert Greene explained it in his *Second Part of Coney-Catching* (1591):

> The *Courber* [i.e. Curber], which the common people call the *Hooker*, is he that with a *Curbe* (as they tearme it) or hooke, do pull out of a windowe any loose linnen cloth, apparell, or else any other houshold stuffe.

Even in the 1930s, when such poles had long since been abandoned, *fish* was being used to mean rob and, in the same period, **pole on** emerged in Australia. However, the pole in this case was a reference to bullock-driving – specifically to *polers*, the pair of bullocks nearest the wagon's pole, seen as most likely to 'take things easy'.

Awdeley called his thief the 'prygman', and this word is a variation of another important 16th-century coinage for a thief: the *prig*, which seems to play on standard English *prick*, meaning 'sting' and thus to subject to crime. In its original sense, a prig or *prigman* was a ne'er-do-well who, accompanied by his woman, wandered the country mixing villainy and legitimate work, but pursuing neither, it appears, with particular enthusiasm (he was sometimes known as the *drunken tinker*). From this aimless vagrancy he progressed to fulltime thieving, specifically of clothes from the hedgerows where they were regularly left to dry, or of poultry from the farmyard (a *prigger of (the) cacklers* was a chicken stealer). To be *priggish* meant to exhibit the characteristics of a thief, while to prig was to steal and *priggism*, *priggery* and *priggyism* all meant theft. Practitioners of priggism included the *prigger-napper* or *prigster napper* and the *prigster*. The *prince prig* was a leading thief, especially one who acts as a receiver for the robberies of colleagues; the name was also given to the current King of the Gypsies.

Sticky Fingers

The image of the thief's 'sticky-fingers' appeared alongside the earliest recorded of names associated with thieving. The late 16th century noted that a thief's fingers are *made of lime-twigs* and are thus 'sticky' – a *lime twig* was a twig smeared with the sticky substance birdlime, in order to catch birds. The thief himself might be a *lime-twig* or *lime-finger* and *birdlime* came to mean larceny in the following century. The 19th century's *pitch-fingers* referred to another sticky substance, *pitch*, which was used (*inter alia*) for sealing ships' timbers. Eventually, *sticky fingers* itself emerged to mean a thief in the 1940s, giving *sticky-fingered*, larcenous, and to *play sticky fingers*, to rob. Providing a similar image, to *glue*, used from the 1920s–70s, meant to steal.

Other early terms
Alongside the prygman, the 16th century also had the **conveyancer**, who 'conveyed' the victim's money or other property into his possession. The 17th century added the **napper** and **nicker**, both derived from words meaning to steal. **Nim** (from German *nehmen*, to take) worked in the same way and could also be a verb: to *nim a tatler*, for example, was to steal a watch. From the same period, the **bloss** was female and linked to *blowse*, defined by Nathaniel Bailey's *Universal Etymological Dictionary* (1731) as a 'fat, red-faced, bloted wench, or one whose head is dressed like a slattern'. The **puggard** expanded the standard English *pug*, to pull or tug (and thus to steal from), while the **sutler** again played on a standard term: a *sutler* was one who sells provisions to soldiers, whether in the garrison or in camp. The era also saw the **abram-man** or **abram-cove** take on a new guise, as a thief who took one's pocket-book or wallet; as a member of the canting crew he had previously been a wandering beggar who adopted tattered clothing and posed as a mad person.

18th- and 19th-century terms
Terms of implied approval are common in cant, as the 18th-century **boman, bowman-prig** and **beauman-prig** demonstrate. All mean a first-rate thief and are derived from French *beau*, handsome. Similarly the 19th century gave rise to the *fly man*, from *fly*, meaning astute or shrewd.

Georgian and Victorian Thieves: a Miscellany

buzz (he 'stings' the victim)
cloy (from *cloy*, to steal, itself based on *cly*, to snatch or
    steal – possibly linked to Erse *cloib*, a snatch; a
    snatch-cly specialised in robbing women)
cribbing cove
faker or **faking boy**
finder
fancy cove

gleaner

gyp (an abbreviation of gypsy, thus a piece of negative stereotyping)

kin (a reference to the 'family' of criminals)

klep or *klepper* (i.e. kleptomaniac)

nabber

nipper

operator

racket man

shooting star (so-called because he travelled from town to town)

snatcher

tradesman (his 'job' was *the trade, fair trade* or *free trade*)

Two key terms appeared in the 19th century. In standard English *cross* means contrary, opposed. It was adopted into criminal use in the early part of the century to mean (of a person) dishonest and (of an object) dishonestly attained. A number of compounds followed to describe those who might be *on the cross* (i.e. involved in crime): the *cross cove, cross-man* and *cross-life man, cross-boy, cross-chap, cross kid, cross lad, cross squire* and *squire of the cross* were all larcenous villains; the *cross-cove and mollisher*, a man and woman who work in tandem as thieves (the *cross mollisher* was a female criminal); the *cross-crib* or *cross-drum*, a public house frequented by thieves; and the *cross-rattler*, a coach (the echoic *rattler*) whose coachman aided criminals by taking their booty away from the scene of the crime. Cross had other uses, too: a *cross-fight*, for example, was a fixed prizefight.

The *gonnof* was also introduced in the 19th century, as well as its numerous alternative spellings, which included the *ganef, gonif, gonof, gonoph,* and *gunnif*. The word came from the synonymous Hebrew *gannabh*, thief; slang lexicographer John Camden Hotten suggested in 1860 that it was 'as old as Chaucer's time', but his mistaken reference was to the standard English *gnoff*, a peasant or lout, which comes from East Frisian *knufe*, lump, and *gnuffig*, thick, rough, coarse and ill-mannered. An *arch-gonnof* was the leader of a gang of thieves. To gonnof was to steal and **gonnofing** theft. In turn, gonnof provided **gun**, which is still a well-known term for pickpocket, and the female version, **guness**. Gun or **gunner** has meant thief as well as pickpocket, and to **punch the gun** was to use criminal slang.

The Rise of Rhyming Slang

Rhyming slang was first recorded in slang dictionaries in 1857, but it seems to have been created around 1820. There are a number of theories as to the originators: they may have been Irish navvies, brought in to build canals and later railways; London costermongers seeking to mask their conversations from the customer; or criminals who needed to replace older terms that were by then well-known to the authorities. As far as the word 'thief' is concerned, the basic rhyming slang was, and remains, the **tealeaf**. It dates from the late 19th century and gives to tealeaf, to thieve, and to be **on the tealeaf** or **tea-leafing**, involved in robbery. Additional rhymes are the **leg of beef**, the **lettuce leaf** and the **corned beef**. Another is **Ted Heath**: pronounced as 'heef' in Cockneydom, it comes ultimately from Edward Heath (1916–2005), the British prime minister from 1970– 74. Elsewhere, the mid-19th-century **eat a fig** rhymed on *crack a crib*, to commit burglary, to **half-inch** is to pinch and the New Zealand **half-hitch**, to snitch. There is also the Australian **rock spider**, a thief who robs courting couples in parks or at the seaside when their attention is elsewhere. It too rhymes, but not in the classic manner, taking itself from the lines of the old nursery rhyme 'Little Miss Muffet': 'There came a big spider/And sat down beside her.'

The Modern Era

Perhaps the most familiar British word for thief today is **blagger**, first recorded in the 1930s when Scotland Yard detective F.D. Sharpe, in his *Sharpe of the Flying Squad* (1938), wrote that 'Hooks, wizzers, blaggers, screwsmen, hoists, and lowly moll buzzers [. . .] abound in the Underworld of London.' It comes from **blag**, a term for a robbery (often with violence, and usually of a bank or post office) first recorded in 1885. The 1950s **blag-merchant** was a pay-roll robber.

Then there is the **chorie**, whose name comes from **chore**, to steal; the words are adapted from the Romany *cor* (to steal), which had been in use since the late 19th century meaning to steal small articles from shops. The ubiquitous **grifter** appeared in the 1910s, although to **grift** (in the sense of to steal) is only recorded from the 1950s.

TO ROB AND TO STEAL

Many verbs have been coined for robbing and stealing. The 16th century's **bird** came from *bird*, a con-man's victim; to **boothale** came from standard English's *booty* and *haul*; to **feng** came from the Anglo-Saxon *feng*, a grasp or hug; while to **strike** was a figurative use of the standard meaning. To **shave** punned on 'trim', and was succeeded a century later by **dry shave**, with the extra image of being 'cheated' of the water required for a proper shave.

Standard English *heave* means to lift and carry away. In criminal use it was to rob, and to **heave a bough** or **booth** was to rob or rifle a *booth* (the contemporary equivalent of a shop) or a house; the 18th-century version was **heave a case** (from *case*, a house). The **booth-heaver** was the thief. To **poll** – another theft from the standard, in this case to plunder or to fleece (and ultimately to cut someone's *poll*, or hair) – was to use trickery rather than violence for one's thefts.

As we have seen, the thief has long been a fan of euphemism. Terms from the 17th century onwards include to **borrow** (thus **borrowing**, theft), to **touch**, to **buss** (literally to 'kiss'), to **touch**, to **tickle**, to **rub**, to **pick up**, to **tuck up** (which also meant to hang), to *attract*, to *bank*, to *claim*, to *serve*, to *sift*, to *sponge*, to *have*, to *say*, to *cadge*, to *sneeze* and to *stroke*. New Zealand's *fend off* was based on the image of 'fending off' the object from its owner so that one may keep it for oneself. To *ease* sounds euphemistic too, but it comes from the standard meaning – to deprive or despoil.

Other terms also reflect the innate physicality, violent or otherwise, attendant on robbery. Again starting in the 1600s, one finds to *pluck*, to *snaffle*, to *crash*, to *do in*, to *skin*, to *beat* or *beat off*, to *bang*, to *bounce*, to *ding*, and to *knock down* or *over*. Pure violence can be seen in *clout*, which was a 20th-century back-formation of the 18th century's *clouter*, one who stole handkerchiefs (*clouts*); to *bump*, an African-American term from the 1980s, is a direct descendant. To *scrag* now means to steal, but formerly it referred to beating and killing, and was based on grasping someone by the *scrag* (their neck). To *scrag a lay* meant to steal clothes that had been laid out on a hedge to dry. The clothes-line, the hedge's modern equivalent, was also vulnerable: to steal from one of those was to *snow-drop* (from the snowy whiteness of freshly washed linen), to *gooseberry* (playing on gooseberry bush) or to *pick a berry*.

Action returned with *frisk* and *put the frisk on*, used especially when targeting a sleeping or helpless person (to *stag* was to rob a man sleeping in the street); to *hobble* and to *muzzle*, subjecting a person to the same restraints as an animal; to *whip*, which in standard use was to take briskly or suddenly; to *blow* or *clean out*; to *gobble*; and to *gun*, which presumably involved using one. To *nail* was a mid-18th-century arrival; in the 19th century to *nail a rattler* was a tramp term for stealing a ride on a moving train. To *ramp* adopted the standard English *ramp*, to act in a threatening manner, and meant to rob with violence. It gave the phrase *done for a ramp*, convicted of a violent crime. The late 19th century also gives *glom* (otherwise spelt *glahm, glam, glaum, glaum onto, glomm, glom onto, gloom* or *glum*), which comes from the Scottish *glaum* – to snatch, to grab, to seize with the jaws, to eat greedily. It was particularly favoured by the authors of pulp fiction. Again from Scottish was to *snam* (literally to 'snap at greedily'), which was defined in the 19th century by John Camden Hotten as: 'That kind of theft which consists in picking up anything lying about, and making off with it rapidly.' Twentieth-century additions include to **roust**, to **pull off** or **down**, to **dig into**, to **root**, to **tip over**, to **bend**, to **dead**, to **zap**, to **hoop** (literally to 'bind or fasten with hoops') and to **stoush**, a black British term that may be linked to the dialect *stashie*, a quarrel or uproar. **Kipe** is probably from the dialect *kip*, to take property through fraud or violence (although the *kyper cove*, a safebreaker, was a 19th-century usage). Dialect was also responsible for the 17th- to 19th-century **click**, which in the north, and spelt as *cleek*, meant to snatch or clutch eagerly.

To Rob and to Steal: a Miscellany

17th Century
to **bite** (to **bite a roger** was to steal a suitcase)
to **bone** (the image of a dog worrying at a bone)
to **fob**
to **kimbaw** (linked to the position of arms akimbo)
to **nab, nap, nip** or **nabble**
to **nick** (from Romany, underpinned by standard English *nick*)
to **strip**

18th Century
to **fly the basket** (to steal a parcel or luggage from the basket, or rear part, of a stage coach)
to **knap** (a development of *nap*, e.g. to **knap a clout** meant to steal a handkerchief)
to **lob** (a *lob* was a cashbox or till)
to **prick in the wicker** (to steal loaves from a baker's basket)

to **work** (still in use in the 20th century in such phrases
as **work the rattlers** (1920s), to rob freight trains or the
passengers on subway trains; **work high** (1930s), to rob
in broad daylight; **work** or **make the hole** (1940s), to
rob drunks who have passed out in the subway (more
commonly known as **lush-rolling**))

19th Century
to **clift** (from standard English *clift*, to split or divide (in
this case possessions from their owner), though note
also the Greek *klephtys*, a thief)
to **crab**
to **dido** (from *dido*, a trick or prank; Australia)
to **dip**
to **frazzle** (i.e. to 'wear away'; Australia)
to **freeze** (i.e. freeze on to)
to **get off**
to **graft**
to **mike** (possibly from Old French *muchier*, to hide or
skulk)
to **mooch, mootch** or **mouch** (possibly from Old French
muchier)
to **pay with a hook** *(Australia)*
to **razzle** or **razz** (variations on *rustle*; Australia)
to **smooch, smootch** or **smouch** (possibly from Old
French *muchier*)
to **smouge** (from South African *smous*, an itinerant
Jewish pedlar)
to **take down** (Australia)

20th Century
to **459** (police code *459* means a burglar)
to **burn** (to **burn someone for a stash** is to steal a dealer's
cache of drugs)
to **dap** (probably linked to standard *dab*, to touch lightly)

to *five-finger* (hence the *five-finger discount*: shoplifting)

to *gaffle* (from dialect *gaffle*, to encumber, to tease, to incommode)

to *gleep* (perhaps linked to *clip* and used by 1950s teenage gangs: to *gleep a cage* was to steal a car; it may be the root of the modern vehicle *jeep*)

to *gyp* (a negative stereotype of the gypsy)

to *have it away* (with)

to *hustle*

to *jimmy*

to *job*

to *oozle* (from standard English *ooze*, to slide and slither around; New Zealand)

to *rat* (note also the gold mining slang *ratter*, one who steals one's finds; Australia)

to *raifield* or *rayfield* (to steal without concealment or regard for the consequence; the root may have been the dialect *raffle*, an idle vagabond)

to *tax*

Heist appeared in the 1920s as a key Americanism meaning both to steal and the hold-up itself. The *heister*, *heist-artist*, *heist guy* or *heist-man* was a hold-up man, the *heist job* an act of robbery, the *short heist* petty theft and, in prison, a *short heist book* was a pornographic one. To steal was to *pull a heist* or *put the heist on*. Heist is a variation on the earlier *hoist*, which had meant to break into since the mid-19th century. As a noun it was even older: a 1703 pamphlet entitled *Hell on Earth* explained:

> the Hoist; that is, two, three or more idle Sparks going together, one of them leans his Head against a Wall [. . .] and another standing upon his Back, he climbs into a Window, and throws what he lays Hands on [. . .] out to his Confederates; then jumping out, away the successful Villains trudge.

More recent are to **gank**, **jank** or **skank**, defined as to steal and then run off. *Skanking* also refers to a dance style, which Richard Allsopp, in his *Dictionary of Caribbean English Usage* (1996), suggests is 'derived from the kind of hip-swinging dancing which is both typical of people of generally low social status and reminiscent of the waist movements of a motorcyclist speeding in and out of other traffic'. Finally some terms from the last decade: to **jay**, from *jayhawk* (referring to the thieving propensities of the bird), to **dee-bo** (from standard English *debit*), to **G-check** (where the *g* stands for gangsta and what is *checked* is one's wallet), and to **schiest** (a variant of the pejorative *shicer*).

THE MANY VARIETIES OF THIEF

The Petty Thief

The first-recorded name for the petty thief – dating from around 1570 – was **hugh prowler**, a generic use of the proper name Hugh plus the standard prowler. (The simple *prowler*, meaning both sneak thief and a housebreaker, was a 19th-century addition.) Soon there were many more terms, often underpinning the paltriness of the objects such thieves managed to steal.

None more so than the humble chicken. The **beaker-hauler** was in the general sense a small-timer, but he was also an actual stealer of chickens. He hawked his feathered booty from door to door, as did the **walking poulterer** and the **beak-** or **beaker-hunter**. The US had its equivalent in the **chicken-lifter** and in Australia he was a **chicken thief** or **chicken snatcher**. The unpronounceable *fhawkner* (perhaps from the standard English *hawk*) stole poultry that had already made its way to a shop. The 18th-century **evesdropper**, punning on the standard *eaves* and *eavesdropper*, was both a robber of hen-houses and a burglar who lurks outside a house waiting for the chance to break in while the owners are absent. In either case, he was not much rated.

Other dismissive early terms included the *bustler* (who elbowed his way through a crowd), the *scrub*, the *snitcher*, the *clip(per)* or *clip-artist*, the *frisker*, the *stoop*, the *louser*, the *mitcher* and the *moocher*. The *snib* came from *snib*, to cut into, and the *snick fadger* from *snick*, again to cut, plus *fadge*, to do. The *fidlum-/fidlam-ben* or *fidlam-cove* was ready to grab anything, irrespective of its value. As George Parker's *View of Society* described them in 1781:

> These are a kind of general tradesmen, who are likewise called Peter's Sons, with every finger a fish-hook. They watch all opportunities, rob at all times and all places, from a diamond ring on a lady's toilet down to a dish-clout in the sinkhole.

Some of the terms coined in the 20th century give a clear idea of the activity being indulged in. The *reader* of the 1930s, for example, followed postmen or delivery men to their destination and claimed to be the official recipient, having sneaked a look at the address label. Then there were the lowly *shoe thief* and mid-century *gas-meter bandit* (whose biggest 'job' was robbing the gas-meter). Australia in the 1960s offered the *tea and sugar bandit* or *burglar*; he had supposedly 'stolen' the commodities, but they had far more likely been offered to him for free. He was as much vagrant as thief, and *tea and sugar burglaring* was travelling as a vagrant. More generic were the early to mid-20th-century *doormat* (*thief*), *doormat grafter* and *doormatter*, who clearly had little to boast of.

The Young Thief

Kid, originally a young goat, has been in use to mean a child since the 17th century; it was taken over to mean a novice or youthful criminal in the middle of the following century. According to James Hardy Vaux, the transported thief whose autobiography (including a glossary of criminal slang) appeared in 1812, the word was 'particularly applied to a boy who commences thief at an early age; and when by his dexterity he has become famous, he is called by his acquaintances the kid so and so, mentioning his sirname [*sic*].'

By the late 18th century, kid had been joined by **kiddy**, a word used variously to mean a fashionable and flashy young man, a rake, a pimp or a thief. In the latter sense, he might also have been a *flash kiddy*, a dandified young thief, or a *rum kiddy*, a popular and successful one. The *rolling kiddy* was either a dandy-cum-thief or a dandy dressed in smart thief's fashions. *Kidling* was a further diminutive (especially if his father was already 'in the trade') as was **kidwy** (i.e. 'kid wee'), a thief's child. To *go upon the kid* was to steal parcels from an errand boy by promising to hold them while he makes another delivery, although this seems to play both on the victim's youth and to kid, to tease or deceive.

The 17th century also used **kinchin** (from the German *kindchen*, a child), thus the **kinchin cove** was a child brought up to become a thief and the **kinchin prig** a young thief. And the theme of fashionable dress continued with the **natty lad** or **natty kid**, although he could be any young thief and the 'smartness' the term implied may well have been in the intellectual sense. Far less obvious as a description of a youngster was the 17th-century **dromedary** or **purple dromedary**, an incompetent or novice villain. It borrowed from the standard English adoption of the name of the Arabian single-humped camel to mean a clumsy bungler (even if the *Oxford English Dictionary* does describe it as a 'a light and fleet breed').

Among the most interesting of the terms for the young thief was the **gaycat**, first noted in the late 19th century as a young or inexperienced tramp but used before the Second World War to denote the junior member of a criminal gang who was employed to run errands or spy out possible crimes (he might also be a tramp's younger, homosexual companion). The term was the title of a novel about hobo life that appeared in 1921: it features 'The Kid', a hobo's sidekick who is not openly homosexual, although this may have been self-censorship on the part of the author.

The **squarehead**, coined in early 20th-century Australia, describes one who is either too timid and conscience-ridden to be an efficient criminal, or who as yet has not entered the files

of criminal records. Otherwise known as the *squarie*, both terms
come from *square*, respectable or honest, or (in criminal terms)
'straight', conventional and naive. Other modern terms include
the *hiram*, a 1910s coinage from the jargon of Freemasonry, in
which Hiram is referred to as 'the Widow's Son'; the American
tinker; the *ziff* (perhaps a slurred pronunciation of the standard
word); the *choirboy*, used by the novelist Joseph Wambaugh to
describe a junior policeman; and the *griff*, which was probably
an abbreviation of *griffin*, a nickname for junior officers of the
East India Company.

The Sneak Thief and the Housebreaker

The Sneak
In the end all thieves (who do not, perhaps regrettably, wander the
streets in masks and stripy sweaters, carrying bags marked 'Swag')
are sneak thieves. They, understandably, don't want to be noticed
– they are not, after all, armed robbers. Sneak thief, however, has a
canonical definition as 'one who steals or thieves by sneaking into
houses through open or unfastened doors or windows' (*OED*).

By the late 17th century one finds *sneak*, first as the theft and
then later as the thief; to *go on* or *upon the sneak* was to be out
thieving. The *evening sneak* worked after dark, and there were
other specialist sneaks. The 18th-century *water sneak* or *water
sneaksman* stole from boats moored on London's river Thames,
while the 19th century's *area-sneak* or *arey sneak* (or *area diver/
lurker/slum*) went in through a building's basement, outside which
was the small sunken court known as the *area*; he might also be
known as a *dead lurker*. The 19th- to 20th-century *lobby-sneak* or
lobby-thief had no special plans: he merely entered a house, took
whatever might easily be grabbed, and left as fast as possible. The
sneak still survives, and in the mid-20th century a *sneak job* was
house-breaking.

Budge and Snudge
A common name for the sneak thief was the *budge*. The word may
seem to suggest the movement of stolen goods, but in fact it refers

to the standard *budge*, a kind of fur consisting of lamb's skin with the wool dressed outwards. The original criminal budge specialised in taking furs, cloaks and coats. A ***darkmans budge*** was not a thief himself; he was the person who climbed into a house through a window and opened the door to admit the rest of the gang, leaving the ***standing budge*** to hang around outside as a lookout. The budge often appeared in conjunction with the ***snudge***, defined in the antiquarian Robert Nares's *Glossary* (1822) as 'a miser, or curmudgeon; a sneaking fellow' but also someone who got into a house and then hid, emerging to commit the robbery once the coast was clear. The pairing is seen in the 1676 work *Warning for House-Keepers*, by 'A Newgate Ex-Prisoner':

> A Budge and Snudge commonly go together, a Budge is one that goes loytering down the street, till he can find somebodies door open [. . .] if there be nobody in the house, then they are so bold to take what stands next them and gives it to his Snudge, who snudges away with it to his fencing cins [*sic*] who buyes it.

Specialists
The 17th- to 19th-century ***glazier*** may sound like a respectable tradesman, but his only concern with windows was removing them in order to break into houses. His peer the ***running glazier*** practised a type of deception that was commonly found in sneak thievery: posing as a window cleaner or mender so as to find empty houses that could be robbed. The ***(rum) bubber*** targeted taverns, stealing the silver tankards that could be found there (a *bubber* was a drinker or a drinking bowl), whereas a ***jilt*** robbed those who were lodging in such places. By the late 19th century, sneak thievery had moved to hotels too, especially in America. The ***gilt-dubber*** (also a term for an expert pick-lock) was a hotel thief, an occupation he shared with the ***hotel barber*** (from *barber*, to steal, i.e. to 'trim') and the ***hotel buzzard***. On both sides of the Atlantic, the ***snoozer*** gave himself a thin veneer of pseudo-respectability by at least taking a room in the hotel before he set about robbing everyone else's.

Sneak thieves were eager to exploit every opportunity for gain, and once in the house there was no need to limit themselves to its contents. The 18th-century *blue pigeon (flyer)* and the 19th-century *bluey-hunter* (from *bluey*, lead) specialised in stealing the lead from roofs – or *flying the blue pigeon* as it was known. Like the earlier running glazier, the blue pigeon would pose as a workman (such as a journeyman glazier or plumber) in order to gain access to the roof, where he would strip off the lead and hide it (often by wrapping it round his body under his clothes) before leaving the house; church roofs were equally vulnerable. Still up high one found the *skylarker*, a thief who doubled as a journeyman bricklayer. Using the legitimate job to facilitate the villainy, he got up early ('with the lark') to spy out vulnerable houses. The *Jacob* (a term playing on the biblical story of Jacob's ladder) used a ladder to assault the upper storeys, while a *dive* was a thief who stood outside a house or shop, inside which would be a small boy who threw out goods that had been stolen; either the thief was forced to dive to catch the falling goods or the goods 'dive' from the window.

'No beast of prey is so noxious to Society, or so destitute of feeling, as these wretches,' declared the jobbing writer George Parker in his *View of Society* (1781). He was referring to the *tinny-hunter*, a thief who, while supposedly offering assistance to people whose homes are burning down, was in fact robbing them. The word tinny may have come from the Gaelic/Erse *teine* (fire) or the standard English *tinder*. Prosperous citizens of the time also faced the *rusher*, explained by Captain Grose as: 'thieves who knock at the doors of great houses in London, in summer time, when the families are gone out of town, and on the door being opened by a woman, rush in and rob the house.'

Points of Entry
Nowhere was safe: the *back-jumper* came in via a back entrance, either a door or window; the *garreteer* or *garreteer* crawled over house-tops and broke in through garret windows; the *parlour-jumper* went through the house's family rooms. From the mid-18th century the *dancer* was either a cat burglar who 'danced' along the

roof and in through a convenient window, or a thief entering a house to rob the upstairs when the residents were not in bed, or were out.

The late 19th century brought in the **second-storey man** or **second-storey mug**, **thief** or **worker**, who climbed into buildings above the ground floor. The **top-storey worker** and the **porch** or **window climber** were his peers. Other cat burglars include the **cat**, the **cat-man**, the **climber** (who is **at the climb**) and the **dancing master**, who was once the hangman. The 1950s added the **stair-dancer**; he stole from offices that had not been properly secured and might have slipped around via the relatively unused emergency stairs. (In Australia he was a **dwelling dancer**, and there we also find the **baster**, from standard *baste*, to hit, thrash.)

Subterfuges used by such burglars included the 18th-century **question lay**, which involved being let into a house by a servant and telling him or her not to wake their sleeping master since the visitor is prepared to wait – and then proceeding with a robbery. In a similar manner, the 19th-century **black cap** befriended a servant girl in order to gain her trust, and thus access to her master's house.

The 19th century's primary term, and one which remains in common use, was **screw**, meaning to rob (originally using skeleton keys). To **screw a drum** or **a chat** was to rob a house. Later, the 1930s coinage **screwer** could refer both to the thief and the burglary that was being committed (the **screwman** is a coinage of the same era). **Drum** was also a key term of the period. As a verb it meant to knock on a front door to ascertain whether or not the home owner was in: if they were not, the house was broken into and robbed. Alternatively it meant to steal from an empty or unoccupied house; thus to **drum up** was to rob and the **drummer-up** a house-breaker. **Drummer**, in the sense of someone who robbed houses while their occupants were out, survived into the 20th century.

This new century introduced the **creep** and the **creeper** (although the **hedge-creeper** had been in use back in the 16th century). Creeper could, in addition, describe a burglary committed while the house owners were at home, while the thief might be described as being **at** or **on the creep**. The 1950s **shack**, to rob a house or apartment when the owner is having dinner in another room, gave the *shacker* (otherwise known as a 'dinner burglar') and the *shacking touch*, the loot gained from such a burglary as well as the crime itself. The modern sneak thief might also be a *gumshoe, gumshoer, gumshoe artist* or *worker*; a *heel* (this had originated as a general pejorative: the individual was either down-at-heel or unwanted, continually at one's heels); a *skinny worker* in America; and a *sleepwalker* or *snelt* in Australia. The *in-and-out boy* or *in-and-out man* was an opportunist who went quickly in and out of the house he was robbing. To *bip, bipe* or *scallybip* was a mid-20th-century term (the root is *bipe*, to rob, a possible play on *biped*, having two feet, i.e. for walking into a house); the thief in this case at least waited until the occupants were asleep before breaking in and robbing their house.

The Shop

The house was the first port of call, but the sneak thief was always happy to disoblige shopkeepers too. The *excavator*, for instance, burgled wine-merchants' cellars. The 18th-century *avoirdupois-man* or *avoirdupois-pincher* went off with the brass weights that were once found on every shop counter; this crime was known as the *avoirdupois lay* and came from *avoirdupois*, which was the standard system of weights that was used in the UK before metrication. The 19th-century *bouncer* or *shop bouncer* was not so much a sneak as an expert in misdirection: his thefts were achieved while he distracted the merchant's attention with argumentative bargaining.

The *lob-sneak* or *lob-crawler* robbed the till, a much less defended object than its modern computerised successors. Also known as the *damper*, it could be *tapped* (by the *damper-getter*). The damper could also be *drawn*. One species of shop thief was less subtle in his approach: he simply smashed the shop window and grabbed what he could. He was known as a *starrer*, from the 'star' he put in the shop window; *star-glazing* or the *starlight glaze* was the smashing and removing of a pane of glass in order to steal items from a shop display (or to break into a house).

The River Thief

The Thames has not been a working river for decades now, nor has it been a target for thieves, but two and three centuries ago things were different. As well as the *water sneak* there was the **water pad**; the **ark man** or **ackman**, who specialised in robbing river traffic; and the more sinister **ark-ruff, -ruffian, -pirate** or **ack-pirate, -ruff** or **-ruffian**, who not only robbed his victims but also murdered them. Similarly ruthless was the **badger**, who first robbed passers-by walking on the riverbank, then killed them and dumped the body in the water. The **river rat** targeted the dead, stripping the corpses of those who had drowned in the Thames and selling off what he found. The **light horseman** preyed on dockside warehouses and the **mudlark** or **mudlarker** was a waterside thief who worked in collusion with a ship's crew; he picked up packages thrown to him by a crew member.

The Horse and Cattle Thief

In a world where horse-power is only considered in the context of what were once termed 'horseless carriages' the crime of horse theft is relatively marginal today. The occasional thoroughbred may vanish, victim of some bookie's racket or trainer's duplicity, but on the whole the crime is uncommon.

In earlier times, of course, the crime was both more common and more serious. Among the earliest terms for a horse thief were **prigger, prigger of prancers** or **paulfreys**, and **prad prigger**. The mid-16th century also offered the **prancer**, which in standard English was a mettlesome, spirited horse but in criminal use was the horse-thief who might steal such an animal. The 17th-century **prig-napper** was synonymous, as was the 18th-century **prad-** or **pred-napper** (a *prad* being a horse). The same era also used the **pad borrower, snaffle biter** and **snaffler of prancers** (from standard *snaffle*, a bridle; a *snaffler* was a street robber, no horse was involved). The **ingler** was a horse thief who toured country fairs looking for victims; the word seems to have come from dialect *ingle*, to fondle – thus he is seen to 'fondle' the horse to persuade it to go with him (in standard English an ingle was a catamite).

Still in the animal world, one has the late 19th-century **cattle-eater**, a cattle thief in the US, and the mid-century Australian **cattle-duffer**. The latter came from *duff*, which had originally meant to sell ordinary goods touted as smuggled contraband but had come to signify the illicit and larcenous alteration of cattle brands. The 17th-century **napper of naps** stole sheep.

The Vehicle Thief

Early vehicle theft tended to involve stealing from a vehicle rather than taking the vehicle itself. For instance, the 18th-century **rum drag** or **rum dragger** posed as a drunkard and persuaded a carter to let him lead his horse so that he (the carter) could get some sleep. Why any carter should have been thus fooled seems strange, but they were; while they napped the 'drunkard' would re-address the parcels that were on the wagon so that they were delivered to houses where his confederates were waiting to collect them. (Less complex, but more immediate, was the **waggon lay**, in which a villain or a team of thieves waited in a suitable street to waylay and rob wagons.) The **dragsman** or **drag sneak** removed the contents of vans or wagons, either by jumping on board while they were moving or by taking whatever possible while the vehicle had stopped and the driver was engaged in a delivery. The **jump-up** (also a verb) and the **van-dragger** did the same. **Dragging** and the **dragging lark** or **game** were terms that lasted while methods of transport changed: it meant stealing from carts or vans in the 19th century and from cars in the 20th.

Amongst its multiple meanings, *peter* could be a piece of luggage or a parcel, and it was used from the 18th century onwards in various compounds and phrases that referred to the theft of such items from vans or carts, and later from railway stations. The robberies did not, however, seem to be carried out on the trains themselves. The earliest term was to **bite a peter**, to steal a suitcases or portmanteau; this was followed by to **nap a peter**, to steal luggage from a (horse-drawn) carriage. The **peterer** or **peteress** was such a thief and the **peter lay** his or her illicit occupation. The 19th century introduced the railway, and with it **peter-claiming**, stealing unguarded parcels and bags from railway stations. The thief was a **peter-claimer** and the 'job' was also known as **peter-hunting** or the **peter drag**. A railway thief might be known as a **rat crusher** or **rattler grab** if he stole from railway wagons, or a **keisterman** (from *keister*, another word for a suitcase) if he stole unguarded suitcases from a railway station.

Car thieves appeared soon after the cars they targeted. Among them were the **heister**, a term that stood for any type of thief, and the **kink**. The acronymic modern term **twock** (from 'take without owner's consent') is described most euphemistically as 'joy-riding'.

The Jewel and Watch Thief

Writing in his pamphlet *The Second Part of Coney-Catching* (1591), Robert Greene listed the **lift**, describing him as 'he that stealeth or prowleth any plate, jewels, bolts of satin, velvet or such parcels from any place . . .' It is probably the first instance of a named jewel thief. The occupation continued, but the remaining terms it created all date from the 19th century or later.

There was, for example, the **bug hunter**. Playing on the schoolboy term for a naturalist, it came from the name for a breast pin (which supposedly resembled a *bug*, i.e. insect), and typified a street thief who specialised in snatching (drunken) men's jewellery – hence **bug-hunting**, robbing or cheating drunks, especially after dark. The **prop-man**, **prop nailer** and **prop worker** all took tie-pins, brooches and other pieces of small jewellery, prop in this case being from Dutch *proppe* (a brooch or skewer), which in English could mean a precious stone. The **spark grafter** went for **sparks**, diamonds (a diamond ring was a *spark prop* or *spark fawney*); the **bagger** or **bag-thief** preferred rings (from French *bague*, a ring). The **stone-getter** was happy with any precious stone. A diamond itself could be a **daisy**, a **fish-eye**, **glass**, a **lustre**, a **rock** (thus the *rock worker*, a seller of cheap jewellery) a **stone** or **white stone**, and **rusty nails**.

Ice and **sparklers** have been the terms favoured by detective fiction. The former was coined in the late 19th century, and the **ice-house** or **ice palace** is a jewellery store. The *sparkler* began life in the mid-18th century meaning an eye, usually an alluring female one. But by the end of the century it meant diamonds, and the eyes had been largely left behind. As the 1825 ballad 'I Am A Knowing Blade' put it: 'The girls would all run after me with their sparkling eyes, [...] But then they're not the sparklers I should ever prize.'

A watch was a **toy** (thus *red toy*, a gold watch and *white toy* a silver one) and the **toy-getter** liked to steal them; so too did the **jerry sneak**, from *jerry*, a watch. **Jerry sneaking** was watch-stealing, an occupation which, says the *Slang Dictionary* of 1873, 'is a distinct form of street robbery, and requires both courage and dexterity; for it is done, as the thieves say, "right afore a bloke's face".' Other watch thieves were the **thimble-twister** (from *thimble*, a watch), the **super twister** (from *super*, another watch – it may have been linked to the standard *soup-plate*, which referred to the shape of early pocket watches) and the **thimble-screwer**. To **draw a thimble** was to steal a pocket watch, while a **thimble-crib** was a watchmaker's or jeweller's shop.

In the late 17th century a **tatler** or **tattler** (from the standard *tattler*, one who tattles or gossips) was specifically a repeater or striking watch; to **flash a tattler** was to wear a watch and to **nim a tattler** to steal it. The synonymous French *horloge* gave the **loge** or **vid loge** (perhaps from Latin *video*, I see), which was also a repeater. The late 19th century used **strike**, and to **nail a strike** for the stealing of it. A **ticker** (referring to the ticking sound) was again something that one **nailed**. The late 20th-century **mug's ticker** is a fake, such as a 'Swiss' Rolex made in the Far East.

Prior to the widespread adoption of wristwatches, personal timekeepers required a chain. That too could be stolen. A watch and chain (often adorned with seals) could be a **block and tackle** or **block and slang**. The **block** was the watch and **block dealer** a jeweller. A **turnip** was large, old-fashioned watch; to **cut turnip-tops** was to steal a watch plus its chain and seals. The watch chain was the **tackle** or **slang**, which has no linguistic connotations but comes from German *Schlange*, a (watch) chain, or Dutch *slang*, a snake. It was also a **front**, from the position in which the chain was worn, and a **drag**.

Slum, which could also mean a wad of notes, was a synonym for jewellery – though it was usually the kind that one would, if smart, avoid. From the 1910s it meant stolen jewellery, cheap or counterfeit jewellery (typically that sold illegally by street vendors), and, in its lowest form, the virtually worthless prizes offered at fairs or carnivals. The **slum hustler** or **slum worker** sold such second-rate fakes, pretending to the gullible buyer that they were stolen property – and therefore, of course, completely genuine. In underworld terms a **slum joint** was a jewellery store.

More recent are the 1930s **chain man**, a thief or pickpocket who specialises in taking watches; the **iceman**, from *ice*, a diamond; the **shoot-flier**, who specialises in snatching wallets, watches and similar small items; and the punning **time bandit**, who prefers expensive watches and whose name refers to Terry Gilliam's 1981 film *Time Bandits*. Some thieves went after silver plate instead, including the **wedge hunter**, from *wedge*, a chunk of solid silver (now, of course, the word refers to a wad of money); the **clank-napper**, from *clank*, a silver tankard; and a **feeder-prigger**, who took silver spoons.

Stealing from Children

There were thieves who were little more than children – such as Fagin's gang – and there were those who targeted children as victims. The late 18th-century **snaveller** and **running snavel** both robbed children, typically when they were on their way to school and might have been given some small coin with which to buy food; the term came from the dialect *snavel*, to remove slyly. Far more sinister were those who didn't merely rob children, but stripped them, quite literally, of the clothes they stood up in. The 18th-century version was the **lully-prigger**, a term that had originally referred to one who stole from washing lines or from wherever washing had been put out to dry. The 19th-century equivalent was either the **skinner** or the **stripper**. In all cases the criminal was usually a woman, who would first strike up a conversation with the child and then lure them into some secluded spot; then, and only then, with confidence achieved, would the thief turn on the youngster, removing their clothes and leaving them naked in the street. More recent is *peel*, though in this case the term means to rob someone of any age.

THE RECEIVER

Had there been no others on offer then a single word would have sufficed for the criminal receiver (itself a word that dates back to the 14th century): the *fence*, which is first noted in B.E.'s *Dictionary of the Canting Crew* (*c*.1698) and remains the most popular non-standard term. The image is one of a metaphorical barrier between the thief and the eventual buyer of the looted goods. He has been at various times a *fencer*, a *fence-master* and a *fencing cully*, and to *fence* is to buy and sell stolen property, to pawn goods with a receiver, or to hide stolen goods. The *fencer's wharf* was a receiver's warehouse, as have been the *fencing crib* and *fencing ken*. *Fencing* is receiving, *fencibles* stolen goods and to *bone the fence* was to find out where goods have been hidden by a receiver and then to steal them. The 19th-century *hedge* and the mid-20th-century *stop* both play on the same image.

Fence may have lasted, but other terms have appeared. In the 16th century were the *rogueman* and the *marter* (or *martar*); the latter was from the standard *mart*, to bargain or to do business, and could also mean a dishonest horse-trader who bought stolen horses and disposed of them at fairs. The 18th century added the *adam tiler*, which most likely combined *adam*, the generic for a man, and German *Teile*, a share or slice: in other words he subtracted his own share from the criminal's profits. The all-purpose *cove* could also be a receiver, as could the *flash cove* and his female equivalent the *flash blowen*. The 17- to 18th-century *lock* and the *lock-all-fast* were ready to help, as was the 19th-century *peter*, which played on the *peter* (strongbox) where he stored the loot. A *fen* was another receiver; the standard meaning of a marshy bog underlined his reputation for 'dirtiness'. Others were the *hifter*, the *shade*, the *gagger* and the *taker*.

The 19th-century *family man* and *father* were yet more members of the criminal 'family'. Both terms played on the mid-18th-century *uncle*, originally a pawnbroker (i.e. a man giving temporary financial aid to out-of-pocket 'relatives'). The 20th-century **buyer** is self-explanatory, while the **placer** is a middle-man who places stolen goods with a purchaser. The Australian **eighteen pence** was presumably named as such by his initial refusal to offer people very much more.

These were all general terms, but there were more specific fences too. As we know from Fagin, the job of receiver was once one of those that 'automatically' fell to Jewish criminals such as the **ikey** and the **ikey-mo**. These come from two common Jewish given names, Isaac and Moses; slang lexicographer Eric Partridge suggests in his *Dictionary of Slang and Unconventional English* (1937–84) that it was 'probably popularised by the Ikey Mo who was partner in the nefarious doings of the original Ally Sloper, the first British strip-cartoon "character", in the series which started in *Judy* magazine, 1867, and ran for many years'. Alongside ikey was **Jack the Jew** or **Jew-Jack**, although he concentrated on less valuable goods. The 19th-century **cystic grist smelter** melted down silver plate (the cystic grist) into unidentifiable ingots; his predecessor in the 18th century, the **melting pot receiver**, did the same with the loot that was passed to him. The early 20th-century **smasher** made counterfeit money from the silver he received, and he was also known to 'launder' stolen cash. The 19th-century **janusmug**, meanwhile, was not quite a fence, but rather an intermediary between a thief and an actual receiver; his name was taken from that of Janus, the Roman god with two faces.

A receiver was not always necessary: sometime the same profits could be made by selling the goods back to the victim from whom they had been stolen. Thus the 17th- to 18th-century **cunning man** was a confidence trickster who used a (spurious) knowledge of astrology to help to convince his or (more often) her victims; the preferred swindle was the 'miraculous' recovery of stolen goods. A similar game was played by the 18th-century **flying porter**, who approached the victim and told them that he could regain the stolen goods on their behalf – and then demanded payment for fetching them.

Then there were those who capitalised on the insatiable appetite of otherwise respectable individuals for something a little 'naughty': the ***broady-worker*** (from *broady*, slang for *broadcloth*, a fine black cloth used mainly in men's tailoring) was a criminal who sells third-rate cloth as the finest material or stolen goods as legitimate. The ***calf-sticker*** (from *calf*, a fool) pretended that perfectly normal goods had been stolen, exciting the buyer; on that basis he was able to ask, and obtain, a higher price than would have been usual.

THE STOLEN GOODS OR LOOT

As fence is to the receiver, so ***swag*** is to the stolen goods that the fence purchases. The original 14th-century term meant a bulgy bag (thus eventually the Australian *swag*, the pack carried by the nation's itinerants or *swagmen*). For criminals in the 17th century it had come to denote a shop (and its contents) – in other words, potential spoils – and by the mid-18th it referred directly to the booty itself, especially linen or clothes as opposed to jewels or plate. There it has stayed, although swag now covers all varieties of criminal loot. The word has given ***swagless***, used of a place that fails to yield the expected prizes, the ***swag-getter***, a thief specialising in silk, the ***swagger*** or ***swag-cove***, a receiver, and the ***swag chovey*** (from *chovey*, a shop), a criminal receiver's shop or store.

Other terms for stolen goods have also existed alongside swag. Standard English *pelf* is now an archaism meaning money, but up until the 15th century it also meant loot. In this sense it was adopted by criminals in the 16th century, and extended as ***pelfry***. The 16th century also used ***garbage***, particularly when referring to stolen parcels or packages. ***Haul***, one of the most commonly used terms after swag, is a late 18th-century invention, while the 19th added ***bonings*** (from *bone*, to steal), ***the lay*** and ***darby***. This last came from the 16th-century standard term *Father Darby's bands*, a money-lender's bond of particular severity which effectively bound the borrower to the lender while the debt remained outstanding.

Bunce also has quite a long history, although it was not until the

1960s that the term was used to mean stolen goods. It came from the costermonger jargon *bunts* and a clear analogy can be seen: they were second-rate apples that were sold off cheap or even given away to market boys, who could in turn sell them at a small profit. Slang lexicographer John Camden Hotten's *Slang Dictionary* (1867) adds the meaning 'money obtained by giving light weight, &c.' Bunts were further divided into *fair bunts* and *unfair bunts*, depending on whether or not the coster was aware of his boy's tricks. As well as bunce, the 20th century contributed **the goods** (and its rhyming equivalent **little Red Ridings**) as well as **things**, **stuff** (and **hot stuff**), **swank** and **mahoska**, which – it has been claimed – is related to the Irish *mo thosca*, my business. If goods were stolen, then the 1940s criminal described them as **tropical**, and if they proved worthless and no fence would touch them, they were deemed **crabs**. And in Australia, when the police came round to ask where something had come from, the traditional answer was *from the man outside Hoyt's*. The phrase referred to the commissionaire outside Hoyt's Theatre in Melbourne, a gorgeously uniformed individual who was here simply used as a verbal deflection.

A number of terms related to stolen goods in a context other than actual receiving. The 18th century offered to **slang upon the safe** (from *sling*, to throw), to remove stolen goods from the scene of the crime; to **ding**, to pass stolen goods to a confederate; and to **pay back**, to return stolen goods for a price (the 20th-century versions are to **blow back** or **kick back**). Moving into the 19th century, to pawn the goods was to **brace up** (the 20th-century equivalent is to **pass**), which may come from the French argot *braser des faffes*, to forge documents. And in Australia to **stook**, which came from *stack* or *stash*, meant to hide stolen goods. The 1970s UK term to **corner** was an elaborate con-trick: the villain arranges to sell stolen goods and then has fake 'policemen' break in, confiscate the goods and threaten the victim with charges of receiving. The charges can, naturally, be dropped in return for a bribe – arranged by a fake 'solicitor', who makes sure there is no real police involvement by assuring the victim that he has no rights in law and that paying and shutting up is the best thing to do, The victim is, indeed, 'cornered'.

THE STORE OR HIDING PLACE

Sometimes, it is necessary to **cool** the hot stuff by keeping it hidden until police activity quietens down. The 16th-century **santar** (based on the standard words *sanctuary* and *sent*) referred to the member of a team of parcel thieves whose responsibility it was to actually remove the stolen goods and take them to a hideout. The earliest term for such deposits and stores was the mid-16th-century **stalling-ken**, which came from *(in)stall*, followed by the 17th century's more secure **lock** (where they were locked up or away). In the 18th century, the **plant** spawned the **outside plant**, a place where a criminal receiver kept his stock, and to **rise a plant**, to unearth loot from where you had hidden it. Occasionally a thief would unearth loot that had been hidden by another thief; in this case, naturally, he would re-steal it. The **dig** (perhaps from the idea of digging a hole for the cache) appeared in the 20th century, as did the **flop** and the **drop** or **drop-house**, which were accessible – and perhaps short-term – deposits where goods could easily be placed in the immediate aftermath of a crime. The **whisper loft** was another place filled with ill-gotten gains. Whisper give sense of secrecy that seems apt, but it has another pertinent, criminal, meaning too – the *whisper* was a lookout or tipster.

Most ill-gotten gains have tended to be sold on surreptitiously, but there have always been (ostensibly 'straight') shops that have indulged in some dodgy under-the-counter work. In the past, the connection between such enterprises and pawn shops was frequently a close one. The 19th century, for example, saw the **dollyshop**. This had started life as a marine store – a shop selling cast-off garments, indicated by a dressed black doll hanging outside as a sign – but it became another name for a down-market or actively illegal pawnshop.

THE SHARE-OUT

Once the loot is safely hidden away, with the authorities having turned their attention elsewhere, it is time for the share-out.

Unsurprisingly, most of the relevant terms deal with cutting. The 17th-century *cut* meant the share itself, as did the 19th-century *cut-in* or *cut-up*. To cut up was to make the division and for a crime to *cut up well* was to give all concerned a good share of the loot (although the phrase was older, and had originally meant to leave a fortune after one's death). A *carve-up* has come to mean the opposite – an unfair division – but when it initially emerged in the 1940s it had no negative connotation.

Aside from cutting, there was the *snack* (a figurative use of the echoic *snack*, a dog's snap or bite), which had been adopted by 17th-century criminals to mean a share of the booty from its standard meaning of a portion. Snacks were equal divisions (there were *half-snacks* too) and to *go snacks* or *go snooks* was to divide up or hand over a share. Lastly one has to *whack up* (from *whack*, a share) and to *single-duke*, a 1920s American term that meant to cheat one's confederates when dividing loot. Based on *duke*, a hand, the image was of one hand duplicitously kept behind one's back.

SHOPLIFTING

In the beginning was the 16th century's *lift* (or *lifter*), and the mid-17th-century *shoplift* was his logical extension, but the term had been consumed by standard English by 1700. The *hoist, hoister, hoisterman* or *hoist merchant* appeared in the late 18th century and to be *on* or *at the hoist* was to be working as a shoplifter. A *hoister-mot* or *hoister mort* was the female equivalent – shoplifting has traditionally been an equal opportunity employer.

For modern shoplifters (at least in the US), or certainly those that work on a large and professional scale, the verb of choice is to *boost* and the noun the *booster*. It gives *booster bloomers* or *booster drawers*: purpose-designed voluminous underwear in which a female shoplifter hides stolen goods. The *booster fold* is a way of carrying stolen goods so as to render them invisible to store detectives, and the *booster skirt* and *booster box* are further ways of disguising what has been stolen. The booster prides him or herself on subtlety and stealth; the **snatch-and-grab** or **boot-and-shoe booster** defines an amateur, lacking in skill and not working with a team. To **boost and shoot** is even less professional: it means to shoplift in order to support a drug habit.

Aside from these primary terms, one finds the *file*, the **cadger**, the **pincher**, the **sneaksman** and the **hooker** (to *fish* was to shoplift), while the **mobsman** was anyone who uses manual dexterity for theft – a category that included shoplifters. The mid-19th-century **palmer** played both on the standard *palm*, to conceal in the palm of one's hand, and on *palmer*, an itinerant monk bound by vows of eternal poverty. He was a shoplifter, but the term could also refer to a beggar who visited shops in order to practice a particular deception; claiming to be collecting halfpence engraved with a harp, he would offer the shopkeeper 13 pence for a shilling's worth and persuade them to empty all their coppers on the counter. While they are busy searching the pile, the palmer hides as many of the coins as possible. The early 20th-century **derrick** and the **elevator** both stressed the physical lifting aspect of the profession, rather than any trickery. A *derrick* was a crane (though before that a hangman) and an *elevator*, of course, is a lift.

Setting aside the obvious *boosting* and *hoisting*, not to mention the ironic *shopping*, there are several more words on offer for the act of shoplifting. The mid-16th-century **nip** was the first-recorded of such terms; it was succeeded by **snatch** in the 18th century. From the same period came the **buckteen** (frustratingly resistant to any etymology); the *fam-lay* (from *fam*, a hand), and thus the *fam-layer*, the shoplifter; **copping**, **coreing** and the **coreing lay** (from Romany *cor*, to steal); and Australia's late 19th-century **chovy-bouncing** (from *chovy* a shop – which in turn offered *ann-chovey* and *man-chovey*, the female and male shop assistant).

More recent terms, from the 1960s on, have been to **slough** (from standard *slough*, to be swallowed up – perhaps inside those booster bloomers), to use the **five-fingered chequebook**, and to **mop**. In Australia, to **rave** is for one member of a shoplifting team to make a fuss so as to cause a distraction while their accomplices get to work, while to **smother**, also Australian, is to use some form of object to obscure the shopkeeper's view while a shoplifter abstracts a targeted object.

THE BANK ROBBER AND SAFEBREAKER

In the traditional hierarchy of crime the bank robber or safecracker has been considered among the elite, and **open work**, as safecracking was termed around 1930, has been at the top of the tree. He requires brains (to plan), skill (to deal with the safe and the security that surrounded it) and, when successful, he makes a good deal more money than the simple housebreaker, let alone a street mugger. His only peer is the armed robber, whose targets – post offices, jewellers, wages, delivery vans – are equally remunerative. In the mid-20th century the bank robber might be a **heavy** (to be **on the heavy** was to work as an armed robber) or a **bankman**. In the late 19th century, the image of burrowing towards his chosen target gave **gopher** (from the animal of the same name). It was a term in use up until the 1960s and produced various others – to **pull a gopher** was to tunnel into a bank vault, and a group of bank robbers was known as a **gopher gang** or **gopher mob**. As the safecracker, it is the **gopher man** or **gopher worker** in particular – as well as his occupation, the **gopher racket** – who has attracted a good number of the terms that surround this particular type of larceny.

In America, safecrackers gained names like **yegg** or **yeggman** (see below) and **Jimmie Valentine** in the 1920s. Jimmie Valentine was the name of the anti-hero of O. Henry's 1910 short story 'Jimmie Valentine'. He was based on an actual safecracker with whom the author served in the State Penitentiary at Columbus, Ohio, when he did 39 months for embezzlement.

However, primarily, the terms cant gave to safecrackers were based on the names for the safe itself. The *peter* was a suitcase to the luggage thief but the term was also used to mean a variety of other containers, from a cash register to the witness box in court. To the safebreaker, the *peter* was a safe, usually as found in a bank or office, but it could also be the nitroglycerine he used to gain access (the implement called the **peter-cutter** was another method the **peterman** might use when **peter busting**). A 20th-century **box** could mean a safe, or other container for cash, and it produced its own set of terms for safebreaking: the **boxer** or **box worker**'s business was **box-busting**,

The Origin of Yegg

Of all the terms used for a safecracker, the most fascinating are surely the *yegg* or *yeggman*, and the related *john* (or *johnny*) *yeg*. Yegg is a term that has produced a number of rival etymologies; all seem feasible, but equally it may be that none are strictly speaking correct. The simplest is that there was a turn-of-the-century villain named John Yegg, who became the first safebreaker to use nitroglycerine in his work. However, the etymologist Gerald Cohen has noted an article in the *San Francisco Chronicle* in March 1904 that cites one John Yeager as the leader of a gang of tramps who robbed the Reading railroad. His name formed the basis of a generic 'John Yegg', the notional leader of all similar gangs. The professional burglar Jack Black, who knew many such leaders, opined thus in his memoir *You Can't Win* (1926): Yegg [...] is a corruption of "yekk", a word from one of the many dialects spoken in Chinatown, and it means beggar. When a hypo or beggar approached a Chinaman to ask for something to eat, he was greeted with the exclamation, "yekk man, yekk man". The underworld is quick to seize upon strange words, and the bums and hypos in Chinatown were calling themselves yeggmen years before the term was taken out on the road and given currency by eastbound beggars. In no time it had a verb hung on it, and to yegg meant to beg. The late William A. Pinkerton was responsible for its changed meaning [...] A burglar with some humor fell into Pinkerton's hands and when asked who was breaking open the country "jugs" he whispered to the detective that it was the yeggs. Investigation convinced Pinkerton that there were a lot of men drifting about the country who called themselves yeggs. The word went into a series of magazine articles Pinkerton was writing at the time and was fastened upon the "box" men. Its meaning has since widened until now the term "yegg" includes all criminals whose work is "heavy".

The American lexicographer Godfrey Irwin, in *American Tramp and Underworld Slang* (1931), suggests an alternative – that the yegg was 'originally a man too wise, too cautious, too old or too cowardly to risk crime in a city, where police and private detectives were alert, and who took to "the road" for easier "graft" and "pickings".' The jury remains out.

and to ***shoot the box*** (crack the safe) he might use a ***jack in the box,*** which was a form of screw used in safebreaking. When he was attempting a ***box job*** he might be up against the ***box screw*** – the bank guard.

There are several further terms based on the safe itself. A ***jug*** meant a safe from the early 20th century and gives a number of compounds, including the ***jug-heel,*** the ***jug-heister*** and the ***jugger.*** To be ***on the jug*** was to be cracking safes, as was to ***shoot the jug.*** The jug was succeeded by the ***can*** as the term of choice in the 1910s–1960s, and the ***can opener*** again equated the crook with his tools – it meant both a skilled safebreaker and any tool used in heists when the noise of explosives was sure to lead to discovery. Last of this group is the 20th-century Antipodean ***tank,*** again a safe, which might be opened by a ***tank blower, tank bloke*** or ***tankman.***

Given the importance of his tools to the safebreaker, it is un-surprising that many terms allude to them. He may be a ***mechanic,*** a ***cracker,*** a ***cranker,*** a ***knob-knocker*** (from knocking out the lock of less well-defended safes) and a ***toolman.*** The tools themselves could be the ***hardware*** or the ***persuader.*** To ***stem*** a safe was to drill out the lock but the most popular method was more brutal: to use an explosive. This could be called ***nitro*** (i.e. nitroglycerine) or ***plastic*** (plastic explosive), and the explosion that followed their detonation was a ***shot,*** a term taken from mining jargon. When tools were abandoned in the favour of the blunter skills of an explosive, the robber was a **blower** or **jelly-baby** (from gelignite, also known as blasting gelatin). The most widely found term, however, was **soup**, first used in the 1910s, which could be either gelignite or nitro-glycerine. It gave the **soup man** and, in the 1940s, the **soup and peter man** who did **soup and peter work**. To **cook soup** was to dissolve a stick of dynamite in hot water to extract the crude nitroglycerine.

Chapter 5

VIOLENT CRIME

Believe me, there is not a game, my brave boys,
    To compare with the game of high-toby;
No rapture can equal the tobyman's joys,
    To blue devils, blue plumbs give the go-by;

And what if, at length, boys, he come to the crap!
    Even rack punch has *some* bitter in it,
For the mare-with-three-legs, boys, I care not a rap,
    'Twill be over in less than a minute!

'The Game Of High Toby' in
W. Harrison Ainsworth, *Rookwood* (1834)

THE HIGHWAYMAN

Prior to the fame (or infamy) achieved by notorious modern gang-sters such as Al Capone or John Dillinger, few groups of villains enjoyed so romanticised a life as the highwaymen of 17th- and 18th-century England. And none more than Dick Turpin, with his faithful horse Black Bess (who never existed), his ride to York (which he never made), and his acts of chivalry (more like brutal thuggery). The romantic image – doffed hats, a kiss for the ladies and a bow for their husbands, a *bon mot* for every occasion including the gallows – is better served by Claude Du Vall, who (as the stereotypes demand) was French, for all that he worked the English roads. As the post-humous *Memoires*, published shortly after his hanging in 1670, put it: 'Here lies Du Vall. Reader, if Male thou art / Look to thy purse: if female, to thy heart.' A former footman, he had doubtless picked up the 'gentlemanly' manners for which, as well as high-stakes gaming, card-sharping and even alchemy, he was renowned.

But Du Vall was an exception and, just like any of the thugs, garrotters or street bullies who operated on foot, most highwaymen – a word first recorded in standard English in 1649 – were simply villains who happened to ride horses. They were no more than rural muggers-cum-hijackers who operated in the dangerous no-man's-lands between the security of towns and cities, even if they did gild the menacing lily with the formulaic cry 'Stand and deliver!', and the threat 'Your money or your life!'

The false romantic image that is so popular is not simply a distortion of historical facts over centuries (although this is undoubtedly a factor); the myth-making was in place at the time, even as they *rode out*, as their own cant would put it, to terrify and despoil. Even a contemporary biographer – Captain Alexander Smith, whose *A History of the Lives of the Most Noted Highwaymen* appeared in 1714 – seemed to have an irrational soft spot for his subjects:

> Though it was the sad fate of these unfortunate creatures to commence and take degrees in vanity and wickedness to the very day of their deaths, yet I upbraid not their miserable catastrophe with rash and uncharitable censures, but only set forth how they laboured to show the world what a latitude there is in villainy.

The Pad

The key to cant's terminology for highwaymen was their field of operations: the highway, commonly known as the **high pad** (the *pad* being the cant equivalent of path), a term which remained in use throughout the centuries in which the highwayman was active. The other basic terms were directly linked – the **high padsman** was the highwayman (although he was known as the high pad, too) and **high-padding** was his specific criminal pastime. The **low pad** of the same era was – logically – a less 'distinguished' criminal; he was the most disdained of footpads, or what Richard Head, author of the fictional biography of Meritron Latroon *The English*

Rogue (1674), dismissed as 'a base Sheep-stealing, half-penny Rogue'. *Pad* itself meant an unmounted footpad (effectively a highwayman on foot), but in Scotland the *paddist* had saddled up, as had the mid-17th-century *rumpad* (in which *rum* meant good) and his slightly later variations *rum padder* and *rome-padder*.

Knights and Gentlemen

The highwayman could also be a **knight of the pad**, another term which juxtaposed the chivalry of traditional knights with the distinctly ignoble pursuits of these particular 'knights' (see page 50), although in the case of highwaymen there was some truth behind the joke as they were, at least, mounted on horses. Other knights of the highway included the **lance-knight** of the late 16th century (possibly from the German *Landsknechte*, a mercenary soldier who, when not actually fighting, terrorised civilians) and the **knight of the road**, who appeared when lance-knight fell out of use in the mid-17th century. The **knight of St Nicholas**, meanwhile, could refer to either a wandering criminal beggar or a highwayman, and two variations on the term were *St Nicholas's clergyman* or *clerk* and *Sir Nicholas Nemo* (in other words 'nobody'). Rather than attaining any real saintliness, this Nicholas was another name for *Old Nick* – the Devil. All these names had a false veneer of respectability, much like the highwayman himself.

If not a knight or an associate of a 'saint', then the robber might at least be a **captain**, which from the late 16th century denoted a success in the trade (the leader of a gang of highwaymen was known as **Captain Crank**), or else a **squire of the pad** by the early 18th century. A similar contrast between name and deed was found in the **gentleman of the pad**, although by 1800 this particular phrase had come to mean a street robber instead. Other gentlemen stepped up, however, such as the early 18th-century **gentleman-outer** (a reference to his being 'out on the road', rather than the later pejorative use of *outer* as a socially unacceptable ne'er-do-well) and the 19th-century **gentleman of the road**. By contrast, the ironic **gentleman's master** posited the victim as the gentleman, referring to the way in which a pair of primed pistols brought temporary ascendancy over the highwayman's social betters.

The High Lawyer and Others

Going back to the scene of the crime, the highway was also known by the abbreviation **high**, and the canters' **high law**, meaning highway robbery, was first cited in 1552. The playwright Thomas Dekker included it in *The Belman of London* (1608), one of his studies of the city's underworld:

> Now must you cast up your eyes and looke aloft, if you have a desire to behold the picture of The High Lawe: which taketh that name from the high exploits that are acted by it: the Schollers that learne it are called High Lawyers; yet they never walke to Westminster to pleade, though oftentimes they are called to the Barre, but then it is to haue them Hold vp their hands, that the Hangman may tell them their fortune. All the former Lawes are attained by wit, but the High Law stands both upon Wit and Manhood. For the High Law is nothing else but taking a purse by the High-way side.

The **high lawyer** that Dekker describes is, of course, the highwayman, but it is a term that was found even earlier, when another playwright, Robert Greene, set down the canonical version of the High Law. In his 1591 pamphlet *A Notable Discovery of Coosnage*, Greene defines a number of participants in the robbery:

> The thief is called a *high-lawyer*.
> He that setteth the watch, a *scrippet*.
> He that standeth to watch, an *oak*.
> He that is robbed, the *martin*.
> When he yieldeth, *stooping*.

The **scrippet** who 'setteth the watch' organised the hold-up; the word came from Latin *scripsit*, which translates as 'he wrote' and which may have referred to written instructions he gave to the rest of the gang. The man who kept a lookout was the **oak**, playing on the tree's solidity, and the **martin** was the unfortunate victim. The latter's etymology is unproved, but as it was supposedly lucky for a martin to nest in the eaves of one's house, perhaps the robbers saw the appearance of a victim as similarly lucky for themselves and so equated the two. *Stooping* presumably referred to the victim's figurative acquiescence.

Those working as highwaymen had their own terminology; to *pull up*, or *pull up a jack*, was to stop a coach in order to rob it. There was also the equivalent of a secret codeword: the word *music* was uttered among highwaymen to signify that an individual was a friend and must not be hindered on their journey (usually in the phrase *the music's paid*).

The High-toby Man

Whether it comes from Shelta *tobar* or Romany *tober*, both of which meant the road, *toby* was usually found to designate the road in the specific context of a highwayman's 'office'. As such it appeared in a variety of compounds throughout the 19th century. Some of these were attributed to footpads as well, such as the *low toby man*, but the *high-toby man* was always a highwayman. The *high-toby spice*, meanwhile, was the robbery that they (and the *spice gloak*) practised. *Spice* was either from a figurative use of German *speissen* (to eat) or from slang to *speak* (to hold up and rob), and gave *spice the swell*, to rob a gentleman. The earlier *high tober* was also an elite highwayman, but one known for his occupational skill rather than his sartorial efforts (although, conversely, the slang lexicographer Eric Partridge has suggested in his *Dictionary of Slang and Unconventional English* (1937–84) that this in fact is a misreading and the term is simply *high toby*, a run-of-the-mill operator. Meanwhile in America, plain toby meant highway robbery from the 19th century up until the 1940s.

The Scamp, Purse-emptier and Others

The term *scamp* has come to mean a loveable – if roguish – youngster, but its original use, while it noted its subject's undoubted roguishness (in the literal sense: a villain), was far less affectionate. In its mid-18th-century meaning of highwayman it was by no means complimentary, but the more recent softening of the term's meaning may well have added to the roseate filter through which the highwayman came to be seen. The word itself seems to have started life as military slang, with roots either in the obsolete Dutch *schampen* (to escape or fly) or the Italian *scampare* (to decamp, run away). Alongside it were the **scampsman** and **scamping blade**, but it was the **royal scamp** who was perhaps closest to the highwayman of romantic fiction than those of historical record. The royal scamp specialised in robbing rich victims and in causing them no physical harm while he did so. Working in quite another way was the **bully-ruffian** or **bully-ruffin** of the mid-17th century. As his name makes clear, he preferred to abuse his victims in order to intimidate them further, rather than bowing to any popular fantasy or pretended chivalry.

Flashman

As readers of *Tom Brown's Schooldays* by Thomas Hughes (not to mention the works of George Macdonald Fraser) will know, Flashman was the bullying braggart who quite literally tortured the priggish hero. Fifty years earlier *flashman* had also meant highwayman, 'scampering', in the words of the raffish Colonel George Hangar in 1801, 'on his prancer upon the high tober'. The use of *flash* here is in its all-purpose sense of pertaining to criminality; although the image of boastful ostentation – still in use today – doubtless played its part.

Equally unromantic was what – it must be remembered – was the highwayman's primary goal: robbery. It won him several names that alluded more directly to his *modus operandi*: the early 17th century's undisguised **purse-emptier** as well as such euphemisms as **collector, rent collector, tax collector** or **collector of the highways**. As such names make clear, this 'collection' tended to focus on cash, rather than jewels or other trinkets that would require fencing. Other than his pecuniary aims, the highwayman's status as a mounted villain was also a point of reference in terms such as *bridle-cull* (simply 'bridle-man' in slang) and **snaffler** (a blend of the standard English *snaffle* meaning a light bridle with the slang *snaffle*, to rob). The **rank rider** too was originally a standard term, in this case a reckless rider and rooted in the Danish *rank* – upright, erect, and thence proud and headstrong. Even the person who provided and stabled the highwayman's horses, usually an innkeeper, had his own term: a **colt** or **coltman**.

THE BUSHRANGER

It is arguable that the *back blocks* and *never-never* (the deep, deserted heartland) of the Australian outback hardly qualify as 'the highway', but there can be little doubt that the last vestiges of the highwayman tradition were found in the form of Australia's bushrangers. The Antipodean successor to the high pad even had his own 'stand and deliver' – victims of the bush-based armed robber might hear **bail up!** (or **bale up!**) prior to having their money or possessions forcibly removed. Used as a verb, *bail* meant to trap or corner, and came from the name for the bar or frame used to confine an animal (usually a cow when milking). Like the highwaymen, bushrangers achieved a good deal of popular celebrity, usually undeserved. And like their British forbears, their eventual fate tended to be the gallows.

Most celebrated of them all was of course Ned Kelly, the late 19th-century Irish-Australian outlaw and 'wild colonial boy' himself. 'Such is life,' he declared on the scaffold, seconds before his death, and his life of outlawry triggered by what he saw as the authorities' injustice to his family, and his refusal to knuckle under to those same authorities, underpins at least some Australians' self-image. The verb to **Ned Kelly** was to take to bushranging as a criminal career, and **game as Ned Kelly**, i.e. plucky and fearless, remains a popular epithet.

A more general term for taking to the bush was to **turn out**, borrowing the standard English expression for leaving home and starting work. There was a definite overlap of vocabulary with the highwayman – the bushranger could be a **captain** or a **knight of** *the road*, as well as a *ranger* and a *bolter*. But despite being a successor of sorts to the criminals of the pad, bushranging was seen as having its birthplace in Van Diemen's Land (now known as Tasmania); thus *demon*, which had in the early 19th century meant a convict, came to denote a veteran bushranger by the middle of the same century. And while in its modern use *bush telegraph* refers to a network of person-to-person communication that exists outside the established systems, it was originally a cant term used to describe a member of a bushranging gang. Like the *bush wire*, his task was to keep his colleagues informed of the whereabouts of potential victims, or of any efforts to capture his fellow criminals.

THE MUGGER

In the infamous (and romanticised) outlaws and bushrangers of the American Wild West and the Australian outback the highwayman had his descendants. In the street robber, who has never gained the slightest degree of romantic associations, he had his antithesis. The street robber's first incarnation was the standard footpad, who was effectively a highwayman without a horse, but the more recent (and still current) version is the *mugger*.

The Origins of 'Mug'

The origins of the word *mugger*, as well as the verb to *mug*, lie in the slang noun *mug*, a face. It is a word that is still in use, and can be traced back to a popular style of 18th-century drinking mug bearing a grotesque human face. (The standard *mug*, pitcher, dates back to the early 16th century.) Mugger was first used not in criminal slang, but in early 19th-century British prize-fighting jargon to mean a blow to the face. As the sporting journalist Pierce Egan, covering a match in his journal *Boxiana* (1821), puts it: 'Oliver put in a mugger that made Donnelly stagger a little.' Mugger was one of a number of similar terms found in the language of The Fancy (as the boxers and their fans were known): a *facer* struck the face, a *muzzler* the chin, a *topper* the head, and a *belly-go-firster* the stomach. It was only mugger, however, by which the violent street robber came to be known, although the linguistic connection between a physical blow and the street robber continued – in the 1940s, **smacko**, from standard English *smack*, was a black-American term for a street robber.

Initially, the word mugger may have referred not to this generic type of criminal but to a specific gang in America, as is suggested by J.H. Browne's mention of the term in his Civil War memoir *Four Years in Secessia* (1865). He notes that 'the Muggers, like most bullies and ruffians, manifested a fine discrimination respecting the party they attacked, selecting those they thought they could rob with little resistance and entire impunity.' Less than a decade later, however, when the last edition of Hotten's *Slang Dictionary* was published in England in 1874, mugger had graduated to near-standard use: he defined both **maceman** and **macer** as a 'street-mugger'.

All that said, it should be mentioned that the journalist and social commentator Henry Mayhew, writing in *London Labour and the London Poor* (1861), took a different view of the term's etymology. Mayhew made his mugger a woman, and her target a mug, in the sense of an innocent or someone ripe for duping. Having picked him up in the street, she

> pays particular attention to his jewellery, watch and everything of that sort, of which she attempts to rob him. If he offers any resist-ance [. . .] one of her bullies comes up and either knocks him down with a blow under the ear, or exclaims 'What are you talking to my wife for?'

And while the actual act of violence was again a blow to the face (albeit its side), it was the woman, and not the blow, that was the mugger in question.

The First Muggings

The mug was another act of physical violence – a stronghold placed on a victim when robbing them, usually an arm lock or a chokehold

– and is first found in 1862, in the records of that year's Old Bailey
trials. In the document, a policeman testifies regarding his arrest of
a man called Roberts: 'He said, "You want me for putting the mug
on, do you? I will put the b—y mug on you,"' and adds 'mug is
slang used by thieves; it means garrotting'. It is around the same
time that one first finds **mugging**, which again means an act of
violence (in this case a beating or fight) as well as an act of violent
street robbery or assault, and to **tobe**, to rob violently. The latter
may have referred to the *toby* (street) on which the violence took
place, but in 1859 the American police chief G.W. Matsell defined
it as: 'Struck on the head and made senseless', and so, with a slight
mispronunciation, it may have originally referred to the *top* (of the
head) instead.

The Earliest Muggers

While the word mugging did not appear until the mid-19th century,
the act undoubtedly came earlier. In *A New Interlude called
Thersytes* (*c*.1538), the anonymous author offers an assonant list
of villains: 'Tynckers [. . .] tryfullers, turners, and trumpers,
Tempters, traytoures, trauaylers, and thumpers'. The list omits the
slightly later **trayler**, whose name comes from 'trailing' a potential
victim before pouncing, but it does include **thumper**, which was
probably the 16th century's preferred synonym for the robber who
would become the mugger three centuries later. This term aside,
however, there does seem to be a dearth of canting terms for street
robbers prior to the mid-19th century. There are thugs galore, but
more often in relation to brothels, and they did not necessarily
rob or even operate on the street. One term does seem to hark
back at least 300 years. It is likely that the **ruffling cove** street
robber takes its root from the **ruffler**, a villain listed *c*.1698 in the
New Dictionary of the Canting Crew as being of the 'first rank of
canters', who posed as a discharged soldier (and might indeed have
been one, although equally may have been a former servant), but
who actually worked as an itinerant. The ruffler came from *ruffle
it*, to swagger, and was linked to the image of a bird ruffling up
its feathers.

Muggers from the 19th Century to the Present

The remaining synonyms for a mugger all date from the 19th century and later. **Gentleman of the pad** had already been ironic when it meant a highwayman, but when appropriated to mean street robber, who did not even have the veneer of gentlemanliness, it was laughably so. The American **sandbagger**, like so many others (including the mugger), evoked the street robber's violent technique. It was from *sandbag*, to ambush or hit without warning; whether an actual sandbag ever entered the picture was irrelevant. Its later Australian equivalent was the **sandman** of the 1910s, who might 'put you to sleep' if you were unlucky enough to be one of his victims. The **bushwhacker** of mid-19th-century America also meant an ambusher. Its origin was quite literally from 'whacking' bushes, as noted by the lexicographer Schele De Vere in *Americanisms* (1872):

> Originally it was a harmless word, denoting simply the process of propelling a boat by pulling the bushes on the edges of the stream, or of beating them down with a scythe or a cudgel in order to open a way through a thicket.

The more menacing meaning presumably came from the bushwhacker's ability to move quietly through the woods in pursuit of his prey, albeit animal prey rather than the humans the later (criminal) bushwhacker targeted. The origins of the word *mugger* in boxing vernacular make the number of terms directly relating to the violence employed by the street robber unsurprising, but some are more forceful than others. There can surely be few that are more to the (unpleasant) point than the mid-19th century's **bludgeon business** and **swinging the stick**, both of which indicate the use of a bludgeon or club.

Certain muggers were more precise. The late 19th-century **smugger** (not a variation of mugger but from the dialect *smug*, to move stealthily) was known for snatch-and-grab thefts, while the **nightliner** preferred to operate after dark. On occasion, muggers work as part of a team and **shoulder-surfing**, from the 1990s, is a general term for a variety of 'distraction crimes' such groups may practise. One member of a team distracts the target by starting an argument or 'accidentally' spilling liquid on their clothes; while the argument is being resolved or the clothes wiped clean, the actual robber has the opportunity to steal.

The *jack roller*, another 20th-century addition, preyed on easy targets – drunk, drugged or otherwise incapacitated victims. The term is made up of two words that date from much earlier: *roll* meant to rob, often when the victim was drunk, while *jack* was a common generic for any man. As such jack was used by Chaucer, but by the mid-18th century the term had come to denote a vulnerable individual such as a gullible peasant or out-of-towner. In the 1930s, the *jack racket* was the act of mugging, while to *run a jack* was to grab a man's shirt and pull it over his head.

From Hijack to Jack

Of course, to *jack* is still a term associated with theft and robbery, but although the word and the meaning are the same, the etymology is different, as the current word is an abbreviation of *hijack* and first appeared in the 1960s. If one is to believe the etymologist Gerald Cohen in the second volume of his *Studies in Slang* (1989), hijack itself was based on *high jack*, a term for zinc ore used *c.*1899 in the mines of Webb City, Missouri – then the world's greatest lead/zinc mine. This zinc ore was more valuable than the basic lead among which it was found, and the criminal link comes from miners stealing it to further enrich themselves. Whether or not Cohen is right, hijack was virtually standard by 1900, and further terms continue to derive from its abbreviation: *jack up*, meaning to assault or attack (usually in a gang), was a black-American coinage in the 1960s; in the 1980s American police might describe an armed robber as a *jack-boy*; and within the last decade in Britain jack has come to mean a street robbery.

To **roll**, i.e. rob, also gives the **fruit roller** – more commonly *gay-basher* – one who enjoys mugging or beating up homosexuals. The term was a 1980s coinage, but *fruit* meaning homosexual – promoting the stereotype of one who is 'ripe' or 'soft' and 'easy picking' – has been recorded since 1900, when the journal *Dialect Notes* coyly defined the word as 'an immoral man'. In the 1950s and 1960s, to **cruise** was also to beat up and rob homosexuals (who were themselves cruising, albeit for something rather different).

Two sets of terms enjoyed a good deal of media attention when they first appeared in the public consciousness in the wake of particular crimes. In Britain the word was **steaming**, which came to light in the 1980s in the aftermath of violent goings-on during several of the yearly Notting Hill carnivals in West London. Presumably based on slang's *steam in*, to rush in energetically, steaming is a form of gang mugging usually performed on public transport – in London, a bus or underground train. Contrary to the usual small numbers involved in muggings, it's a crime based on numerous participants: the multiple muggers making their attack, and the multiple victims who lose their money and jewellery as a result.

America's **wild** and **wilding** appeared in more specific, but even more unpleasant, circumstances when they were featured in reports of the savage rape and beating of New York's 'Central Park jogger' in 1989. According to the accused, wild was used by them alone and means simply going wild. In theory, it was only elevated to a more general slang term when it was used in the *New York Times* on 22 April 1989. However, actually, the criminal sense of the word can be found earlier on the rapper Ice-T's 1987 album *Rhyme Pays*: the track 'Radio Suckers' includes the lyric 'Gangs illin, wildin' and killin'.

THE GARROTTER

The Notting Hill carnival muggings and Central Park jogger case were not the last occasions where media involvement brought widespread attention to a particular crime – and thus the language associated with it – and they certainly weren't the first. Over a

century before, London found itself in the grip of the great garrotting panic of 1862.

The origin of the word garrotte lies in the Spanish *garrote*, a
packing stick used to tighten the cord around a package to make it
more secure and easier to transport. The criminal meaning (half
strangling someone so that he is easier to rob) is derived from the
use of such a stick in garrotting, the preferred form of capital
punishment in Spain. In what was no more than judicially sanctified
strangulation, the stick tightened a cord around the condemned's
neck. Once again, when looking for a contemporary report on the
crime, one can turn to the journalist and social commentator Henry
Mayhew:

> The garotter tries to get his arm under [the victim's] chin, and presses
> it back, while with the other hand he holds his neck firmly behind.
> He does it so violently that the man is almost strangled and unable
> to cry out [. . .] Should the person struggle and resist he is pressed
> [i.e. throttled] so severely that he may be driven insensible.

And, adds Mayhew, 'it may be some time before he recovers his
presence of mind'.

Garrotting was by no means a 'new' crime when the panic spread
in 1862. It had been on the increase throughout the previous decade,
but it took the garrotting and robbery of a public figure – the MP
Hugh Pilkington – for it truly to be brought to the attention of the
press (and the police). The crime made all the London newspapers
and led to a panic that was, as so often happens, out of proportion
to the relatively small number of cases that occurred. Garrotting
was not, fortunately, a long-lived phenomenon, but the terminology
accrued nevertheless.

Flimp, to mug someone in order to steal a watch, could also
imply this act of semi-strangulation (also known as to **put the flimp
on**). The mugger was the flimp or *flimper*; his name came from the
western Flemish *flimpe* (to hit in the face). To *yoke* was to garrotte
in a team of two: one does the 'yoking' by choking or strangling
the victim, either with a rope or stick, while the other rifles the
victim's pockets. Other than this, the majority of terms for

garrotting or the garrotter were based around the idea of the neck and/or hanging. Links to capital punishment could be seen in **quinsey**, to garrotte, an abbreviation of the *hempen quinsey*, a blackly jocular euphemism for the hangman's rope. It played on *quinsey*, a swelling of the throat that typically resulted from tonsilitis. The later verb to **scrag**, derived from the slang for neck, was another term that referred to hanging as well as robbery by strangulation, as could **hemp**, **hang up** and **string up** (when used for hanging, however, the latter phrase is standard English rather than slang). In the 1940s, Australia added **necklace artist** or **necktie artist** for a garrotter, while the **necklace** won a grim celebrity in 1980s South Africa, but for denoting another type of violent crime – the gruesome act of placing a petrol-soaked tyre around a victim's neck and setting it on fire.

THE WORLD OF GUNS

The Gun in General

'Listen, snoop. This cannon ain't stuffed with feathers, see? Make just one wrong move and I'll feed you a lead supper.' So wrote Robert L. Bellem in a 1936 issue of *Spicy Detective*, one of the many pulp magazines that did so much for the vocabulary of crime, and most especially its weaponry – its *gats*, *equalizers*, *cannons*, *rods* and *roscoes*, to name but a few. Whether the real-life villains picked up their scripts from the pulps or whether the pulps and movies truly represented criminal vocabulary doesn't really seem to matter. And in the end, it was all about lead.

Lead was used to mean a bullet as early as the mid-19th century, although it had been recorded in standard phrases, for example a 'piece of lead' fired from a gun, at least a century before that. The first non-standard use of the word is found earlier in a parody written in 1812, in the lines 'Make Nunky surrender his dibs, / Rub his pate with a pair of lead towels.' Used to mean pistol, the term **lead towel** was modelled on the earlier *oaken towel*, a cudgel (one way or another both kinds of weapons gave their victim a 'rub-down'). Soon after, both **cold** and **hot lead** were used for a bullet, and by the 20th century 'lead' was to be found throughout the vocabulary that surrounded the gun and its use.

Lead Means Dead

Bullets
cold lead
hot lead
leaden capsule
lead pill
lead plum
lead sandwich

Guns
lead-chucker
lead-pusher
lead-spitter
lead-sprayer
lead towel

To Shoot
feed someone lead
pump lead
sling lead
squeeze lead
throw lead

The Victim
eats lead
gets (a) lead cocktail, lead medicine, lead poisoning, lead supper
gets the lead
leads up

After lead came the **gat**, an abbreviation of the Gatling gun, a form of machine gun invented by Dr R.J. Gatling (1818–1903) and first used in the American Civil War (1861–5). The term dates from the late 19th century and has a long history. Coined to mean a gun (usually a pistol or revolver), it would also come to mean a gunman in the 1920s (and to **gat up** was to commit a hold-up), and during the 2003 Iraq invasion the British Army used the variant **gatt** to describe their rifles. Another recent variation in current use is the **gak**, while gat itself has taken on an additional meaning, a prison-made knife.

As popular as gat, and first recorded in 1904, **rod** simply points to the weapon's shape. A pistol or revolver at its inception, like gat it came to mean the gunman who wielded it. Once armed one was **rodded** or **rodded up**, and one could rod a citizen – that is, hold them up. A **fast rod** was quick on the draw, and **tommy dodd** its rhyming slang equivalent. The Second World War had its own variation on the rod, unsurprising given its dominance of global events. The **Dutch rod** was a Luger, but despite appearances it had nothing to do with the Netherlands – *Dutch* was slang's version of *Deutsch* (i.e. German).

The origin of **roscoe** (or **John Roscoe**), the weapon of choice for any self-respecting hard-boiled operator, remains unknown. Coined in the 1910s and still going strong, it certainly sounds as if it must be anecdotal, but as far as anyone has been able to tell, no relevant story featuring a Mr Roscoe exists. The **shooter**, now a staple of any 'realistic' British cops and robbers show and usually describing a shotgun, was actually coined in the 1840s. Finally, a term that refers not to the gun's shape, power or function, but to its effect: the **equalizer**. As the one-time Black Panther Nathan McCall put it in his memoir, *Makes Me Wanna Holler* (1994), 'For me guns were life's great equalizer,' and he was hardly the first to realise that. Indeed, any weapon could be thus named, whether gun, club, cosh, knife or bomb: all bring everyone before them down to the same abject level.

Some of the vocabulary is based on the physicality of the weapon – **steel** is one, used in the late 19th century for a knife it is now a gun as well. The finish applied to many models of pistol or revolver gives **chrome**, while **metal**, coined in the 1970s, can mean both a weapon and its ammunition (apparently an abbreviation of *precious metal*, a nod to the weapon's utility). The gun's solidity and weight, rather than the aesthetics of its physicality, are reflected in the current African-American **four pound** and the **clog**, which is also a squat, heavy 'lump'.

Most of the above terms are, if not euphemisms, then still unwilling to offer any suggestion of what the weapon is actually used for: to kill. Less so are the **waster** (from *waste*, to kill), the **blaster** (a less powerful pistol is merely a **squirter**) and the **toast**, which is what it turns its victims into.

Phallic Guns

Rod falls into that group of macho terms which equate the gun with the penis, especially terms like **big rod**, a machine gun in the 1940s, and **long rod**, a rifle from 20 years earlier. Nor was rod the sole phallic weapon: one finds the **cannon** (a large variety of both 'weapons'), the **peashooter** (in either sense, presumably small and ineffectual), the **shooting stick** (which punned on *shoot*, to ejaculate) and the **tool**. Of course, even gun itself has been used to mean penis from the mid-17th century onwards. For example, the ubiquitous US Army boot camp chant sung by a recruit referring to, respectively, his rifle and his penis: 'This is my rifle, this is my gun. This is for fighting, this is for fun!' It would seem that firearms are toys for boys and guns can be for fighting *and* fun. Less obvious is the 1930s **biscuit**; why the penis should have been so named is debatable (perhaps its role as something that can be 'eaten'), but in the case of the pistol the allusion is undoubtedly to something one 'snaps'.

The Shotgun

The shotgun, especially the sawn-off variety, was for many years the villain's weapon of choice, spreading its deadly circle of pellets in a way that required relatively little marksmanship, as opposed to the single shots fired by a pistol. This no longer seems to be the case, especially in the States where the criminal's firepower has been vastly increased by the new technology that created such machine pistols as the Glock, the TEC-9 or the MAC-10, which have entered mainstream public consciousness thanks to their frequent appearances in hip-hop and rap lyrics.

The first slang term for a shotgun was probably the mid-19th-century American **scatter**, a musket that fired shot that 'scattered' as it left the muzzle. By the end of the century the default term had become the **gas pipe** and in the 1940s, when shotguns became double-barrelled, it was a **two-pipe**. Gradually, a shotgun of the sawn-off variety increased in popularity – being less conspicuous to carry and ideal for armed robberies – and it gained its own set of terms. The most common of these entered use in the 1920s: the **sawn-off**, **sawed-off** and **sawyer**. The 1930s **blow gun**, in standard use a weapon that fires a blow-dart, was a short-barrelled shotgun, as was the **blower**. Both were rooted in the standard **blow**, meaning to explode, but were underpinned by the slang term for killing, to **blow (someone) away**. The **alley-cleaner** of the 1950s also reflected the end aim – the killing of the target – as well as the scatter of the multiple pellets and the breadth of their effect: they would 'clean out' those standing in a narrow alley. The early 20th-century **broomstick** is a term for a pistol that potentially has a similar etymology: while it may appear to refer to the shape, the weapon also 'sweeps up' the opposition. The **street sweeper** is the modern equivalent, and just as the area it refers to has increased from alley to street, the firepower has been augmented too. A revolving cylinder loaded with shotgun cartridges is a terrifying magnifier of force. And the action of the shotgun has its own associated terms: to **trombone** is to rack the slide, loading a cartridge into the breech, and the way in which the weapon is 'broken' between the barrel and stock gives the **break-down** for the gun itself.

Whether double-barrelled or a single-barrelled **poker**, sawn-off, or pump-action like the **pom-pom** (originally a quick-firing gun used by the military), the shotgun is seen as a big weapon in comparison to the handgun, and the 1970s made this distinction with the terms **big boy** and **big toter**. This era also offered the British villain's **happy bag**, which was not the shotgun itself but the bag in which it was carried on an armed robbery: the threat of a gun meant that the victim was 'happy' to pass over the money. The newest coinage is the simple **shottie** or **shotty**, and it is one that shares the rap culture origins of the Glocks and MAC-10s that have, at least in some circles, succeeded them as the weapons of choice.

The Handgun

The most recent generic term for a handgun is probably the **strap** (one 'straps' it to one's waist or into a holster), but unlike the shotgun, handguns are more often named after the specific ammunition they use. The celebrated 'Police Special' that was the standard service cartridge for American police departments throughout the best part of the 20th century is a **spechie** (although the less impressive **Saturday night special** is any old cheap handgun, even a malfunctioning one, that serves for a one-off robbery, a salutary wounding or whatever 'job' is required). More usually, terms are derived from the calibre.

The Magic Numbers

.22 calibre
deuce-deuce
double-deuce
twenty-two

.25 calibre
deuce-five
two-fifth

.38 calibre
trey eight

.45 calibre
four-fifth

Nine-millimetre ammunition
milli
9 or nine
nine-mil
nine-milly

Machine pistols requiring nine-millimetre ammunition are perhaps most present in mainstream slang due to their frequent appearances in rap lyrics, although they are often known by an abbreviation of the particular model. Thus, the **ten**, the **mack** and the **big mack**; all are terms for the **spray and pray** (or, to give it its technical term, the Ingram MAC-10 sub-machine gun – also known by the punning and deceptively innocuous sounding *raincoat*). The *mag*, beloved of Hollywood cop Dirty Harry, is an abbreviation of Magnum, but the similar sounding *maggie* was an automatic pistol from the 1910s that was named after its magazine of bullets, rather than any brand name. *Snubbie* is another more general term – since the 1960s it has been a cheap, short-barrelled (in other words 'snub-nosed') revolver.

Despite the dominance of ammunition-related terms, the handgun also offers terms associated with the sound of the equipment. The *pop-nine* falls into both categories, coupling the nine-millimetre ammunition it uses with the sound it makes. It unites the very modern 'nine' with this onomatopoeic tradition that extends from the 1990s *oo-wop* (echoic of the noise of firing) back to the 18th century, when a pistol was a *popper*, a pair of pistols *popps* and a *pop* was a bullet. The 18th century also coined a number of other noise-related terms, all with a distinctly canine bent – the *barker*, the *barking iron*, the *bull pup*, the *bulldogged pistol*. All are so called because they all 'bark', as does the even more obvious mid-19th-century *dog* (or to give its alternative spelling, *dawg*).

Still auditory but more human was *Mister Speaker*, which as well as associating with sound referred to the political office of the Speaker, who 'lays down the law' in the US House of Representatives or the British Parliament. The ironic *persuader* was another: coined in the mid-19th century it had already been a spur and a cudgel before it was used for a gun (and later, like so many 'gun' words, it would be used to refer to a penis).

Moving from emphasising sound to emphasising action and effect one finds the 20th century's *burner* which represents the 'heat' of the fired gun – an image which produced its own set of terms in different milieus: the current black-American *flamer*, the mid-20th-century American *torch* and that pulp writer's standby the *heater*. It could also be linked with the early 20th-century American term *pepper-box* and its predecessor *pepper-castor*, although both these presumably come from the scatter meaning of the verb pepper, despite the neat 'hot pepper' link.

And when it comes to real guns, as well as their phallic

equivalents, size matters. Large pistols include the **hand artillery**, the **horse-pistol** (defined in the *Oxford English Dictionary* as 'a large pistol carried on the pommel of the saddle while on horseback') and the more recent **howitzer**, which borrows the proper name of a light cannon. On the other end of the scale is the **belly gun**, so named because it can be tucked into one's waistband and because it is most effective when fired at short range, especially when aimed at a victim's abdomen.

The Machine Gun

National stereotyping is of course invidious, but one has to admit that the British criminal just didn't get the machine gun. His American cousin most definitely did. The Thompson sub-machine gun was invented in 1919, fractionally too late to be tested out on the First World War killing fields. It gained its opportunities, however, with the almost immediate advent of Prohibition in the United States, a 'war on liquor' of which the primary effect was offering a massive boost to emergent, and highly lucrative, organised crime. The **tommy gun**, otherwise known as the **chopper**, the **Chicago piano** or **Chicago typewriter**, and less commonly the **Chicago atomizer** or **mowing-machine** (the latter group of terms honouring the Windy City's reputation for gangland on-street shoot-outs), was the weapon of choice at the time, or at least the weapon with the highest publicity value. The machine gun's wielder was a **tommy gee** or **tommy man**, and by the time Prohibition had ended in 1933, a new name had emerged for the weapon: the **tomcat**.

Similar weapons included the **brownie** or **browney** (the Browning machine gun), the **coffee-grinder** (like the gat this was originally a Gatling gun, but in non-military use it could be any machine gun), the **woodpecker** (reflecting the tapping noise) and the **sho-sho** or **sho-sho rifle** (presumably also echoic of the noise it made).

The Gunman

The killer-for-hire in the American underworld had carried his **trinkets** since the mid-19th century: they were his personal weaponry, often a knife and revolver. But while the profession was there, the names came later. The ***loogan*** was perhaps the most unusual. Used in the 1980s, it might have originated from *lug* (a big, dumb man), but it was more likely based on negative racial stereotyping – in this case through a concocted 'typical Irish' surname, presumably an extension of Logan. The American loogan elevated himself from his 1910 beginnings as a fool or newcomer by becoming a petty crook or ruffian and in due course a gunman, gaining the authority that the weapon he carried afforded him.

More usual, however, were the words that rendered the killer at one with his weapon. The easy one was the simple ***gun***, used since the 1910s for a professional gunman, and its extension the ***hired gun***, who kills, wounds or merely intimidates as required by his employer. His girlfriend was the ***gun moll***, but she too could carry a weapon and carry out her own work. And if the name did not equate the wielder with the whole weapon, then it could do in part: the ***trigger***, ***triggerboy***, ***trigger guy*** and ***triggerman*** appeared in the 1930s (although the important part of its meaning was the weapon-carrying sense rather than the criminal one – as well as the hired hand it has meant an armed bodyguard or prison guard).

Nowadays, of course, someone who is armed may be said to be ***packing heat***. We've noted the link between the 'heat' of the fired gun and some handgun names such as the burner, but ***heat*** by itself also means gun, and thus the gunman can be a ***heat-packer***, combining the term with the late 19th-century ***pack***, to carry a weapon. He can ***pack a heater*** and, when required, fire his weapon, or rather ***turn on*** or ***up the heat***.

Stick 'Em Up

'People kill people, guns don't kill people,' intone the National Rifle Association. Nevertheless it often seems that the rule remains: have gun must use it. And if there's money in it, then all the better for the hold-up man and his successor, the armed robber. He was nameless until christened the ***hold-up man*** in the United States in the mid-19th century, but his crime dates back at least to the previous century, when the ironically euphemistic *speak*, *speak to* or *speak with* meant to hold up. *Hold up* itself has two possible roots: the fact that the victim was 'held up' in what he or she was otherwise doing, or in the robber's cry of 'Hold up your hands!' A similar cry ('stick up your hands!') is the basis of the mid-19th-century coinage *stick-up*; however, the *stick-up man* and his equivalents (*stick-up artist/boy/nut* and *stick-em-up kid*) all emerged in the 20th. The raising of the hands also lies behind to *put up*, and the punning *elevate* (to 'hold up'), which was for the robber (or *elevator*) to rob at gunpoint and for the victim to put their hands in the air. The 1940s noun *raise-up* was another variation on hold up.

In the hierarchy of criminal acts, armed robbery might be seen as the antithesis of petty crime, and its gravity is reflected in its recent names: for example *the heavy* and a *knock-over* (which can also mean a police raid), while *hit a lick* is to commit such a violent robbery. Robbers of the 1920s used the verb *charge*, but their 1930s successors preferred *fade*; meanwhile to *prime* (from the 'priming' of an old-fashioned gun) and to *jack up* (from *hijack*) are both post-1950s coinages. Jack up gave the *jack-boy*, who, in Britain at least, can be said to be working *on the pavement*, the reference being to armed attacks on security vans and suchlike. The 1960s *face* was picked up by the period's young Mods (they of the scooters, parkas, mohair suits, purple hearts and The Who) to define an outstanding member of their peers, but he was an armed robber first of all. And a retired face might be a *rusty gun*: defining the gunman by his gun and suggesting that both weapon and wielder are no longer in working order.

Carrying and Shooting

Like gun for gunman, to *carry* was easily assimilated from standard English. (An extension was to *carry iron*, especially when used of a gangster's bodyguard.) *Pack* is still dominant in current use, but it has another popular descendant in to *run heavy*, a phrase that relates to that weighty iron again. So too does to *iron-whip*, meaning to 'pistol-whip' – a brutal piece of intimidation, using the gun as a blunt weapon, which has been euphemised as to **comb someone's hair**, **head**, **noddle** or **wool**.

The basic late 19th-century phrase for pulling a gun in preparation to shoot (but not yet fire it) again went for the simple route: to **pull** or **pull down on** (or to **throw down on**). To **flash the muzzle** used flash in the sense of show; again, the trigger remained unpressed. In keeping with the whole group of terms that double for the gun and the penis, the 1940s offered what is probably the most obvious allusion to the link yet – the phrase **get a hard-on**, which meant (as it still does) to have an erection, but also to draw a pistol.

Once the gun is drawn, then it's usually **out of the pocket**, the modern gang term for using it. To shoot has been to **flip**, from the standard English **flip** (to strike at sharply) and to **smoke**, a rather straightforward image of smoke coming from the fired weapon. A 1920s coinage, smoke has proved durable and adaptable – it has meant to kill, to murder or just to shoot at, while a **smoking** was a killing or shooting and to be **smoked** to be murdered or shot.

To smoke someone is still around today, but there are other recent terms too: to **break**, **bust slugs**, **bust a gun** and **bust** or **pop a cap**. Bust and pop a cap are much older than their place in current mainstream slang suggests, having made fleeting appearances in the American Civil War before usage lapsed for another century or so (the synonymous **snap a cap** did not survive beyond the 1890s). The use of **cap** for bullet began in the 1930s, and in the 1970s the term became a verb meaning to shoot or kill, as well as producing a word for gunfire: **capping**. More metaphorical, and more melodramatic, was the 1960s to **hold court in the streets**. This term, which means to engage in a gun battle on the street, smacked of the 'Wild West' and the clichéd image of its pairs of faced-off gunmen. It pits villain against 'the law', with the implication that the former would rather die than face the latter's prison. However, police presence in the 'court' is not mandatory: the first recorded use was by the black power militant Malcolm X in his recollection of a 1940s encounter between two pimps.

KNIVES, COSHES AND
OTHER WEAPONS OF CHOICE

The Knife

The gun is useful, but unless silenced it is noisy and has been rela-tively hard to obtain in Britain (where villains as well as policemen allegedly preferred operating without one). So, if circumstances permit, the chosen weapon may be the knife, and the word of choice is undoubtedly *chiv*. A Romany term, it was appropriated in the late 17th century and since then has produced a multitude of vari-ations and extensions within the language of knife crime, from the mid-19th-century *chive-fencer*, a street-seller of knives, to the *chiv-mark* of the last decade, by which the scar left by a knife slash may be known. Also recent is the 1990s *chivvy*, to slash with a knife, but a century earlier *chivy* was an adjective relating to the use of knives and the *chivy duel* a knife fight. Even earlier was the *chiving-lay*, a form of robbery practised in the 18th and 19th centuries in which the robber cut the braces (the strong leather straps that suspended the body from the springs) of a coach so that coachman was forced to dismount. While the coachman's attention was distracted by one thief, an accomplice could empty the boot of its contents. The same term was used to describe another form of coach-related crime too. In the days when every man who could afford such a thing wore a wig over his shaved scalp, the chiv could be used to cut open the back of a coach to nab the large (and valuable) wigs straight from the heads of the passengers.

Of the other terms, the mid-19th century's **breadwinner** and the more recent **edge** are harshly practical, and others were even more callous. The **bleeder** of the 19th century and the **carver** of the 20th were both matter-of-fact and ostensibly violent, as is the American gang term **bora** (probably a misspelling of 'borer'). Modern American prisons have the **bonecrusher** and the home-made **Christmas tree**, which may sound innocuous enough but is so named because its triangular shape and damaging serrated edges resemble the stereotypical shape of the Christmas pine. The 20th-century rhyming slang *charming wife* may also seem to provide a slight lightening in tone, but again it is ironic, providing the 'wife' with a more lethal alternative to the traditional rolling pin.

The Razor

There is something dreadfully intimate about the use of a razor as a weapon – the cut-throat variety of course; one wouldn't get very far with even the fanciest of safety models. It tends to be aimed at the face, and where a knife might puncture, the razor slashes and leaves a scar that rarely goes completely away. Not for nothing did the Scottish gangs of the 1920s and 1930s use *brand* to mean both to razor-slash and to scar. As with the British tendency towards knives, the razor could be the preferred choice in places where firearms were hard to come by, or when the penalty for carrying one was deemed too severe. At the same time as the Scottish razor gangs were operating in the East End of Glasgow, their Australian equivalents were slashing their way into the Sydney crime scene. Grim humour underlined the use of *Bengal lancers*, an Australian term for the razor gangs that flocked (as they did in Britain) to the racetracks in the 1930s and 1940s. Australia also produced the rhyming slang *Dawn Fraser* and *Malcolm Fraser*. The first was named after the swimming star Dawn Fraser (b.1937) and the second after Malcolm Fraser (b.1930), the country's prime minister between 1975 and 1983.

Certain modern terms for a razor-slashing focus specifically on the scar that the weapon is so infamous for leaving. The *Chelsea smile* is a knife slash that runs from the corner of the mouth up and across the cheek. The name, first noted in the 1990s but as an act probably somewhat older, is from the supposed origination of such cuts, which were inflicted by the more violent of Chelsea Football Club's fans (and their blades) on the supporters of rival teams. Football being the tribal sport it is, other fans have replaced 'Chelsea' with their own team, but whatever the name the scar remains the same. The *buck-fifty* is a razor-slash too, but it runs either over the top of the skull or from ear to ear. In monetary slang the term means $150, but in the criminal parlance of American prisons it has nothing to do with money – the number denotes the number of stitches that is required to close it.

The Club, the Cosh and the Blackjack

By the standard of the gun or knife the club is indeed a blunt instrument, and may seem far from efficient. Yet the club, the cosh, the blackjack or any other form of bludgeon can do serious damage and, unlike the gun in particular, it can be controlled damage: you do not have to beat the victim to death, you can just break whichever bits of their body you choose instead.

The *cosh* or *kosh* has no definite etymology, and the best guess is that it's simply echoic of the weapon swishing through the air (prior to its landing with a sickening crunch). Dialect does offer *cosh*, a stick of any kind, but chronologically it appears that slang got there first. Cosh was first recorded in the slang sense in 1868, when the anonymous author of the article 'Six Years in the Prisons of England' explained to the readers of *Temple Bar Magazine* – the 'London magazine for town and country readers' – how a prostitute worked with 'her accomplice the coshman (a man who carries a "cosh" or life-preserver)'. Defined as a stout stick, bludgeon or truncheon, a cosh was carried by a *cosher*, *cosh-bandit* or *cosh-boy*, and *the cosh* was the action of knocking a victim out or down.

In the terms that follow we see a general strain of personification, borrowing from what would otherwise be proper names. In Britain the *neddy* came from the slang *kennedy*, which meant a poker and was allegedly from a real-life – but frustratingly undocumented – Kennedy who used such a household implement to murder someone. The United States, meanwhile, had the *bessie* and the *billy*, the latter having survived up to the present day. Also known as a *billy stick*, it started life as a short iron crowbar used by criminals but progressed to mean weapons used by both sides of the law: the policeman's truncheon (originally of untanned cowhide and covered in wool) and the villain's cosh, which was usually 'loaded' with lead shot. The *eel skin* was also loaded for increased effectiveness, but it was a canvas tube stuffed with sand, and the 20th-century *bag* was a descendant of both. It was made from several socks placed inside each other; a solid, ball-shaped object was placed inside them and the whole thing was then packed with sand. Similar objects are found in American prisons today, such as the *slock* – a sock filled with something heavy (such as a few large batteries or a chunky padlock). The slock's main advantage is that it can be broken down quickly into its constituent parts to disguise its application as a deadly weapon when whole. The etymology, too, is a combination of innocuous and violent. In part it comes from the sock that acts as the vessel, but it is likely that *slug* made a contribution, too. Like *slog*, slug meant a blow in the early 19th century, becoming a blackjack in the 1920s and the thug who probably used one 20 years later. Such a thug might **put the slug on** an unfortunate victim, leaving him suffering the after-effects (or rather, making him *slug-nutty*).

The mid-19th-century **bully** may have been a variation on *billy*, but on the other hand it might just have been another use of bully's basic meaning – a thug. One would have to be a thug to wield the era's **drumstick**, so named because it beat out a 'rhythm' on the victim's body. In the mid-19th century the standard English *blackjack* was abbreviated to **jack**, which was to beat with a blackjack but which has gained additional, and no less nasty, meanings: to stun a fellow prisoner with a blackjack before raping them, and most recently to stab or to punch.

Aside from the late 19th-century **stick**, which needs little explanation, the remaining names for the club were relatively short-lived. Among them were the **squeegee** (1920s), the **rubber** (1930s) and the **strap** (1940s). The **blackie** of the 1950s may have been another abbreviation of blackjack, or it may have been due to the mental blackout it might cause; the same decade's **beanie** was so called because it 'beaned' you. In the 1970s the **swailer** may have been linked to the dialect *swail*, to swing the arms while walking, and thus implied the swinging action of the bludgeon. The **stonikey**, also from the 1970s, was originally a nautical term referring to a rope's end. But even here it was used in a violent sense, as the rope's end was used for punishment. Finally a current term, and a rare one that eschews violent connotations in favour of a simple visual link: the **beavertail** is so called because it resembles the animal's tail – broad at one end and narrow (for gripping) at the other.

Chapter 6

GANGS

Thus far our Riots with Success are crown'd.
Have found no stop, or what they found o'ercame;
In vain th'embattled Watch in deep array.
Against our Rage oppose their lifted Poles;
Through Poles we rush triumphant, Watchman rolls
On Watchman; while their Lanthorns kick'd aloft
Like blazing Stars, illumine all the Air.

John Gay, *The Mohocks* (1712)

EARLY GANGS

There have always been criminal gangs, be they of pickpockets, confidence tricksters or bank robbers (all of which groups tend to operate 'mob-handed'), and of course there is 'organised crime', whether the US mafia, its more recent immigrant Russian rivals or indeed the UK's homegrown firms, such as those of the Krays and Richardsons in the 1960s. But while, thanks to Mario Puzio and his many clones, we know all about *made men, dons, caporegimes, consiglieres, skippers, crews, going to mattresses* and all the rest, the day-to-day language – referring to guns, money, women – is pretty run-of-the-mill. After all, the aim of such gangs has always been to keep a low profile. The street gang is different, especially in its current incarnation: the young men and women of the US ghettos for whom belonging to a gang (and proclaiming the fact) is a central factor in their identity. For them, establishing a language is as important as the wearing of colours (red for *Bloods*, blue for *Crips*), sporting tattoos, and tagging walls with their coded gang names, slogans and insignia.

Street gangs have existed as long as the cities in which they resided. And they were often, at least to start with, an upper-class amusement. Thus in the late 16th century we find the **damned Crewe**, upper-class roisterers who, in the words of contemporary clergyman Stephen Gosson, were 'without feare or feeling eyther of Hell or Heaven'; the **roaring boys** or **roarers**; and the **Mohocks**, named for the supposedly 'savage' Indian tribe the Mohawks. All of which were mainly aristocratic rowdies who delighted in terrorising the unfortunate citizenry and caroused through the streets of London beating up passers-by, attacking watchmen, molesting women and smashing windows. The 17th century brought in the **scourers**, from standard *scour*, to move around hastily and energetically, while the 18th added Dublin's **chalkers**, who specialised in roaming the streets and **chalking** – slashing the face of any unfortunate victim. Also Irish were the **pinkindindies** or **pinking-dindees** (literally 'a turkey-cock given to pinking with a rapier'), who deliberately picked arguments that could be ended by a sword-thrust, and the **tittery-tus** or **tityre-tus**, who took their name from the first words of Virgil's first eclogue: *Tityre, tu patulae recubans sub tegmine fagi*. The Latin tag implied that these privileged rogues were men of leisure and fortune, who 'lay at ease under their patrimonial beech trees'. Such gangs did not have their own particular slang, or if they did it is unrecorded. They were written of; they did not write.

THE BIRTH OF THE AMERICAN GANG

The 19th century ushered in the working-class gang, especially in New York, where one might find the **Dead Rabbits**, who would parade brandishing such a corpse as their standard and a symbol of their defeated rivals, as well as the **Whyos**, the **Forty Thieves** and the **Shirt Tails**. The **Gophers** preferred to congregate in cellar hideouts around their West Side turf, which was best known as 'Hell's Kitchen'. The origin of the name of the **Plug Uglies** is debatable. It may have been from the large *plug-hat* stuffed with paper which each member wore for protection from the clubs of their rivals, or it might have blended ugly and *plug* (a face). The Plug Uglies had an offshoot in Baltimore, where they doubtless fought the local **Blood Tubs** who had, according to John Farmer's *Americanisms* (1889), allegedly earned their name from having 'on an election day, dipped an obnoxious German's head in a tub of warm blood, and then sent him running through the town.' It is of the Baltimore Plug Uglies that a correspondent of *The Times* was writing on 4 November 1876, when he suggested an alternative origin of their name: 'it was derived from a short spike fastened in the toe of their boots, with which they kicked their opponents in a dense crowd, or, as they elegantly expressed it, "plugged them ugly".'

As well as representing antagonistic communities – such as Irish Catholics versus 'native American' Protestants – New York gangs were often allied to one of the city's fire engine companies, who fought fiercely for the honour of tackling a fire (so much so that by the time the fight was over, so too was the fire), and they were regularly employed by political interests to bring in the vote, usually via intimidation or the dissemination of bribes. Again there does not seem to be a proliferation of gang-specific language. A few terms have been recorded: **the boys** were the gang members, as were **round rimmers**, which presumably referred to a style of hat; the **kentry** was the gang's territory. But, in general, they seem simply to have spoken the slang of their era.

The **b'hoy**, a phonetic spelling of the immigrant Irish pronunciation of 'boy', denoted any sort of lad (Irish of course) living on or around New York's downtown, and downmarket, Bowery. Thus the **Bowery B'hoys** were a gang, but the term also referred to a proletarian New Yorker who worked as a fireman but whose main occupation was running with a gang, mixing street thuggery with life as a political mercenary. The b'hoy went on to 'literary fame': Edward Judson (1823–86), a political fixer and bullyboy, wrote a number of blood-and-thunder burlesques featuring Mose, Lize and their friend Sykesy. Mose, who also featured in B.A. Baker's play *A Glance at New York* (1848), was a mythical, larger-than-life gang boss based on the real-life Moses 'Old Mose' Humphreys – leader of the real Bowery B'hoys, a ferocious street brawler and a fireman of Lady Washington Engine Company No. 40.

Perhaps the most important word of the time was **hoodlum** (and its abbreviation **hood**). The term was coined in San Francisco c.1870–2 and had spread across the US by the end of the decade, generating a number of popular etymologies. Among them, according to H.L. Mencken (1880–1956), was the idea of a local newspaperman who, keen to coin a term to describe the street gangs that were plaguing the city's streets, decided simply to reverse the name of a leading gangster, one Muldoon. This created *noodlum*, and a printer's error that substituted 'h' for 'n' did the rest. Other theories include a reference to a gang rallying-cry – 'Huddle 'em!' – and to roots in the Bavarian dialect term *Hodalump*, which carries exactly the same meaning; as well as links to various terms in Spanish and also Native American languages. It is tempting to suggest the near-synonymous *hooligan*, but that word was British and was noted only when it began appearing in London police reports *c.*1898. In his history of San Francisco crime, *The Barbary Coast* (1933), Herbert Asbury offers highly persuasive evidence for the 'huddle 'em' theory.

THE AUSTRALIAN LARRIKIN

Across the world in 19th-century Australia one found the **larrikin**. Another street villain, the word has no precise etymology but might be linked to the Warwickshire/Worcestershire/Cornish dialect *larrikin*, a mischievous or frolicsome youth. Other theories include the elision of *leery* (untrustworthy) and *kinchin* (a child or youth), or dialect *larack*, to lark or lark about. The term gave the **larrikiness** or **larrikina**, the female equivalent, and **larrikinism**, hooliganism. There was also the **larrikin push**, often abbreviated to **push**, which had a variety of meanings, including not merely the criminal gang but also a gang of tramps and a prison work gang. There was the **upper-ten push**, upper-class criminals and prisoners; **pushism**, the world of such gangs; and the **pushman** or **pushite**, a gang member.

THE GROWTH OF AMERICAN TEEN GANGS

Come the mid-20th century, the emphasis had moved again this time on to the teenage 'juvenile delinquents', with their switchblades and leather jackets, their jailbait and their gangbangs. Like their

19th-century predecessors they too were encountered in the cities of America, where teenage members of different ethnic groups fought, in every sense, to maintain their sovereignty over a local area, which was sometimes no more than a block or two in size. It was gangs like these whose existence resulted in the hit musical *West Side Story*, as well as a wide range of cheap, lurid novels from authors such as Hal Ellson (*The Knife*, *The Golden Spike*), Wenzell Brown (*Cry Kill* and *Teen Age Mafia*), Edward de Roo (*Go, Man, Go!* and *The Big Rumble*) and Vin Packer, actually Marijane Meaker (*The Young and Violent*). Given the number and variety of such gangs, their territories were sometimes limited to a minuscule fraction of a city and so there would have been a wide range of localisms. However, all the terms that follow appear to have been in general use between the 1940s and 1970s.

The juvenile delinquent was a part of society – and thus of English – as early as 1817, but the term was used then as a synonym for 'juvenile offender'; the modern version, embraced by those it described, did not appear until the 1940s. This was a new variety of young criminal, who was known in the UK by such names as **cosh-boy** or **Teddy-boy**, though these British delinquents would not have aspired to the ubiquity of their American counterparts. The Teddy-boy was thus named for his clothes, grotesquely parodied versions of supposedly Edwardian male fashion, c.1900. The style had first been sported by upper-class dandies around 1945, but when they moved on, the Teds took over. Gangs, as noted, had been a part of city life for decades in the US; what was new was the racial spread. There were now black and Latino gangs as well as white ones (divided by their immigrant background), and as 'white flight' took every white parent who could afford it away from the inner city to the suburbs, it was they who would set the pattern for today's mainly ghetto-based associations.

Among the earliest gang terms were those pertaining to the still new Latinos, and of these **pachuco** was the earliest. Recorded since the 1930s, it stood for a Mexican-American, especially a member of a street gang, and usually of those in the Mexican *barrios* of Los Angeles. *Pachuco* was a Mexican-Spanish derogative meaning flashily dressed or vulgar, and was commonly abbreviated as *chuco* or *chuc*.

It was these Latino gangs who adopted – as their preferred 'uniform' – the *zoot suit*, a term possibly originating in the New Orleans Cajun *zoot*, cute. The suits were characterised by a long, draped jacket with padded shoulders and high-waisted tapering trousers. In 1943 the locally based US servicemen, fired up by the racist demagogy of the *LA Times*, launched widespread vigilante attacks on the Latino youths. Despite the sadistic violence of the white instigators it was announced by the local authorities that the *zoot-suiters* were communist-inspired, while the beleaguered troops were acting 'in self-defence'.

By the 1950s the word had been largely replaced by *cholo*. Taken from Cholollán (now Cholula), a district of Mexico, the name had been used since the mid-19th century to describe a Mexican or South American, especially one considered lower class or of mixed blood. It was used of teenage gang members from the 1950s on.

Members of these gangs revelled in their own image. The gangster lifestyle was *la vida loca*, the 'crazy life' – sometimes personalized as *mi* [my] *vida loca*. One who led such a life was a *bato loco* or *vato loco*, literally a 'crazy dude'. The term was, and still is, used for any member of a Mexican teen gang, especially an individual who has a reputation for over-the-top violence, but also poise, courage and other admired attributes of street life. It could, in addition, mean a madman and could be abbreviated as *loco*, 'crazy'.

A gang leader was the *aceman* or the *Prez*. A lower-ranked member was a *diddy-bop* (also *diddley bop* or *ditty bop*), but the *boy* had the lowest status. One's fellow members were *my people*, but a *cokie*, with no apparent link to cocaine, was a member of a rival gang. A gang member who was disloyal was a *chump*, while a *snake* or *cheeser* was a spy; cowards were *one-ball*, i.e. weak and worthless (semi-gelded as it were), and a *turkey* wouldn't or couldn't fight, and so was allowed only such menial tasks as running messages or bringing the gang's food and drink. A *hook* was a weakling or a conformist, and usually not a gang member. The term may have been comparing such individuals to the stereotype of the studious Jew – in slang a *hook* (from image of a hooked nose) – who is seen as unlikely to join a gang. One may also note the First World War military use of *hook* to mean a shirker.

Gang members were not exclusively male, but the women – the *debs*

– who took part were seen as second-class citizens; and they had a role to play. While a *wife* was the steady girlfriend of a gang member, a more common term was ***pulling a train***, submitting oneself to sex with multiple partners, also known as ***pulling a G*** (the 'g' in this case standing for gangbang). ***Food*** could mean any victim, but was often a sex object, and the ***Midnight Revue*** referred to an act of group sex, as well as the girl (often a prostitute hired by a group of boys) who was its focus.

While gangs of juvenile delinquents undoubtedly consumed drugs, and doubtless involved themselves in small-scale dealing, there was nothing like the levels of drug selling that can be found amongst modern gangs. Far more important was the defence of one's own turf and invading that of one's rivals. The gang that fought was a ***bopping club*** or ***bopping gang***, from *bop*, to hit. A fighting member was a ***bopper*** or ***bop***, and a ***diddlebop*** or ***bebop*** was a fight. Perhaps the classic term was ***rumble***: meaning both the fight and to fight, it was immortalised on stage and between paper covers.

The fight itself could be a ***fair one***, conducted under some sort of mutually recognised set of rules, and possibly preceded by a verbal argument, or a ***jap***, a surprise attack. The latter referenced the stereotype of the Japanese, as epitomised by their unannounced attack on Pearl Harbor. To declare gang war was to ***put it on*** (a rival gang), while to attack was to ***fall down*** or ***whip it on*** that gang. To attack without warning was again to jap, as well as to ***snag***. Other terms included to ***jitterbug*** and to ***thump***. To win was to ***waste*** one's opponents. A ***face-up*** (a variant on the standard *face-off*) could be a full-scale gang-fight or an encounter between two individuals, which was otherwise known as a ***one-on-one***. Meanwhile a ***jump*** was a fight, but it could also be a dance party.

Juvenile gang members carried ***blackies***, blackjacks, guns and ***burns***, although the latter were less common than in succeeding decades. The weapons of choice were the ***button***, a switchblade knife activated by a button on the handle, and the home-made but still effective ***zip-gun***. This was constructed by taking a short length of pipe, 4–10 inches long, with an inside diameter the same as that of a bullet; a bullet was placed at one end and detonated by a sharp tap from a pointed steel rod (which was hit by the heel of one's hand or by a small object). The word *zip* mimicked the sound of the fired bullet. There was also the

Webster Avenue walking stick, a baseball bat studded with razorblades
that originated from the 5.8-mile-long Webster Avenue in the Bronx.

Various other terms were found among the gangs. The police
could be the **Gestapo** and their cars **hunt-buggies**. A **prayer meeting**
was a game of dice: all the players were down on their knees. To
cat was to hang out, to loaf about, while to **sound** was to chat. **Smooth
smooth** meant peacefully, or in a law-abiding manner; **tight as a tick**
was to be well-prepared. **Dickies** were the baggy trousers favoured by
teenage gang members; the term was the brand-name of one of
America's biggest manufacturers of work clothes. More violent was
the **cocktail**, in which the 'drink' of choice was a Molotov cocktail
that was tossed into a rival clubhouse, and the acronym **l.a.m.f.** ('like
a mother fucker'): when added to a gang name it implied the toughness and aggressiveness of the person who could be so defined.

THE MODERN US GANG

The juvenile delinquent gang may have been the precursor of the
modern gang as it is found in America's cities, but as regards size,
multiplicity and breadth of language there is no comparison. A
current Wikipedia listing of America's primary gangs runs to more
than 150 names, broken down into Asians, bikers, blacks, whites,
Hispanic/Latin and prison-based. There are also the more traditional
varieties of Irish and Italian gangs (the latter the crime 'families' of
the US Mafia), plus a new candidate: the Russian 'mob' who have
established themselves over the last couple of decades. Among
America's modern gangs are the **Asian Boyz**, the **Gypsy Jokers**
(bikers), the **United Blood Nation** (black), the **Rollin 60 Neighborhood
Crips** (black), the **Maniac Latin Disciples**, **Nuestra Familia** (prison-
based Latinos) and the **Potato Bag Gang** (Russian). To list every
variety of language, not to mention the particular initiatory and
declaratory tattoos and gang 'tags' spray-painted on to walls, one
would need a similar level of dedication as those who pore over the
minutiae of the German armed forces of the Second World War,
with their seeming infinity of uniforms, ceremonial daggers and

American Biker Gang Slang

Most bikers are just that – bikers – but like other groups they have coined their own vocabulary, a very small selection of which is included below:

BTBF   Bikers Together, Bikers Forever

1%   The 1% of all motorcycle riders who are outlaws

13   denotes marijuana or methamphetamine use

chopper   cut-down motorcycle, with only the bare essentials and with handlebars set high

colors   the official uniform of all outlaw motorcycle gangs: a sleeveless denim or leather jacket, with club patch on the back, and various other patches, pins and Nazi medals attached to the front; colors belong to the club, are worn only by male members, and always are held sacred by members

DFFL   Dope Forever, Forever Loaded

filthy few   an elite group of bikers found within the Hells Angels; they are the enforcers of discipline. In order to wear the Filthy Few tattoo, the biker usually must have committed murder

HOG   Harley-Davidson motorcycle

MAMA   a girl available to all club members, usually sexually

MC   patch on colors: Motorcycle Club

nomad   non-affiliated motorcycle gang member; used by some clubs as an enforcer

old ladies   women associated with motorcycle gangs (may be attached to a specific member or the gang in general)

originals   a member's first set of colors, which are never to be cleaned

probate or *prospect*   a person pledging to become a member of a biker gang. After completing a probationary period and being voted into the gang by 100% vote, the probate receives his colors or patch and is accepted as a full member

wings   an emblem worn by 1 percenters as a pin or patch: a cloth attached to the colors. All wing-earning must be witnessed

indeed tattoos. The internal jargon of the **Aryan Brotherhood** (white and racist, prison-based), and the different flavours of **Bloods** or **Crips** (black, rooted in city ghettos) or **La Raza Nation** (Latino, again ghetto-based), would be impossible to include here. Instead, what follows is a round-up of a relatively small subset: the general terms that are common to a number of these organisations.

The basics are very simple, and they start with the letter G. G for **gangster** or, as it is often written, **gangsta**, an apparent misspelling that deliberately underlines the gang's outlaw status (in language as in life). G creates a number of compounds: the **G-ster**, a synonym for gangster; to **G down**, to get dressed up; **G-name**, a street name (also *placa* in Latino gangs); **G-check**, to rob; and **G-ride**, any type of automobile favoured by teen gangs, and usually a stolen vehicle. **G-money** is a term of affectionate address, while a **G-thang** or **G-thing** has two uses of the initial letter: for anything that is seen as a male preserve, i.e. a 'guy thing'; or anything that concerns a street thug, i.e. a 'gangster thing'.

The image of the gangster or gangsta, especially as propounded through rap music, offers an alluring mix of sex (often coerced), violence, drugs and illicitly gained money, but those same characteristics have made it a threatening force for conformists – whether black or white. The word was coined in the 1890s to define a member of a gang of criminals. The term has persisted in this original use, which still works, but it has taken on a secondary sense: the rebellious, non-conformist individual who refuses to accept establishment (i.e. white) authority. By the 1980s, still some years before the advent of gangsta rap, the term had been taken up by the US black underworld and formed a number of compounds: **gangster doors**, the four-doored saloon that was the vehicular preference of prominent ghetto criminals (**gangster walls** were the white-walled tyres such a car might feature); **gangster front** (from *front*, a suit), a double-breasted suit in the style worn by the (movie) gangsters of the 1920s–1930s and adopted by latter-day ghetto criminals; **gangster pills**, barbiturates, and **gangster stick**, a marijuana cigarette.

The advent of gangsta rap created a number of new compounds (all of which can also be spelt in the orthodox manner): **gangsta-ass**, pertaining to the street culture of a black urban gangsta; **gangsta** *bitch*, a woman who associates with a male gang and may participate in its activities; *gangsta class*, the style affected by a young street thug and/or drug dealer; *gangsta juice*, Olde English malt liquor and *Night Train*, wine (after a brand of low-end fortified wine); and *gangsta roll*, a large wad of paper money. There are also two references to the physical style adopted by such young men: the *gangsta lean*, their supposedly sophisticated way of driving a car, with an elbow out of the window and the body leaning in the same direction; and the *gangsta limp*, a style of walking, characterised by a slight dip in the stride, adopted by young urban black men.

After G was the gang. *Gangbanging* has traditionally been associated with sex, but since the 1970s it has evolved a parallel, and equally widespread, sense: to be involved in gang activities. In context it means fighting with another gang, and the gang member is known as a *gangbanger*. The abbreviation *HBS* stands for the three givens of gangster life: *hanging*, *banging* and *slanging* (hanging out, gangbanging, and selling drugs).

Banging abbreviates gangbanging, and a *banger* is a gang member. The leader can be the *big boy*, the *shot-caller*, and – if he's making money (usually from crime) – a *baller*. The soldier (just as it is used in the American Mafia) is a lower-ranked member; juniors are known variously as a *YG*, a *young gangster* or new member, a *TG*, a *tiny gangster*, or a *BG*, *baby gangster*. Both the TG and the BG are children used by a gang to act as lookouts and hold drugs, guns, etc. (also known as *pee-wees*). A baby gangster can also be someone who has not shot anyone yet. The antithesis of BG is *OG*, *original gangster*, which can mean a veteran, but also someone who has shot or killed an enemy, as can *OB*, *original banger*. The more general terms *homes*, *homeboy* and *homey* can all be used to refer to fellow gang members, as can *player*. In Latin gangs, a fellow-member is a *carnal*, while female members are *carnalas* or *queens*. Some gangs have white members: men are *peckerwoods* and women *featherwoods*. The ideal member is *down* (i.e. loyal), but some are failures, such as the *buster*, who does not live up to gang standards, and the *chip dog*, who steals the gang's money or drugs. They may fall foul of the *enforcer*, who disciplines members for violations of the rules. The all-purpose condemnation *bitch* – here used of men – refers to anyone failing to meet the gang's standards. To have no gang affiliation is to be from **nowhere**. Of the many antagonistic terms, the Crips' dismissal of Bloods as **slobs** is one of the best known. The Bloods opt for **crabs**, and the slogan **B's Up C's Down**. If the gang has many members it considers itself **deep**. The gang itself is the **posse** (a mainly East Coast term) or the **set** (i.e. a subset of a larger 'nation' of gangs); the term can also refer to a neighbourhood. To go **set-tripping** is to attack a rival gang, while to be **down with the set** is both to affirm one's loyalty and, self-referentially, to express a peaceful, secure state of mind.

Initiation

One does not merely walk into a gang. To be **blessed** or **married** requires, as one might expect, that the **mark**, the prospective member, first must experience (often painful) initiations. **Courting in** and **jumping in** both mean the same thing: the mark must fight two or more members of the gang for up to two minutes. He is not expected to win, though he may, but he must acquit himself honourably. If at some later stage, assuming he remains alive and out of prison, he wishes – perhaps through age – to quit, he cannot walk away: he is **courted** or **jumped out**, and another two minutes of fisticuffs must be endured. Some gangs, however, are not satisfied with a mere fistfight. The meaning of **blood in blood out** is that to gain membership one must shed blood, probably by committing murder (sometimes by going on a drive-by shooting), and, to round off one's days, one must do it again. **Blood out** has an alternative, still violent, meaning: the gang member has to endure a severe beating from his former friends if he wishes to leave.

Colours

Once one has been initiated, one may sport the gang colours or more properly – since we are talking about American gangs – **colors**. To do this can be to **fly the flag**, to **dress down** or to **drip colors**. The colors of the Bloods, to give an example, are red; those of the Crips are blue. The rapper Snoop Dogg, once part of the *Long Beach*

155

Rollin 20's Crips, can often be seen sporting clothes that have enough blue to make his affiliations clear to those who understand. The main garment is often a bandana handkerchief, known as a **rag**, **flag** or **bandera** (Spanish for 'flag'). A **do-rag** or **durag** (originally a cloth used to preserve the look of one's *do*, i.e. hair arrangement) can also be coloured as required. Perhaps the most extreme example of such devotion is the **five-point star**, whereby, in this particular gang, membership is signified by wearing or orienting everything on the left: hair 'fade', hand in left pocket, earring in left ear, teardrop on left, hat cocked to the left, bandana knot on left, untied left shoe, left knee bent, etc.

Still related to clothes is the concept of **saggin'**: wearing one's trousers very low and exhibiting a large band of one's underwear. This may have become the style of choice of the world's young men – rich and poor alike – but it began life as a symbol of gangster life. It comes from one's arrival in jail: the belt is removed because of the supposed risk of suicide and so one's trousers slip from one's waist. Saggin' mimics this, and suggests that those whose trousers droop thus have suffered the rigours of the jailhouse. Not clothing as such, but certainly allied to the colors, are gang tattoos – known as a **brand**, **ink** or **tat**. Not all gangs sport them – the Crips supposedly resist – but many do. A tattoo that covers one's arm from shoulder to wrist is a **sleeve** and to wear one is to be **sleeved**. Some gangsters sport a solid teardrop beneath an eye. It means the death of a close family member in the US (whereas in the UK, where one may see similar tattoos, it means a spell in jail).

Graffiti

Gangs are big on graffiti, sometimes known as **pieces**, which a writer will **hit up** on to a suitable yard, area, or place where tagging is done. Pieces are usually unsanctioned but there are legal yards, where graffiti is permitted by the local authorities. A writer's signature with marker or paint is known as a **tag**, thus **tagging** or **tagging up** is placing such marks on a wall; to tag a bus is to **comb**. Second-rate graffiti can be **generic** or **wack**, while a mark that deliberately erases the **placa** (gang-sign) of a rival gang is a **puto** (literally 'pimp').

Fighting

Much gang slang overlaps with the wider world, and its main preoc-cupations – prisons, weapons, murders, assaults, and of course drugs – are very much those shared by contemporary criminal youth. The 'banging' of HBS means fighting, and it has produced a variety of terms, not all of which exist only in gang talk. Synonyms include to **bump titties**, to **throw down**, to **go up from the shoulder**, to **blast**, to **bust**, to **squab**, to **get down**, to **get off the gate**, and **get some down** or **gone**. To **get jammed** is to be accosted or challenged. To talk aggressively, with a fight in mind, is to **talk smack** or **talk head**, and to tell someone to come with power is to tell them to come back team-handed. To **get real** is to prepare for a full-scale war, and to start a fight is to **gun-up** or **head-up**, often backed by the spoken threat *I'm going to get stupid*. **Doing a rambo** is making an attack (possibly with one's **Rambo gauge**, or shotgun – otherwise known as a **breakdown** or **thumper**) and to **ride on** is to enter a rival gang's territory with violence in mind.

THE BRITISH TEEN GANG

There are, of course, gangs in London and other UK cities. Some even claim to be affiliated to such US equivalents as the Crips. However the language does not seem to have crossed the Atlantic. When UK gangs speak slang, then it is currently what is known as Multi-cultural London English (incorrectly nicknamed as 'Jafaikan'), but that, while 'state of the art' as regards current youth-speak (and used by all: black, brown and white), is only coincidentally used by young gangsters. MLE is a mix of Caribbean (mainly Jamaican) terms, traditional Cockney, and of course the ever-pervasive language of rap and hip hop. The latter has showcased some gangsta terms, but still, the hardcore gangsta jargon remains very much of the US and not the UK streets.

Chapter 7

DRUGS

Cocaine's for horses and not for men
Doctors say t'will kill you but they don't say when.
Ho, ho, honey take a whiff on me.
Traditional American Folk Song

DRUG NAMES

The vocabulary of recreational drug use has tended to originate in the United States and cross the Atlantic thereafter, a direction that can be assumed for the majority of the terms that follow. It has been recorded since the late 19th century, when opium and then morphine were the best known. After that came cocaine, heroin, marijuana, amphetamines (and other forms of 'uppers'), barbiturates (and other 'downers'), and – beyond them – hallucinogens and 'designer' creations such as MDMA, better known as ecstasy. There is now a vast and ever-growing number of specific terms.

However, there is one term that has been the word of choice since the 1930s for any drug – ***dope***, which comes either from the standard English *daub*, the axle grease used on wagons, or the Dutch *doop*, sauce. It began life meaning sauce but by 1872 was recorded as a name for any form of unspecified mixture, often an adulterant, including dubious or otherwise nameless medicines. The first recorded use in the drug context came in 1888 when the *Los Angeles Times* used the word to mean opium when reporting on the arrest of 'a couple of Chinamen' in possession of an ounce of the drug.

Its variations and extensions have been numerous. The ***dope addict*** is a narcotics addict (originally the dope in question was opium); the ***dope booster*** (using *booster* to mean one who praises) was a drug seller, especially when proselytising new customers. A seller could be a *dope peddler*, a *dope man* and most recently a *dopeslinger* or *dope boy*. A *dope crew*, a 1990s coinage, is a group of drug dealers who divide up, package and then retail the bulk purchases of the drug (usually crack cocaine). The narcotics addict is best known as a *dope fiend*: the original use, popularised in the American tabloid press of the late 19th century, referred to opium; the current incarnation refers to crack cocaine. Thus the phrase *dope fiend move*: any wild, bizarre or extreme action taken out of desperation. The *dope doctor* is a general practitioner known for his or her (over-)prescribing of narcotics; more recently the prescriptions are for narcotic-based painkillers. A doctor can also be a *croaker*, so a *writing croaker* was one who was willing to write prescriptions for narcotics or medicine from which they could be extracted.

Popular Terms

Opium
black stuff   1930s to present
dream   1920s to present
gow   1920s to 1950s
gum   late 19th century to 1950s
hop   late 19th century to present
mud   1910s to present
O   1930s to present
poppy   1910s to present
tar   1930s to present

Morphine
cube   1910s to present
M   1910s to present
Miss Emma   1930s to present

Since the 1950s the **dope city** has been any area of a town known for its high level of drug sales/consumption. Today such areas are more likely to be known as **corners**. The **dope house** and **dope pad** both mean any room or apartment in which drugs can be consumed; while the **dope trap** or **dope shop** give a base for those who are selling; it can also be a **grease pit**. The classic term for the place where narcotics addicts can consume their drugs is the **shooting gallery**, from *shoot*: to inject a drug. The **dope stick**, now obsolete, was a marijuana cigarette (and occasionally a 'straight' one), while the **dope gun** was a hypodermic syringe. The modern **dope rope** refers to the gold chains sported by well-off drug dealers.

DEALING DRUGS

While the extent of drug names is seemingly inexhaustible, the world of drug dealing and its slang terminology can be more easily captured. The words **dealer** and **pusher** are used interchangeably (although the latter tends to attract more negative adjectives in popular mythology); however, technically, a dealer is a wholesaler, while a pusher, hanging about street corners, very likely outside the local school, is the retailer, selling in quantities that are affordable by the street-level user.

Both dealer, a standard English term since the 17th century, and pusher, which had been used to define any salesman since the late 19th century, were first recorded as drug 'industry' terms in 1928, both in the context of heroin. The *Philadelphia Evening Bulletin* set out the relationship between the two in an article on 'Racket' vocabulary: '"pusher," a "small-time guy" who sells for a large dealer'. The pair were slightly predated (to 1920) by the **peddler**, another term which has been overtaken by conventional use.

As will be seen below, neither term has ever been used widely by those who actually sell, buy and consume drugs. The moralising attention of government and the media has ensured that such use tends to the ironic. In any case, one does not wish to advertise one's occupation or tastes.

Popular Terms

Marijuana
blow 1970s to present
bud 1980s to present, American campus
charge 1940s to present
cheeb 1970s to present, America
chiba 1970s to present
chronic 1990s to present, black-American
collie 1970s to present, West Indies/Jamaica
dacca 1970s to present, Australia
dank 1990s to present, black-American
doobie 1960s to present, originally American
gage 1930s to present, America
ganja 1920s to present
grass 1930s to present
greefo 1930s to present
green 1950s to present, America
hay 1930s to present, America
herb 1940s to present
locoweed 1920s to present, America
mary jane 1920s to present, America
mary warner 1920s to present, America
moota 1930s to present
muggles 1920s to present
pot 1930s to present
reefer 1930s to present
skunk 1980s to present
spliff 1980s to present
weed 1920s to present
whacky baccy 1970s to present

The Major Dealer

The man, otherwise unqualified, denotes a holder of authority, whether in an institutional or non-institutional context. In the former he can be a senior policeman, in the latter a major drug dealer from the 1940s onwards. The **connection** was coined in the 1920s to deal with the illegal liquor that was sold during Prohibition; the term soon passed into the drug trade to mean a bulk supplier. Thus **connection money**, money for drugs, and the modern term **house connect**, a dealer who works from their home rather than the street. To **connect** or **make (a) connection** is thus to obtain drugs, usually by arranging a specific appointment with the dealer. Coined in the 1990s, the **bundle connection** is a mid-level drug dealer who links the bulk wholesalers and street-level retailers. He packages the drugs into saleable units – *bags, wraps* or *decks* of heroin, *bottles* of crack – and sells them on to the street crews. To be a major dealer in modern times is to **pack**, i.e. to make up the packs of a drug which are then sold on to the dealers who trade on the street.

The Drug Seller

Some terms are not drug-specific and have been used for anyone selling drugs, be the product narcotics, hallucinogens or pills; one can only tell from the context. These have included the 1920s **dopester**, which given the era probably opted for cocaine, heroin, morphine and opium, the **shover** and the **pitcher**, both synonyms for pusher, and used from the 1930s to 1970s, and the **head doctor**, a 2000s coinage. Other terms from the 1980s onwards have included the stingy **chooch** (possibly from *chinch*, a bug), the **paper chaser**, for whom paper is money, the **roller** and the **pin** (perhaps from kingpin).

The Narcotics Seller

The term of choice for narcotics, especially heroin and morphine – and before that opium – has been **junk**, first noted in a prison dictionary of 1916. The range of products covered by this one word (including hashish, surprisingly) was seen in a Montana newspaper the *Helena Independent*, reporting on the aftermath of a big drug raid on 30 December 1926: 'Bundles and packages of morphine, cocaine, opium, yenshee [opium residue] and hashish [. . .] were burned in the kitchen range of the county bastille. The "junk" [. . .] would have meant pipe-dreams for many addicts.' The narcotics dealer has been a *junker*, a *junkhead* (which also denotes the buyer), a *junkman* and *junk guy*. Even *junkie* was transferred from the usual addict to his supplier in the 1950s, albeit rarely.

Since the 1920s names for the narcotics seller have varied – the industry always wants to stay one step ahead of the police – but those who needed to know doubtless always did. Such a dealer could be a *mother* (who takes care of your troubles); a *fixer*, playing both on the political *fixer* and on the *fix*, the injection of heroin or cocaine; a *narco*, which could also mean an addict as well as a member of the narcotics squad; a *bingle*, presumably from the *bindles* (small packages) of narcotics he sells; a *copman*, from *cop*, to score drugs; or a *jones man*, from *jones*, a narcotic addiction. The roots of this last, recorded since the 1960s, are unknown, although the *Online Rap Dictionary* suggests that it comes from Jones Alley in Manhattan where junkies, always desperate to feed the 'monkey' that lived on their backs, used to hang out. Despite the sound, the *pillman* did not sell uppers or downers but pills of, originally, opium or morphine and, since the 1930s, heroin. By the 1950s, pills were known in British rhyming slang as *jacks*, i.e. jacks and jills.

In the 1950s, the *ice-cream man* took his name from the whiteness of his narcotic product as well as the pleasure it provided; in the 1960s and beyond the *candyman* offered similar delights, but he also sold cannabis and other drugs too. In the 1990s the *G-man* was based on a gram (in weight) but deliberately teased the seller's enemy, the G-men of the FBI. The 1930s *Chino* was a Chinese drug dealer, and the 1990s *German*, although less obviously, a Dominican cocaine seller. *Snow* has meant cocaine since the 1910s (giving rise to merry remarks about *sleighbells*, a dealer in or at least a possessor of coke, and the *sleigh-ride*, the experience of cocaine and its white 'brother' heroin), while the *snow man*, *snow peddler* or *snow merchant* have been its dealers.

The 1980s also launched *clocker* (best known from Richard Price's 1992 novel *Clockers*), a dealer of crack cocaine. The name has been attributed to the users' ongoing (if not incessant) need for the drug and the appearances of the dealer: both seem to occur at regular intervals, and these dealers are on call 'around the clock'. The verb *clock* means to earn money and thus to sell drugs (i.e. to make money from drug dealing), as does *clock paper*, while *clocking* is selling crack cocaine.

The Marijuana Seller

Despite the widespread consumption of the product, the cannabis seller has attracted fewer names than his narcotics peers. The *ganja man*, *herbman* and *herbalist* all come from Jamaica where *ganja* and *herb* are popular synonyms for marijuana. More recent is the American *budman*, from slang's *bud*, used particularly on American campuses. The *fatty* means a dealer and refers not to his size but to the cannabis cigarettes he sells, taken from *fat one* (*fattie* or *fatty*), which has meant a (usually large) marijuana cigarette since the 1960s.

WEIGHTS AND MEASURES

Narcotics

Opium, which boasted an entire vocabulary of its own, mainly based on Chinese or a pidgin version thereof, was sold in *toys*, *hop toys* or *pin-yen toys*. The toy was a small ball of opium, about the size of a pea; it also referred to the opium container, approximately one inch in diameter; between the 1960s and 1980s it came to mean a hypodermic syringe.

But opium was replaced by heroin, and for heroin, at least since the Second World War, the key container has been the *bag*, whether literal or, in compounds and phrases, figurative. *The bag* in general is much prized, being the symbolic, if unmeasured stock of drugs held by a given dealer. The dealer is a *bag man* or *bag dude* and is said to **hold the bag**, and those on the street often ask 'Who's holding the bag?' Thus, the container became the contained and the word began to be used for the narcotic itself, usually heroin. A **big bag** was a large quantity. At street level one purchases **nickel bags** ($5) or **dime bags** ($10). Synonyms, always for small amounts of drugs, are the **nickel**, the **nickel deck**, the *five-cent bag*, *five-cent balloon* and *five-cent paper*. A **nickel-** or **dime-bag dealer** or a **nickel-bagger** is considered very low in the hierarchy. A *fifty-cent bag* is in fact $50 worth of marijuana, and a **quarter sack** or **quarter-bag** $25 worth of a given drug. A single bag could also be a **balloon**, into which the priced quantity was placed prior to sale. Such balloons were considered easy to swallow, if one faced arrest. Since the 1980s the bag has been used in the context of cannabis, usually marijuana, and means a quarter-ounce (7g) measure. The verb **bag** or **bag up** means to divide bulk purchases of drugs into smaller quantities for dealing. The **bag-chasing**, i.e. obsessed, **baghead**, who is **hooked through the bag**, pursues the drug intensely, while the contemptuous **bag bride** is a prostitute who is addicted to crack cocaine.

Narcotics became available in capsules in the 1920s and the word **cap** came with this new form of packaging. More recently the word has come to cover first hallucinogens, then crack cocaine and in the modern American prison a measure of marijuana: as much as can be fitted into a small cap, such as that of a toothpaste tube. To **bust a cap** (which also means to fire a gun) has meant to inject a shot of heroin.

While crack cocaine is sold in glass or plastic vials, heroin arrives in **folds** of paper. The shape of packet is known as the **junkie fold** from the method of folding up the necessary small square of paper: one end is tucked into the other and the top folded into the resulting 'slot' so that the measure of narcotics is held securely inside. Such folds have also been known as **bindles** (from the standard word *bundle*, although the slang *bindle* had also referred to a tramp's pack), and this gave **bindle Kate**, a female narcotics addict, and **bindle stiff** or **bindle bum**, which meant both a narcotics addict and a hobo. The **bundle** itself is variously a package of 25 (occasionally 24 or 12) bags of heroin (which in its original 1960s retail value came in at $5 per bag) and later a quantity of any drug available for sale. The current use of bundle is for ten one-gram bags of heroin. Further terms include the **deck** (from a deck of cards), which is prepared by **decking up** the bulk drug, and the current term **wrap**, which may also hint at the fast-food staple. Ten bundles is a package.

A **go** was a single injection of a given drug and later a small quantity of drugs wrapped in paper. A **good go** was seen as a fair amount of drugs for the money paid; a **bad go** was the opposite. A **hit**, which usually means a single injection, sniff or a single puff on a joint or pipe, has also meant a single drug purchase. And a **taste** is a sample of drugs, and thus any small portion. It gives the 1960s **taste face**, a heroin addict who rented out his drugs equipment in exchange for small amounts of the drug.

Meanwhile, in Australia, the modern terms **one-spot** and **two-spot** refer respectively to A\$100 and A\$200 worth of heroin. What you get, of course, depends on the current market.

Cocaine and Crack Cocaine

Wholesale cocaine comes in kilograms: and names for one kilogram since the 1980s have included the **big thing**, the **big bird**, and the **pie** or **cake**, a round disc of crack cocaine which will be 'sliced up' into smaller weights. Serious importers can look forward to a **ride**: a quantity of free heroin provided to a purchaser of bulk cocaine, e.g. 5kg of heroin for every 100kg of cocaine. Down on the corner things are less generous, although when a new brand is due to be put on sale, users can look forward to a **C.C.** (i.e. calling card), a dealer's sample of cocaine, given away to enlist new customers. There is also the hope that the crack seller, like his peers in the conventional world, will decide to offer 'two for the price of one', a process known as **doubling up**. This should not, however, be confused with the **double-up**, a \$20 piece of crack cocaine that is broken into two pieces, each of which is then sold for \$20. A crack vial is known as a **bottle**, and the different stoppers, which notoriously litter well-known **crack spots**, give the various brands such names as **red-cap**, **blue-cap** and the like. The use of **monkey nut** for a given measure of crack makes the dealers' views clear, while a **slang** is a measure based on the verb *slang*, to sell (usually drugs).

Popular Terms

Cocaine
bernice/bernies   1930s to present, America
blow   1960s to present
(Bolivian) marching powder   1970s to present
C   1920s to present
candy   1930s to present
charlie   1930s to present
coke   1900s to present
girl   1950s to present
snow   1910s to present
sugar   1930s to present
yeyo   1990s to present

Crack Cocaine
base   1980s to present
bump   1990s to present
crack   1980s to present
rock   1980s to present

Heroin
boy   1950s to present
brown   1980s to present
chiva   1960s to present
duji   1930s to present
H   1920s to present
horse   1930s to present
junk   1920s to present
scag   1960s to present
smack   1930s to present
stuff   1920s to present

Cannabis

In the days when joints were sold in singles, like some brands of cheap cigarettes, a **stack** was a pack of them. At the same time – the 1950s – one could also obtain a **tin**, some 28g (1oz) of marijuana, which was based on the size of the tin of a then-popular brand of tobacco. The **lid** was slightly smaller, about 22g (¾oz) or 40 cigarettes' worth; such a quantity filled the lid of a tin of Prince Albert, a popular brand of tobacco. The 1960s added the **bar**, which resembled the usual shape of a piece of hashish and was considered to weigh around one ounce; thus quantities were known as a five-bar, nine-bar and so on. More recent use has defined the bar as an ounce of heroin. From the 1980s onwards, the relatively indeterminate **draw** has been used to measure cannabis and weighs around one ounce; it is often cited in multiples thereof, e.g. five-draw, seven-draw and so on. The term is old; it was originally used for a single pipeful of opium in the 1920s. A large portion of marijuana was a **keg**, which weighed five pounds and may have represented the amount that could be stashed in a beer keg. But returning to manageable quantities we have the **deal**, which had meant a purchase or sale of drugs, especially cannabis, since the 1910s. In the days when an ounce of hashish cost British buyers under £10, a popular 'entry-level' purchase was the **quid deal**, which would have given the buyer enough for a good few joints. With the rise of the American term **bud** for marijuana from the 1980s onwards, the popular word for a container-ful is a **bud-sack**, although there is no specific amount attached. Bud-sack can also refer to crack.

Turning to South Africa one finds an elegant hierarchy of modern marijuana measurement. Starting at the top one has the **arm**, a measure approximately the size of a maize cob and weighing about two kilograms (4.25lb); after that comes the **hand**, proportionately smaller. We then have the **kaartjie** which borrows the Afrikaans *kaartjie*, literally a ticket or a card. This in turn looks back to the American term **card**, a small measure of opium, but there may also be a link to Mexican Spanish *cachuca*, a capsule of drugs (from Chilean slang *cachuca*, a small comet). Whatever the etymology, all mean a very small measure of cannabis. Finally there is the smallest of all, the **stop**, from Afrikaans *stop*, a plug or fill of tobacco. The post-1940s term means both marijuana as a drug generally and the amount that is enough for a single pipeful of marijuana or a single cigarette (also as **stopper** or **stoppie**); such a quantity is the smallest amount sold.

Selling Product

To sell drugs – the **product** – often uses the same terms as exist for selling anything else: **hustling, grafting** (a **grafter** can mean a dealer's assistant), **working, pitching** and indeed **dealing**, and the buyer, like any other sucker, can be the **mark**; but certain specifics have accrued to the trade. In the 1950s **in biz** meant to be working as a seller (*biz* was also the kit of eye-dropper, needle, spoon etc. used by a narcotic addict for injections and a bag or portion of drug), while the 1980s saw **chill out**, extending the more general use of the term, to mean working on a street corner or from a bar. From the 1980s, when a dealer is **piggybacking** he is occupying several floors in a building; when one is raided others are still available. Since the 1960s **front money** has been money advanced to a dealer for the purchase and from the 1910s onwards a **panic** is a period when drugs are hard to purchase. Finally a pair of terms from the mid-20th century, both using a form of American carnival slang that inserted a 'z' into certain words to supposedly render them incomprehensible: **mezonny** was the act of arranging for and taking the delivery of drugs from one's dealer and **sizendizup** indicated that the drugs were on their way. The insertion of the extra 'z' re-emerged in the 1980s, and remains a trademark of rap slang.

Short Measures

To **scale** is to weigh a measure of a drug. All scales are supposedly accurate but all **scale boys**, those who perform the weighing and measuring of the street-sized portions, are perhaps not.

The American term **short** began in the 1930s to mean a short measure of drugs, and to **push shorts** was to sell short measures (or occasionally to sell only small amounts, albeit at a fair price); since the 1980s short has been a measure of drugs, especially crack cocaine, that is sold at a reduced price. When the buyer is **short** or **on the short** they are trying to get away with making a buy without paying the price required. When the dealer offers a **short go** it is a short measure for the money; such a deficiency is also known as a **bad bundle** and a **bad**, **low** or **short count** (all of which come from boxing imagery, where such counts are unfair to a man who is knocked down).

The Ounce

Price all depends on the drug, of course, but the ounce remains a primary measure. From the 1930s to the present, it has been known as an **o.z.** (using the American 'zee' rather than the British 'zed' pronunciation). **Bozo**, a 1950s term, plays on it as it seems likely do today's **zip** and **zone**, an ounce of crack cocaine. When the dealer sells single units, he is an **ounce-man**, and as such is seen as a small to medium dealer, but still better than a pusher. Since the 1930s an ounce has also been a **piece**, although this is used only of heroin, cocaine or morphine. Thus one finds the **half-piece** and **quarter-piece**. A **short piece** is a purported ounce that has in fact been **shaved** (a term originally coined for the actual shaving down of a one-ounce cube of morphine) or otherwise reduced. A **load** represents 25 or 30 packs of heroin held together in a bundle and the package is the equivalent of an ounce weight.

The **half** or **halfie** is a half-ounce of any drug, and the **quarter** logically a quarter-ounce. In rhyming slang, and with reference to cannabis (which also has the term **q.**), the quarter can be a **bottle**

Popular Terms

Amphetamines
Billy Whizz   1990s to present
bombita   1960s to present
crank   1960s to present
pep pill   1930s to present
speed   1960s to present
uppers   1960s to present
whites   1960s to present
whiz   1990s to present

Barbiturates
down   1960s to present
downer   1960s to present
goofball   1940s to present
spoor   1970s to present

LSD
acid   1960s to present
microdot   1970s to present
orange sunshine   1970s to present
windowpane   1970s to present

MDMA
E   1980s to present
ecstasy   1980s to present
X   1990s to present, America
XTC   1990s to present

(of water) or a **Janet (Street-Porter)**, a rhyme based on the British journalist and broadcaster.

A *half-quarter* or *h.q.* is one-eighth of an ounce (4g) of cannabis. The *eighth* is one-eighth of an ounce, whether cannabis or narcotics, as is a *henry* or *Henry VIII*. *Eight* can mean heroin in general (since H is the eighth letter of the alphabet) but also refers to an eighth of an ounce or an eighth of a kilogram of narcotic, usually heroin. An *eight track* is actually five grams of crack cocaine; it may be partial rhyming slang with 'crack', or based on one-eighth of an ounce (4g).

The smallest unit of cannabis is a *teenth* (one sixteenth of an ounce), while the *spoon* was once the popular equivalent weight of heroin or cocaine – approximately one standard teaspoonful, or two grams. It gives the phrase *in/into the spoon*, that is, addicted.

The Pound

It may not mean much in terms of, say, flour, and it still requires 2.2 of them to make the even more substantial kilogram, the *key*, but in drug terms the pound is a substantial quantity. It can be an *l.b.* or *el-bee* (from the standard abbreviation lb). The most widely used synonym for the pound is *weight*, which in turn can be generic for any substantial amount of drugs, and thus the quantities purchased by dealers rather than street-level users. It has meant a pound of cannabis since the 1960s; it can also mean a large amount of heroin, but here the weight is one ounce. Weight can be qualified by number, e.g. five weight of hash, five pounds of hashish. Its most recent use is less specific, and refers to any measure of a given drug, differing as to the drug in question.

Chapter 8

PROSTITUTION

Lalun is a member of the most ancient profession in the world. Lilith was her very-great-grand-mamma, and that was before the days of Eve as every one knows. In the West, people say rude things about Lalun's profession, and write lectures about it, and distribute the lectures to young persons in order that Morality may be preserved. In the East . . . nobody writes lectures or takes any notice; and that is a distinct proof of the inability of the East to manage its own affairs.

Rudyard Kipling, 'On the City Wall' (1888)

THE PROSTITUTE

Whores, Hos and Hookers

Prostitute (from the Latin *prostituere*: to offer for sale, to prostitute, to put to an unworthy use, to expose to public shame or to dishonour) was first recorded as a verb in 1530; the noun form joined it in 1607. Neither entered cant nor slang, but given the near-taboo status of the 'oldest profession' (Kipling is acknowledged coining the phrase, but he had in fact called it 'ancient'; not until 1922 did the common form appear, set down by the American critic Alexander Woollcott) the vast majority of terms dependent on the job undoubtedly are slang.

Indeed, the synonymous and earlier *whore* (noun from before 1100, verb *c.*1530) is also standard and comes from a range of north European languages – Old Norse, Gothic, Old Teutonic, Old English – in which the cognate terms mean adulterer, and before that from an Indo-European root *qar-* which can also be found in the Latin *carus* (dear), the Old Irish *cara* (friend) and the Lettish *kars* (lascivious). Its compounds, however, frequently are not standard English: *whore's bird* (in the 16th to 19th centuries), a debauchee; *whore-pipe* (late 18th to early 19th centuries), the penis; the American *whore-hopper* or *whore-fucker* (1940s to present), a sexually voracious man who frequently visits prostitutes; the Irish *whore's ghost* (1970s to present), anything seen as intractable or obnoxious; and that charming phrase dating back to the early 18th century but still in use today, *as demure as an old whore/harlot at a christening*, meaning extremely demure and well behaved. And yet, while these words and phrases may be slang, they are not cant.

The working girl, however, does play her role in certain cant compounds. The 18th century produced **whore-eater** for a pimp; and the **whore's curse** was the pre-decimal sum of five shillings and three pence, or one quarter of a guinea. The term springs from the then current rate for a prostitute's favours: half a guinea (ten shillings and sixpence); less generous customers who liked to be seen giving the woman gold, but saw no reason to be over-generous, would substitute a less valuable gold coin, the quarter guinea (minted only in 1718 and 1762), which was worth only half the going rate. The 'curse' was presumably the obscene scolding one received for offering so mean a sum. The last half-century has added the **whore car**, an unmarked car used by police to patrol street prostitutes, and the **whore splash** or **whore's bath**, a brief, cursory wash, often a quick shower, as taken by a prostitute between clients.

The modern whore, or at least as named in the American ghetto and thus propagated worldwide through the lyrics of rap, is a **ho** (**hoe** or **whoe**), a term that is no more than a black-American pronunciation of the standard English word. It was first recorded in the 1950s, unequivocally describing a prostitute, but since then (especially in hip hop, where it is synonymous with the equally demeaning *bitch*) the commercial aspects have been abandoned – even if the background implications are quite consciously retained by many young men unable to throw off such misogynistic stereotyping. The current American campus derogative *ho-bitch* combines the two; the parallel use of *ho-ass* for a disdained man probably offers insufficient compensation to women.

Certain compounds of ho are used in the game. The **ho stroll** describes the street or streets in a town or city where prostitutes work regularly; a **ho jockey** is a successful pimp or womaniser; a **ho-catcher** is not a person but the smart suit that a pimp sports when looking to impress a new girl; a **ho train**, a group of prostitutes that accompany their pimp on the street. The girls in turn may well be tricked out in **ho boots**, ostentatiously sexy, tight, high-heeled woman's boots – when, of course, they have not opted for their *(follow me and) fuck-me shoes*. To ho is to work as a prostitute (and in figurative use, to sell out or to prostitute oneself).

One other key term is **hooker**, which has meant a prostitute, originally and still mainly in America, since the mid-19th century. It provides us with **hook house** and **hook shop**, a brothel, and **hook joint**, which was both a brothel and in extended use anywhere that swindles its patrons. To **hook** is to work as a prostitute, as is to **hook it up** (which can also mean to act like one). Its etymology is arguable. The obvious link is to the standard English *hook*, and earlier cant hookers included the 17th-century confidence trickster and the 16th- to 19th-century thief who used a form of 'fishing rod' to extract goods. Hook also means to catch, lure or entice – the prostitute's primary objectives. Popular etymology, however, has always preferred a link to *Corlear's Hook*, known as 'The Hook', a red-light area on the New York City waterfront and the first recorded use of hooker, in the *New York Transcript* of 25 September 1835, comes within a courtroom conversation that seems to bear the theory out: 'Prisoner: [. . .] he called me a hooker. Magistrate: What did you call her a hooker for? Witness: 'Cause she allers hangs around the hook, your honner.' The sense of 'picking up' also underpins a supposed link to the city's *hookers*, tug boats that cruised to pick up incoming schooners off Sandy Hook. Hooker was also a sailor's affectionate term for any vessel and is thus synonymous with the various terms that equate a prostitute with a ship.

The Ship and the Prostitute

In the 16th and 17th centuries the image of choice for a prostitute appears to have been some kind of boat. There was the **pinnace**, from standard English *pinnace*, a light vessel in attendance upon a larger one; the implication is that she is aged between the juvenile punk and older bawd or 'madam', but there was possibly a nod to *pin*, the penis. The **land carrack**, taking the term for a large ship, 'sailed' the streets. In standard use the **tilt-boat** was a large passenger-carrying rowing boat having a tilt or awning, and used on the Thames. The **frigate** was properly a light, swift vessel; there may also be some punning connection to slang's verb to *frig*, which referred to sexual intercourse as well as masturbation. The **light frigate** played on the boat and the slang use of *light* to mean immoral, and the **frigate on fire** carried venereal disease, rendering the girl in question more than usually *hot*.

Early Prostitutes

The 16th Century

If whoring is indeed the oldest profession (some say lawyers, others see no difference) then it certainly started, as Kipling suggests, long before the 16th century. However, the recording of canting terms comes only with the 16th century.

Of the contemporary terms the first to be recorded, *c.*1535, is **dell** (**del** or **dill**). Its roots may be no more demanding than the proper name *Doll*, but there are possible alternatives. Just as the Welsh *cwm*, a valley, may lie behind *cunt*, then so too may standard English *dell* (also meaning valley) relate to this young woman whose vagina is, as the late 19th century put it, her **moneymaker**. Less coarsely, C.J. Ribton-Turner in his *History of Vagrants* (1887) notes another Welsh word: *del*, pert or smart, and a Lowland Scots one: *dilp*, a trollop. In all cases the word refers to a young woman on the tramp, and more specifically a young or as yet virgin prostitute; a **wild dell** was either a 'born' whore or one who had been at the very least conceived beneath a hedge. Harman, in *Caveat for Common Cursetours* (1566), described her thus:

> A Dell is a yonge wenche, able for generation, and not yet knowen or broken by the vpright man [i.e. a leading villain]. These go abroade yong, eyther by the death of their parentes, and no bodye to looke vnto them, or els by some sharpe mystres that they seme, do runne away out of seruice; eyther she is naturally borne one, and then she is a wyld Dell: these are broken verye yonge; when they haue beene lyen with all by the vpright man, then they be Doxes, and no Dels. These wylde dels, beinge traded vp with their monstrous mothers, must of necessytie be as euill, or worsse, then their parents.

An **arch-dell** was the senior female in a gang; by the late 18th century she too was simply a whore.

Harman also includes the 16th century's primary alternative: the **mort**. The etymology is unknown, although Ribton-Turner suggests the Welsh *modryb*, a matron, or *morwyn*, a virgin, and others have put forward standard English *mort*, a salmon in its third year (which relates to the popular equation – at least in a number of less than congratulatory slang terms – of women with fish). The mort played the same role as the dell: a tramp's companion who boosted their joint income by working as a prostitute. To complicate matters she might also be a **mort dell**, which meant either an unmarried woman or a virgin girl – she seems to have stayed that way – who accompanies a mendicant villain. The mort was part of a number of compounds. The **kinchin mort** blends mort with German *kindchen*, a little child. It too referred to the usual 'virgin'-cum-whore, but also to a beggar's child or any child carried by a beggar in order to excite pity. From the mid-17th century, the **strolling mort** (also **strolling punk**) was an unmarried female beggar, often accompanied by a child, who claims to be widowed and begs for her and her offspring's keep. She and her hapless child, often borrowed for the day, can still be seen on the streets of Europe. The **rum mort** originally meant 'the good woman' and was coined for Elizabeth I; with her gone, it gained less savoury associations as a synonym for prostitute.

Unlike her younger 'sisters' a ***mort wap-apace***, in the 17th to 19th centuries, made no bones about it: she was either an experienced prostitute or a sexually active woman and the term's literal translation ('woman fuck fast') is reminiscent of the modern staple of American jokes 'Little Johnny Fuckerfaster'. Wap-apace combines standard English *apace*, fast, with *wap*, to have sexual intercourse, which itself may have been echoic of the slap of flesh on flesh but may also have come from standard English *wap*, to throw violently or to pull down; there may have been a further link to slang *whop*, to beat, itself meaning to copulate from *c.*1660. They both underpin the basic sense of most slang terms for intercourse: man hits woman. (Thus the 17th century's ***thrum***, which can mean a prostitute and to have sex, but in standard English again means to hit, and also ***striker***, a prostitute.) The writer James Hencke suggests a link to *wap*, a mongrel and thence a play on *bitch*. All of which said, it may just be a matter of a coarsely affectionate nickname: the playwright and author of 'canting' pamphlets Thomas Dekker, in *O Per Se O!* (1612), claims that the name was anecdotal, noting that 'there was an abram [i.e. a beggar], who called his mort Madam Wap-apace . . . '

Wap gave ***wapping***, sexual intercourse, the ***wapping dell***, ***wapping moll*** and ***wapping mort***, all meaning a prostitute, literally a 'fucking woman', and their client the ***wapping cove***, the 'fucking man', who enjoyed their company in the ***wapping ken***, the brothel or 'fucking house'. Then there was the popular adage, at least in male circles, *If she won't wap for a Winne, let her trine for a Make*, i.e. 'If she won't fuck for a penny, let her hang for a Half-penny.'

First found in the 16th century, and still in use to mean a prostitute until the 1920s, was the widely used ***punk***. It came from standard English *punch*, to pierce, and is thus linked to slang's *punch*, to have sex. As one 'L.B.' put it in the *New Academy of Complements* (1671): 'The Pimp, the Punk, and the Doctor are three / Which cannot but thrive when united they be. / The Pimp brings in custom, the Punk she gets treasures / Of which the Physician is sure of his measure, / For work which she makes him in sale of her pleasure.' Punk could also mean to work as a prostitute, and the related ***punchable*** referred to a woman considered ripe for seduction; thus the ***punchable nun*** was a prostitute posing as a virgin.

John Florio, in his Italian–English lexicon of 1598, explained the Italian *trucca* as 'a fustian or rogish word for a trull, a whore, or a wench'. It was linked to the standard English *truck*, to barter or exchange commodities, and is thus the root of the same era's **trug** or **trugmallion**, a prostitute; the variant **trugmoldy** lasted until the 19th century. Further terms coined in the 16th century include the **vaulter**, from *vault*, to have sex; **trull,** which borrowed from the synonymous German *Trulle* and is still present today; and the **pagan**, which referred to a paganic, i.e. Greek or Roman, worship of physical beauty.

The 17th to 19th Centuries
Moll, coined in the 17th century, was a prostitute (and still is in Australia). The **posture moll** specialised in stripping and adopting sexually arousing positions before her audience. This time there is no doubt about etymology: moll is simply a diminutive of the proper name Mary. The modern **ship-moll** or **shippie** works on ships docked in the ports of New Zealand; she is a descendant of the 19th-century Maori **ship-girl**. Also coined in the late 17th century and lasting into the 19th, **strum** abbreviated the standard word *strumpet*, while **tackle** meant equipment in standard English and thus equated the prostitute with the primary tool of her trade.

The 18th- to 19th-century **mot** or **motte** most likely comes from the Dutch *mot*, a woman; less likely is that it is an abbreviation of French *amourette*, a girlfriend. However, the *Oxford English Dictionary* simply classifies it as an alternative spelling of mort. **Motting** meant frequenting prostitutes, **mottism** was prostitution, the **mot-cart** a smart carriage owned by a kept woman or well-off prostitute, and the **mot-case** (from *casa*, a house) a brothel.

The 18th- to 19th-century underworld also offered **blowen**, **blowing**, **blower** and **blow**, all of which meant a prostitute and all of which, according to the 19th-century expert in Romany language and culture George Borrow, came from the Romany *beluñi*, 'a sister in debauchery'. Slang lexicographer John Camden Hotten's *Slang Dictionary* (1864) prefers the German *Bluhen*, bloom, and/or *Buhlen*, sweetheart, as its origin but acknowledges that 'the street term *blowen* may mean one whose reputation has been "*blown on*", or damaged'. Blower was additionally qualified as the specific antonym of *jomer*, a respectable girlfriend. Similar in meaning and chronology but of a separate etymology was **blowse** (variously spelt **blouse, blouz(e)** etc.), all of which may be linked, perhaps ironically, to the Dutch *blos*, blush. Nathaniel Bailey's *Universal Etymological Dictionary* (1731) defined her as 'a fat, red-faced, bloted [*sic*] wench, or one whose head is dressed like a slattern' but it was simpler for most people to say whore. **Mob** and **mab**, both 18th-century terms, were also slatterns before they were prostitutes.

Prostitutes in Rhyming Slang

No job so well known as that of a prostitute could possibly avoid attracting its share of rhyming slang. Like all such slang, it has been coined at any time since the mid-19th century, although most have appeared since 1930. The majority rhyme on *whore*:

five to four

Jane Shore (ultimately Jane Shore (d.1527), the mistress of Edward IV)

Noah's (ark) (slightly anomalous, as it rhymes on the first element of the phrase – the Cockney pronunciation of Noah as 'ore, i.e. whore)

(Rory) O'Moore (although according to St Vincent Troubridge's 'Some Notes on Rhyming Argot' (1946) this may have 'derived from the tremendously popular song of that name, sung by Madame Vestris in the 1830's and 1840's')

six and four

six to four

sixty-four

sloop of war

swinging door

two by four

Other rhymes include:

brass nail   (= tail)
charlie   Australia (probably an abbreviation of *charlie wheeler* = sheila)
kewpie (doll)   Australia (= moll)
mallee root   Australia (a semi-rhyme, since it rhymes only with *root*, an act of intercourse; *mallee*, from an Aboriginal language, is eucalyptus)
twist and twirl   American prison (= girl)

The Image of the Prostitute

Setting chronology aside, at least some of the terms for prostitutes fall into a variety of thematic groups. Before moving on to those who resist such classification, let us assay those that do.

Night
Like Dracula, although eschewing his monochrome rigidity of dress, a prostitute is a creature of the night and has been so categorised since the 17th century. Not invariably – streets can be walked, clients 'escorted', brothels up and running while the sun still shines – but such is her stereotype, and at least one subset of her names reflects this. Exclusive to the 17th century, there is the euphemistic **nightgown lady**, the honestly commercial **night trader** and the **nightshade** who one may assume was seen as 'deadly'. Coined then but still in use, the **night walker** and **night-stroller** reflect what might be termed her 'office' address. Also present from the 17th century to the 20th, the **night bird, bird of the night** or **night fowl** all 'fly at night' and are linked to the standard term *night bird*, meaning anyone who goes about at night but especially a thief. The **night hunter** and **night poacher** are openly predatory. The early 20th century's **nightcap** is not as cosy as it sounds; it is a blend of night and an abbreviation of capture, while 20th-century Australia offers **nighthawk**.

The early **nightingale** takes one punningly back to night bird, while the 19th century's **nocturne** uses the painting jargon *nocturne*, a night-piece (which in this context may or may not pun consciously on slang's *piece*, a woman, especially considered as a sex object). Like the creature in question the **bat** comes out at night from the 17th century to the present day, while an 18th-century variant was the **bat of Venus**. The modern phrase **on the bat** is to be working on the streets, while a **bat house** is a brothel in Australia. The 19th-century coinage **alley bat** brought in a generic use of standard English *alley*, as any unsavoury area of a town. The most recent variation on night-time shenanigans is the black-American term **moonlighter**.

Geography

Early Londoners tended to go outside City walls, and even over the river, for their pleasures. Brothels in these locations had existed since Roman times, and would go on until the 17th century. But no terms, if ever they existed, seem to have survived for or from the brothels of Bankside – across London Bridge on the south bank of the River Thames – other than the names they bore during their 16th-century pomp: the **Holland's Leaguer**, the **Cardinalles Hat**, the **Pope's Head**, the **Gun**, the **Cock** and many more.

What has survived, and in a very different form to that in which it was initially used, is the word *suburb*, plus its adjective *suburban*. Literally 'beneath the city', such early suburbs – Holborn, Wapping, Mile End, Bermondsey, Clerkenwell – may have become parts of central London now but, in the 16th and 17th centuries, they were beyond the City and its walls, and, as such, were home to various 'stink' industries – tanning, leper hospitals, playhouses and brothels. And most notoriously the last. Thus the contemporary terms **suburb wench**, **suburb lady**, **suburb whore** and **suburban strumpet** were not, as they might be today, some porn queen wannabes out of 'Reader's Wives', but prostitutes who worked in the suburbs rather than the West End of London.

A **sixpenny suburb-sinnet** (also **sixpenny damnation/sinfulness** or **suburb sinner**) was also a prostitute and came from the prostitute's usual fee of sixpence, plus a play on the standard words *sinnet*, a trumpet-blast that introduced actors on to the stage, and, of course, sinner. The **suburban trade** was the world of prostitution; the **suburbian** the prostitute herself and the **suburbian-trader** her client. Other brothel-related terms from the period included **suburb tricks**, sexual variations as offered by a whore; a **suburban roarer**, a pimp or male 'heavy' in a brothel; an **aunt of the suburbs**, a prostitute; a **house in the suburbs**, the brothel itself; and a **minion of the suburbs**, a male prostitute.

By the 19th century, even outside the profession, suburban had become, as John S. Farmer and W.E. Henley put it in *Slang and Its Analogues* (1890–1904), a 'generic for disorder and loose living'. The suburbs were further from the City now and the house in the suburbs (with a possible extra nod to the slang term *house*, a brothel) now referred to the reputation of the then quintessentially suburban St John's Wood as a place where a man could set up his mistress at a decent distance from his respectable West End family home; it could also be a **suburb garden** or **garden house**, defined by the unsparing Farmer and Henley as a 'private fuckery'.

Other than suburbs, the gradual movement of London's centres of commercial sex are reflected in a variety of terms. The 16th-century **Smithfield jade** was properly an inferior house which had been smartened up to deceive a prospective buyer; in extended use she was a prostitute. The term came from the Smithfield market, London's horse and cattle (and later meat) market – chronology renders the pun wholly coincidental – which has existed on the same site since the 12th century. Further east and from a century earlier one finds the **Spital whore** (or **Spittle whore**), **Spital lady** and **Spittle sinner**, all of whom frequented the area of Spitalfields. In later years the area would typify the tough East End, but then the word may well have played on standard English *spital*, a hospital (the area was named after the medieval priory and hospital, St Mary Spittel) and thus the physical perils of prostitution. Other 17th-century terms include **angel** or the punning **fallen angel**, which was first applied solely to those prostitutes whose beat ran near the Angel public house in Islington, north London.

Perhaps the best-known geographical link of the time was to the fruit and vegetable market of Covent Garden, centre of metropolitan prostitution from the mid-17th to the early 19th centuries. As an adjective, the phrase came to mean pertaining to sexual excess and is usually found in a variety of pertinent compounds. The **Covent Garden abbess** was a procuress; logically enough the **Covent Garden nun** or **Covent Garden lady** was a prostitute; the **Covent Garden ague** or **gout** was venereal disease, especially gonorrhoea. To **walk the piazzas**, i.e. those that formed a feature of the market and provided a useful area of operations for the girls, was to (start) work as a prostitute. Whoring spread as time passed, and in the 18th century a prostitute might be a **Drury Lane vestal**, while into the 20th century she might have been a **Fulham virgin**, probably from the louche reputation of Cremorne Gardens in neighbouring Chelsea, a **Seven Dials raker**, whose home was in Seven Dials (north of Covent Garden) but who pursued her trade elsewhere, or a **Piccadilly daisy**, who flourished up to the 1950s alongside the girls who were known to the 1940s British Army as the *Piccadilly commandos*.

There was, of course, sex outside the big city. The 16th-century **hedge-whore** or **hedge-wench** plied her trade in the open air, possibly even beneath a hedge; so too did her 19th-century successor the **hedge prowler** and **hedge ranger**. And nor was it restricted to Britain. A 17th-century **Dutch widow** was a prostitute and seems to have been a precursor of the later slang term a *Dutch wife* which was a bolster, otherwise defined as a 'masturbation machine'; in modern use, a blow-up sex doll. The Dutch had been the nation's enemy, as had the French, but it took until the 20th century – when we were ostensibly their allies – to properly equate our nearest neighbours with whoring. Meanwhile the equation of the French and filth, be it literal or figurative, is vast. For these purposes, however, it can be restricted. **French**, as used by a prostitute, was an all-purpose reference to oral sex and **French girl** a whore who was happy to offer it. The client who asked her for the service was a **French date**, a term which has also meant the paid-for act of fellatio itself. This same act could be a **Frenchie** and came under the general and long-lived rubric of **French tricks**, a phrase coined in the 17th century to mean any form of degeneracy but which by the 1960s referred specifically to oral sex. A prostitute who was **French by injection** preferred to go with foreign customers, although these were not restricted to the French.

The Animal Kingdom: Birds

Poor animals (and that's birds and fishes too): how language abuses them. Not content with consigning them to our plates, imprisoning them in zoos, and wiping them out by our occupation of their habitats, we have to recruit them as descriptions for human types – reverse anthropomorphisms as it were – and the prostitute has grabbed on to a positive menagerie.

If there are two supposedly positive images attached to women and girls, and found across the linguistic spectrum, they are the equation with sweetness (the idea of being 'good enough to eat') and with some form of bird (which sports attractive plumage but which one also desires to tame). Other than those mythical beings with their 'heart of gold', whoring has somewhat underplayed the sweetness, but bird imagery, whether domestic or otherwise, is common, and has been right from day one.

The first use of **bird** as a term for a woman appears in 1560 referring to a prostitute, and soon afterwards she was qualified as a **brothel bird**. The imagery has been found ever since, with most coined in the 17th century. **Bird of the game** refers to prostitution but played as well on the 'hunting and shooting' aspect of male pursuit. As sporting journalist Pierce Egan explained of the term *fancy piece* (a kept woman) in his *Life in London* (1821): 'A sporting phrase for a "bit of nice game" kept in a preserve in the suburbs. A sort of Bird of Paradise!' Other such 'game' has included the **partridge**, the **plover** and the **quail** (celebrated as a supposedly amorous bird). Quail has lasted, although the commercial sense has gone: since the mid-19th century it has meant a young woman, usually attractive, and no longer invariably promiscuous. However, the late 19th century's **dicky-bird**, often **naughty dicky-bird**, returns to the commercial world.

Like the bird, the **hen** could come solo or as part of a phrase – the **hen of the game** – both were coined in the 17th century.

From the same era, the **guinea hen** puns on the farmyard bird and on this upmarket trader's price of a guinea (a great deal at a time when sixpence or a shilling might be the best her lowlier sisters could manage). Such a high-class prostitute, a courtesan rather than a humble street-walker, was known in the 20th century as a **poule** or **poule-de-luxe**, both of which borrowed outright from the same terms in French slang where *poule* means chicken. The 1950s **hip-chick** was an American prostitute who worked hotels (using one of slang's favourite terms for women: *chick*, in use since 1608). The **band**, used at much the same time in the United States and Australia, is seemingly from *bantam* (hen), and as such is another member of prostitution's poultry-house.

Other domestic birds include the 17th-century **duck** and the 16th- to 17th-century **green goose**, a young, innocent girl, soon to be made into a prostitute; and thus the **green-goose fair**, a figurative 'fair' where innocent girls are encountered. The roots are in standard English, either *green goose* (a gosling and a simpleton) or *green* (naïve) plus *goose*, a fool. In the 1950s and beyond in South Africa, **goosie** can refer to a prostitute, one's girlfriend, or – in prison – the passive, 'female' partner of a homosexual couple. The *Oxford English Dictionary* terms **tib** as 'a typical name for a woman of the lower classes' and presumably equated the word with its alternative meaning of a cat, but in cant, it meant a goose (usually as **tib of the buttery**), and a prostitute too in the 16th and 17th centuries.

Elsewhere, the birds are wild. The **jay**, which took flight in the 16th century, is a showy bird and thence a showy woman as well as a prostitute (the jay also 'chatters' just to pile on the clichés). The **pye** or **magpie** was used as a 17th-century synonym for the penis; the **py-woman** would service its needs. The prostitute as predator or 'bird of prey' lies behind the mid-20th century's **kite** and its much earlier predecessor **puttock**, which in dialect meant a kite or buzzard. The modern Australian **crow** or **cro** is not, however, a bird, even if the Italian *cornaccia* means literally a crow and figuratively a tart. The word actually comes from slang's *chromo*, a prostitute, which is itself an abbreviation of *chromolithograph*, a picture printed in colours from stone: the image equates an overdressed, over-made-up prostitute with such a picture – both are colourful and flashy, but neither resembles natural beauty. A *charity crow* did not charge (especially to the impecunious troops of the Second World War) while a *society crow* worked the toffs. The *wren* who specialised in army camps charged full price.

The 17th-century *owl* was definitely avian and referred to one who, like the bird, 'flies after dark'. More elaborately she could be a *Madge Howlet* (also *howlet*, *Jennie Howlet*, *madge*, *Madge-owlet*, or *Margery Howlet*) from dialect's *madge howlet*, a barn owl. *Madgyland* or *maggyland* was the world of prostitution. Last of the bird prostitutes was the genteelly euphemistic *soiled dove* or *dove of the roost* – which gives the deceptively gentle *dovecotery*, prostitution.

The Animal Kingdom: Horses
The equation of sexual intercourse and 'riding' is old: 'He rydyth well the horse, but he rydyth better the mare,' wrote Skelton in *Dyvers Balettys and Dyties Solacyous* (*c*.1495) and he may not have been the first to use the image. The first borrowing by prostitution is in the *hobby horse* or *she-hobby* used between the 16th and 18th centuries, both of which draw on the tradition of the morris dance, wherein the 'hobby horse' ties a rough representation of the animal around his waist, and who executes 'various antics in imitation of the movements of a skittish or spirited horse' (*Oxford English Dictionary*); such 'antics' might also be seen as those of intercourse. The contemporary *horse leech* is quite straightforward, equating the working girl with a sucking worm. In standard English the *bobtail* is a horse or dog with its tail cut short; slang's human variety has been both an impotent man and a sex-peddling woman in the 17th to 19th centuries. The term puns on both the standard word *bob*, to go up and down, and slang's *tail*, which can mean variously the vagina, the penis or the buttocks. And a horse, as ever, is 'good for a ride'. *Bangtail* similarly plays on tail, and on *bang* which means to copulate; bangtail appeared in the late 17th century but vanished from Britain in the 18th, only to be revived in 20th-century American black use.

Human Tails

From the late 18th century to the present day *tail* itself has been used to mean a prostitute, following earlier uses dating back to the 14th century for buttocks, penis or vagina. *Tail-trading* (prostitution) has been recorded since the 15th century as has *tickle-tail* for a prostitute. The 19th century saw *tail-piece*, *tail-trader* and *tail worker* also meaning a prostitute. Like many synonyms, the *wagtail* or *up tail* was either a promiscuous woman or a full-on prostitute in the mid-16th to 19th centuries; for a woman to *wag her tail* was to act in a promiscuous manner, but this was again usually in the context of prostitution. The 19th-century *flashtail* specialised in seeking out wealthy customers who were then robbed by her pimp. In the mid-16th to 19th centuries, *curtal*, *curtail* or *curtall* also used the image of that which had been docked or cut short and originally referred to a horse. The 17th-century *doxy* may well fit this bill with its possible link to standard English *dock*, to cut short. That said, there are also claims for the Dutch *docke*, a doll, or Lowland Scots *doxie*, lazy.

From the 1950s onwards, the simple noun *horse* was used to mean a prostitute working for a pimp; she was part of the group of his girls known as the *stable*; however, it is worth noting that the pronunciation is almost identical to that of *ho*. Maintaining the racetrack imagery, in the 1970s there is the *thoroughbred*, a prostitute with style, sophistication and knowledge, generally considered among the élite of her profession. Yet the use may not be that modern; in his *Memoirs of a Woman of Pleasure* (1748–9) John Cleland writes, 'Phoebe herself, that hackney'd, thorough-bred Phoebe, to whom all modes and devices of pleasure were known.' Cleland uses hackneyed to mean 'available for hire as a prostitute' rather than tired and predictable; **hackney** (also **hack** and **hackster**) meant prostitute from the late 15th century, and came ultimately from the 14th-century *hackney horse*, a run-of-the-mill horse (i.e. not a warhorse or hunter) that was used for everyday riding, typified by the sort available for hire.

The racetrack also brings another pimping term used from the 1930s in America. **Mud-kicker** refers to a slow racehorse that gets stuck in the mud; the obvious use in whoring is for a second-rate prostitute – one who fails, either through laziness or lack of appeal, to make enough money for her pimp (she can also be one who prefers to rob rather than have sex with her clients). Yet mud-kicker can be positive, too, symbolising a dedicated prostitute who works hard, against all odds.

The Animal Kingdom: Domestic and Farmyard
The linking of cats to women, and in this context to women who sell sex, dates from the 16th century. Although her *pussy* has since been *peddled*, *slung* and simply *sold*, in the realm of feline imagery the prostitute herself was first a **kittie** or **kittok**, a **mawkes** or **maux** or a **tabby**. The first of these used the diminutive, itself often an affectionate name. The last designated a cat's colour (from *tabby*, the striped or watered silk that was originally produced in the Baghdad suburb of Attabiy) rather than a name; its attribution to a prostitute runs against its more common use, which was to define an old woman. Mawkes is based on Scots *malkin*, a cat, and as 'Grimalkin' it has often been the name of a witch's feline familiar. Malkin itself also means hare, suggesting a link to the rabbit (a traditionally 'sexy' animal), which may or may not be coincidental. **Hare** itself is also a synonym, and appears to offer a connection to dialect *puss*, a hare, and a play on standard English *hair*, in this case of the pubic variety. In the 19th century, the **rabbit pie** was the metaphorical home of the *live rabbit* (penis); the **rabbit-pie shifter** was a policeman who moved prostitutes on.

Mutton, used from the 16th to 19th centuries for a prostitute, is seen rather poetically by the *Oxford English Dictionary* as 'food for lust', but it seems far more likely that it indicates no more than a tough old sheep rather than a sweet young lamb. It has been extended in the 19th-century **bit of mutton** and in the 1960s and 1970s **hawk one's mutton** (based also on slang's vagina sense of mutton), and it was paralleled by **laced mutton**, first found in 1578, in which the lacing (i.e. of stays or corsets) embellishes a young figure, or disguises an ageing one. It could also be a pun on the culinary term 'lacing', making incisions into a duck or chicken's breast, but the latter, at least as recorded, comes slightly later. By contrast, a **heifer** or **heffer** has no embellishments, appearing from the late 16th century to the present day; neither does a **cow** (first used in 1607) nor the recent verb **cow** (**it**), to work as a prostitute. The 17th-century **twigger** comes from standard English *twigger*, a ewe that is a prolific breeder.

Finally the pig, whose linguistic alliance with prostitution began in the 18th century. The **still sow** was taken from the proverb 'the still sow eats up half the draff', i.e. the quiet pig eats more than its share of fodder, and presumably alluded to the prostitute's appetite for money and perhaps sex (the idea being that the 'respectable' married woman would be more restrained). Australia's **grunter** in the second half of the 20th century either plays directly on pig (it has been a slang word for a pig since the 17th century) – never a flattering description of a woman – or applies to the (simulated) grunts of passion with which she embellishes her services. The mid-20th-century black-American term **pig meat** meant sexual intercourse, and more recently a prostitute.

The Animal Kingdom: Fish
Women have regularly been equated with fish. The connection is simple and, like so many slang-based stereotypes, an association made by men: the fish smells, so does the vagina. It is predictable, therefore, that prostitution would attract a small subset of terms making the same equation, and so it did for 300 years from the 16th century. Thus in that period a prostitute could be a **fishmonger's daughter**, a **mackerel**, a **shrimp** or a **scat** (i.e. skate). Still fishy were the 19th-century **loose fish**, taken from a whaling term for a whale that is fair game for whoever can catch it, and the 16th- to

17th-century *mermaid*, a rather more romantic association with the mythical fish-women (based on the Greek sirens) who were reputed to lure sailors to their doom.

Less obvious is the 19th-century *dollymop*, which mixes *dolly*, a young woman, with another fish, in this case the *mop*, a young whiting or gurnard. As such the term is similar to the German slang *Backfisch*, a teenage girl (literally a 'fish for baking'). The dollymop was usually a part-timer, often a servant or shopgirl, frequently a milliner, and was the London equivalent of the Parisian *grisette*, who might sell her body to supplement her otherwise meagre income.

The Animal Kingdom: Monsters
The idea of the prostitute as a fatal lure is found in the 17th-century *scolopendra*, defined in prosaic reality as centipede or millipede, but presented in a much more alluring manner by the lexicographer William Bullokar in his *English Expositour* (1616) as 'a fabulous sea-fish which feeling himselfe taken with a hooke casteth out his bowels vntill hee hath vnloosed the hooke and then swalloweth them vp againe'. The prostitute as monster has been a recurring trope. In the 16th to 19th centuries, *cockatrice* for a prostitute was derived from a hybrid monster with head, wings and feet of a cock, terminating in a serpent with a barbed tail and which apparently, Medusa-like, could kill with a single glance; it has been suggested that the term was specifically attached to the mistress of a ship's captain. The mid-19th-century *goatsucker* or *goatmilker* was also the name given to the bird *Caprimulgus europæus* from the belief that it sucks the udders of goats. The modern Caribbean *leggo beast* (which can also mean a tramp) is taken from the standard English *let go*, i.e. uncontrolled, without an owner.

Proper Names
The first use of a proper name as a synonym for a prostitute was that of *kate*, *cate* or *katy*; these emerged in late 15th-century Scotland, but usages south of the border appeared about a century later. A *Cyprian*, *Cytherian* and *Cyprian Queen* were all on the game and members of the collective *Cyprian corps*. All came

from the word for the inhabitants of Cyprus, an island that had once been celebrated for the worship of Aphrodite or Venus; the variation **Cytherian** was from Greek *kuthereia*, Aphrodite. **Paphian** was another reference to Aphrodite's island – she had supposedly been born in its southwestern city, Paphos. The **Paphian game** was prostitution, while to **dance the Paphian jig** meant to have sexual intercourse. Moving from paganism to early Christianity in the 18th century one finds the **Athanasian wench** defined by Captain Francis Grose in *A Classical Dictionary of the Vulgar Tongue* (1785) as 'a forward girl, ready to oblige every man that shall ask her'. The phrase puns on the Athanasian Creed, which begins with the words 'quicumque vult' (whomsoever wants), and this also gives the synonymous **quicumque vult** and its variation **quicunque vult**, which may play on *cunt*. The Latin tradition was maintained in **quaedam** (from *quaedam*, 'one of those'), which was in turn 'Englished' as **one of them**.

There were other 'real' names during the period from the late 16th century onwards: **Maid Marian** referenced the morris-dancing tradition of having that character played by a local prostitute; the 17th-century **Maggie, mag, Margaretta** and **meg** were all variations on Margaret; the late 17th- to 19th-century **Madam Van** or **Madame Ran** may originally have been the name of a contemporary prostitute, although given the then role of the Dutch as our 'national enemy' it might have been based on the common *van* prefix used in Dutch. Appearing in the 16th to 19th centuries, **miss** (a heavily ironic use of the standard English), sometimes extended as **miss of the town** or **town miss**, was 'a Whore of Quality' (B.E.). Slightly later in the 18th and 19th centuries, **Miss Laycock** or **Lady Laycock** punned on *lay*, to have sex, and *cock*, the penis.

More recent additions to the roll-call have been mainly 19th century. **Poll** and **polly** either used the proper name or were a rhyme on *moll*; **jude** came from *judy*, a woman. **Sal slapper** was used by London's costermongers: the obvious link would seem to be the modern *slapper* but chronology suggests otherwise, and the name is more likely based on *Sal* (Sarah) and the slapping of her feet on the pavement. (*Slapper* itself comes from either Yiddish *schlepper*, an unkempt, untidy person, or the 'slapping on' of make-up.) In the 20th century, *flossie* or *flossy* (specifically Antipodean and South African use) came from slang's *floozy*, a promiscuous young woman, and gave *flossiedom*, the world of prostitution. **Tottie fie** or **tottie hardbake** is, if not a committed whore, then at least an 'enthusiastic amateur'. These names combined *tottie*, a prostitute or a promiscuous woman, with the exclamation *fie!*, usually used to signify shock, and *hardbake*, which was almond toffee – 'hard' albeit sweet.

South Africa gave **gentoo** for a prostitute and the **gentoo house** for a brothel, wherein clients were usually serenaded by a Malay band. The term came from the *Gentoo*, a ship which arrived at Cape Town in the mid-19th century with a group of women passengers on board who became prostitutes; 'the countries of origin of the women and the ship, and the circumstances of their arrival at the Cape are obscure and in dispute' (*Dictionary of South African English*, 1996). The main theories point to Britain, whose authorities sent out 46 women recruited for the task, or the French. A century later, post-war New Zealand features the **Jap moll** or **Asian moll** as a prostitute who specialises in Asian or Japanese customers. A **Fifi** was a French prostitute working in London in wartime and immediately after.

Finally a little class – or lack of it. Before the Street Offences Act of 1958 removed them from the pavement, those girls who worked Piccadilly, Bayswater Road and other 'cheap' streets in London were known as **edies** (the image of Edie being that of a poor person's name), while **tom** (from an earlier American term **tommy**) applied to those who worked the more exclusive streets of Mayfair. For their pains they were subject to the **tom patrol** or **tom squad** – the Metropolitan Police Vice Squad.

Euphemisms
Simplest of all, if just a little jaundiced, is the 18th- and 19th-century **froe** or **frow**, which comes from Dutch *vrouw* or German *Frau*, both of which mean a woman. Indeed the slang had already been used to mean a woman, especially a female pickpocket, for more than a century. Some women like to see themselves as ladies: through the 20th century, a **lady** was an independent high-class prostitute, while

in the pimping world of the 1970s she was defined as a prostitute belonging to a specific pimp. As a euphemism for prostitute the word had a long pedigree, however, and was found from the 17th century, usually in some variation of compound. Thus there was the *lady of pleasure*, who might equally be a *pleasure/pleasurable lady* or a *daughter/woman of pleasure*; a *lady of the game* or *female of the game*, a *lady of the lake* or *laker lady*, which came from standard English *lake*, to play amorously and perhaps ultimately from standard English *lark*; the *fancy lady* or *fancy woman*; the *lady of the town* or *lady of the evening*. America's *sporting lady*, *sporting girl, sporting woman* or *sportswoman* (and in the modern West Indies a *sportgirl*) was most likely employed in a *sporting house* or brothel. Nor did one even need to be a lady: simply being female and in the big city, rather than the allegedly untainted country, was enough: a prostitute could be a *woman about town* or a *woman/girl of the town*. Euphemistic, but still pejoratives – compared to the *man about town*, who was, on the other hand, an admirable figure.

Damned with equally faint praise were the 17th- to 18th-century *belfa* or *bilfa*, perhaps from the French *belle*, beautiful, and *good girl* or *good one*, which sound ironic but were in fact practical: if nothing else she was good for sex. In the same era, there was also the *pure*, although this reappeared in the 1990s, and the *puritan*, which factored in a jibe at the too overtly religious. Paradoxically, in the 18th and 19th centuries the *impure* also appeared as a prostitute, as did the *unfortunate* with its sanctimonious overtones of pity for the 'fallen woman', and the similar *misfortunate*. Morality also seems to underpin the early 17th-century *backslider*, but the reference actually might have been to the movement of her body during sex. More ironic wit is found in the *light o' love*, first appearing in 1589 and playing on an old name for a dance (and thus pointing to the many terms in which dancing was equated with sex); it was still in use into the 1930s. *Kootcher* was a feature of the 1970s and looked backwards to the *hootchie-kootchie*, again a dance.

Less condemnatory were the 19th century's *gay bit, merry bit* or *merry legs*, all of which allowed for sex as amusement. Gay meant cheery, but it also pertained to sex-for-sale. From the mid-17th century, the *nymph* meant a prostitute, while her standard English counterpart was a semi-divine being, a mythological maiden inhabiting the seas, rivers, fountains, hills, woods or trees, who was a young and beautiful woman. It was all very different for her flesh-and-blood, not to mention commercial sister, whether she appeared as a *nymph of darkness*, *nymph of the shade*, *nymph of delight* or *nymph of the pave/pavé* (or indeed a *pet of the pave/ pavement*). A similar loan from France was *joy girl* (also *joy lady* and *joy woman*), a simple translation of the French *fille de joie*. A *joy house*, *joy club* or *joy shop* has been the brothel in which she would be employed.

All of these terms at least recognised a degree of humanity. Neither *commodity* in the late 16th to 18th centuries, nor *convenient* or *conveniency* in the late 17th to 18th could even manage that. A commodity being something available for sale or trade, the woman and her body are seen as no more than pieces of merchandise. Showing the same disdain was the *convenient house*, a brothel, and in the 20th century *public convenience*, doubling as a punning term for a prostitute and a euphemistic one for a public lavatory. More puns came in the late 19th century with the *public ledger*, named after a real-life journal founded in 1760; Captain Francis Grose in *A Classical Dictionary of the Vulgar Tongue* (1796) was keen to note that 'like that paper, she is open to all parties'.

Bed is a euphemism for intercourse, and so the 17th-century *Bedfordshire woman* also euphemised prostitutes; so too did the 19th-century *bed-presser*, *bed-faggot* (also found as a simple *faggot*), *palliasse* (from the standard English *palliasse*, a straw bed or mattress) and *dossing moll* (literally 'sleeping girl'). As a verb, the black-American *sit on one's stuff* was to work as a prostitute in the 1970s, although one might have thought that sitting was the least of her occupations. Similar euphemisms include the *pillow-mate*, which, according to the antiquarian Charles Hindley in *The Old Book Collector's Miscellany* (1873), served 'as a little Side Pillow, to render the Yoke of Matrimony more easy'; the antithesis, presumably, of the contemporary *bride*.

Some men flaunted their temporary bed-mates; others were deeply shamed. In the 17th century a prostitute became a *cousin* and was quickly introduced as such on meeting an acquaintance. Or one could opt for a profession in the 16th and 17th centuries, such as a *laundress* or *sempstress* or *seamster*, or in the 19th century a *needle woman* (which also played on *needle*, the penis). In the 20th century, other 'jobs' were the black-American *kitchen mechanic*, otherwise a cook, and the American *industrial debutante*, a prostitute who specialises in attending business conventions. Another 17th-century ploy was the *niece*, but if she had any relationship it was to an *aunt*, a bawd. Likewise a *daughter* did not compound one's immorality by incest: she was a *daughter of the game* (sometimes a *gamester*). The *spinster* worked too, in a period when the standard English meant any unmarried woman, rather than today's old maid. The late 19th-century *spoffskins* defies etymology (a possible link is to dialect *spoffle*, to hurry along), but the word's meaning, at least, is known – a prostitute who posed as her regular client's 'wife'.

Diseased

Euphemisms are in the end only . . . euphemisms. If you want a good word for a prostitute try *filth*, or maybe *fen*, with its back-drop of gas-filled rotting putrefaction, or perhaps *scab*. All three were 17th-century coinages, as was the era's *barber*, specific to a prostitute who is carrying syphilis. One of the disease's symptoms was hair loss and thus the diseased whore 'cuts' her client's hair; that and a link between the barber's shaving water and the vagina – both of which are 'hot' (i.e. in slang infected). Equally un-appealing was the *dripper*, which had meant the disease itself (a pus-like discharge is a primary symptom of gonorrhoea), but since the 1930s the prostitute who, almost inevitably, can be assumed to be rotten with some form of clap. The modern *skank*, which was originally black-American usage, may not be diseased as such, but skankiness implies dirt and the equation of prostitute and filth is inescapable. Equally modern, and equally repellent, is the *glueneck* or *gluepot*.

Clothing
Given that a number of the terms that follow were intended to point up the fact that one could recognise a 16th- or 17th-century prostitute by her distinctive clothes, the sheer variety of those clothes must have led to a number of embarrassing misapprehensions. There was the *white apron*, which referred to the garment that was seen as the prostitute's 'uniform'; the purported aim was 'the better to be seen'. There was also the *bluegown*, based on the blue dress worn by prostitutes who were confined in a house of correction. The *brown Bessie* presumably referred to a distinguishing brown garment, backed by the generic female name. Finally the *red petticoat* although that can hardly have been limited to a street-walker's lingerie. The *waistcoateer* depended not on a colour, but on the waistcoat that served her as a 'badge of office'.

Even less easy to discern as innately 'bad' or 'good', and similarly plucked from the underwear drawer, was the *smock*, a generic use of standard English *smock*, a chemise or shift; the term was used from the 16th to 18th centuries for 'womankind' in general and an immoral one in particular. The term was mainly found in compounds. *Smock Alley* was any street occupied by brothels, but there was an actual Smock Alley, running off Petticoat Lane in London's East End, an area well known for its brothels. *Smock fair* was a place where prostitutes gathered, and a group of such women were known as *smock vermin*; a *smock hunter* (also *smock hero* or *smock soldier*) was a womaniser. The *smock merchant* (also *smock agent*, *smock attorney*, *smock tearer* or *smock tenant*) was a pimp, as was a *smock pensioner* – the latter might also be a prostitute's kept-and-paid-for lover, also known as a *smock toy*. The *smock rampant* or *smock servant* was the prostitute herself and the *smock shop* a brothel.

The *placket* represented another borrowing from a hitherto blameless piece of dressmaking; a *placket* was the slit at the top of an apron or petticoat that facilitated dressing and undressing. Used between the 17th and 18th centuries, it could mean both the vagina (as could *placket-box*, *placket-hole* and *placket lace*) and a prostitute, who was also a *placket-lady*. To *search the placket* was to have sexual intercourse, especially with a whore or one's mistress, and this pleasure might be provided by a *placket broker*, a pimp; the woman had long since *torn her placket*, lost her virginity, and she might even render her unfortunate partner *placket stung*, i.e. venereally diseased, giving him a pain in his *placket racket* (his penis).

Like the coloured garments above, the *loose-bodied gown, loose gown* or *loose-kirtle*, present in the 16th and 17th centuries and then again in the mid-19th, worked via metonymy; the antiquary Robert Nares, in his *Glossary* (1822), explained: 'This being a very customary dress of abandoned women, was sometimes used as a phrase for such ladies.' Presumably the loose body exposed some extra cleavage and being loose, was easier to remove at speed. The Australian *bag-swinger* was specifically a street-walker in the 1950s and 60s, and highlighted an essential part of her equipment.

The *muff* had meant the vagina or the female pubic hair since the 17th century; it also meant a prostitute for the first half of the 20th. A *muff merchant* was both the woman and her pimp. The 20th century's *fleabag* is not quite a garment, but as a sleeping bag (even overlooking the pun) one can stretch a point. The term referred to an old, worn-out prostitute (it was equally applicable to an ageing dog) forced to seek equally rundown clients, often on Skid Row; the term is usually found meaning a cheap hotel and around 1910 there was an actual Fleabag in New York City, a cheap saloon at 241 Bowery.

Selling It

Of course the prostitute is selling sex; what else is she there for? Not every term for a whore says it so baldly, but these do.

In the first place she's a *pro*, an abbreviation, coined around 1930 to mean professional woman rather than prostitute. Since then, a part-timer has become a *semi-pro*, and a *baby pro* is under the age of legal consent. Earlier terms include the late 16th- to 18th-century *traffic* (also *trafficker* or *traffique*), based on standard English *traffic*, the buying and selling of goods or the goods themselves; the late 17th- to early 18th-century *plier* who plies her trade, or the late 18th- to early 19th-century *pintle-merchant* or *pintle-monger*, from *pintle*, the penis. In the 19th century, she could be a *receiver general*, who 'receives' lovers that pay their money, or a *purse-finder*, which played on standard English *money-bag*. Around 1880, based on the rates she charged, she could be a *twofer*, which meant either two shillings or perhaps two pounds, and an *onicker*, which elides one *nicker*, i.e. one pound. She (or indeed he) has been a *piece of trade* since the 1930s, or an *ass, butt* or *hip peddler* in America since the 1940s. Rarely, but sometimes in the 20th century, she gave it away, offering a *freebie, free ride* or *free shot* (she was also known therefore as a freebie or free ride in America). Such generosity made her *charity goods, charity stuff* or a *charity worker*. Australia's *charity moll* still charges, but she is an amateur or a professional who undercuts her peers.

While the 17th and 18th centuries' *lechery-layer* – with its use of *lay*, to have sex – is relatively restrained, one cannot be much blunter than the 19th century's *fuckstress* (and *on the fuck*, working on the game), although at the time, the *charvering/chauvering donna* or *chauvering moll* was equally blunt. In all cases these came from the slang verb *charver*, to 'fuck'; the *charvering dodge* was prostitution. The root word is most likely the old Italian slang *chiavare*, to fuck, and charver first emerged in the Italianate language Polari. *Donna* is of course originally Italian for woman. More recent variations on 'fucking girl', and both imitative of the rhythm of intercourse, are the *boom-boom girl* (and thus the *boom-boom parlor*, the brothel) and the *pom-pom girl* (not, even if pornography tends to suggest otherwise, to be confused with the teenage cheerleaders of the same name), who may work in a *pom-pom house* and pay her dues to the *pom-pom man*, who is either the establishment's owner or her pimp.

Strip away the moralising and prostitution is a trade much like any other. Thus *trade* has meant prostitution itself since the late 16th century, and to work as a prostitute since the early 17th. It could also mean the prostitute's client from the 1950s, while a whore herself from the 17th century was variously a *trader, civil trader, she-trader, town-trader* or *trading dame, trading lady* or *trading woman*. The late 19th century added the verb to *hustle*, or *hustle one's bustle*; thus the *hustling broad, hustling dame, hustling girl* or *hustling woman* was *on the hustle*. From the 1930s the term *peddle* entered the field: one might *peddle one's ass, arse, butt, gash, hips, hump, shape, stuff* or – if male – one's *peter*. One could, if a pimp, peddle someone else's ass. Synonymous were *sell body* and *peddle/sling/sell pussy*. In Australia one could *sell one's crack* as well as *crack it (for a quid)*; it, in this case, referred to her legs. To *hawk one's fork* is another Australianism – the 'fork' is the juncture of the legs and thus the vagina; *hawk one's greens* harks back to the 19th-century use of *greens* to mean intercourse.

The 18th-century *market dame* made it clear what prostitution was about: money, and the market was that of Covent Garden, the great whoring centre of its day. It foreshadowed the 20th century's *business girl* or *business woman*, the *sales lady*, and most recently the *working girl* or *working broad/chick/woman* and the plain Australian *worker*. Not to mention the late 19th-century American *horizontal worker* whose French 'cousin' was the *grande horizontale*, the classiest of courtesans. Business was a popular image: to *do (a bit) of business*, i.e. have sex with a prostitute, dated from the mid-19th century. To *work the cuts* is currently used of a prostitute who works on the street rather than in a brothel and refers to the standard term *cut*, a passage or route, and other modern sales talk includes *work the biz*, *go commercial* and *earn*.

The Pick-up

The prostitute attracts clients: she also picks them up. She has been a *picker-up* and, more recently, a *barfly* working from a bar wherein she finds her customers. Trinidad adds the *wajan*, a term that appears to be based on the local enunciation of the phrase *wait, John* (i.e. a *john*, the client).

Walking the Street

In theory at least, the literal street-walker is a thing of the past in Britain, the Street Offences Act of 1958 having driven the girls off the streets and into a new world of 'call-girls' and 'escort services'. The reality is otherwise, and street-girls and their attendant kerb-crawlers can still be found in most cities, though the days of girls openly offering 'business' in the main streets of London (not to mention Paris, New York and every other major conurbation) have indeed gone. It was different once.

The early prostitutes in the 17th to 19th centuries were *rangers*, literally 'wanderers', and *range* meant to work in her occupation.

The *pad* was the road or street, thus a ***pad*** was a prostitute and to pad – for others simply to walk – was for her to ply her trade. Some terms took on a military tone: in the same era there was the ***trooper*** (which could also refer to her client) and the ***she-trooper***, both of whom 'trooped' along. In the 16th century, a ***trot*** worked the streets as well, but that was coincidental: the term derives from a standard word for an old hag, and further origins have been lost. From the 19th century, ***turf*** has been used to mean an area of ground, typically for a street gang (or their rivals the police), but it could also be a prostitute's beat. The ***turfer*** was the working girl, and to ***turf it*** or be ***on the turf*** was to work the streets. The modern American ***gypsy*** travels the country looking for trade; alternatively she is based in a trailer park.

The 19th century provided pavements, which the girls of an earlier era had not been able to enjoy (there had been a ***stone-thumper***, but the stones she 'thumped' were the testicles); in a modern world the terminology duly noted the change. There was the ***curbstone sailor***, the ***pavé thumper*** (by using a French term, this made the usual acknowledgement of 'naughty' Paris), and there was also ***sidewalk Susie***. The ***pavement pounder***, ***pavement pretty*** and ***pavement princess*** were mid-20th-century coinages.

Australia in the 20th century offers the ***lowheel*** and the ***lowie***. The first undoubtedly looked to the state of a girl's shoes after pounding that unyielding concrete, the second possibly factored in a sense of her being 'low'; she was also defined as the female equivalent and accomplice of a ***rev-head***, an ultra-hedonistic young man.

Troll, ***troll about*** or ***troll around*** had come from Old French *troller*, to search for game (without purpose), and had entered Middle English in the 1300s, meaning to wander around; it took some time, but by the 1930s it meant for a prostitute to seek out clients and offered ***trolling***, working on the game. From the 18th century to the present, a prostitute could also be ***on the town***, which had originally meant to be in the swing of fashionable life, while to ***take to the town*** was to work as a prostitute. Other terms included the mid-19th-century ***on the seek*** or, from the 1930s onwards, ***on the bash*** (her feet 'bashing' the pavement), which provided ***basher***, a prostitute. In the 20th century, to ***batter***, to work as a prostitute (whether male or female), and the phrase **on the batter**, combine two earlier uses of the verb: first to have intercourse (again, the image is of man hitting woman) and second to beg. Australia's **battle** and **on the battle**, usually implying the struggle with life, can also be used of a prostitute, who has herself been a **battler** from the late 19th century, though the term is more regularly found as characterising one who uses natural rather than social or economic advantages to pursue the struggle for existence (and is seen as brave in doing so). The simple act of walking, irrespective of where, gives **step** and **stepper** for a prostitute in the 1970s and 80s; hence **stepping**, working as a prostitute.

Two primary terms exist for the street itself: the **stroll** and the **track**. Taken from standard English *stroll*, to wander along, the original stroll was situated between 26th and 63rd Streets on New York's West Side, the centre of the black population in the mid- to late 19th century. During the 1890s the stroll moved to Seventh Avenue between 23rd and 34th Streets, and when the focus of black life moved again – to Harlem (*c*.1920) – the stroll moved uptown, on Seventh Avenue between 131st and 132nd Streets. In 20th-century pimp slang, stroll meant a prostitute as well as the streets she worked, and was also used as a verb. The track embraces the entire world of whoring, pimping, hustling and the rest; the Eastern cities are the 'fast track', California and the West are the 'slow' or 'soft' one.

Tricks of the Trade
Setting aside the prostitutes who work with pickpockets, and those who practise their tricks in brothels (see Criminal Practices in Brothels, page 218) one finds many whores defined by their particular style of tricking innocent punters. In the early 17th to 19th centuries, **jilt** or **gilt** meant any prostitute who tricked her client. It is defined in standard use by Dr Johnson as 'a woman who gives her lover hopes, and deceives him' and comes ultimately from *jillet/gillet*, a loose or wanton woman. Among the tricks a prostitute could 'pull' was claiming to be a virgin, a status which allowed her to command a higher price than her experienced sisters could, although it was also invariably true that she was as far from virginity as they were. Such a girl had been a **puzzle** in the late 16th to 17th centuries, from

dialect *puzzle*, a slut, and before that from French *pucelle*, a virgin. The miraculously 'renewed' maidenhead was also offered by the mid-19th-century **shoful-pullet**, which came from the Yiddish *schofel*, worthless stuff or rubbish, and was ultimately a variation on Hebrew *shaphal*, low. *Pullet* had meant a young girl since the 1570s.

Flash was an all-purpose 18th- and 19th-century term for a criminal; thus the **flash girl**, **flash hen**, **flash madam**, **flash lady**, **flash woman** and **flash mollisher** might all be assumed to be up for a little trickery if the chance presented itself. And since the re-creation of virginity did depend on a girl who still looked as if she might vaguely remember her rural upbringing, there were other tricks at a prostitute's disposal. In the 18th century, a **buttock and twang** was a robbery executed by a prostitute: she picked up a client in a tavern and led him down an alley, where she picked his pocket and her male accomplice knocked him down. In the 19th century, the **cross-girl** propositioned sailors, taking their money and then vanishing.

In the early 20th century a **lusher** preyed on *lushes* or drunks, while the **lumberer** was a prostitute or pimp who specialised in robbing the clients; the word comes from *lumber*, to hide oneself. (A **lumber gaff** was the flat from which a prostitute worked.) Also in the 20th century, Australia's **ginger**, **ginger-cake**, **gingerer** or **ginger girl** was a prostitute who robbed her customer of his wallet, based on the idea behind the standard word *ginger*, which is both 'sweet' and 'spicy'. The ginger was also the robbery itself, often carried out in brothels (known as **gingering joints**). Across the Pacific one finds the **georgia**, which abbreviates the old carnival use the *Georgia scuffle*, a form of confidence trick. It can be any swindle, but especially one worked by a prostitute on a customer. Georgia, **george** or **georgy** first meant to play a confidence trick on a person who has newly arrived from the south and is thus naïve as regards the northern, urban world. As played by a prostitute (who might also be said to **do the G** and **send to Georgia**), it involved offering her services, getting the money 'up front' and then disappearing. The trick played by the American **mush-worker** was relatively painless – only one's wallet suffered: the prostitute obtained money from men by simply playing on their sympathy, giving them a 'sob story'. They may have even had sex first.

Turning Tricks

Trick has meant an act of sexual intercourse since the 16th century. Like the standard use it meant an act or habit, usually, as the *Oxford English Dictionary* notes, 'unpleasant'. And although such tricks could be performed by prostitutes and gentlewomen across the centuries, the modern use, specific to paid intercourse, is a coinage of the 1920s. It is most regularly found in the phrases **turn a trick** or **turn tricks** but also **do a trick**. Whether the philologist of black-American English J.L. Dillard is right to suggest in his *Lexicon of Black English* (1977) that 'the term trick for the sexual performance of a prostitute probably comes, ultimately, from the voodoo term for achieving control (often sexual control)' is debatable. The synonymous 18th-century **do the story with** once again points up the 'old, old story' – the basic falsehood underlying the exchange of counterfeit affection for money.

From the 1920s onwards, *trick* has meant a prostitute's client; any casual sex partner; and a general term of abuse. It can also refer to the prostitute herself and to anyone who can be easily manipulated. As an adjective, trick relates to commercial or casual sex. It also means to work as a prostitute, giving the noun **tricking** and the image, as explained by the husband-and-wife sociolinguists Milner and Milner in *Black Players* (1972), that 'one is literally tricking a man by taking money for doing what women should do for free'. For a man, it is to pay for sex or to spend money on any woman in the hope of being repaid with sex. A **trickster** or **trick broad** is a prostitute. To **get up to tricks** was to work as a prostitute but its date, *c*.1890, may suggest a literal use of the phrase. To **beat a trick** is to rob, i.e. 'beat' a client. **Trick-ass** is a general put-down: the implication is of sexual inadequacy (for a man) or promiscuity (for a woman).

Trick has generated a number of compounds. A **trick baby** is a prostitute's illegitimate child (the **trick daddy** is the father). **Trick dough** or **trick money** is the money earned and turned over to a pimp; a **trick house** is a brothel and a **trick pad** or **trick room** is any room used by a prostitute to entertain her clients. A **trick suit** is a dress that can be removed easily; a **trick towel** is used for wiping oneself after intercourse. **Trick willy** (in which the name Willy is used as a generic for 'man') is a gullible black man. A **straight trick** is a client who requires no 'extras' beyond normal intercourse and a **freak trick** is one who requires out-of-the-way sex or who attacks the woman physically; a **boss trick** or **champagne trick** are both well-paying customers; a **cheap-trick** is their antithesis.

THE CLIENT

No clients, no prostitutes. Not a great deal of gratitude, though, let alone respect. One of the earliest terms is the 16th-century **simpler**, who was the gullible victim of a conman as well as the prostitute's despised customer; similar is the **flat**, coined in the 18th century and still found: its generic use is a peasant, a rustic and, as such, a fool or innocent; the step to a whore's punter is a short one.

Less disdainful are the mid-20th century's **action**, which is what the client is after, and serves as his name as well; a **date**, which covers the paid sex as well, and a **fare**, another play on 'ride' – the fare is what he pays to take such a ride. Other terms include the 16th- to 19th-century **rifler**, which is based on standard English *rifle*, of a hawk, to tread the hen, as well as having overtones of the standard sense, meaning to despoil, to plunder; in criminal use it meant to have sex. A *bully* could be a client in the 18th century but was more likely to be a pimp or brothel thug, meanings present from the 17th to 20th centuries. A *bit of mess* played an anomalous role in the 1950s onwards: that of a prostitute's male lover, who is neither ponce nor client. The *john* (thus *john catcher*, a prostitute) was born in America in the 1910s and is probably still the number one term for a prostitute's paying customer. If the john has a rival, at least in Britain since the 1930s, it is the *punter*, which in 'civilian' use has meant a bettor since the 18th century. Clients come and clients go, not so America's *steady*, present from the 1960s onwards, although the word is more commonly known in its standard sense of a regular boy- or girlfriend. From the beginning of the 20th century, a *live one* has been a rich and generous client of a brothel, specifically the client of a male prostitute; like so many others he is probably gullible too, since the term is also used by confidence men of one whom they can exploit.

The usual paid encounter, known in the early 19th century as the *move*, is relatively short – around 15 minutes – but a *long shot* may stay longer and pay for more than just the basics, while an *all-nighter* is a client who stays and pays for a whole night. A client who prefers his appointments in the afternoon is a *matinee*. The basic appointment is known as the *short time* from the mid-19th century onwards, allowing for a single copulation. The *short-timer* is one who frequents a prostitute for a brief visit, involving a single act of intercourse. From the 1920s onwards, a *quickie* is a very short time indeed. The total of clients a prostitute has serviced within a given time is her *catch*.

Ultimately it is all about the transaction, and to pay the prostitute is to *lay the note* in 20th-century America. Again there is a sense of duping the client, as the phrase has also meant to short-change; while in the 19th century to visit a whore was described as the seemingly strange *Joe Blake the Bartlemy*. This is a mix of rhyming slang – Joe Blake (= *fake*) was loosely 'do', therefore extended here to mean visit, plus Bartlemy for Bartholomew Fair, a once-notorious annual festival held in Smithfield. A modern version is *pay and lay*.

THE BROTHEL

While the word brothel is and always has been standard English, it is nevertheless something of a misnomer, since *brothel* in its original, 14th-century usage meant simply a disreputable person, of either sex. A century later the disrepute had overtaken the individual, and brothel meant first and foremost a prostitute; it was not for another century that, as an abbreviation of 'brothel's house' or 'brothel-house', it replaced the person with the place. Meanwhile, there already existed a perfectly good word for brothel: *bordel*, from *bordar* – a feudal term meaning the owner of a hut or cottage, which in turn came from the Latin *bordarius* (cottager) and hence from Latin *borda* (a cottage or hut). Bordel vanished from popular use as brothel took its place, but the late 16th-century slang synonym **bordello** is still in use, if usually, and quite consciously, as a mix of the exotic and the archaic.

The Brothel in Slang

Most often, the slang terms for a brothel have been based on the idea of a 'house' of prostitution, as well as various other slang synonyms for the word 'house', such as 'crib' or 'joint' and similar buildings such as religious institutions.

The House
There is, as at one time or another most of us have discovered, a **house** in New Orleans and while, floods permitting, its doors are doubtless ever open, we also know – as the celebrated American madam Polly Adler entitled her memoirs – *A House is Not a Home*. Indeed not. By the time those who consulted an *Impartial List of the Ladies of Pleasure in Edinburgh* by 'Roger Ranger' in 1775 found that 'Miss Walker [. . .] keeps a very genteel house', the equation of house and whorehouse, i.e. brothel, was long established; its first record being some two centuries earlier. The term was found without embellishment, but it often attracted some form of descriptive modification, usually euphemistic. Between the 16th and 19th centuries

one could encounter a *house of profession, of resort, of sale, of state, of conveniency* (as well as a *convenient house*), *of delight, of pleasure* and *of civil reception* or *civil entertainment*. The 1950s added the *house mother* or *house-keeper*, i.e. a madam, and the *house girl*, a resident prostitute.

The 16th century offered the *vaulting* and *leaping houses* (both from terms for having sex); the *victualling-house*, which doubled as a tavern and was run by the *victualler*, both an innkeeper and a pimp; the self-explanatory *naughty house* and the *occupying house*, from *occupy*, to have sexual intercourse. The *trugging house* was linked to *trug*, a prostitute, taken from the synonymous Italian *trucca*. The image of 'heat' in *scalding-house* may have suggested the possibility of getting a venereal disease from its whores, certainly a *hothouse*, 'a very ill house too' writes Shakespeare in *Measure for Measure* (1603), was one to avoid. (A 1980s version is the *clap-trap*.)

Casa, which means house in either Italian or Spanish, was adopted as a brothel in late 17th-century England, and in time would refer particularly to those establishments open on the Haymarket, the centre of whoring in London's 19th-century West End, as would the term *case*. Case gave *case-fro* meaning a prostitute, and based on German *Frau* or Dutch *vrow*, a woman. The *vrow-case* was the brothel itself again, as was the mid-19th century's *mot-case*. In the 20th century this became the *case house* and *caseo* or *caso*, with a *case keeper* for its owner.

Back among the houses of the 17th century, there was *garden house*, either a place where a mistress was lodged (the garden in question being the vagina) or a brothel (in which case the reference was probably to Covent Garden: a placename used as a generic for prostitution). Other synonyms are the *playhouse*, the *nanny house* or *nanny shop* (from a generic use of the proper name *Nanny*, i.e. Nancy), the *nugging house* (from *nug*, to fondle) and the *punch house*, a tavern-cum-whorehouse that drew its name from its provision of alcoholic punch.

A century later one finds the *accommodation house* or *house of accommodation*, a term that had begun life meaning an innocent lodging house; such places may have begun as respectable buildings, but soon changed their use to that of brothel. By the 19th century, they provided a 'hotel' where rooms could be hired for short times by lovers or a prostitute (an *accommodation beauty*) and her client. The verb *accommodate* was a back-formation meaning to work as a prostitute. The *call girl* – summoned by her phone or via an agency, these days frequently online – seems a modern concept, but the original *call house* or *house of call* in which such a girl might work was a 19th-century brothel to which men could 'call' or arrive without making any prior appointment. This developed *c*.1910 into a hetero- or homosexual brothel to which women or men were summoned by telephone after they had been selected, via some form of visual 'menu', by the visiting male clientele; the *call trade* was prostitution arranged on this basis. The period also offered *call flat* or *call apartment*, a brothel. The other major development in the 18th century was the *molly house*; based on a term for a male homosexual that dated back to the late 17th century, it was the first name to be used for a gay brothel. The same period's *gay house*, and the 20th century's *moll shop* or *molly shop*, however, were all heterosexual.

The brothel was hardly unknown in America prior to the 19th century, but it was only then that the nation began contributing to its nomenclature. A *hooker* was a prostitute, and a brothel a *hook house*, *hook shop* or *hook joint* (see page 174). The *sporting house*, *sporting crib*, *mansion*, *resort* or *room* was a brothel (see page 193 for its inhabitants), although the equation of sport with sex had long been made already. The link has remained – modern Caribbean has *sport house*. Equally American was the *parlor house*, which lasted well into the 20th century. It was a high-class establishment, situated in what was ostensibly a fashionably furnished middle-class house; the place was run by a complaisant 'aunt' whose bevy of attractive 'nieces' gathered in the front parlour to meet and make themselves available to visitors. The nieces were properly known as *parlor girls*, *parlor house girls* or *parlor queens*. In this kind of set-up the Americans were starting to ape the French, whose upmarket *maisons closes* provided the same kind of 'beauty parade' to their moneyed clients. (Cheaper brothels had little more than bedrooms in which one had sex.) As such places developed, dining and gambling facilities might too, until the sex was seen as just a pleasant facet of a gentleman's (expensive) evening out.

Not everyone could afford the parlor house, and America offered its antithesis in the late 19th to 20th centuries: the **barrel house**, named for the barrels of beer on tap. It was these rough and ready whorehouses that gave the musical jargon *barrelhouse*, 'swing music played in a "dirty and lowdown" style' (*Downbeat Year Book of Swing*, 1939) not to mention such lyrics as W.C. Handy's 'Mr Crump Blues' (1909): 'Mister Crump won't 'low no easy riders here, / Mister Crump won't 'low no easy riders here. / I don't care what he don't 'low, / I'm going barrelhouse anyhow.' An **easy rider** was of course a prostitute, appearing long before the phrase's brief fame as the title of the hippie dystopia movie of choice. The era also coined the **fast house**, and the **cathouse**, from the identification of cat with woman – and of course prostitute – and which term has lasted ever since. Variations have included the **cat flat**, **cat shop**, and **cats' nest**. Also, before the anti-'white slavery' legislation of 1910 that outlawed the 'interstate commerce' in women, many cowboys enjoyed the ambulating pleasures of the **cat wagon**, a horse-drawn covered wagon that carried a group of prostitutes who followed the cattle trails and offered lonely cowpunchers a pleasurable break in their solitary existence.

Also in America, there was the **bed-house**, which as well as a brothel was a 'short-time' hotel – the precursor of today's **hotbed**, **hot-sheet** or **no-tell motel**. The first **circus houses** were found in New Orleans, and the name refers to the *circuses*, the 'live sex shows' the patrons could watch. Early jazz was supposedly performed in such places; the **jazz house** itself – slightly later and also known as a **jazz joint** – joined the ranks of brothel synonyms. In this case the reference was to *jazz*, to have sex, and the musical background was coincidental, although both uses are generally seen as coming from *jism*, meaning spirit or energy (and thus semen). The **nautch house** or **nautch joint** came from Urdu/Hindi *nach*, dancing. The attendant image of the 'exotic' East led inevitably to assumptions of sexual licence, and a **nautch girl** or **nautch broad** was a brothel prostitute. The 20th-century **notch house** or **notch-joint** was less exotic, and depended on slang's *notch*, a 17th-century coinage meaning vagina. To *grind* meant to work hard and to have sex, and a **grind house**, **grind joint** or **grinding house** could be a place of business or work, or a brothel (of course, for some these were the same thing).

The UK offered the **fancy house** and the **dress house**, with its **dress lodgers**, whose wretched career was best described by sporting journalist Pierce Egan in *Finish to the Adventures of Tom and Jerry* (1830):

> Corinthian Kate became the inmate of a dress-house! [. . .] kept during the day in beggary, and almost in rags, and at night dressed up like a painted doll, sent to the Theatre on speculation, watched by her landlady or old procuress hired for the purpose, to preclude her from robbing her mistress of her wages of prostitution, and also prevent her running off with the clothes belonging to her iniquitous employer.

The Ken

Ken, in cant use, meant a house, a term that is possibly an abbreviation of standard English *kennel* (in a non-canine mode) or from the Hindi *khan(n)a*, a house or room. Although the compound *bawdy-house* has been restricted to standard English, in which it is first recorded in 1552, **bawdy-ken** was slang for a brothel in the 19th century, and the **bawdy-ken dodge** was the robbery of a brothel prostitute's client by her pimp or 'husband'. Slang compounds involving the bawdy-house have been recorded from the 17th century, including the miniature **bawdy-house bottle**, specially designed to be sold at brothels and offering the owner yet another means of fleecing clients. It was presumably drunk in the similarly miniaturised **bawdy-house glass**.

Between the 17th and 19th centuries ken itself provided the **flash ken** which might also be found as the **flash house** or **flash panny** (from slang's *panny*, a house, itself a possible generic use of *pantry*), the **snoozing ken**, the **wapping ken** (from slang's *wap*, to fuck), the **smuggling ken** (from dialect *smuggle*, to smother with hugs and kisses) and the **rum ken** in which *rum* meant 'first-class'.

The Crib

The standard English *crib*, a small house or narrow room, has been linked to low-status brothels since the early 19th century. The **crib** or **dossing crib** (later **crib-joint** and **crib-house**) meant the brothel, and the unmodified crib was also the actual room where the clients were serviced by the prostitute – the **crib-girl** – whether within a brothel or for her own use only. Its compounds, all meaning brothel, included the **moll-crib**, the **pegging-crib** and the **touch crib**. There was also the **goosing crib**, **goosing slum** (from *slum*, a room) or **goosing ranch**; the etymology here remains obscure – chronology makes impossible the otherwise logical link to slang's verb *goose*, to fool, or the rhyming slang *goose (and duck)*, to fuck.

The Joint

Like crib, **joint** had multiple uses. It appeared as a brothel in the late 19th century and in time gave **joint togs**, the clothes in which a working prostitute displayed herself. All its compounds arrived in the mid-20th century. They include the **boff joint** (from slang's *boff*, to fuck), the **jig-a-jig joint** (again based on a term for intercourse), and the American **chippie joint** or **chippie house**, which came from *chippie*, a prostitute. Also in America, a **boogie joint** or **boogie house** referred to slang's *boogie*, i.e. to have sex, a meaning that followed the primary ones of having fun or dancing. Entertainment was available at the **jump joint** too, a cheap roadhouse or brothel, which provided food, drink and music for dancing, as well as sex; *jump*, like boogie, referred to both the dancing and sex. A **cracker joint** was based on Australia's term for a prostitute (who 'cracked it' for the customers, see page 199).

The Shop

Given the commercial reality of the game, the use of **shop** to mean brothel, first noted in the 16th century, is wholly logical and, in the years since, a number of compounds have naturally followed. The **warm shop** or **warm show** played on slang's *warm*, i.e. sexy; the **banging shop** made its sexual function very clear, as did the **crack shop**, **bum shop** and **buttocking shop**. The 18th century's **gig shop** was based on an old term meaning a foolish, coquettish or lewd

young woman, although *gig* could also mean a 'flighty fellow' and
so the reference may have been to the client rather than the prostitute. In addition were the late 19th-century **girl shop** or **girlery**
and the Australian **cake shop**, based on the 20th century's *cake*, a
prostitute, and one of a string of terms that equates sexually available women with edibles such as 'jam', 'biscuit', 'confectionery' and,
of course, 'tart'. The image of 'banging' also underpins what is
possibly the best known use of shop as brothel: the mid-19th-century
coinage of **knocking-shop**, still in use today. There is also the modern
rub-a-tug shop or **rub and tug shop**, which mixes slang's *rub-a-dub*
(-dub), sexual intercourse, with *rub off* and *tug*, two terms meaning
to masturbate; it is either a cheap brothel or an escort agency.

The Religious Foundation

'Get thee to a nunnery, go: farewell. [. . .] To a nunnery, go, and
quickly too.' This is Prince Hamlet offering what, outside of his talk
of 'country matters', is his best-known *double entendre*. From the
16th to 19th centuries, the conflation of self-denying chastity with
all-indulgent sin, made a **nunnery** a brothel, a **nun** a prostitute and
an **abbess**, **lady abbess** and (in time) a **Covent Garden abbess**, a
brothel-keeper. An **abbot** was her husband or lover and the **croziered**
abbot or **abbot on the cross**, which punned on the standard English
croziered, bearing a crook, and cant's *on the cross*, criminal, was a
man who runs a brothel that is designed less for providing sex, and
more for robbing or blackmailing the clients.

The Academic Institution

The British male's love of the traditional schoolgirl uniform –
whether worn by others or indeed by himself – is long established,
but the use of schools and colleges to denote brothels is much older.
Indeed, with the exception of the punning **riding academy**, a black-
American term from the 1930s to 1950s that plays on *ride* (to have
sex), and the recent **toss parlour**, which presumably offers more
than a mere toss (i.e. masturbation), nearly all such terms would
run their course between the 16th and 18th centuries.

The oldest, recorded in 1593, was the **dancing school**, which again
played on the use of *dancing* to mean sexual intercourse. A wide

range of terms then appears, all coined in the 17th century. They include the **academy, college** or **ladies' college**; the **cavaulting school** (punning on Lingua Franca's *cavolta*, riding); the **pushing school** (referencing the standard use of *pushing school* for a fencing school, and thus linked to slang's uses of the *dagger* and other pointed weapons to mean the penis); the **school of Venus**, the *firking school* (which despite appearances actually uses standard English *firk*, to move about briskly, to whip or to beat); the **topping school** (from slang's *top*, to have sex); and another pun, the **seminary**.

A century later one finds the **boarding school** (and in the 1930s the **star boarder**, the best-performing prostitute in a brothel) and the *finishing academy* (which probably puns on the image of finishing as both ending a girl's education and achieving orgasm).

Animal House
The mid-20th-century **zoo** was a brothel whose workers came from 'all nations', and the animal kingdom, as it has in other areas of criminal language, provides a number of useful terms. Earliest is the **cony-burrow** (also **cunniborough** and **cunny-borough**) which literally means a rabbit warren and puns on slang's *cunny*, vagina. From rabbits to birds in the 19th century, where one finds the **bird-cage**, **hen-coop** and **pheasantry**; a **covey**, more usually applied to feathered game, was a group of prostitutes, usually those found in a brothel. The era also produced the **chicken ranch** or **chicken house**, the original of which was at Gilbert, Texas. Popular legend claims that the local farmers who made up the clientele paid for their pleasures with chickens, but disappointingly the name is actually far more likely to have come from slang's *chicken*, which has meant a prostitute since the 17th century. The **hog ranch**, another 19th-century coinage, may commemorate an actual place; what is certain is that it does the women no favours, and nor do the early 20th-century **cowyard** and **heifer den**. The modern **beaver palace** is linked to slang's *beaver*, both the woman and her pubic hair, and finally the **snakepit** possibly comments quasi-moralistically on the goings-on within, but it might just be a reference to slang's *snake*, the penis, and *pit*, the vagina.

Geography and Location

As with the names for the prostitute herself, geography played a part in identifying brothels. In the same way that the classics provided *Cyprian* or *Paphian* as generics for the world of commercial sex (see page 190), they gave **Corinth** for a brothel and **Corinthian** for a courtesan or a regular brothel client. Taken up in the early 17th century, the Corinth referred to the Greek city that was home to a celebrated temple of Aphrodite, goddess of love, a place renowned for its depraved and licentious lifestyle. (A **temple**, unadorned, was also used for a brothel in the 1700s.) Corinthian had the same root but also echoed some Greek slang which translated as *corinthianise*, to associate with courtesans.

Even earlier was the **picked-hatch** (**pick-hatch** or **picthatch**), which combines the standard words *picked*, spiked, and *hatch*, a half-door designed to prevent unauthorised entrance; such an image was commonly used as a brothel sign. The original Pickthatch was a tavern-cum-brothel in the notorious red-light area of Turnmill Street, in the suburban district of Clerkenwell. The term provided **picked-hatch captain** for a pimp, **picked-hatch vestal** (an ironic use of Rome's Vestal Virgins – although putative virgins or not, they too have been linked to sexual excesses). The best-known brothel sign is of course a *red lamp* or *red light*. Before them, however, was the 16th- and 17th-century **red lattice**, a popular tavern sign and, if the tavern was thus inclined, the indication of a brothel (at one time an actual Red Lattice inn stood at Butcher's Row, off the Strand). Since then the red light has become the best-known sign of a sinful area; and working girls can be **red lighters** or **red light sisters**.

The 17th century also offered the **place of sixpenny sinfulness** and a **hole in the wall**, which may or may not pun on slang's *hole* meaning vagina. The etymology is linked either to the holes in the walls of English debtor prisons, through which the inmates could obtain supplies and money to alleviate their situation, or to the small shops and similar establishments found in the broad stone walls of fortified medieval cities. The term crossed the Atlantic and in the 1860s New York City boasted the notorious Hole in the Wall tavern on Water Street, where its proprietor, the **strong-arm woman** Gallus Meg (a monstrous Englishwoman), bit the ears off ill-behaved customers and preserved her trophies in a pickle jar displayed behind the bar. Still in 19th-century New York one finds a *cowbay*, a cheap brothel or a prostitute's room, based on the city's 'red-light area', which was known as Cow Bay (presumably from the *cows*, whores). *Sugar Hill* was another American term, used for the brothel and 'red-light' area of the black part of any southern town. It was also a gross libel on the original Sugar Hill area of Harlem (otherwise known as Coogan's Bluff), bounded by Amsterdam and Edgecombe Avenues, between 138th and 155th Streets. As well as the rich, many black intellectuals and artists chose to live in the area, known for its grand apartment houses, once the original white population had moved out during the 1920s.

Finally there is the 16th and 17th century's *go to Westminster for a wife*, which meant to visit a brothel. The concept was based on the proverb: 'Who goes to Westminster for a wife, to St Paul's for a man or to Smithfield for a horse, may meet with a whore, a knave and a jade.' If one found such a 'wife' one could celebrate a *Westminster wedding*, defined by B.E. in 1698 as 'A Whore and a Rogue Married together'.

The Brothel Whore

If it wasn't the streets and one was not fortunate (or attractive) enough to charm a rich keeper, then it might well be the brothel as a place to earn a living. Most of the terms have been listed already as terms for prostitutes, but there are some to be noted. In the punning 19th-century group that includes the *academy* for a brothel in which the *academician* was the whore (as was the *pensionary miss*). Anti-clericalism gave the 17th-century *parnel*, a more specific use of the standard term *parnel*, a priest's concubine or mistress. The mid-20th century abandoned subtlety to give *whorehouse broad*, *girl* or *woman*. Within the brothel the *line* was the parade of available prostitutes; on the street it meant the women employed by a single pimp; thus *on the line* was working – according to context – either in a brothel or on the street. For a brothel girl to out-earn her sisters in any given period was to *top the house*.

The Brothel Bawd

If the brothel whores were *daughters of the game* then the bawd for whom they worked was logically their **mother**. The 17th and 18th centuries note several such dubious maternal figures. There was **Mother Cunny**, whose name advertised the commodity she sold; **Mother Knab-cony**, whose name was literally 'Mother Snatch-Sucker'; **Mother Midnight**, whose second job was as a midwife (especially in the context of delivering or aborting illegitimate children); and **Mother Damnable**. This last lady may actually have existed, although her 'sisters' are simply generic. The author and print-seller James Caulfield's *Blackguardiana* (1793) has a picture of a bawd entitled 'Mother Damnable of Kentish Town Anno 1676' with an accompanying verse from the same year which notes that 'So fam'd, both far and near, is the renown, / Of Mother Damnable, of Kentish Town'. The **Mother of the Maids** played on her standard English equivalent – the governess to the Queen's maids of honour. Equally euphemistic, though few again would have been fooled, was the **aunt**, which lasted from the 17th century into the 20th.

The equation of woman with fish lies behind the 17th-century **fishmonger**, while a **mackerel** (also **macquerella** or **macrio**) came from the French *maquereau*, a pimp, and has been used for a madam from the 15th century and for a pimp from the 16th. In the 17th century, the **bronstrops** or **brainstrap** came from standard English *bawdstrot*, a pander or procuress, while the **buttock broker** made her commercial interests clear. Last is the 19th century's **Mrs Lukey Props**, who one must assume was a real-life brothel-keeper, although history sadly preserves no record of her existence.

The Brothel Bouncer

Not all the men to be found in a brothel are clients. One at least may be an employee, not for sex but for violence, just in case one of the customers hasn't rid himself of quite all his testosterone-based urges.

The mid-16th-century **ruffian** hired himself out for various jobs, and brothel bouncer was among them; the century also had the *hector* or *bull-hector*, a name that refers to the Trojan hero Hector, son of Priam and Hecuba, husband of Andromache (who in turn is abbreviated to *dromaky*, a prostitute in northern England). He was succeeded by the *bully-rock*, *bully-rook* or *bully-back* (from the standard verb *back*, to support, to back up), who worked both as a bouncer and as the occasional lover or 'husband' of either the madam or one of the prostitutes. The 18th century added the *flashman* and the 19th the *bludgeoner*, who was another one available to play the 'outraged husband' when an unfortunate client was to be menaced out of his purse. The *knight of the petticoat* sounded gentler but wasn't. More recent are the American *john walker*, from the popular term for a client plus standard English *walk* (i.e. to remove), and Australia's *bumper-upper*. Rather than a thug, the latter is a handyman who works for a prostitute; hence the derogative phrase *he couldn't get a job as a bumper-upper in a brothel*.

It was not all violence; like other less than respectable places of amusement, the brothel needed someone to point the client in the right direction. The mid-18th-century *wagon-hunter* was a brothel-keeper's agent who solicited customers at coaching inns, while the 19th century's *poundage cove* was defined in the *Modern Flash Dictionary* (1835) as 'a fellow who receives poundage for procuring customers for damaged goods'; standard use *poundage* was 'an impost, duty, or tax of so much per pound sterling on merchandise' (*Oxford English Dictionary*). The *capper*, the *outside man* and the *lighthouse* would wander the adjacent streets, ready to 'steer' the enquiring passer-by to their house of ill-fame. Another jack-of-all-trades employed by a brothel was the mid-20th-century Australian *condy boy*; his task was to ensure a good supply of Condy's fluid, a disinfectant used post-intercourse. The fluid had made its appearance in the Second World War, when Australian troops in the Eastern Mediterranean used the phrase *maleesh* (i.e. never mind) *the condy's*, forget the preliminaries, let's get on with it, and any local menial was christened *Abdullah with the Condies*.

Finally, the late 18th century's *burning shame*. This far from obvious term was a form of sexual 'game', whereby 'a lighted candle [is] stuck into the parts of a woman, certainly not intended by nature for a candlestick' (Captain Francis Grose, *A Classical*

Dictionary of the Vulgar Tongue, 1796). Playing on that, the phrase also referred to a night watchman placed at the door of a brothel, holding a lantern, even in daylight, to deter people from wandering in and out.

Criminal Practices in Brothels

> The Cros-biting law is a publique profession of shameles cosenage, mixt with incestuous whoredomes, as il as was practised in Gomorha or Sodom, though not after the same vnnatural manner: for the method of their mischieuous art [. . .] is, that these villanous vipers, vnworthy the name of men, [. . .] doth consent, nay constrayne their wiues to yeeld the vse of their bodies to other men, that taking them together, he may cros-bite the party of all the crownes he can presently make, and that the world may see their monstrous practises.

> Robert Greene, *A Notable Discovery of Coosnage* (1591)

It might not have happened in Nell Kimball's establishments, let alone at Chicago's Everleigh Club where even the spittoons were solid gold and cost $650 apiece, but lower down the scale there was always the possibility that a brothel client might fall victim to fraud, extortion and simple violence. So widespread were these hazards that a mini-lexicon evolved to accommodate them. While the tricks had surely been played for years, the associated language developed in the mid-19th century.

One particular trick must have existed for as long as men went to prostitutes, and was noted by Robert Greene as the **crossbiting law**: the whore picks up her client, they go to her room, the sex begins . . . and in bursts the **crossbiter**, posing as a 'brother' or 'husband' (in some cases the real one – a 'villainous viper . . . an excremental reversion of sin' says Greene – but in most a pimp or helpful thug), railing against their 'sister's' or 'wife's' defilement and threatening a violent reprisal. Only with a substantial payment can her honour be appeased. The victim, probably a country farmer up to sell his cattle or crops to the London markets, has little option but to fork out.

By the 19th century the primary fraud, on which all others were merely variations, was known as the **badger game**, named after the **badger** or **badger moll**, any prostitute who participates in a scheme to rob her clients. (The game could also be played by a man, who for the purpose dresses as a woman.) Like the animal which is nocturnal and carnivorous; the prostitute also 'devours' her victims after dark. To 'play' the game was to **badger** and the male accomplice was the **badger-man** or **badger-worker**. The brothel that hosted such frauds was the **badger-crib** or **badger house**; it could also be the **trap-house**.

A popular variation was the **panel game**, **trick** or **dodge**, played in a purpose-built room of a brothel (the **panel crib**, **den**, **house**, **joint** or **store**). In this case the accomplice was the **panel thief** or **worker**. Unlike the badger game, no violence need be involved or threatened. The New York journalist James D. McCabe, in *Secrets of a Great City* (1868), explained:

> The girl in this case acts in concert with a confederate, who is generally a man. She takes her victim to her room, and directs him to deposit his clothing on a chair, which is placed but a few inches from the wall at the end of the room. This wall is false, and generally of wood. It is built some three or four feet from the real wall of the room, thus forming a closet. As the whole room is papered and but dimly lighted, a visitor cannot detect the fact that it is a sham. A panel, which slides noiselessly and rapidly, is arranged in the false wall, and the chair with the visitor's clothing upon it is placed just in front of it. While the visitor's attention is engaged in another quarter, the girl's confederate, who is concealed in the closet, slides back the panel, and rifles the pockets of the clothes on the chair. The panel is then noiselessly closed. When the visitor is about to depart, or sometimes not until long after his departure, he discovers his loss.

A less sophisticated version of the panel game was the **creep** or **creep game**. In this the accomplice simply crept into the room while the prostitute made sure her client was otherwise engaged, and rifled through his clothes for the wallet; since the client has always had to pay in advance, it is unlikely that he will check the wallet until, long gone, he next requires it. Brothels in which such incidents occurred were known as **creep houses**, **pads** or **joints**.

Last, and today perhaps the best known of these tricks, is the **Murphy game**. This variation does not require a brothel but it is far more likely to involve violence. A prostitute lures the client either to a room or, more usually, to a deserted alley, hall or suchlike; before sex even begins her accomplice appears, and assaults and then robs the victim. He may play the 'aggrieved' husband, lover or brother and halt at mere intimidation but, given the relative openness of street robbery, the need for speed makes violence far more likely. Where the name comes from is unknown, although it has been suggested that the game's first practitioners promised the victim a meeting with 'a lovely woman called Mrs Murphy'.

THE PIMP

Pimp Names

Pimp is standard English. Its roots have been linked to the French words *pimpreneau*, a scoundrel, *pimpant*, alluring or seducing in outward appearance or dress, or *pimpesouée*, a pretentious woman. In all cases the *Oxford English Dictionary* is unimpressed and declares its etymology 'unknown'.

The Mack
The mack is the best known of the pimp's non-standard peers. The original 16th- to 17th-century form is **mackerel**, a pimp or pander (a century before it meant procuress), who resurfaced around 1930 in American use. This word borrowed from the synonymous French *maquereau* but the background has been debated, with allusions made to the 'bottom-feeding' habits of the fish; the most likely origins lie in the Dutch *makelaar*, a broker, and in parallel to that the medieval French *macque*, as explained by French slang lexicographer Lorédan Larchey in his *Dictionnaire Historique* (1878): 'In the Middle Ages the word *macque* signified *vente*, the profession of

a merchant. From this came *maquerel* and *maquignon*. The *maquereau* is nothing more than a merchant of women.'

Mack itself (also spelled *mac, maq* or *maque*) is an American coinage from the early 20th century, or possibly the late 19th (as a verb it has been found as early as 1887). *The mack* or *mack talk* is his seductive, persuasive talk, especially the 'chat-up' line used to recruit a new woman. Officially, as it were, the pimp is a repellent, exploitative character; in reality he has become romanticised, especially in sections of the black community to whom his material success, seemingly sophisticated style and undeniable power over women have rendered his a lifestyle to which one can aspire. Thus a mack can also be a 'smooth operator', especially one who deceives or tries – often successfully – to seduce a member of the opposite sex. The mack as pimp has been extended as *mackman* or *mac man*, and found as *macker, magoofer, magiffer* and *McGimp*, the last of which is semi-rhyming slang. To *make mack with* or *get the mack on* is to flirt or to pick up a woman and to *put the mack down* is to act in a smooth, sophisticated manner reminiscent of the idealised pimp. Thus the adjectival use, while primarily referring to anything pertaining to the pimp such as attitude, philosophy, automobile or clothes, can also simply mean masculine in appearance and behaviour.

The same pattern continues. To mack is to work as a pimp but extended as *mack down* and *mack on* it can also mean to talk seductively and to flirt (specifically as a pimp does to recruit a prostitute). Mack can also mean to swagger, to lie or exaggerate in order to deceive, exploit or influence someone, to have sex, to steal and most recently to be successful, usually sexually. *Macked out/up* means stylishly or flashily dressed or decorated, *mackadelic* refers to one who is self-promoting, parading the qualities otherwise attributed to a pimp, and *mackery* is pimping. The *mack daddy* or *macdaddy* is an exemplar of pimping qualities, and outside the pimping world he is an important, influential black man, a power in the community; usually successful, handsome and virile. The term is used on American campuses, irrespective of colour, for anything or anybody that is considered the best.

16th- and 17th-century Terms

Mack may be among the most ubiquitous, but the first recorded slang term for a pimp appears to have been the **captain**, initially the *captain of the stews* (i.e. the brothel area), as found in the satirical poem *Cocke Lorelles Bote* (1515), which mentions 'Fraunces flaperoche, of stewys captayne late', and *Nicols Narratives* (1579), which states that 'He made hym capteyne of the stews and all the whoores therto belongyng. And in dede he proved an excellent cutter [i.e. thug] and ruffyne.' The **striker**, with its equation of sex and violence, was an ancestor of the modern **hard mack**, a pimp who maintains discipline with blows (as was the 17th-century **carrion-flogger**, *carrion* being both flesh and a whore), while the **bellswagger** was another 'ruffyne' who literally 'swaggered his belly'. The **apple squire** and **apron squire** teased the aristocratic esquire – the 'apple' possibly links to *apples*, the female breasts. He might also be an **apple-monger**, literally a dealer in apples, thus 'ripe fruit', thus 'ripe' women. Other squires included the **squire of the body**, **squire of the petticoat** and **squire of the placket**, while to *squire* was to pimp someone.

At the same time, there was also the **pensioner at the petticoat** and the **pensioner of the placket** (also just the **pensioner**), and the **petticoat merchant**. A **petticoat pensioner** was a kept man (whether or not an actual pimp), common from the late 17th to 19th centuries, and the money that the prostitute gave her pimp, or the mistress gave her kept lover, was a **petticoat pension**. The petticoat could be replaced with another garment: the same era saw the **knight of the gusset**, **squire of the gusset** and **brother of the gusset**. And where the 16th century had a captain of the stews, the 17th had the **led captain** or **led-friend** for a pimp. In standard English, the *led horse* was a riderless horse that is often seen in the retinues of the rich and powerful, underlining the extent of their possessions, and the fact that they own extra horses, even if they are of no real use; its initial meaning was as a toady or sycophant. Also in the 17th century, but far less euphemistic, were the **broker** and the **bully**, the latter of which practised **bullying**.

Other terms from the 17th century include the **mutton-tugger** or **tug-mutton**, in which the mutton was the woman's flesh; the **setter**, otherwise a species of hunting dog; the **drab-driver**, from *drab*, a slattern, and the **cock-pimp** who posed as his prostitute's 'husband'. The pimp's sexual abilities are seen in **stallion**, a term that in 20th-century America can also refer to a prostitute – although was used in the 16th and 17th centuries for a courtesan – as well as the still-extant slang term for a womaniser or sexual athlete. A **town bull** from the same period also might mean a local Casanova; the *town trap* punned on the standard verb *trap*, to ensnare. If a prostitute was a punk, then her pimp was a **punk-master**; he could also be a **rumper** or **cully rumper**, both of which drew on standard English *rump* and could also be used to refer to the punk's client. The **Turnbull Street rogue** took his name from a London street well known for prostitution – this location also gave the **Turnbull Street bee**, a whore who might 'sting' her clients with venereal disease or if nothing else leave them with a case of **Turnbull Street fleas** (crab-lice).

18th- and 19th-century Terms
In the 18th century the **badger**, best known as the larcenous whore who played the badger game, could also be a pimp. The bully extended to become a **bully-hack**, drawing on *hackster*, a variant of hackney and thus a prostitute. From the late 18th century, he could also be a **gap-stopper**, which suggests he sampled the merchandise, a **whore-eater**, or a **jockum-gagger**, **jack-gagger** or **jock-gagger** (literally a 'penis-beggar'), who even if not a pimp certainly lived on his wife's prostitution. The **twang** (in 20th-century Irish use a **twangman**) was a prostitute's male accomplice; he would arrive to beat up the victim she had already robbed under the guise of offering intercourse. The term usually occurred in the phrase *buttock and twang* (see page 202).

The perennial usefulness of such an accomplice meant that the figure of the captain reappeared in the 19th century: he was now christened **Captain Shaddy**, and took his name from the shadow wherein he lurked. Such a pimp-cum-mugger might also be a **bearer-up** or a **bouncer**. (In the 1930s he had become an **alley rat**.) Both the **fucker** and **holer** were unashamedly sexual, as were **pinch-bottom**, **pinch-buttock** and, above all, **pinch-cunt**. The **bruiser** and the Australian *bludger* (which simply abbreviated the standard term *bludgeoner*) were another pair who used violence, whether on the client or the girl or indeed – as was quite likely – both. The back-formed verb *bludge* meant to live off a prostitute, although it developed to cover any form of exploitative idleness. A *Haymarket hector* made his pimping home at the centre of London's West End whoring. The *prosser* was briefly a pimp, but coming from the slang verb *pross*, which meant to sponge on one's acquaintances, was better known via the celebrated Prossers' Avenue in London's Gaiety Theatre, the theatre bar where the more raffish elements of society were wont to promenade. More prossing came from the *cunt pensioner*, both a kept man and a pimp. The *split* was remarkably generous: he split the girl's earnings 50–50 with her. A *dona jack* was literally a 'woman man', and while the era's *faggot-master* or *faggoteer* dealt only in heterosexuality, the 1960s *faggoter* specialised in selling the services of male prostitutes (one sees the progress of slang's *faggot* from meaning a woman to meaning a gay man).

The *pounce-shicer* or *ponce-shicer* were extensions of the far better known *ponce*, a mid-19th-century coinage. Its true etymology remains unknown: the *Oxford English Dictionary* suggests standard English *pounce*, while in 'Shelta and Polari' (1984) Ian Hancock notes the French argot *pont (d'Avignon)* or *pontonnière*, a prostitute (who works from the arches of a bridge); Eric Partridge in *Dictionary of Slang and Unconventional English* (1937–84) offers French *pension-naire* (pronounced 'ponce-ee-onare'), a lodger, and thus there is a possible link to the earlier *pensioner*. As for *shicer*, it was based on Yiddish, and that Germano-Hebrew dialect also gave *shundicknick* for a pimp.

The 19th century also allied the adjective *sporting* both to sex and to the 'fast' life of gambling – and by extension to pimping. It in turn gave the 20th century's *sporting life*, meaning the 'good' life, i.e. money, liquor, women and all the desired pleasures of the flesh; the term became particularly popular as a description of the lifestyle of a American pimp and was popularised in the 1950s as a term of address, often ironic, after the success of the 1951 George Gershwin musical *Porgy & Bess* and its eponymous 'city slicker' character.

Modern Terms

Of the less immediately obvious terms was the early 20th-century use of **cadet** to mean a pimp, or more specifically a man who abducted young women and forced (or otherwise persuaded) them into turning tricks. The term came from French *cadet*, a younger son of the nobility: to be a cadet implies inexperience and a suggestion that such young gentlemen spent much of their time in mischievous idleness. Thus it was extended to the procurer and what became known as the **cadet system**, explained in 1909 by American author C.B. Chrysler in his book *White Slavery*:

> The boys commenced to bring in the girls. They had nice clothes; their hair was allowed to grow long and hang away down on their forehead. They wore white mufflers around their necks, and this was the origination of the famous 'cadet' system of New York. Thousands of boys from fifteen to twenty-two years [. . .] joined the 'cadets' and went into the tenement district corrupting young girls and inducing them to enter the life of shame.

The commercial basis of prostitution was underlined by **salesman**, as well as **meat salesman**, **crack salesman**, **muff merchant** and **hustler**. The **poultry dealer** plays on *chicken*, a young gay man, and is thus a pimp who trades in young homosexuals (as also is the **queen of tarts**). Food is represented in a number of names: the pimp can be a **macaroni** (a play on mack), a **candyman** or **pudding eater** and, less obviously, an **Eastman** or **easeman**. This last is based on the black pronunciation of *yeast* as 'east'; one has the image of yeast as expanding and making a 'big man', or alternatively, yeast is required to make *dough* and thence *bread*, both of which are slang terms for money. Violence underpins the imagery of the **twat-faker** (literally 'cunt-maker'), **twat-masher** and **beard-jammer**.

The pimp can be a **player** or a **gamer**, a **boss lady** and a **stud**. Since the 1930s he has been commonly known as a **daddy** – extended as **daddy-o**, **swing daddy**, **big daddy**, **sweet daddy** and also as **puff daddy**, a pimp whose girls specialise in oral sex. The pimp can be a **jockey** or **ho jockey**, a **lowrider** (from a figurative sense of his morals being 'low') and an **easy rider**.

Australia calls the pimp a **red bob** or **red quid**, which extend and personify the basic term, the *red shilling* (also *red deener* or *red penny*), that is the money that has been earned by a prostitute and passed to her pimp; thus the **red penny man** is that pimp (red, like scarlet, has sinful connotations). The **hoon** is another Australian term, dating from the 1930s and meaning both a flashy lout and a pimp. The slang expert Sydney Baker suggested that it is a contraction of Jonathan Swift's *houyhnhnm* (the anthropomorphic horses of *Gulliver's Travels*, 1726), but they are seen as intelligent beings. Rather it is their human slaves (the yahoos) who are the fools – and noted as such in dictionaries.

Finally a pair of definite literary references. A **pal joey** comes from the book *Pal Joey* (1940), by American novelist John O'Hara, while **iceberg slim** (ultimately from the standard English *iceberg*, an unemotional person) immortalises the street name of Robert Beck (1918–92), the one-time pimp and author of a series of autobiographical books. With his professional expertise Beck was doubtless ranked among the **hard legs**, men who devoted all their time and energies to pursuing the street life and the world of strictly male endeavour.

A Hierarchy of Pimps

The Superior Pimp
Whatever the outside world may think of them, pimps themselves have a hierarchy. It has been in place since the 17th century when a **pimp whisk**, **pimp-whiskin** or **pimp-whisking** was the name of a first-rate pimp. The term also came to mean a mean-spirited bigot, which is more logical, since *whisk* usually equates with the wholly derogatory *whipper-snapper*. Other terms post-date the 1960s: the euphemistic **account executive**, the **boss player**, a thoroughly experienced, professional, worldly wise pimp who may even transcend pimping for superior occupations, and the **promoted pimp**, a veteran who gives advice to other pimps or to their prostitutes.

The Pimp in Rhyming Slang

In pimping as in much else, one cannot avoid rhyming slang. *Pimp* itself gives **fish and shrimp** but the majority rhyme on *ponce*:

alphonse
candle (and) sconce
Charlie Ronce
Harry Ronce
joe bonce
Johnny Ronce
Jo Ronce

The remaining terms are Australian and rhyme on *hoon*:

dish ran away with the spoon
egg and spoon
loon
silver or **silvery spoon**
terry toon

The Inferior Pimp

Where there is good there is also bad, and the second-rate pimp has his own nomenclature. In the 1930s to 1950s, the **coffee-and pimp** or **coffee-and-mac** was a small-timer, whose women barely made him a living, let alone provided the high style to which he would aspire. The term comes from the tramp use *coffee-and*, meaning 'coffee and cakes' or 'coffee and doughnuts', as provided in cheap cafes; the resulting adjective referred to anything seen as cheap, minimal, second-rate, in other words worth little more than the barest of snacks.

Others made a similar connection. The **chump** offered a new interpretation of the long-standing word for a fool, and meant,

in 1970s black-American use, a pimp who barely got by; its extensions *chile-chump* or *chili-chump* were based on the stereotypical
incompetence of small-time Mexican pimps and referred specifically
to a pimp who has only one woman working for him. It was also
found as *chile* or *chili pimp*, *chili-bowl pimp* or *chili-mac*, and the
reference to 'bowl' may suggest that for once chile/chili was not a
generic for Mexican but a reference to another cheaply purchased
dish. In the same period, a *cigarette pimp*'s women make him
no more than cigarette money and he may even have to do their
soliciting for them, while the *simple pimp* is another who barely
manages. From the 1960s, again in black-American use, a *popcorn
pimp* made just about enough for popcorn, while the contemporary
welfare pimp was forced to collect the welfare checks properly due
to his prostitutes.

The Violent Pimp and the Kindly Pimp
Pimping is by its very nature violent, even if that violence is
destructive of the spirit rather than the body. From the 1960s,
black-American terms for a physically violent pimp were a *gorilla
pimp* or *hard mack*. Perhaps surprisingly, there are, at least as
recorded, more terms for those who prefer the carrot to the (pimp)
stick, and all are based on the word 'sweet'. From the 1920s in
America, the *sweetback* or *sweetback man* took his name from
his physique, which women like to touch, but there was also the
sweetman in the same period, and this term crossed the Atlantic
as well. In the 1970s, there was the black-American *sugar pimp*,
also known as a *sweet pimp* or *sweet sugar*, or *Sweet Willie*, who
was any kindly and attentive man; he could be a pimp too, but
the term usually referred to a pose used when 'catching' a new
whore.

The Pimping Life

If the prostitute, at least in Britain, is *on the game*, then the pimp,
across the Atlantic, hopes to *have game*. The game had meant sexual
intercourse as far back as 1460, and it was first used for a prostitute,
as a collective noun describing a group of brothel girls, in 1593. The

pimping sense, that of an ability to manipulate humanity (usually for financial gain), is an 18th-century coinage, although the modern underpinning, which adds in urban sophistication and street wisdom, is only recorded from the 1960s.

The game appears in a number of phrases from that period, primarily in black-American use. To **get one's game together** as a pimp is to define one's image by a variety of material/symbolic 'props'; to **run down the game** is to explain the principles of the pimping business, whether an experienced pimp educating a novice or the pimp telling his prostitutes the tricks of their trade. To **talk** or **spit game** can simply be to talk, but in the context of the pimp's life it is to discuss pimping, whoring and those involved; to **reverse game** is for a pimp to manipulate the relationships of his prostitutes to his best advantage.

Freelancers and Part-timers

Despite all the elaborate structure, some girls remain impervious and prefer to **freelance**, a contemporary term for working without a pimp. They reject the supposed security of the stable, and their status is either that of the **orphan** or the **outlaw** (terms used in America from the 1930s onwards). In the 1980s, they were said to operate an **open game**. Last of all these independent operators is the contemporary **weekend ho**, a part-time prostitute without a pimp, although she may be helping out her boyfriend with some extra cash.

The first recorded term for pimping was the verb to **man**, seen in the 17th century; but while the pimp himself has attracted a number of names, his activities have accrued far less. There is the late 19th-century **carry the cosh**, but this London term was hardly a tribute to modern pimping skills as feted in New York and other

American cities: it referred to the ambushing and robbing of the prostitute's client. Far more pertinent is the (again) black-American term used from the 1960s onwards – *the Book*, and the associated phrase to *work by the book*. The capitalised Book (comparisons with the Bible are not coincidental) has never been written down: it is the oral tradition that forms the basis of black pimping. Thus to conduct one's professional life by its tenets was to keep to the recognised 'rules and regulations' of the pimping life, supposedly enshrined in its authoritative pages.

Finding and Keeping Women
Before a pimp sets about organising his women and profiting from their work, it is necessary to find them. All the following terms appear from the 1960s onwards, mostly (or at least origin-ally) in America. The pimp either has to *hit on* suitable candidates or use one of his experienced women to *cast the net* and bring a new girl into the team. If he does it himself then he will don his *copping clothes*, a particularly smart get-up worn specifically to maximise his charms; if all goes well he seals the deal with a *copping fuck*. This done he *downs*, *turns her out* or *puts her on the block/corner*: all mean to launch her into her career on the street.

In turn the prostitute who wishes to work for a given pimp is said to *choose* him, and on joining his 'team' offers him a financial gift – the *choosing money* or *claiming bread* – which both initi-ates and cements the relationship. He will kit her out in the working clothes known as *bonds*, since his money has paid for them and they thus symbolically bind her to him. It is then up to her to make her *trap*, the number of customers a prostitute's pimp assigns as a daily tally to ensure she reaches a specified financial target. If she fails, her daily take is considered *short money*. The *short-money game*, however, is the money that a pimp can make from a prostitute who works for him for only a short period. The *share certificate* (the pimp has invested in her) and the *stick*, the 'tool' whereby he can solve any financial problems, reflect the essentially commercial relationship between the pimp and his stable of women.

The Stable

Whether or not the term is a conscious reference to the slang term *ride* for sexual intercourse, the pimp's girls are known as his *stable* (a term that can also be used of a girl's regular clients) from the 1920s onwards. An individual prostitute can be a *stable sister*, while the pimp is the *stable boss*. To stable is for the pimp to enrol a whore, and to *stable up* is for the woman to agree to join those already working for him. His stable might also be the *flock*, the *nest*, the *family* and the equestrian *corral* or *string (of ponies)*; the pimp *strings* or *pushes ponies* and the working girls are *in harness*. An alternative name is the *line*, and when such a group walk the streets alongside their pimp they are known as a *ho train*. A single prostitute – other than his favourite and thus most privileged woman – can be a *lady*, an *old lady*, a *wife* (also a name for his favourite) or *sister-in-law*. The pimp himself could be a *brother-in-law*.

The stable is by no means equal and there are prizes, albeit titular, for the number-one worker. The most reliable and experienced of its members is the *bottom woman* (also *bottom*, *bottom baby*, *bottom bitch*, *bottom ho* or *bottom lady*), which is based on the standard English *bottom*, a foundation. Logic suggests that the *top woman* is her opposite but she is not – she is her peer. So too is the *stomp-down woman* or *stomp-down whore*, the hardest working of the stable. If one isn't a woman, then one is a bitch, and the same privileged position is held by the *main bitch*, *mama bitch* or *boss bitch*. She can equally be a *main chick*, *main girl*, *main ho*, *main lady*, *main stuff* or *main whore*, the *head chick*, or the *star (of the line)*.

The pimp's overriding philosophy is summed up in the phrase ***cop, lock and block***: to obtain a prostitute, to secure her to his stable and to ensure that no other pimp is able to lure her away. It comes from slang's *cop*, to obtain, the standard word *lock*, which here means both to secure the girl in the stable and maintain her emotional and economic fidelity, and *cock block*, usually used of sexual advances but here of resisting any other pimp's attempt to lure her away; such an invader is known as a ***pirate***. That is the perfect theory; it may not work, in which case the aim is to ***cop and blow*** – to exploit an unsatisfactory prostitute for as much money as possible and then abandon her.

Chapter 9

THE AGENTS OF
THE LAW

I guyed, but the reeler he gave me hot beef
And a scuff came about me and hollered;
I pulled out a chive but I soon came to grief,
And with screws and a james I was collared

'Dagonet', 'A Plank Bed Ballad' in
The Referee, 12 February 1888

Although the police could claim a substantial pre-history, with the constables, bailiffs and watchmen of earlier centuries all possessing various powers of arrest and control, and earning a wide variety of canting names to accompany them, the police 'proper' do not appear until the establishment of the London Metropolitan Police – popularly known since the 1940s as *the Met* – in 1829.

THE MANY NAMES FOR THE POLICE

Proper Names

Of all the proper names that have been used to identify a policeman (because historically they almost always have been male), none comes within striking distance of the popularity of the very first: the ***bobby***, with its short-lived but related 'cousin' the ***peeler***. 'Bobby' himself is generally accepted as having been the then British prime minister Sir Robert Peel (1788–1850), who established the force. In popular and immediate use this was surely true, but the slang lexicographer John Camden Hotten writes in the 1860 edition of his *A Dictionary of Modern Slang, Cant and Vulgar Words*:

> The term is, however, older. The official square-keeper, who is always armed with a cane to drive away idle and disorderly urchins, has, time out of mind, been called by said urchins Bobby the Beadle. Bobby is also an old English word for striking, or hitting, a quality not unknown to policemen.

Bobby has also given a number of compounds: ***bobby's labourers***, volunteers who joined up as special constables during the Fenian scares of the 1860s; ***bobby twister***, a thug who will stop at nothing, even killing a policeman; and ***bobby peeler***, a policeman. The peeler or *Mr Peeler* did not really outlive the 19th century, other than in Northern Ireland, and was originally restricted to the Irish constabulary.

Other proper names are many and varied. The ***jack***, yet another generic use of the given name, appeared in the late 19th century, as did the ***cook's own***, with its semi-military suggestion of a 'regiment' of policemen and referring to the alleged propensity of policemen for flirting with the 'below stairs' servants of London houses. At the same time, ***demon*** appeared, meaning a detective or a policeman; it was often abbreviated to *D* in Australia. While ***dick*** is usually used today to refer to the detective branch, it started as a more general term in the 1910s. A popular etymology sees this linked to the fictional Dick Tracy, but as he was created in 1931, chronology mitigates against this derivation; a more likely root is in the gyspy term *dicked*, being watched (itself from *dekko*, a glance). Dick is often found as a compound, e.g. the ***house dick***, a hotel detective.

Subsequent 20th-century terms include a ***roger***, ***Johnny Nab*** and ***Uncle Nabs*** (from *nab*, to arrest), and ***charlie nebs***, which combines slang's black-American *Mr Charlie*, a white man, and *neb*, a beak (and thus linking back to the much earlier *harman beck*, a constable or bailiff). The identification of the white man with an oppressive authority continues in the native Australian ***gunji*** (otherwise a white man), and the West Indian (originally Rastafarian) ***Babylon*** (or ***bab***), which covers the entire white power structure as well as the police ensconced in their ***Babylon House***. America's ***three-bullet Joey*** makes general use of the proper name, as do *irv*, *irvine* and ***Charlie Irvine*** (which may have been based on a specific investigator).

Fiction and Show Business

More proper names have been culled from the worlds of fiction and show business. If there were justice in fiction, the name adopted by slang for a policeman would possibly be Lestrade, but the reality is that it is that of ***Sherlock (Holmes)***, with or without his surname. The great consulting detective, created by Sir Arthur Conan Doyle (1859–1930), was first co-opted to the United States in the 1950s. Almost as popular, at least in this context, is ***hawkshaw***, taken from Hawkshaw the Detective, a character created by Henry Cecil Bullivant for such books as 1935's *The Ticket-of-Leave Man* (the title of which was itself taken from *The Ticket-of-Leave Man*, an 1863 play by the English dramatist Tom Taylor); the name also appears in the comic strip 'Hawkshaw the Detective' by the American cartoonist Gus Mager (d.1956). As noted above, ***Dick Tracy***, a cartoon strip created by Chester Gould in 1931 for the Chicago Tribune/New York News syndicate, was not in fact the root of *dick*, but rather an adoption of that name, plus the standard verb *trace*, to uncover. His own name was swiftly added to the roster of police, and was joined in the 1960s by a punning female counterpart, the ***dickless tracy***. A final Americanism was the ***keystone***, drawn from Hollywood's Keystone Kops, a group of comical, incompetent policemen created by director Mack Sennett (1884–1960) in 1912; they featured in a number of films made by his Keystone Studios.

Back in Britain one finds ***the Bill***, or more usually ***the old Bill***, a name that was originated by Captain Bruce Bairnsfeather for the cartooned British soldier he drew for the First World War. Many such soldiers, if they survived the trenches, were taken on by the London police, and Old Bill, once a *tommy*, was now in new employment. The name gave the ***bill-shop***, the police station, and the ***bill wagon***, yet another synonym for the black maria, as well as the localised ***Bill from the Hill*** – the police of Notting Hill Gate in west London.

Given the volume of TV cop shows, it is hardly surprising that they too have made a mark on the vocabulary. Thus ***dibble***, taken

from Officer Dibble, a character in the TV cartoon series *Top Cat*;
five-oh (or *5-0*) which comes from the 1960s show *Hawaii Five-0*;
and the ***Kojak with a Kodak***, a police officer manning a radar speed
trap whose name acknowledged the Telly Savalas vehicle of the 1970s.
Given the vast popularity of *The Muppet Show*, created by Jim
Henson in 1976, it is perhaps surprising that ***muppet*** is invariably
used to sneer, as much at the police as at civilians.

Gay Men and Policemen

The gay world, at least in its camper side, has always gone
for proper names, usually those that deliberately 'effeminise'
the consciously macho police who traditionally manifest a
good deal of homophobia. Thus one encounters **Lucy**, **Lily**
or **Lillian Law**, **Miss Lily**, **Tilly (Law)**, **Brenda Bracelets**,
Jennifer Justice, **Hilda Handcuffs** and the vice squad's **Vera**
or **Victoria Vice**. Present-day gay South Africa uses some of
the above, as well as the surname-free **Priscilla** and **Theresa**.
The same circles have **Betty Blue** (which is the title of a
French film from 1986) and **betty bangles**, referring both to
the officer and his handcuffs. Gay slang also offers **our friend
with the talking brooch**, i.e. the walkie-talkie radio clipped
to the front of the uniform.

   Prior to laws against entrapment the ***crapper dick*** was a
plain-clothes policeman who specialised in hanging around
public lavatories in the hope of entrapping gay men into
having sex; the term also applied to an extortionist who
poses as a policeman to blackmail homosexuals.

   The American term ***Bobsey Twins*** takes a new look at the chil-
dren's adventure story characters created in 1904 by 'Laura Lee Hope'
(Edward Stratemeyer), as well as giving a nod to British bobbies.
Stratemeyer was also responsible for the ***Rover Boys***, another

fictional creation who gave their name to the police. Other real-life celebrities have been turned into cant coppers, such as **Sam and Dave** and **Junior Walker and the All-Stars** (who in this incarnation don't sing, but walk the beat).

The Uniform

Plain-clothes detectives aside, and they came later, what distinguished the world's first police force was the uniform. It was dark blue (a deliberate antithesis to military red) and the bulk of terms that reflect on the uniform have maintained that link. (The high top hat they also wore didn't have the same appeal.) Indeed the link of blue to authority goes back earlier; the **admiral of the blue** had been used since the early 18th century to refer to bailiffs or beadles, while a **bluecoat**, again a beadle, dated back to the late 16th century.

However, the mass of terms followed 1829 and there were plenty to choose from. The *lobster* had meant a soldier (from their red coats, although the term had originally been used for the full suits of armour worn by Hazelrigg's Cuirassiers, a unit who fought with Cromwell's New Model Army in the English Civil War); the **unboiled lobster**, however, is blue-black, and thus the term, along with its synonyms **raw lobster** or **uncooked lobster**, suited the new policeman's uniform. (In the 1930s in America, the **lobster-box** was a cell in a police station.) Since the mid-19th century, related names have included the **blue devil**, the **bluejacket**, the **bluey**, the **gentleman in blue (and white)**, the **royal blues**, the **blues**, and the **boys in blue, bellies in blue, blokes in blue, boys blue** or **men in blue**. To **wear the blue and buttons** was to be a member of the police, but to **bilk the blues** was to evade capture by them. The **bluebottle** of the 1830s leads to America's 1850s *fly* (later **shoo-fly**), coined around 1890 and based on the traditional song lyrics 'Shoo fly! Don't bother me'.

A range of mainly American terms kept up the flow for the new century: a policeman might be a **little boy blue**, a **blue boy** or a **blue light** (also a police car) or the **blue light special** (which plays on American restaurants' blue plate specials). The 1970s **blue pig** combined the colour with the hippies' term of choice (see Pigs and Other Animals, page 241), while the 1950s gave **baby-blues** and, with a slight twist, the *sky* (who might also be a prison warder if he wore a blue uniform). The 1918 song 'My Sweet Little Alice Blue Gown' gave the camp *Alice Blue Gown* or *Miss Alice*.

Not all police uniforms are blue: the *black beetle* was a mid-19th-century term for a constable in the Thames River police (the 1950s *beetle* was any policeman), a *brown bomber* was an Australian parking warden c.1950. A *khaki* has been a county police officer in America, a *ginger* plays the same role in brown-uniformed South Africa, and the *green bean* or *greenfly* is a township municipal police officer there too. (A *green hornet*, with its additional reference to the NBC radio series *The Green Hornet*, was a New York City police patrol car in the 1960s, suggested by the colour scheme of the time.) The *red seam* has been a Caribbean policeman since the 1910s: it refers to the stripe running up the uniform trousers; the same red stripe also gives *woodpecker*, which is similarly marked.

Colours aside, the 20th century contributed the simple *uniform* and the *brassey* (from his brass buttons). England has *tithead* (a general insult that also notes the shape of the policeman's helmet), while the *big hat* is the American equivalent, referring to the headgear used by many police officers and state troopers. Perhaps the best-known reference is to the *harness*, the Sam Browne belt favoured by some American forces. The term had meant clothes since the 17th century; the police use was coined in the mid-19th century. It gives the *harness bull*, *harness boy*, *harness cop*, *harness gent*, *harness guy* and *harness man*.

The Badge

The main identification of authority is the *badge*, which itself can stand in for its wearer. America has coined many other terms based on this important accesssory. Sergeants in the mid-19th-century New York police carried copper badges (patrolmen had brass ones; those of lieutenants and captains were silver, while a *gold-badge man* was a city detective). It was this badge that led to what remains the best-known term for a policeman: the *copper* or *cop* (the use was strengthened by the slang verb *cop*, to capture). In compounds it adds the *copper house* or *copper's shanty*, the police station, and *copper jitters*, an excessive fear of the police that verges on obsession.

The use of *tin*, another word for the badge, has been recorded since the early 20th century (although *tin ribs*, a policeman, appeared in the late 19th). It can be used to mean to take advantage of one's position, obtaining a range of gifts and favours – free meals, drinks, etc. – by showing one's official badge. The *tinner* or *tin shield* was the policeman and the *tin wife* his own 'better half'; the *tin star* is usually a private detective or a country police officer. The badge is often shaped like a shield, and thus *shield* too stands for its wearer; the *star* plays the same role. The *buzzer*, another alternative, comes from the officer's 'buzzing' it in one's face and can mean the policeman as well as the badge. Finally, the *tomato can* is the badge worn by a local or small-town police officer; the inference is of course of the cheapness of its manufacture.

The Truncheon

Other than handcuffs, which seem to have inspired nothing but the camp Brenda Bangles and Hilda Handcuffs (see page 236), the final element in the police uniform is his truncheon. The earliest term for this was America's *locust*, from locust wood, the material from which the early clubs were made. The United States also offered the *shill*; this came from the Irish *shillelagh*, a cudgel, and underpinned the links between the Irish and the police. The late 19th-century *tomahawk* and the modern *nigger stick* both played to racism in the force, while the 1970s British policeman personalised his truncheon as *Mr Wood* or *Charlie Wood*.

The Irish

In the big cities of America policemen have always been associated with 19th-century Irish immigration and what are seen as 'typical' Irish names have often been used to denote a policeman. From the 1960s to the present day, there's been *Muldoon*, *Murphy* and *O'Malley*, but the most famous dates from the 1940s: *Paddy*, itself an all-purpose term for any Irishman. Paddy gives the *paddy wagon*, a piece of racist stereotyping that has long since been overlooked, and this is one of most widely used equivalents of the black maria. Other 'Irish' policemen include the 1900s **biddy**, i.e. Bridget, and the English **jerry** of the 1910s. The team of **Gallagher and Shean**, used around the 1910s–1920s, was not as Irish as it may have seemed. The real Gallagher and Shean were contemporary vaudeville stars; Gallagher was Ed Gallagher (*c*.1872–1929) and genuinely Irish; Shean, however, was the Jewish Marx Brothers' equally Jewish uncle, Al Schoenberg (1868–1949), who in 1914 had written their hit show *Home Again*.

The Police in Rhyming Slang and Backslang

The main source for rhyming slang policemen is *copper* or *cop*:
bottle (and stopper)
clodhopper
dime a pop
ginger-pop
grasshopper (used in First World War as a military
   policeman)
greasy (mop)
lemon drop
lollipop
pork chop (also of course linked to *pig*)
silk and top
spinning top
string and top
woodentop (refers to the BBC children's TV series,
   launched in 1965)

Australia also rhymes on *cop* with:
hop

---

hot scone (= john = *john hop*)
john hop
johnny hop
jonn
jonnop

Other rhymes include:
blueberry (hill) (= Old Bill, also underpinned by the blue
    uniform)
club and stick (= dick)
hammer and saw (= the law)
Uncle Wilf (= the filth)

The police were also recognised in the short-lived backslang
of the 19th century:
esclop (the police, pronounced 'slop')
nam (the man)
namesclop (the policeman, pronounced 'namslop')

Pigs and Other Animals

The police, of course, liked to pretend that the word was an
acronym, for 'Pride, Integrity and Guts', but not many outside the
squad room were listening. For most people *pig* appears to be a
coinage of the Sixties, used by black militants and white hippies.
The reality is that it has been recorded since the early 19th century,
as seen by the example cited by the *Lexicon Balatronicum* in 1811:
'The pigs frisked my panney, and nailed my screws; the officers
searched my house, and seized my picklock keys.' The use lapsed
by the 1870s, but was back in force for the 1960s, notably in the
slogan *Off the pigs!*, i.e. Kill the police! Since then one finds the
pig brother, used of any black (i.e. a *brother*) who informs against
their own people to the (white) police; *pig heaven*, the police
station, and *pig wagon*, a police van. The police as a whole have

become *pork, porker* or *bacon,* and a policeman might be a *grunter,* an *oink* or *oinker,* a *hamhead* (which originally meant a fool) or a *cozzer* or *cosser* (based on the Yiddish *chaser,* a pig). South Africa's *vark,* from the Afrikaans term for pig, is another general term of abuse used for a specific insult. *Johnny ham,* a detective, was coined in the 1930s.

Not all animals are pigs; neither are all police. The most widely used animal alternative has been America's *bull,* which comes from the synonymous German slang *bulle* (or possibly Spain's *bul*) and has been used since the late 19th century. A variant is *bulladeen,* used in the 1960s, and the *bull wagon* is a black maria. Bull has given the *bullbuster,* one who is obsessed with assaulting the police, the *fresh bull,* a police officer who cannot be bribed, and the *wise bull,* a detective. The bull can be job specific, e.g. the *narcotics bull* or *motorcycle bull*; the *night bull* works nights. The *bull trap* impersonates an official in order to extort money (although as *bully trap* the term was used from the late 18th century and as such may not in fact be linked to the animal); to be *bull simple* is to be frightened of the police and the *bull horrors* are that fear turned into terror, and often experienced by heavy drug users.

Animal has been used since the 1910s, while the *beast, beastman* and *beastboy* emerged among the British black community of the 1970s; the *beast wagon* is a black maria. Dogs give the early 19th-century *bloodhound* and the 20th-century *bandog,* although that term had been in use since the 17th century to mean a bailiff or his assistant. The word combines the standard word *band,* a chain, and dog. A *bandog* was originally a large guard-dog, and the term re-entered standard use in the 1980s to describe a cross-breed of Neapolitan mastiffs and American pit bull terriers. The *bear* had a short-lived popularity during the Citizens' Band radio craze of the 1970s; it was an abbreviation of the US Forest Service's mascot Smokey the Bear, used in United States fire prevention campaigns, and *smoky* or *smoky bear* were used for a traffic policeman and Highway Patrolman, while a *smokey beaver* or *mama smokey* was a female (motorcycle) police officer.

Generic Terms and Proper Names

Gendarme is one branch of France's police, and the word has been borrowed to mean a policeman in Britain from the early 19th century onwards; synonyms exist in the forms **jenny** and **johnny darby** (in both of which the *darby* refers to the *darbies* or handcuffs he carries). **John Dunn** is an even more tortured pronunciation. The **Feds** and their former boss the late **J. Edgar** (Hoover) have also been used to mean the mainstream police, and the American **Statie** is a state police officer. Finally Irvine Welsh's *Trainspotting* introduced readers to the **labdick** – not, as might appear, a forensic scientist, but a member of the Lothian and Borders (LAB) Constabulary.

Violence

The police, at least in Britain, are a force, and one cannot avoid the existence of a degree of violence in both their policing and their slang-based nicknames.

The imagery began in the 19th century with the **tapper** (who had been a 17th-century bailiff) and the **land shark**, who had begun life as a ruffian or thug. **Scuffer** is based on dialect's *scuff*, to strike, and underlined by Yorkshire's *scuff*, 'a mean, sordid fellow, the scum of the people' (*English Dialect Dictionary*); alternatively it refers to the standard word *scurf*, the back of the neck, and thus one who grabs you by it. A variant is the **skupter**, and the **judy scuffer** is a policewoman. The mid-19th century added the **crusher** (hinting at the policeman's large, booted feet), a term also used in the Royal Navy for a ship's corporal; to **put the crusher on** was to mount a police raid.

At the end of the 19th century, forceful images persisted with Australia's **cosher**, Britain's **rozzer**, **razzer** or **roz** (most likely derived from the Romany *roozlo*, a villain, and still in use today), and America's **clubber**. This last was used specifically of the New York policeman Alexander 'Clubber' Williams, known as the Czar of the Tenderloin. It was Williams who seems to have coined the use of 'Tenderloin' for a city's red-light area and entertainment centre:

when in 1876 he was transferred from the city's Gas House District (around impoverished East 35th Street) to West 13th Street station, at the heart of Broadway's nightclubs, casinos and brothels, he announced: "'I like it fine. I have had chuck [i.e. a cheap cut of steak] a long time, and now I'm going to eat tenderloin.' The area would be duly rechristened.

The 20th century brought in the **slapman**, the **skull-buster**, the **pounder** (who pounded a beat as well as heads), the **paddler** (from standard English *paddle*, to beat) and Australia's **walloper** or **wal**. Alongside these were the **head-whupper**, **head-knocker**, **head-beater**, **head-breaker** and **head-buster**. The 1970s **whips** was self-explanatory, a black term that could refer to the entire white establishment. A policeman could also be a **door shaker**, from the way in which patrolling police or security guards shake doors to check that they are locked. Two modern terms are the **buster** and the **G-smack**, in which G stands for *gangsta*.

The police might also be equated with notorious agencies of violence: the term **Cossack** was used between the mid-19th century and 1930s, especially of police used for strike-breaking. The ultimate reference was to the Turkish tribe living to the north of the Black Sea, who were organised into cavalry and fought for the Polish army, then the Russians. The 1950s added the **gestaps** or **Gestapo**, from the German *Geheime Staatspolizei*, the internal police force used by the German Nazi regime 1933–45.

Violence can also be seen as underpinning the 19th century's **blooming six foot of tripe**, the **block** (i.e. his hardness of heart) and the **bulky**, which mixes the standard use of *bulky*, sizeable, with the word's 17th-century sense: pompous, self-important. More recent variations offer the **drack**, from Dracula, and the **knocko**, **knocker** or **knockman** (especially used of the drugs squad, who may pause to knock on the door before kicking it down and then possibly knocking on skulls). The 1970s–1980s British black **radication** contracts the standard English word *eradication* and reflects what was seen as the Metropolitan Police's violent and racist attitude towards black youth. Finally, since the 1950s **the heat** has meant both police pressure and the police themselves.

The Peasant and the Fool

Early policemen were often recruited from the countryside, and those they encountered in the big cities tended to use the same insults for these new recruits as they would for any peasant, seen as lacking the sophistication of a born city-dweller.

Among such terms were the *lob*, a country bumpkin since the 16th century, a *five-barred gate* (a countryside staple), and America's *hoosier*, which had originally been used for a native of Indiana and thence for any peasant or rustic simpleton; the 1910s saw the term used for a local small-town police officer. The countryside also underpins the *clown* or *town clown*, the local officer, and the *nod*, *noddy* or *noddy man* which, with its extension the *noddy bike* (a police motorcycle), is linked to Enid Blyton's *Noddy* books (first published in 1949). However, the policeman there is Mr Plod, while Noddy is in fact a wooden toy, therefore the link must be assumed to be to a policeman's perceived stupidity rather than to his actual profession. Alternatively, there may be a connection between the police helmet and Noddy's pointed hat which, if nothing else, is blue.

On the Beat

A *flat* in slang is a sucker or a fool, usually up from the country, and it is hard to state unequivocally whether the mid-19th-century *flattie*, *flatty*, *flatty-cop* or *flatter* refers to this aspect of a recruit or to the contemporaneous nickname, the *flatfoot*, which undoubtedly stems from his large, perambulating boots; to *flatfoot* was to walk like a policeman.

Other terms offer no such problems. A *trot* and a *stalk* are from the 19th century (although the latter may just refer to the officer's height); more recent are the *pavement pounder*, the *sidewalk snail* and the *beat-basher* or *beat-pounder*. The *lumberer* is an Australian traffic cop. Direct references to the boots are found in *beetle-crusher*, *rubber sole* and *squeaky shoe*, the last of which tends to be a detective. The *rubber heel*, *rubber glue* or *soft heel* is also a detective, and often a private one. Finally, while noddy may seem mis-characterised,

Mr Plod is spot-on. Toyland's policeman entered the canon in 1954 as a real-life policeman, often abbreviated as *plod*.

The Arresting Officer

If the policeman has any primary role it is the making of arrests, snatching up the villains and taking them away. Thus the earliest such form, the 17th century's *prig-* or *prigger-napper* was literally a 'thief-taker'. The prig in this context most likely comes from standard English *prig*, to prick or sting and by extension to rob or to cheat.

The literal meaning of *charpering omee*, a term drawn from the theatre's quasi-Italian Lingua Franca and used in the mid-19th century for a policeman, is 'catching man'. It is based in the far older Italian slang *chiappare*, to catch or seize. *Charper* also leads to the *charpering carsey*, the police station. The period also gives the *nabman* and *nabbing-cull* (the *nabber* is a 1940s usage; at this stage it meant a thief), and of the many other terms around, *trap* was more than averagely popular. Used most often in the plural – *the traps* – the word meant what it said and had been recorded since at least 1707. It was still found in Australia and the United States in the mid-20th century, but it sounds very archaic.

On the same theme the policeman can be variously a *catcher*, a *grab*, a *claw*, a *nailer* and a *snatcher*. He can be a *frog* (who 'leaps' on to criminals). Australia offers the *hoonchaser* (from slang's *hoon*, a flashy lout), while South Africa has the *gata*, from a Sotho word *legatha* (literally 'catch a thief') or perhaps from their *gats* (guns).

Miscellaneous Names

The remainder of the names for police are unclassifiable and are best considered in chronological order. The *forty-pounder* was a 19th-century usage based on the £40 cash bonus awarded to any policeman who secured a 'Tyburn ticket', i.e. captured a murderer. Other terms coined in that century include the *ossifer*, still considered a 'funny' variation on the standard English *officer*.

The 20th century added *the boys* and *the chaps*, Ireland's *shade* (from his 'shadowing' a villain through the streets), the **ready-eye** (another surveillance artist) and the **hack** (possibly a descendant of *hawk*, a bailiff). The 1920s coined a term that remains among the most popular, even if it reached its peak in the 1960s and 70s: the **fuzz**. Its first appearance was in the *Los Angeles Times*, 30 January 1924, even if the journalist was hardly helpful to his uninitiated readership:

> A 'mob' can 'beat a pap' to the 'leather' and get away with it with the ordinary 'fuzz' lookin' on. But it's a twenty-to-one shot when the 'cannon coppers' are wise.

The origins of fuzz are sometimes claimed to be in the phrase 'the man with the fuzzy [i.e. manly] balls', but are probably more prosaic: standard English *fuss*, which is what an investigating policeman makes. The term is thus linked to slang's policeman the **busy**, often **the busies**, usually used of the detective force, who – again – are rushing around.

Let us conclude what is really a near infinite list with the otherwise obscure **mermaid**, based on the mythical fish-women (themselves taken from the Greek sirens) reputed to lure sailors to their doom. In modern New Zealand the mermaids are police officers manning a weigh station. Why? Because they are 'cunts with scales'.

THE DETECTIVE

The Plain-clothes Man

The standard English *plainclothes*, as in the clothes worn by a police detective, was first recorded in 1852, although its next appearance had to wait a further half-century. Since then it has been common and if a single thing defines the detective department of any police force it is that they no longer wear the uniform that makes their colleagues so conspicuous. *In clothes* meant working as a detective in the 1970s, while the **quiet-clothes boy/bull** appeared in the 1930s.

Once garbed in his inconspicuous outfit, the detective supposedly became invisible and thus took on what was seen as his primary
role: that of a spy (and thus effectively an informer). He would be
off to **work up**, or follow his suspects, and once he had tracked
them down he would **pipe** (i.e. peep at) them. From the 1930s he
worked **undercover**, a word that could also be used for the man
himself. The same period suggests a detective is an **eagle-eye**, a
dummy (he kept silent), a **nose**, a **ferret** (he 'ferrets out' crime), a
plant, who lurked unseen, or a **shadow**. The 1920s **elephant ears**
presumably suggested an image of the pachyderm's large ears,
implying that the detective has the ability to hear more than normal.

The image of the detective's noiseless feet is found in such
20th-century terms as **slewfoot** (although that had originally meant
a shambling or clumsy person), a **pussyfoot, goosefoot** or **heavy foot**
(referring to the size of his boots – noticeable even if the rest of his
clothes were inconspicuous – rather than the sound of his footfalls),
which last was eventually abbreviated to **heavy** in Australia. And
once the spying was over, then came the arrest; thus such terms for
the detective as the **snatcher**, the **roper** (as in to *rope in*, to catch)
and the **stop** were all found in the 19th century. A more obvious
term was and remains the abbreviation **'tec**, first found in the 1880s.

Less classifiable terms (all coined in the late 19th century) are the
bloke, the **confidence-queen** (perhaps so called because in plain
clothes this female detective 'cons' her criminal victims), and the
elbow, a term that either played on the detective as the 'long arm of
the law' or as suggested by Patrick and Terence Casey, the authors
of *The Gay-cat* (1921): '"Elbow" comes from the detective's way of
elbowing through a crowd.'

Among the best-known terms of the 19th century, certainly in
America, was the *fly cop*. He might also be found as the *fly, fly bull,
fly copper, fly dick, fly man, fly mug, fly peeler* or *fly sleuth*; in all
cases the compound depended on slang's *fly*, meaning alert or aware.
The unspoken back-story was of course that their uniformed
colleagues were usually deficient in such intelligent qualities,
although fly cop could on occasion mean an alert or experienced
police officer. The 1920s–30s American *flyball*, however, means a
detective but seems to have taken its origins from baseball, where

a flyball was one that can be caught 'on the fly' or simply as an image is of a ball that travels far and fast.

Looking at the names accorded to police of all sorts, it is perhaps remarkable how forgiving are the criminals; very few are out-and-out abusive. But one that is, however, is *the filth*, a British term that has been used for plain-clothes men since the 1960s. And while it may not be an insult as such, the old stereotype that links the Irish to the police is found in *shamus*. Although suggestions have been made linking the word to the Hebrew/Yiddish *shames*, a synagogue official, the origin is far more likely *Seamus*, an Irish name once common among American policemen. As viewers of the 1940s film of Raymond Chandler's *Big Sleep* will know, the term is also used for a private eye, although Humphrey Bogart's pronunciation of the word as 'sharmus' continues to baffle fans.

The Private Detective

I reached for the doorknob of Linda LaMarre's dressing room. Before I could turn it I heard a gurgling screech from inside, followed by a heavy thud. I yanked the portal open, catapulted over the threshold. Then I froze as I lamped the gorgeous LaMarre cupcake writhing on the floor. Her squirms reminded me of a gaffed eel on a hot rock. I knew she was a goner the instant I hung the focus on her glazing glims, her bluish-purple mush, her protruding tongue. A guy doesn't have to be a doctor to recognize the symptoms of suffocation. The quail on the carpet was obviously passing to her reward; and not from natural causes, either.

Robert Leslie Bellem, 'Dead Heat' in
Hollywood Detective, January 1944

It's a very long way from the home (and indeed professional life) of Britain's plain-clothes fictional police detective Inspector Morse. The master of the private eye genre, Raymond Chandler, may have described his own Philip Marlowe as a 'private detective' when first we encounter him in the opening lines of *The Big Sleep* (1939), but to most fans of his favourite stamping ground – the pulp magazines of the 1930s and 1940s – he was a ***private dick***, ***private star***, ***private ticket*** or ***private eye***, the last of which tipped his fedora in the direction of Pinkerton's National Detective Agency (founded 1852), the epitome of establishment sleuthing, the logo of which was an eye.

He could be an ***operator*** or an ***op*** (the name used by Dashiell Hammett for his un-named hero, who was employed by the fictional Continental Detective Agency), a ***bishop*** (who 'searches out sin'), a ***gumshoe***, ***gumshoer***, ***gum boot*** or ***shoe***, ***squeaky shoe*** and a ***rubber heel***, all of which referred to the quietness of his footsteps as he tracked down some lowlife. Like a policeman he could be a ***copper***, the ***law*** or a ***piper*** (from ***pipe***, to look at). Less flattering were ***peeper***, ***snooper*** and ***weasel***.

Railroad Detectives

A small sub-group of detectives were those hired by American railroad companies, whose main job was to stop hobos from riding the rails for free. They could be ***shacks***, ***mugs***, ***cinder bulls*** or ***cinder dicks***, ***yard bulls***, ***railroad bulls*** or ***railroad dicks***. The yard being the railroad's marshalling yard, at which point a hobo might try to board a wagon of a stationary train. A ***fly mug*** was both a police detective and a railroad detective.

THE CORRUPT POLICEMAN

Heaven forfend, but one must admit: the police, while still quite possibly wonderful, are not quite the saintly examples of myth and self-promotion. Anyone who has enjoyed America's pulp magazines, dime novels and movies will know perfectly well that that country's police work hand-in-glove with villainy – whether professional or political – almost as a matter of occupational course. Britain has always professed to set its own officers above such venality, but a history of the force, especially that in London, will show that ever since the Met began, it has required some form of purging on a regular basis.

The Bent Copper

The **bent copper**, who has abandoned the straight and narrow and whose morals have been loose since at least the 1910s, is also the **right copper** – right, that is, as assessed by his villainous confederates in the 1930s to 1950s. 'Right' in this context has also created the **right town**, any American town or small city where the authorities – police, local politicians – have been bribed into allowing criminal activity to flourish. The phrase was popular in the first half of the 20th century, as was **right up**, which meant to corrupt those same authorities. Bent also lies behind the 1970s term **bananas**: it was used during the investigation of the (now-disbanded) London-based Special Patrol Group, the members of which were declared by their colleagues to be 'yellow, bent and hanging around in bunches'.

Briefly popular during a major 1970s investigation of the New York Police Department were **grass-eaters** and **meat-eaters**. The former accepted only small bribes, but the latter, not content with the payoffs, bribes and perks that are freely offered, actively compelled people to offer him such monies. That said, it may have been that these terms were more journalistic inventions than daily police (or criminal) usage.

Nor can one even trust that once bribed a policeman stays bribed. Unlike the **fresh bull**, who simply won't take a payoff, the **doubler** (used in Britain since the late 19th century) not only takes the offered bribe but still arrests you for the crime. There ain't, as they say, no justice.

The Payoff

Terms for corruption, if not corruption itself, seem to be relatively modern, as all these payoffs are 20th-century coinages. Once a policeman has made it clear that he is *on the make*, then the next step, at least in America, is to be enrolled on the *pad*: defined as the regular bribes paid to members of a United States police department in the form of an actual list (albeit not written down) laying out exactly who gets what, from the street-based patrolman right up to the Chief. In Britain, it is known as being *on a pension* and the bribe itself is known the *pension*, *rent* or in Australia *dog food*. The best-known term in Britain is the euphemistic *drink*: 'do you drink?' asks the villain after he has been arrested, sounding out the possibility of corrupting the officer. If the answer is 'yes' then the bribe itself is a *drink*. Literal drinking underpins the British term *freemans*, which refers to anything obtained for free, and particularly of a bribe given to a corrupt police officer. The word comes from the longer phrase to *drink at Freeman's Quay*, originally referring to the free drinks that were distributed at this quay near London Bridge to porters and carmen in the 19th century. The Royal Navy amplified it to *Harry Freemans* (and used it for anything, not merely drink, that was free), while the British Army shortened it to *Freemans*, a usage followed in the police.

There are, of course, no free lunches, and once *on the take* it is expected that the policeman gives as good as he gets. Thus the term *copping*, a British usage defined as turning a blind eye when necessary, including dropping charges, losing evidence and so on. Also in Britain, the police may *license* a favoured and generous villain, giving them permission to commit a given crime, e.g. prostitution or drug dealing, in return for bribes. Such protection is known in America as an *umbrella*, under which the criminals are safe from being 'rained on'.

To bribe a policeman was to *bug* him in the late 19th century and for him to accept the money was to *cop the drop* from the 1910s. He could also be *squared* and *straightened*. To *earn*, more euphemistically, meant to take bribes, and the *earner*, often as in 'nice little earner', is a bribe, especially when it is paid as regularly as more legitimate wages (the earner is not automatically corrupt: it can simply be a commercial opportunity). The 1940s *on the earn* meant to make money by illicit means, but one does not even need to be a real policeman to make money out of the uniform: the 1980s *rush act* is the impersonation of the police in order to extort bribes from fellow criminals.

THE INFORMER

'What is honour? A word. What is in that word honour? What is that honour? Air.' Like Falstaff in Shakespeare's *Henry IV Part I*, villains are not much impressed by honour and for all the theories of 'honour among thieves' there are more crimes solved by plain and simple informing than by police work, however dogged.

Informing Across the Centuries, from Boiling to Dobbing In

Informing is so widespread and long-recorded a phenomenon that not every term fits into a thematic group. Thus one is forced back on chronology, starting with the earliest recorded terms. Of the earliest is the late 16th-century *boil*, to inform on, and its noun form *boiling*, a betrayal. The image is of 'putting someone in hot water', although the presence of steam during boiling may link the words to standard English *smoke*, to unmask.

The 19th century was generous with its synonyms. To inform on or betray might variously be to *blow the gaff/gap*, to *put the light on*, to *put someone flash to*, to *give the cross-hop* or *the cross* (a *cross* was an informer), to *give the snap away* (possible reference to slang's *snap*, a share-out of booty) or to *throw over the bridge* (the image is of two confederates getting together to throw a third party from a metaphorical bridge). To *sell down/up the river* or *down the drain*, coined in America, is believed to refer to the practice of selling an errant slave to a Mississippi sugar-cane plantation; the journey to the plantation, where work was especially hard, was literally 'down the river'. One could *come it, give up, turn over* and *turn up, sell, shop, spot* or *do a sneak* (predating the school tell-tales of the 20th century).

The new century kept up the flow. The *gumshoe worker* was an informer; so too were the *funk*, an indirect use of *funk*, meaning fear (from Flemish *fonck*, fear by way of undergraduates at Oxford), the Australian **smoodger** (from *smoodge*, to ingratiate oneself) and the **spotter**. To inform was to **sink**, to **flop** and to **score on**. The 1920s added the **shelf** or **shelfer**, an Australian coinage based on the standard verb *shelf*, to place something, in this case information, aside. One might **put the blast on** or **put someone in** (i.e. prison), **turn on the leaks** (a *leak* was an informer). The tale-bearer might be a **brassey**, a **welcher** (a nationalist slur which usually applied to those who failed to pay their debts) or America's **faded boogie**, the origins of which are considered by the American lexicographer Geoffrey Irwin in his *American Tramp and Underworld Slang* (1931): 'Why the adjective "faded" is applied is hard to say, unless it is felt that the negro who turns informer has still less claim to identity than as a negro, and that he has faded from what small importance he formerly had.'

For whatever reason – the rise of fascism with its legions of informers? – the 1930s were prolific in coinages. Ever-inventive Australia offered the **gig**, the **top-off**, **topper** or **topper-off** and the **lemon**, who earned his name from his being 'squeezed' by an interrogator. This created the **lemon twist**, which described a gang's employment of a known police informer to give information about rival gangs to the police. To **jump** and to **put the arm** or **pin the rap on** (from *rap*, a criminal charge) and to **rattle the cup** (more usually associated with street beggary) were also popular new terms. The **bat carrier** seems sport-based, but there seems no logical connection to baseball (nor indeed cricket); instead the reference may be to *bat*, a Hindi term for language that had moved into slang via the Indian Army and the First World War. Meanwhile, the Second World War introduced the **wrong guy** – wrong that is from the criminal perspective – and to **go wrong**, to inform.

The post-war decades brought the **flip** (who 'turns you over'), the **backmark**, suggesting secrecy and deliberate concealment, and the **peasoup**, presumably a human version of London's dense and impenetrable fogs. In Australia, there was the **dobber**, which comes from *dob in*, to betray, itself based on the dialectal *dob*, to put down with a sharp, abrupt motion; thus the informer 'drops you in it', and can also be known as a **drop** (in which the primary meaning is underpinned by his willingness to 'drop a word in'). He also **puts** *a name up, cops out, cools in, gives up, fronts off, sends over, tips someone in* or *tips the pot.* The black-American term *tom slick* refers to one who first charms their criminal friends and then turns their names over to the police (there is perhaps a nod to an *Uncle Tom,* a black person who courts white approval). *Pussy claat,* from the Caribbean, is uncompromisingly insulting – the term properly means a cloth used to soak up menstrual blood. After that the *buster,* who gets one 'busted' or arrested, the *pop-off* (i.e. at the mouth), the *hater* and even the *shit-heel* or *shit-heeler* are positively affectionate terms for a police informer.

The Nose

The concept of the nose as an intrusive object is old. The standard use *poke/stick one's nose into* dates back to the early 17th century, as does to *nose something out;* to *nose around/about* is slang from the mid-19th century. The transfer from simple enquiry to the world of informing is hardly surprising.

As informers, the 18th-century *nose* and 19th-century *noser* make themselves clear; nose had meant to inform since the 19th century, while to *blow one's nose* appeared in the 1950s. *Snout* (ultimately another standard term for nose) was coined in the 1920s. The *conk* is also an informer, he 'sniffs things out', a thief who betrays his accomplices. The *conk* or *konk* is itself slang for nose and has been linked to the Latin *cocha,* a shell, and the Greek *kogcha,* anything hollow. Used verbally it means to 'poke one's nose in'. The mid-19th-century *smellerwank* sounds like a schoolyard insult; but *smeller* is another slang term for nose and thus this, too, is yet another derogatory term for an informer.

The best-known use of a nose-based term, however, is *snitch.* Its first use, in the late 17th century, was as a blow on the nose; then it meant the nose itself and, a century on (*c.*1790), the term was first employed in Britain to mean an informer (i.e. one who 'sticks their nose in'). It remains in use, especially in America, and since the 18th century, such variants as *snich, snitcher, snitching-rascal* and the early 20th-century Harlem *boot-snitch* have all emerged. The etymology is unknown, although there may be a link to dialect *snite,* to blow the nose with a thumb and finger. Since the 18th century, **snitch** and **turn snitch** have meant to inform, as do their variants **snitch off**, **snitch on/upon** and **snitch out (on)**. *Snitching* is informing and a **snitch-off** an act of betrayal, and the word has inspired a number of compounds, usually found in American prisons. The best known is the **snitch jacket**, a reputation as an informer (a *jacket* being a prison file in which one's records are kept), and to **hang a jacket** on someone is to accuse them of informing. The **snitch-box** is a box used both for institutional correspondence and for passing on messages that accuse fellow inmates of illegal activity; such tale-telling is written up as a **snitch-kite** (from slang's *kite*, any form of communication passed within the prison or sent outside it), a note passed by a prisoner to the authorities.

Like snitch, **nark**, which comes from Romany *nak*, literally means a nose; its variants are **narc**, **narko** and **knark** (although, confusingly, a *narc*, i.e. an abbreviation of narcotics, is a member of the drugs squad). The late 19th-century **narking dues** refer to an arrest made on the evidence of an informer, while to **nark the lurk** was a 1930s Australianism meaning to betray a plan (the *lurk* was any kind of criminal 'dodge', but had originally referred to raising money under false pretences).

Rats and Other Animals

Among the many anthropomorphisms laid on that scapegoated, intelligent rodent the rat is that of informing. Does anyone *not* know James Cagney's snarl of 'You dirty rat!' (even if he never actually said it: what he did say was 'Mmmm, that dirty, double-crossin' rat' in *Blonde Crazy* (1931))? The **rat** has been smeared as a tell-tale since at least 1818 when the poet Thomas Moore, writing as 'Thomas Brown', in his *Fudge Family in Paris*, requested: 'Give me the useful peaching [i.e. informing] Rat.' More recent, and originally if not wholly American, synonyms are the **cheese-eater**, a play on murine appetites (although the later **cheesy rider**, while playing on rat again, is more immediately linked to the 1969 movie *Easy Rider*), and the **rat fink**. The latter is essentially a double-strength insult, since **fink** has meant an informer and to inform since the 1920s (its extensions **fink on/out** mean either to inform on or to brand as an informer). Its etymology must strictly be marked 'unknown' but there have been a number of theories. In January 1926 the language expert H.L. Mencken's journal the *American Mercury* claimed that 'dating from the famous Homestead strike of 1892 is the odious fink. [It] according to one version was originally Pink, a contraction of Pinkerton, and referred to the army of strike-breakers recruited by the detective agency'. The only drawback to that popular belief is that no citations of fink for strike-breaker have been found prior to 1914. Jonathan Lighter's *Historical Dictionary of American Slang* offers one of two German words: *Fink*, 'a student not belonging to the students association [. . .] hence, not one of the guys', and *Schmierfink*, 'a low dirty hack'.

The animal kingdom has also given the late 19th-century coinage *mouse* (a less confident rat, perhaps); the 1940s *ferret*, who 'ferrets things out'; the 1950s *rabbit*; the 1930s *ringtail*, an American/Australian prison reference to the ringtail possum known for 'playing dead' when threatened; and the *weasel*, first found in the mid-17th century and revived in the 1920s. From the 18th century to the present day, there has also been the *stag*, named for the belief that deer turn on any one of their number that is being hunted. The South African *impimpi* may be based on Zulu *iphimpi*, a species of cobra; on the other hand it may come simply from standard English *pimp*.

The most (or least?) popular animal is the dog. *Dog* itself has been an all-purpose put-down for an untrustworthy man since the 16th century (similar to the standard English *cur*), but has been used specifically for an informer since the mid-19th century. Similarly, *hound* is now an informer in contemporary Australia. To *turn dog* in an Australian prison has been to turn informer since the mid-19th century; thereafter one is *on the dog*: branded as an informer and duly ostracised. Earlier synonyms include the 17th- to 19th-century *setter* and the mid-19th-century *pointer*, both breeds of dog. The more recent *dog's nose*, a paid informer, is from 1960s America. Australia's term *Baskerville*, as in Arthur Conan Doyle's *The Hound of the Baskervilles* (1902), puns on hound, while the *tuckerbox* is for Aussies only: it refers to the Jack Moses poem (*c.*1920s) 'The dog sat on the tuckerbox / Nine miles from Gundagai', a verse in which 'sat' is usually spoken as 'shat' and is, thus, another pun on the tell-tale canine. The late 19th-century **bark** was to inform.

Productive of some confusion is the **gonsel** (and its various spellings, which include **gunsel** and **gonsil**), a term that remains best known from its use as the description of Elmer, the young, inadequate hoodlum of Dashiell Hammett's *The Maltese Falcon* (published in 1930 and filmed in 1941). Given that Elmer carries a gun and is an older man's sidekick it is perhaps unsurprising that the term has often been defined as a gunman. However, this is not the case, and the word is not based on gun or gunslinger: it comes from the German *gänslein*, a little goose, and thence the Yiddish *genzel*, a man's young male lover, a catamite. In American cant it means an informer or a criminal's young sidekick.

Stool-pigeons

Birds usually 'sing' but in the case of the **stool-pigeon** (also **stool**, **stooler**, **stoolie**) he is not so much an informer by choice as by persuasion, and his decision to **stool** or **stool on someone** tends to come after pressure, typically the police interrogator's notorious 'third degree' (i.e. physical violence). A *stool-pigeon* was a bird that was tied to a stool in order to lure other birds towards the waiting hunter. In the case of the informant, there is also often literally a stool – that found in a police station interrogation room – while the 'pigeon' is the unfortunate suspect. According to the journalist Herbert Asbury the term first emerged not under the bright lights of the station basement, but as used in the game of faro. As he explained in his *Sucker's Progress* (1938): 'A few years before the turn of the nineteenth century [stool-pigeon] came into general use among American gamblers to designate a capper [i.e. a tout] or a hustler for a Faro bank, and was still used as late as 1915.' The term's more general use to mean an informer has been recorded since the mid-19th century.

Helping the Police with Their Enquiries

Copper means a policeman and thus, in criminal eyes, can equally well mean an informer, which it has done since the late 19th century. Therefore *turn copper, come the copper, call copper, scream copper* all mean to become an informer. To raise the alarm is to *cry copper*; one can also *holler copper/cop*, *yell copper* or *squeal copper*. One who is *copper-hearted* is an informer by nature and to *turn copper-hearted* is to betray one's associates. Possibly best known is the *copper's nark*, the police informer.

Other police-related terms include the *policeman* and the *police pimp*, which gives *pimp (on)*, to inform (on). The *bogies* are the police, hence the 1900s term *work with the bogies*, to inform; however, the 1920s use of *bogey* to mean informer (and thus *boggy up*, to inform), was taken from *bogie*, the devil, a figure who also provided the late 18th-century *black spy*, both constable and informer.

Talking Indiscreetly: from Peaching, Squeaking and Squealing to Singing

One of the earliest terms based on the idea of speech being the method of informing was *peach*, first recorded in cant in the late 16th century as a simple abbreviation of impeach (itself from the Latin *impedicare*, to entangle, and *pedica*, a fetter – and ultimately from *pes*, a foot). Equally established is *split (on)*, which was explained in a glossary of 'Cant Language' in the *Monthly Magazine* of 7 January 1799: 'He has Split or turned Snitch against his Palls, He has turned evidence against all his Companions.'

The idea of indiscreet talking may underpin Australia's 20th-century informer the *fizgig*, *fizzgig* or *phizgig* (and the variants *fizz* and *fizzer*); the term can also mean one who runs around and chatters indiscreetly. Unrestrained speech also stands behind Britain's late 18th-century *squeak* and its 19th-century variant the *squeaker*, especially used of one who turns informer to save themselves after being arrested. To *put the squeak in* or *put in the squeak* is to betray to the authorities, while to squeak is just to inform. From the mid-19th century to the present day, a *squealer* can be an informer, as can a *squeal* from the 1980s. From the late 19th century, squeal has also been, in America, the report of a crime by a member of the public (or an informer), and, from the 1950s, the actual investigation by police of a crime (using an informer to help them). Alternatively, one can *squeal on*, *put the squeal on* or *do a squeal*.

Singers

Alongside squeaking and squealing, singing has become closely associated with informing. The following terms play on the verb *sing*, first used in this sense in the 1920s (although *sing out* dates from the early 19th century):

budgie   1970s to present
chirper   1930s
dicky-bird   20th century, America
nightingale   1930s to present
pigeon   mid-19th century to present (based on
   stool-pigeon)
psalm-singer   1910s–40s, America (also a prison 'trusty')
singer   1930s–50s, America
songbird   1970s, America (an informer-crammed
   American prison is a *song factory* in the 1910s)
squawker   1920s–40s
whistler   1940s, America (who 'blows the whistle on' a
   criminal or crime)

The 18th century's *queer rooster* was a police spy who frequented thieves' haunts, often feigning sleep (i.e. 'roosting') in order to listen to their conversations; it gave the phrase *dorse a darkey on the queer roost*, to fake sleep in order to overhear conversation. Equally noisy are the 19th century's *belcher* and *buzzman*, the mid-20th century's

American **bigmouth** and **bleater** (who would **bleat** to the authorities), and the modern **mouthpiece, yelper** and **croaker**. To be **satchel-mouthed** (literally 'big-mouthed' and better known by the abbreviation 'Satchmo', the nickname of jazz superstar Louis Armstrong) is to be an informer. Modern usage also gives a **dime dropper**, referring to the fast-fading world of street phone-booths, into which a dime was dropped to obtain a connection to the police. The **telephone** itself is a grim warning: a scar in the form of a curving line from the corner of the mouth to the earlobe, inflicted on an informer's face. In the late 19th century to 1960s, a **beefer** came from the old cry of *hot beef!* (stop thief!) or from slang's *beef*, to complain; while Australia's **sling/chuck (someone) the whisper** also means to inform.

Fingering

Rather than 'speak', the **finger, finger man, finger guy** or **finger merchant** all 'point the finger' at the criminal, while the 1930s–40s **finger mob** was a criminal gang who had paid off the police, often adding a little information on rival gangs. The finger can also be working for the criminals, acting as an **inside man** (himself an informer) who directs robbers to a lucrative target. To inform is to **put a finger on**.

Rhyming Slang

The most famous piece of rhyming slang for an informer is still Britain's favourite term, the **grass**, coined in the 1920s. The word is an abbreviation of *grasshopper* and rhymes with **shopper**, which in turn comes from *shop*, which originally meant to imprison and thence to inform, i.e. to give information that will send someone to prison. Rhyming slang also provides **grass in the park**, which rhymes with nark, and offers a bonus reference to grass.

More terms for an informer are derived from rhymes based on

other slang terms, such as rat: *cabbage-tree hat* or *cabbage hat*; and nark: *carpark*, *Hyde Park* and *Noah's Ark*. Nark also lies at the root of *nause*, an unpleasant person: although they may indeed be 'nause-ating', the source remains the Cockney pronunciation of Noah's, thus *Noah's ark*, nark. The *chocolate frog* and *hollow log* are both current Australianisms and rhyme on dog; a *Johnny Walker* is a talker, while *bubble (and squeak)*, *bubble up* and *put the bubble in* all rhyme on to speak. The *pen-and-inker* is a stinker, the *conger (eel)* will squeal and the *garden hop* is a cop. In Australia, the *Morton* or *Moreton* are abbreviations of *Moreton bay fig* (= fizgig), which takes its ultimate root from Moreton Bay, the penal settlement sited at the mouth of the Brisbane River, Queensland, from 1824 to 1839.

THE ARREST

The Moment of Arrest

It is all very primal: terms for an arrest had existed before, but the echt-term, created in the late 19th century and still going strong in the United States, is the *fall* – that is, the 'fall from grace', the villain's expulsion from the Edenic garden of liberty. And once arrested the plunge continued, taking the criminal through the conviction and the imprisonment that followed. To be arrested is to *fall*, *take/get a fall* or (even more evangelical) to *stumble and fall*. One may also *take a tumble/drop*, *tumble*, *trip* or *flop*. To *take the fall* may offer some atonement: it is to volunteer oneself to be the alleged perpet-rator of a crime, standing in for the real villain; the phrase is also used of being accused (and condemned) unfairly. There is no such thing as a good fall, but there is a *bad fall*, an arrest and charge from which one cannot escape, despite one's best efforts to intimi-date or bribe the plaintiff or a prosecution witness. The prudent villain maintains a store of *fall money*, *fall dough* or *fall scratch*, all of which are funds that have been set aside for bail and legal fees, or, if circumstances permit, for bribing policemen or judges. A *fall partner* is one of two or more people who are arrested or sentenced to prison at the same time for the same crime (it is also one of a pair of thieves working together). One's *fall togs* are the respectable clothes worn for a court appearance.

Central to American crime is the *beef*, which meant an arrest in the 1960s, but is much older, dating from the cry of *hot beef!* which was used for 'stop thief!' in the 18th century. In the 1930s beef became a criminal charge and Damon Runyon could write in 'Breach of Promise' (1931): 'He is one of the surest-footed lawyers in this town, and beats more tough beefs for different citizens than seems possible.' Subsequent uses have included a crime under investigation, an act of criminality, a jail and a sentence. A *beef baby* is a child fathered by a gangster who is living temporarily with a girlfriend or mistress while hiding from the authorities; a *bum beef*, any charge that is considered unfair (at least by the accused villain). To *chill*, *cool* or *square the beef* all mean to escape a criminal charge by paying a bribe. Finally the American prison term *street beef* refers to any crime that, while committed inside prison by a serving prisoner, is tried in a normal court rather than punished with internal prison discipline; such crimes include murder, escape, sex- or drug-related offences.

The earliest terms for an arrest are from the 17th century, and all reflect the moment of seizure and the actual 'laying on of hands': the *clap on the shoulder*, the *cog-shoulder* (from standard English *cog*, to place an impediment in front of) and the *tap (on the shoulder)*. The mid-19th-century *collar* (from standard English *collar*, to get hold of) is still the term of choice in American police departments. Britain has preferred to *feel someone's collar*, used since the 1950s. A *come-along* was an early 20th-century form of handcuff (without locks) used by the American police; it also meant an arrest and to *pull the come-along* was to be arrested. And while to pinch has meant to rob since the mid-16th century, the *pinch* has meant an arrest since the 19th century, giving *hang a pinch on* or *make a pinch*, to arrest, and *take a pinch*, to be arrested.

The 19th century added the *cop*, here the policeman's triumph rather than his person and traditionally found alongside the images of the mask and stripy sweater in the phrase 'It's a fair cop, guv, slap the bracelets on.' But as the etymologist Michael Quinion notes in his discussion of the term: 'This is, and always has been, an entirely fictitious view of the relationship between British criminals and the police.' The **pull** is not recorded before the 1950s but to **pull in** was used from the early 19th century; the related phrase **Mr Pullen is concerned** was used for when an arrest had been made. The **capture** can also be the victim of arrest, and to **get a capture** is to be arrested (as is the abbreviation **cap**). The 20th century has the **jackpot**, which in general terms means any problematic or troublesome situation, as well as the ironic **free ride** (i.e. in the black maria), a **pop**, a **knocker** and the Australian **stingo** (the police 'sting' their target). From the 1940s in America, the **humble** or **hummer** (based on the late 17th-century slang *hummer*, an obvious lie) was what villains termed an arrest on false or petty charges (to **hum** was to arrest). In America in the 1930s, the **blind jam** was an arrest without a specific charge, so called because one could not 'see' it. The arrest warrant has been a **brief** (coined in the 1970s, from Latin *breve*, a letter or note), and in America a **tag** (1930s to present) or **hooker** (1930s–50s), while to be wanted on the basis of a warrant is to **have smallpox** (1940s).

Although for a short time in the 18th century *rap* meant a theft from a purse, its primary use is in terms that imply speech, but all have the image of 'rapping' or hitting. From the late 18th century, it has meant a reprimand, and this use has been much extended. As first recorded in 1903, a **rap** is a judicial charge. One's **rap sheet** is a criminal record, a **rap partner** is someone who is on the same charge sheet as oneself and/or someone who is jailed for the same crime; a **rap buddy** is a friend with whom one suffers an arrest (but the term may also mean someone who is a close friend and nothing more); a **bad rap** is a serious or unfair criminal charge. To **beat the rap** is to be found not guilty in a court; to **hang, lay** or **pin a rap on** is to charge (fairly or otherwise); to **put in the rap** is to inform. To **stand** or **take the rap** is to take a punishment, often a prison sentence, that is actually due to someone else, and to **square a rap** is to have a criminal charge dropped.

A **strike** (taken from baseball imagery), used since the 1910s, was an arrest and the prison sentence that followed it; it is mostly found in multiples: thus two strikes, two terms in prison; three strikes, three arrests and the mandatory life sentence that follows in many states (from baseball again: three strikes and you're out). A *jacket* is a criminal record in America, and thus to *fit someone for a jacket* is to threaten someone with arrest and a prison sentence (the link to Britain's *fit someone up*, to 'frame', may not be coincidental). The British *coat* plays on the same imagery but refers to the actual arrest only.

To Arrest or Be Arrested

Setting aside the 'action' verbs that emphasise the arrest's phys-icality, there are various others on offer. In chronological terms the earliest slang word meaning to arrest is the 17th-century *romboyle*, which defies any etymology; it means to seek out by hue and cry and after that to arrest on a warrant, and one who was *romboyled* was wanted by the watch. In the 18th century, to *bum* came from the bum-bailiff who carried out the arrest, while *nig* was a vari-ation on *nick*, but has not lasted so well. To *nipper*, to *lumber*, to *copper* and to *snake* emerged in the 19th century, as did *clink*, from the prison of the same name. Of the 20th-century terms, perhaps the most enduring is *bust*, which was one of a number that also meant to break in: it is first recorded in the 1940s and is usually linked to arrests for drug possession. The United States produced to *jam up*, to *chalk*, to *gag* and to *gow*, which came from *hoosegow*, a prison. The black militants of the 1960s and 1970s opted for *vamp on* (as in vampire), which meant to make an unjust attack as well as to arrest, and cropped up in such comments as 'The pig is vamping on the people.' To *put the cock to* was a semi-euphemism for a figurative use of to *fuck*; while the recent slang *f.* stands for felony, so to *catch an f.* is to be arrested for a felony.

A small group suggest that the arresting officer is 'eating' the criminal. The earliest of these is the 18th-century *snabble*, which in dialect meant to eat greedily; in the late 20th century *nyam* comes from *nyam*, to eat (originally used in West Africa), while *chaw* borrows a dialect term meaning to chew.

A Form of Attack

There are many verbs which underline the physicality of an arrest, whether violent or surreptitious. These include:

bangle 1960s (from the standard *bangle*, i.e. handcuff)

choke off mid-19th century (from the use of a choke to force a bulldog to relinquish its grip)

clamp mid-19th century to present, America

claw 1920s–30s, America

collect 1960s, Australia

drop the arm on 1950s, America

feel 1990s to present

gather 1910s to present, Australia

harvest 1920s–30s, America

haul in 1910s to present, America

jerk up mid-19th century to 1910s, America

land 1900s–30s (from fishing terminology)

lug 20th century

mitt 1910s, America (also means to handcuff)

put the claws on 1960s–70s, America

put the sleeve on 1930s–50s, America

put the snatch on 20th century, America

scurf 19th century (probably from the *scruff* of the neck, by which one may be grabbed)

spear 1930s–40s, America

The Search

Once one has been stopped one may be searched. In the 19th century the terms were **turned over** and **turned up**; the mid-20th added **jacked** (i.e. hijacked), **shaken up** and **rumbled**. Modern American use is to **take on**. In Britain from the 1950s, the most controversial is **sus** or **suss**, i.e. suspicious, especially in terms of the **sus laws**, controversial powers that permitted the police to stop and search persons allegedly suspected of a crime and that were considered as racist by the black and Asian communities.

The Interrogation

Once arrested the alleged criminal will be questioned: put **on the mat, on the line** or in the **hot seat**. In the context of police work the questioning is an interrogation. The earliest recorded terms for it were the early 19th-century **whiddle**, which comes from slang's *whiddle*, to speak. Standard English meanwhile yielded *grin*, here used in the sense of a snare.

The questioning takes place in an interrogation room that is unlikely to be especially friendly, but nowadays it will probably not feature the stereotypical hot, bright lights, swirling cigarette smoke and isolated stool on which the suspect sits. The room was known as the **dry room** or **drying room** in the 1930s, although the lights would be more likely to have elicited sweat, hence another name (popular in the 1900s–1930s), the **sweat-box**. The latter also served to name a punishment cell, the cells at a magistrate's court and those set into a prison transport van; from the mid-18th century on, to **sweat** a prisoner was to subject them to intense pressure. In Australia from the 1950s, it might be the **blue room** (from one's 'blue' feelings when sitting there), or in America in the 1930s to 1950s, **Coney Island**, an ironic use of the name of New York's much-frequented beachside fun fair. There was also the **goldfish bowl**, found in America in the 1930s to 1960s, where the prisoner was the hapless fish, isolated from the outside world. The **goldfish** itself could be the rubber hose, a popular form of weapon for the extraction of confessions, and to **see the goldfish** meant to suffer a beating, while to **show someone the goldfish** was to beat them up.

The following terms for interrogation, all from the United States, leave one in little doubt as to its style: the **bake** (1990s), the **going-over** (1940s), the **treatment** (1980s); only the **bull session** (1960s, but originally just men gossiping, 1910s) and the **rap session** (1970s, otherwise used for group therapy) were neutral, if ironic. To be questioned was to be **pumped** (in use from the 17th century in

Stealing and Arresting

Somewhat ironically, the following terms mean both to
arrest and to rob or steal:

bail up   mid- to late 19th
century

bone   late 17th to 19th
centuries

bounce   1980s, America

bust   1940s to present

choor   2000s

claim   late 19th century to
present

clip   1940s–70s, America

clout   1920s–30s, America

cloy   late 16th century

cop off   1920s, America

cop out   1900s–70s

gaffle   1950s to present,
America

glom   1910s–50s, America

glue   1900s–30s

grab   mid-18th century to
present

grip   2000s

half-inch   1950s to present

have   19th century to
present

hobble   early 19th century

jump up   1960s, America

knap   mid- to late 18th
century

knock over   1920s–60s,
America

nab   late 17th century to
present

nail   late 18th century to
present

nick   mid-18th century to
present

nip   mid-16th century to
present

off   1970s, America

pinch   late 18th century to
present

pluck   20th century,
America

roust   1960s to present

snaffle   late 16th century to
1910s

snag   20th century

snake   mid-19th century,
America

sneeze   1910s–50s, America

snitch   1990s to present,
Australia

sting   1940s, America

swoop   1980s to present,

take down   1940s to present,
America

take in   late 19th century to
present, America

yank   late 19th century to
present

similar senses), and the tough prisoner would tell his interrogators 'your pump is good but your sucker is dry': your questions are good, but I have nothing to offer. Few police saw any reason not to use physical force as well as verbal pressure, and the best-known term for this is the **third degree**, first recorded as 'police slang' in 1890 by the ex-chief of the NYPD, George Washington Walling. It involved, he explained, 'a bad quarter of an hour' for the prisoner. Equally unpleasant is the 2000s coinage **mattress job**: the victim is placed under a mattress and then jumped and stamped upon, so no visible marks are left on the victim's body.

To be interrogated in a violent way has been to be **massaged** (1930s), to be **put** or **run through a/the wringer** (since 1910s) or to enter the **bull-ring** (mid-19th to mid-20th centuries); this last term was coined to refer to the notoriously harsh British Army training centre at Étaples, northern France, during the First World War. From the 1920s to 1950s, **gaff** meant an interrogation and to **stand/take the gaff** was to suffer it without breaking down. The word has a variety of etymologies: standard English *gaff*, the steel spur attached to a fighting cock; France's *gaffe*, a verbal blunder; Scotland's *gaff*, to talk loudly and merrily, or dialect's *gaff*, loud, coarse talk.

To Confess

Those who manage to resist fists and rubber hoses or simply the relentless questioning have been said to **sing dumb** or **dummy** in the 19th century; in Australia since the 1990s to **stick solid**; and in America in the first half of the 20th century to **ace** (from that card's supremacy in most games). They are **stand-up guys** in 20th-century America. But most suspects do confess. Those who do are said in contemporary America to **fold**, another card reference, meaning to throw in one's hand, or to **knuckle**, that is knuckle under, which dates back to the 18th century.

Vomiting and Coughing

The bulk of images for confessing are those of bodily fluids and their expellation. All are from the 20th century, and first and foremost is vomiting:

come one's cocoa	*spill one's nut* (i.e. head)
come one's fat	*spill one's tea*
come one's guts	*spill (out) one's insides*
come one's lot	*spill the beans*
open up one's guts	*spill the cherries*
spew	*spill the dice*
spew one's guts	*spill the dirt*
spill	*spill the dope*
spill one's brains	*spill the gravy*
spill one's guts	*spill the works*

If not vomiting, then coughing and sneezing:

Other bodily fluids include tears, spit and excrement:

cough	*bawl*
cough it	*cry off*
cough up	*dump*
sneeze	*spit up*
sneeze it out	*spit up one's guts*

Many confessions are based on speech. The 16th century launched **blab**, the 17th **squeak** (and thus **put to the squeak**, to demand a confession), the 18th had **whittle**, from *whiddle*, to talk, and the 19th to **peach** (i.e. impeach) and to **come it** (later uses are **come across** or **come through**). The 1950s **come down front** offered the image of a congregant approaching the front of the church to confess their sins; religious auto-destruction also underpins the abbreviation **fess (up to)**. To **sing** has meant to make a confession since the 1920s, and one can *sing like a canary*, *a bird* or *the birds*, *a lark* and *a nightingale*. In the early or mid-20th century, there is also *holler*, *pop off (at the mouth)* and simply to *talk* (still in use today), while in America at the same time there was *shoot the works*, *yell* and *do a solo*.

The contemporary *stand up* and *put* or *stick one's hand up* are reminiscent of a classroom. In the 1900s one could *round* (i.e. on someone), while from the mid-20th century onwards, one can also *cop for* (or *cop out* in America) or *level*. Later on, towards the end of the century, *bend over* and *roll over* appeared, linking the act of confessing with a compliance with sodomy. In Australia since the 1970s to *sign up* is to make a written confession and a *shoppying blue* (from slang's *shop*, to inform, and *blue*, some form of note) is the signed confession itself.

Chapter 10

TRIAL AND SENTENCING

In a box of the stone jug I was born
Of a hempen widow the kid forlorn,
And my father, as I've heard say,
Was a merchant of capers gay
Who cut his last fling with great applause
To the time of hearty choke with caper sauce
Nix my doll, pals, fake away

W. Harrison Ainsworth, 'Jerry Juniper's
Chaunt' in *Rookwood* (1834)

THE TRIAL

From the criminal point of view the trial is rarely a positive event. He does not see it as an even-handed assessment of unimpeachable evidence, argued by skilful experts and presided over by a scrupulously fair judge who is, like all attending, wholly immune to corruption. One of cant's terms for a trial with the oldest roots is a ***whiddle***, from the early 19th century; it ultimately comes from slang's 16th-century *whid*, a word, but relates directly to the verb *whiddle*, explained in B.E.'s *Dictionary of Cant* from *c.*1698 (note 'c.' in this passage means 'cant'):

Whiddle c. to tell or discover. He Whiddles, c. he Peaches. He Whiddles the whole Strap, c. he discovers all he knows. The Cull has Whiddled, because we wou'd n't tip him a Snack, c. the Dog has discover'd, because we did n't give him a share. They Whiddle beef, and we must Brush, c. they cry out Thieves, we are Pursued, and must Fly.

In other words the trial is merely a betrayal, a theatre of grass, a means of informing on what should best be ignored: the doings of a criminal about his work. Add to that the early 19th-century *stammer* (or, in Scotland, *stammery*), which points up the tongue-tied lies of those bearing witness, and the trial loses some of its supposed majesty. From the criminal point of view, in the mid-18th to 19th centuries, the whole event was nothing but a *patter*, usually used to describe duplicitous talk and in this context dismissing the entire event. To be sent for trial was to be *fullied*, as used in the phrase 'the prisoner was fully committed for trial', popular in the mid-19th century's penny-a-line journalism, and thus the trial itself was the *fully*. The event gained no more respect from the 1930s usage *circus*. More specific to the courthouse, the steps that lead from the cells beneath the Old Bailey up into the dock offer another image: to *go up the steps* or *stairs*, to go on trial; to *go down the steps* or *stairs* is to go off to prison. Then there is the otherwise strange number *13½*, usually seen in tattoos, which in today's American prisons sums up the trial as 12 jurors, one judge and one half-chance.

To Plead

As regards the moment of pleading 'guilty' or 'not guilty', the lexicon offers nothing to cover the latter other than the Australian *jack up*. Perhaps all villains know it is indeed 'a fair cop'. Perhaps, in common with the resolutely sceptical tone that informs the majority of their courtroom references, their experience of 'justice' has convinced them of the futility of fighting the system. Real trials, of course, throw up many claims of innocence, but for whatever reason the concept has been overlooked in cant.

The nearest one finds for terms that are not pleading guilty is the equivocal *cop a plea* or *cop out*, American coinages from the 1920s that mean to plead guilty to a lesser charge in return for the dropping of a greater one (based on slang's *cop*, to take or grab). This system has been institutionalised in American courts, where it is seen as a necessary means of reducing a vast caseload. However, the terms can also mean to plead guilty as charged (although still hoping for a lesser sentence) and simply to plead guilty come what may. Cop out can also mean to confess and worse, to inform. A more recent variation is **plea out**, again from America. ***Cop-a-plea*** has also been adopted as a nickname for a lawyer, suggesting a lack of real commitment or ability.

The remaining terms, all Australian, relate to the bowing of the head by the accused, in acknowledgement of their guilty plea. Since the 1930s they have included **bow the crumpet, duck the scone, get one's head down, nod the nut** and simply **nod**.

The Lawyer

Talking for a Living
No single officer of the court has earned so many synonyms as the lawyer. They are (almost) invariably derogatory. The profession's overall image – and not merely among crooks – is best summed up in the traditional sign for the once-widespread pub name 'The Honest Lawyer'. It shows a headless man dressed in lawyer's robes, the implication being that his honesty is only possible since, headless, he is bereft of the chance to speak.

Lawyers are paid to talk. Their names reflect this essential function, as seen in the 18th- to 19th-century **son of prattlement**, the mid-19th-century **mouthpiece** (perhaps the longest surviving of such terms), the **loudmouth**, the **tongue** and the **mouth** of the mid-20th. Along similar lines were the 19th century's **belly-ache belfry** (literally the 'lawyer's mouth'), **jaw-cove** (literally 'talk-man'), **stammer-hankey** and **mangsman**, from slang's *mang*, to speak (and ultimately the Romany *mag*, to beg). Pointed as ever, the 20th century added **yeller**. The Australian **spruiker** (from Yiddish *shpruch*, a saying, or Dutch *spreken*, to talk) borrows the slang term for the touts who are employed by fairgrounds and carnival sideshows or a cinema, theatre or similar entertainment. They also deal with the law, a creature of infinite fissiparousness offering a chance for the infinite splitting of hairs. Two terms from the 17th to 19th centuries reflect this: the **councillor of the piepowder court** and the **split-cause**. The last is self-evident, while the counsellor took his name from the actual Court of Piepowders, the court of wayfarers or travelling traders; this court's name stemmed from the French *pieds poudreux,* dusty feet.

Incompetent, Unscrupulous and Corrupt

Many lawyers were perceived to be entirely incompetent, such as the 18th- to 19th-century **puzzle-cause** and **puzzle-cove**; 'puzzle' meant to work out, but the implication was perhaps that law was something of a puzzle to this hapless practitioner. In the 19th century, the **jackleg** applied not merely to lawyers but to any incompetent, unskilled or unprincipled worker or professional. *Jackleg* began as an American regionalism, meaning unskilled, and can be traced back to British dialect *jack-a-legs*, a large clasp knife, as used by a second-rate carpenter.

Completely unscrupulous lawyers included the early 20th-century **law sharp** (an extension of slang's *sharp*, a cheat), and the **shark** and the **land shark**, both coined in the 19th century. The 18th-century **Philadelphia lawyer** – stereotyping the duplicitous Yankee – was shrewd or unscrupulous, an expert in exploiting the minutiae of the law, while the 20th century's **slicker** or **sleeker** is not merely a shrewd and predatory lawyer but any variety of cunning or dishonest person (e.g. the *city slicker*). Similarly, in the 17th and 18th centuries the **ambidexter** was 'ambidextrously' skilled at taking fees from both plaintiff and defendant. From the 19th century the **longshore lawyer**, which used the term *longshore* to mean tough and villainous, and the **trimmer** played both sides against his own lucrative middle. Terms from the 20th century have included the **steerer**, who was either a crooked lawyer or the agent who supplies such a lawyer with clients; the term was more usually associated with the touts who guided the unwary into crooked casinos or brothels.

Of course while some lawyers are merely incompetent or unscrupulous, there are those that are out-and-out corrupt. The best-known term remains the **shyster** (coined in the mid-19th century; for a full discussion see SWINDLERS, CONMEN AND FRAUDS, page 28). Equally well known is the **ambulance-chaser** or **ambulance lawyer**. This term, first encountered in the late 19th century, means a lawyer (rarely a first-rate one) who specialises in representing the victims of street and other accidents, to whom he offers his services – often appearing at the victim's hospital bed promising the launch of a substantial claim – which tend to be accepted since the victim is still too shocked to make proper and rational arrangements. A variant of **ambulance-chasing** is **wagon-chasing**, pursuing the police wagon from the crime scene to the lock-up in the hope of picking up otherwise unrepresented cases.

Given the negative burden of so many of these terms, it might be assumed that any lawyer is seen as pretty contemptible but some specific terms have been used. The 18th- to 19th-century **Newgate solicitor** was a no-hoper who hung around prisons (including, but not invariably, Newgate) in the hope of picking up work. More recent are America's **dirty shirt** and **penitentiary dispatcher**. The first is an incompetent lawyer who is given clients by court or jail officials; he has no substantial legal knowledge, charges minimal fees, and usually loses: his fees do not run to laundry. The second highlights what are considered the professional inadequacies of court-appointed lawyers, whose clients are all too likely to end up in the penitentiary rather than back on the street.

Fee-chasers

Other than their failure to keep one out of prison, one of the great sources of criticism aimed at lawyers is their fee, which is invariably seen as inflated. The early 19th-century term for both fee and lawyer was **snipe**. It puns on the *snipe*, a bird with a 'long bill', as well as a possible borrowing from the dialectal *snipe*, an avaricious person (presumably from the same root). By the 20th century, he was simply a **fee-chaser**. Even when it was not seen as inflated, the lawyer could be defined in terms of their fee. The 18th- to early 20th-century **six-and-eightpence** was a solicitor, whose basic fee originally came to this amount, worth one-third of a pound. There was also an earlier 17th-century use of the term, but this referred to the accepted fee demanded for the removal of a felon from the gallows and for their burial in sacred ground.

Attire and Appearance

The distinctive attire of the lawyer provided one of the earliest terms, dating from the late 17th century: the **black box** turned one of his basic pieces of kit, his black-painted deed box, into the man himself. On the same basis he was also known as a **black boy** or **black knob**. Similar, and also coined in the 17th century, was **green bag**, and its adjective form **green-baggish**. Captain Francis Grose explained in his *Classical Dictionary of the Vulgar Tongue* (1785): 'These gentlemen carry their clients' deeds in a green bag; and, it is said, when they have no deeds to carry, frequently fill them with an old pair of breeches . . . to give themselves the appearance of business.' In time the green bags were replaced by blue bags (for barristers, thus the **priest of the blue bag**, a barrister) and red bags (for King's or Queen's Counsel). The still popular British **brief**, from the 1930s, is similar, in this case equating the man with his legal commissions or brief. Lastly, from the 18th century, is the **jet** (referencing the jet-black gown that he wore) and the less than flattering **slabbering bib**, which played on standard English *slobber*, and was used of the neckband worn as part of a lawyer's robes.

A Miscellany of Other Terms
There are other terms, one of the earliest of which is the 17th-century **trample**. It referred to the metaphorical 'trampling' of a path between individuals, in this case the lawyer's role as middleman. The **limb** or **leg of the law**, coined in the mid-18th century from standard English *limb*, an extension or branch, was often used to typify a second-rater (a **limb of the bar** was a barrister). High legalese was involved in the 16th-century **latitat**, rooted in the Latin *latitare*, to lie concealed, and embodied in the legal jargon *latitat*: 'a writ which supposed the defendant to lie concealed and which summoned him to answer in the King's Bench' (*Oxford English Dictionary*). The 1930s **needle-nose**, a probable back-formation from the anti-Semitic adjective *needlenosed* for Jewish, underlines the assumption of the law as a stereotypically Jewish occupation. The modern American attorney, at least when prosecuting, is a **cutor**, **cuter** or **cutter**; a **big cutor** is a district attorney.

And, for once, the underworld offers something positive in America in the 1960s: the **fire-burner**, a very enthusiastic, passionate lawyer.

The Judge in Rhyming Slang

Beak
bubble and squeak
once a week

Magistrate
garden (gate)

Judge
Barnaby Rudge (from Charles Dickens's eponymous 1841
  novel)
elmer fudge (from the *Looney Tunes* cartoon character
  'Elmer Fudd')
inky smudge
vanilla fudge

The Judge and Magistrate

Of all the terms for a judge, or his less grand colleague the magistrate, the longest lasting is the **beak**, first recorded in the 16th century and showing no signs of disappearing. While popular imagery may equate the term with some bird of prey, the most likely root lies in the Old English *beag*, a necklace worn as a badge of office. The 19th-century use of the word beak expanded, sometimes as **beaky**, to include a sheriff's officer or a policeman, as well as a **beak-runner**, an officer of the law (literally 'a runner for the judge or magistrate'), and a **beaksman**, a policeman or police-office clerk. Compound terms included the **milky beak**, who was a drunken magistrate. (That this character engendered his own specific term suggests that his type was far from uncommon.) The 18th- to 19th-century **queer beak** was a magistrate who was impervious to corruption; his opposite number was the **rum beak**, open to pecuniary suggestion. (The use of *queer* meaning bad and *rum* meaning good – from the

criminal perspective of course – illustrates the underworld's topsy-
turvy sense of values.) When early 19th-century magistrates went
on their evening rounds, this patrol was known as **beaks (out) on
the nose** (from slang's *on the nose*, on watch or on the lookout).

Both judge and magistrate were also found in the 17th and 18th
centuries as **cuffin**, most likely from *cove*, a man, and in the 19th
century as **bloke**, another term that usually means no more than
man. At a stretch, they can both therefore be seen as precursors of
the 20th-century slang for anyone in authority – **the Man**. The
cuffin-queer was a magistrate, and like the queer beak he could not
be bent. Equally incorruptible was (and remains) the late 19th
century's **wrong 'un**, a severe judge or magistrate, and a term that
stems from racing jargon's *wrong 'un*, a horse that has been deliberately pulled up during a race. The wrongness, of course, is from
the criminal's perspective.

A number of terms cover both magistrate and judge but there
are others that work only for the former. The earliest of these was
the 16th-century **harman** (see Sentencing, page 304). By the 19th
century he could be a **squire**, and indeed that was often his social
position in the local countryside; if paid, and thus a stipendiary, he
was a **stipe**; if severe he was known as a **six monthser**, who, whenever
possible, gave the longest sentence (six months) that the law at that
time allowed him to pronounce. A derisory 1980s coinage, meaning
either a magistrate or a policeman, was **muppet**, a dubious honour
for the puppets created by Jim Henson and featured on TV's *Muppet
Show* in the latter half of the 1970s.

Like everyone else on the official side of a British court, the judge
has a 'uniform', the most prominent aspect of which is his full-
bottomed wig. Thus since the 18th century he has been a **wig** (the
term extends to the equally bewigged barrister, although his or hers
is naturally smaller), a **full bottom** or a **jasey**, which most likely
comes from *Jersey*, a variety of flax used in the making of a certain
type of wig. And if not the wig then his ermine-trimmed gown,
giving the 17th century's **lambskin man** and the mid-19th century's
nob in the fur trade.

Conjuror, in the 17th century, could mean pickpocket (from his
dependence on sleight of hand), but it could also mean a judge,

and to *go before the conjuror* was to be tried at the assize. What he
'pulls out of his hat' is a sentence. The same air of magic pervades
the period's *fortune-teller* (in this legal sense what he is predicting
is the sentence), and linked is the 18th century's *cunning man* (a
cunning woman was a witch). The 19th-century *floorer* was a judge
in the act of passing a sentence of death; the term had originated
in the prize-ring for a knock-down blow. South Africa has *sticker*,
for the man who 'sticks you' with jail time, and *stretcher*, the man
who gives you a *stretch*. In America in the 1920s–50s the word was
rapper, from slang's *rap*, to talk (specifically to criticise), while the
Harlemites of the 1940s went up before *the man with the book of
many years*.

The Jury

The jury, or *tomato purée* in today's rhyming slang, was known in
the 18th century as the *twelve godfathers*, or simply *the twelve*. They
are those who 'give a name', i.e. guilty or not guilty, to one's crime;
thus a criminal, or perhaps a badly behaved youngster, might be
told: *you will be christened by twelve godfathers someday before long.*

Evidence

The witness box seems to have earned its synonyms only in late
19th-century Australia, where it was a *peter* – more usually known
in criminal circles as a cell – or a *jump-up*, giving the phrase to
jump (in) the box, to give evidence. One could also *do a mount*.

Assuming that the villains have failed to complete their *spring
cleaning* (a contemporary term for getting rid of the physical
proofs of the crime), they will find themselves in court. The idea
that evidence was invariably injurious underpins the 20th-century
phrase *put someone in*, to tell a story that incriminates the
accused; the 'in' refers to prison. America's late 19th-century
lace-work came either from the world of seamstresses (i.e. the
'embroidery' of the facts), or from that of boxers, specifically
the idea of confusing and half-blinding an opponent by rubbing the
laces of one's gloves against their face and eyes. *Dock asthma*, a

British term used since the 1970s, is the ironic description of the gasps of alleged 'surprise' from the accused when the police produce their evidence in court.

From the criminal point of view, the whole event, from fraudulent arrest to grossly unfair sentence, is no more than an example of flagrant and calculated miscarriage of justice – known, since the 1930s, as a *fit-up*, *stitch-up* or *frame-up*. All these terms can be used as verbs, and all refer to the concoction of negative evidence by the planting of evidence, the faking of confessions (known as *verbals*; to *verbal* was for the police to concoct a statement – incriminating, of course), and the use of false accusations or perjured evidence in order to have an innocent suspect (albeit one who may have a criminal record) arrested and found guilty.

The defendant had only one recourse, the hiring of a *stag* (originally a dialect term meaning a deer that turns on any one of his peers who is being hunted), a man who attends courts in order to hire himself out as a defence witness, usually to provide a false alibi for a guilty defendant. Up to the late 19th century, the range of professional perjurers available to both prosecution and defence – whoever was paying most – was substantial. The *knight of the post* or *post-knight* flourished in the 16th century and earned his living by giving false evidence; it may be assumed that the 'post' in this case was a whipping-post or pillory. The 17th century had the *napper*: otherwise known as a thief, here he *napped* or grabbed a fee rather than stolen goods; and the *affidavit man* who took his name from the standard *affidavit*, a sworn statement that can be used in evidence. The *Kerry witness* (from a negative stereotyping of Kerrymen as corrupt) was an 18th-century coinage, as was *Irish evidence*, which stood both for the perjurer and his perjury. This same century also had the *accommodation man* (like the *accommodation house*, he was up for rent).

The Verdict

No-one, of course, is guilty, even if they have pleaded so to the charge. To be charged or sentenced unfairly is to get a *stiff rap* (1950s America) or a *bum rap* (1920s onwards, originally in America), while to be convicted falsely is to be **bum rapped**. In contemporary Australia to be found guilty is to be **sunk**.

However, the majority of the terms here refer to acquittal. Perhaps the best known is a **result**, beloved of every TV villain since the 1950s. **Turnips** for an acquittal in the late 18th century may be linked semantically, if it comes from a *turn-up (for the books)*, a fortunate event. The term also provides the 19th-century verb **turn up**, usually used of an acquittal that has been achieved through lack of evidence rather than actual innocence of the crime. The late 19th century had **music** (doubtless to one's ears) and a **chuck**, both meaning a not guilty verdict, and to be **chucked** (or **slung**) was to be set free. In 1930s America, one can be **in the blue** (i.e. released into the 'wild blue yonder') or **kosher**, a figurative use of the Yiddish *kosher*, acceptable according to the Jewish dietary laws. To **fade** was to be declared not guilty in the 1960s (and one can promptly 'fade away'), while 20th-century America gives us to **beat** or **beat the rap**. This is perhaps the most widely used term and means to win out over the prosecution; of a lawyer, to beat means to defend successfully. From the 1910s onwards, to **ring the bell**, with its image of the 'try-your-strength' machine found at a traditional fairground, has meant to carry off a prize, and for the criminal there is surely no better prize than being acquitted.

SENTENCING: PRISON

Although the concept of imprisonment was hardly novel in the vocabulary of cant, the terms that accrued to sentencing and imprisonment are very much a development of the 19th century and beyond. This is because, prior to the 19th century, the prison was simply a holding pen, existing only to contain defendants awaiting trial or convicts due for punishment (which was often that of hanging). Minor crimes, such as petty larceny (theft of goods worth less than a shilling), were punished with public shaming, such as a spell in the pillory or stocks. Major crimes were divided into two sorts: 'clergyable', those for whom one could plead 'benefit of clergy' (i.e. claim clerical status – by 1700 merely a matter of showing oneself able to read the line *Miserere mei, Deus, secundum misericordiam tuam* ('O God, have mercy upon me, according to thine heartfelt mercifulness') from Psalm 51 – and thus be tried in the church courts, which did not use capital punishment), and those which were not.

To quote the American jurist David D. Friedman, writing in 1995: 'For clergyable felonies, the convicted offender was either branded on the thumb and sent home or (especially after 1718) transported. For non-clergyable capital offenses, of which there were a great many, the convicted offender was either pardoned, pardoned and transported, or hanged.' It was not until the system began to misfire, and the prisons to fill up with individuals still awaiting either punishment or release, did things change and simply putting a person in prison began to be seen in itself as an alternative means of punishment – the time to be served being supposedly proportionate to the severity of the crime.

Doing Time

In the end – not to mention at the beginning and indeed throughout – it is all about time. Time spent in prison. Time waiting to get out of prison. Time, as the uncharitable warders say, before, inevitably, you'll be back in prison. Thus *time* has been a prison sentence since the mid-19th century, and to *do time* is to serve it. Still widely used is the rhyming slang *birdlime* from the same era, also found as *bird's lime* or *bird shit*; all are often abbreviated to *bird*, which has given the contemporary playful synonym *sparrow*. In addition there have developed a number of terms related to time, the source of which is primarily American jails.

One can enjoy *good time*, which from the late 19th century referred to time off for good behaviour – more recently this is known as *copper time* (1940s), equating good behaviour with behaving like a policeman – but since the 1970s good time has meant a sentence that is suffered without any particular problems. Its logical opposite is *bad time*, incarceration that causes the subject, one who cannot acclimatise to prison, a great deal of suffering. Similarly there is **hard time** and **easy time**, the latter being also known as **light time**. From the 1930s onwards, **big time** has meant a lengthy sentence (at least three years), thus a **big-timer** or **longtimer** (1970s) is the person serving it. **Short time**, obviously, is a short sentence, also known as **sleeping time** from the 1920s, a sentence 'one could sleep through' (an alternative modern name is the **lie-down**); to **sleep off** in the 1950s meant to serve the sentence without problems, as if one were doing no more than taking a nap. From the 1940s onwards, **wino time** in America or a **tramp's lagging** in Britain are short sentences, since habitual drunkards generally receive minimal sentencing, i.e. days rather than years in prison.

In the mid-20th century, to be imprisoned is to **pull time** and to serve the term is to **build time** while **full time** is a life sentence. In the 1970s, **dead time** denotes both any time spent in prison that does not actually diminish one's sentence and any period of a sentence when one is prohibited from associating with other prisoners, while to be **time drunk** is to be intellectually depleted after a long jail sentence. The contemporary **Buck Rogers time** is a sentence for which the parole date has been set extremely far in the future; it refers to the fictional space hero Buck Rogers, who may have been launched as a comic hero in 1929, but whose adventures take place four centuries hence.

Finally an exclamation from the 1970s, aimed at the incoming convicts: **do your own time!** that is, mind your own business! and keep out of anyone's else's; used as a verb it means to serve a sentence without becoming involved in any of the gangs, illicit businesses and the like. Alongside this, from the 1960s and still popular today, *if you can't do the time, don't do the crime* was originally aimed at criminals whose bravado outpaced their intelligence, but it has been carried into mainstream life, where it warns against taking an action if you can't deal with the concomitant responsibilities.

Do a Bit

If time implies extent, then **bit** or **bid** (an alternative pronunciation), an equally well-used word for a jail sentence from the mid-19th century onwards, seems to suggest a mere segment. But as its

– mostly American – compounds make clear, a bit can be just as substantial as any amount of time. Such lengthy sojourns behind the bars can be a **long bit**, coined in the late 19th century and still in use today for any term of imprisonment over 38 months that must be completed before the prisoner becomes eligible for parole. From the 1930s and 1940s onwards, a **big bit** or a **nice bit** meant ten years or more, while a **telephone number bit** was a sentence of 20 years plus, but not a life sentence. Defined as a 50-year sentence in the 1970s, **four bits** is based on the old monetary *bit*, of twelve and a half cents. From the 1950s, the **split bit** is an indeterminate prison sentence, subject to the decisions of the parole board, while the **short bit** (from the 1910s onwards) is logically a short one. The 20th century's **soft bit** (also **soft time**) is a system of imprisonment whereby an inmate must serve at least half the sentence before becoming eligible for parole. Given the length of many American prison sentences, this seems far from 'soft'.

From the mid-19th century, to **do a/one's bit** has meant to serve a sentence, while to **pull one's bit** from the 1960s (based on standard English *pull through*) is to survive it relatively unscathed. In the mid-20th century, to serve a **flat bit** or **flat time** (from standard usage of *flat* meaning complete, utter) is to remain imprisoned with no remission for good behaviour. Finally, during the same period the **phoney-baloney bit** is what the prisoner sees as a clearly unjust or discriminatory prison sentence, especially one based not on sound legal principles but on a technicality.

Spots and Other Terms

Used as a suffix in the 20th century, **spot** – in combination with a given number – denotes a term of imprisonment; the default spot is a **one-spot**, a single year's jail, but any pertinent digits can be inserted.

Other terms for serving one's time in America include **take** or **wear the stripes** (late 19th to mid-20th century), which calls up the traditional striped uniforms as worn in dozens of Hollywood's Big Houses, and **jack** from the 1950s onwards, based on the idea of being beaten with a blackjack. The phrase **get the glory** was popular in mid-20th-century Britain and meant to become suddenly and fervently religious while serving a prison sentence. Such religiosity may be presumed to be temporary and counterfeit. As Paul Tempest notes in his *Lag's Lexicon* (1950), prisoners who display it 'imagine that by crawling round the chaplain or priest they will get preferential treatment'.

And last, but very far from least, is **porridge**, a term current throughout the 20th century but vastly popularised by the TV series that ran from 1974 to 1977. It refers to this staple of British prison breakfasts and adds a pun on *stir*, meaning the prison itself. It also provides the phrases **dish out the porridge/gravy**, used of a judge who hands out a heavy sentence.

A Sentence

A prison sentence has earned many names:
bat   mid-19th century (from dialect *bat*, a stroke, a pace)
bit   mid-19th century to present
hitch   1920s to present, America (from standard English *hitch*, a temporary fastening, as with a loop or knot)
jolt   1910s to present, America
lot   1920s
porridge   20th century
shopping   1930s
tariff   2000s
time   mid-19th century to present
trip   1900s–50s, America
wallop   1950s
whack   1940s, America

Sentences in Days

The traditional magistrate's offer, usually to drunken vagrants, of 'One pound or one day' – that is a day in prison – has presumably been lost to a new economic climate, but sentences were once weighed out in mere days. A century ago the equation was **five or** *seven*, a five-shilling fine or seven days in prison, a sum that by metonymy came to define the drunkard themselves. More recently, in 1970s America, a *stone* (the imperial measurement of 14 pounds) was used to mean a sentence of fourteen days. Other terms for a very short period in prison include the late 19th-century coinage *cells* from the idea of a *night in the cells*, and the mid-20th-century *weekend*. Finally, and timelessly, is Australia's resigned reference to *another day up the Queen's arse*, a phrase that signifies the passing of one more day of one's sentence.

Sentences in Months

Starting with a single month's imprisonment, one encounters the obsolete 19th-century *flummut*, which comes from tramping use and refers to the *flummut* (ultimately from standard English *flummox*, to confuse), a mark placed on a door to indicate a house that will be unfriendly to begging tramps. The mid-20th-century *acre (of corn)*, found in Australia and America, was a sentence cited variously as one month, twelve months or simply 'plenty'. In all cases the 'corn' refers to hominy, a staple of prison food; one will eat an acre of the stuff during such a sentence.

A short sentence, whether in months or years, was a *haircut* from the 1940s onwards. The length served depended on whether one entered a local prison (from a few weeks to two or three months) or a convict prison (three to five years); both referred to the relatively short period and the idea that one just had time to get your prison haircut before being freed. The *beggar's lagging* was a sentence of 90 days' imprisonment, commonly that meted out for vagrancy.

In 1960s Scotland a *deuce* lasted two months (although it's much more common from the 1930s onwards as an American term for a two-year sentence) and, logically, the 19th-century coinage *tray, trey* or *treymoon* (from Italian *tre*, three) runs for three months, although it can also mean a three-year sentence. Other words for three-month terms in the 19th century include the *tail-piece* and the *spell* (from standard English *spell*, a short time). The *braggadocio* specifically referred to a known thief or regular offender, and played on standard English *braggadocio*, an empty, idle boast or boaster – in this case the boast was 'you'll never catch me'. Australia thought of a three-month prison sentence as a *snooze* from the 1940s onwards.

The mid-19th-century to present-day usage *drag* and the 1920s–1930s term *Brussels (carpet)* are also three-month sentences, and both are linked to one of the better known of such terms: the 20th century's *carpet*. Carpet has two possible etymologies; either the rhyming slang (*carpet-bag* = drag, although nobody knows why drag means three months in the first place – perhaps simply because it drags by), or the earlier assumption that prison workshops took just 90 days to produce a particular type of regulation size carpet. However, this meaning of carpet is questioned by a 1903 text, *Mark of the Broad Arrow* by the ex-prisoner 'No. 77': 'Your "Auto-leyne" cares little about a "drag" (three months), a sixer (a "carpet" it is generally called), or a "stretch".' What an *Auto-leyne* might have been remains lost to researchers, but the widespread use of carpet as meaning three months – and the absence of any other recorded examples of it meaning six – makes one inclined to agree with etymologist Michael Quinion when he says that 'No 77 made a mistake'.

Some indisputable terms for a half-year incarceration are generally based on those which already mean six in one form or another. Thus the Antipodean *zac* or *zack* from the 1930s onwards, which was otherwise used to mean sixpence; and the British backslang *exis,* which had meant a sixpence or the number six from the mid-19th century but was appropriated for a prison sentence in the 1980s. It had appeared in its full form from the mid-19th century: *exis sith-noms* (literally 'six months') was used for the period of time, whether in prison or not. *Six* and *sixer* have both been used to mean a six-month term from the mid-19th century onwards, although briefly in the 1920s they were a six-year term. America's 1950s term the *five twenty-nine* was a sentence of five months and 29 days, doled out for 'jostling', i.e. robbing a drunk. The *pint* and *length* both represent a half (that is, of a full year). The 1950s West Indian term pint meant half a *quart* (see page 289), while the 19th-century length, at least in racing jargon, was *half a stretch* (a phrase that also meant six months, whether in or out of prison). Finally, a *ninepennyworth* lasted nine months in the 1940s and 1950s.

Sentences in Years

One

The term **stretch** again takes one back to time, since it abbreviates the standard phrase *stretch of time*. A 19th-century coinage, it means a 12-month sentence and is often found in specific combinations, e.g. **two stretch**, two years; **three stretch**, three years; etc. It could also be a sentence of undetermined length and offered the synonymous **stretcher**. In mid-20th-century America **boffo** or **boppo** meant a single year in jail; 25 **boffos** still means a 25-year sentence, and if one is hit with imprisonment one is said to be **boffed**. The **quart**, a West Indian term from the 1950s, lasts a year (i.e. a 'double' pint), as does backslang's 19th-century **evlenet sith-noms** (i.e. twelve months) and Australia's **all the year round**, first used in the 1920s. In America a **bullet** can mean a single example of anything, including a one-year sentence. So too can a **george**, for which no apparent etymology exists but which appeared a decade later in the 1970s. In Australia in the late 19th to mid-20th centuries, a **rest** is a euphemism for a year in prison, while **resting** meant being in prison, on the same lines as the theatre world's term for being out of work: *resting* (although cant seems to resist what would be an even greater irony, any play on the American thespian's equivalent: *at liberty*). Finally the somewhat anomalous **eleven, twenty-nine, twenty-three**, a phrase from 1920s America that means a jail sentence of one hour less than a whole year. The reason for this was that in some states a full 12-month sentence required that the criminal automatically lose his or her citizenship – the more humane judges used this otherwise strange calculation to get around so draconian a rule.

Two

All the terms for a two-year sentence are based on words that already mean two, the most obvious being the 20th-century term **two** itself. Also present in the 20th century, there is **bice** or **byce** (from French *bis*, twice) and the American **deuce, deucie, deuceburger** or **duce**. **Swy, sway** or **swi** comes from German *zwei*, two. A **twicer** means two of something, e.g. two strokes of a whipping or a two-year prison sentence. **Twoer** has also multi-tasked: in the late 19th century it was a two-wheeled cab or a two-shilling piece, before becoming a two-year sentence in the 1930s. America offers the 20th-century **two spaces**, i.e. two year-long spaces in one's life.

Three Years and More

Prison sentences involving the less obvious numbers have also generated their own slang terms:

Three
threepen'orth   1930s
three-er   1940s

Four
rofe (backslang)   1940s–50s

Seven
nevis/neves (backslang)   late 19th century
nevis stretch   mid-19th century
seven   late 19th century (thus in Australia a **sevener** is a convict sentenced to seven years)
sevenpence   early to mid-19th century (specifically seven years' transportation)
seven pennorth   mid-19th century (also as seven months, as well as transportation for seven years)

Fourteen
fourteen penn'orth   early 19th century (specifically fourteen years' transportation)

Fifteen
wolf   1970s, America

Five

Other than the 20th century's predictable *five*, the bulk of cant usage for a five-year sentence simply borrows from words that mainstream slang has created for describing sums of money.

America's **nickel** is worth five cents, and it has meant a five-year sentence since the 1950s, while the dime is ten cents and provides the 1930s term **dime store**, a sentence of 'five to ten years'. America's **pound** dates back to the 1950s, an era when the pound sterling equalled five dollars. A *flim* (from slang's *flimsy*) had also meant a five-pound note but was used for a five-year sentence from the mid-19th century onwards, as did the slightly later *fiver*, which could mean not just the sentence but the person having to serve it. Meanwhile, in the late 19th century *five pennyworth* was a British tramp usage for five years in prison. Australia's mid-20th-century term **caser** comes from Yiddish *kesef*, silver, and thus the long-obsolete silver five-shilling piece. The *fin* appears in 1930s America and Canada and is still in use today for a five-year sentence. It is primarily an abbreviation of *finnif* or *finnip*, a five-pound or five-dollar bill, and ultimately another Yiddishism, borrowing from the word *fünf*, or five. It provides the extended term *fin up*, a sentence of five years to life. Finally, Australia's **spin**, current from the 1940s onwards, at first glance appears to have nothing to do with cash. Yet the word is an abbreviation of the standard term *spinnaker*, which is a large three-cornered sail carried by a racing yacht; it was once used to refer to the old 'white' five-pound note, far larger than its modern successors.

The exceptions to money-based imagery include the 1970s term *fever (in the South)*, an American nickname for the point of five in craps dice since the mid-19th century, as well as America's *five specker* (1920s–30s) and Australia's **hand** (1960s), i.e. based on its five fingers.

Ten

If a nickel is five cents then a **double-nickel** is ten and also an American term for a ten-year sentence. The **dime**, also ten cents, is another synonymous American term, present since the 1930s, while from the late 19th century both America and Britain have used the **tenner** for ten years in prison. The **sawbuck** (also **sawski** or **sawzie**) is an American term still popular today; it originally meant a ten-dollar bill from the mid-19th century and has been used for a ten-year sentence from the 1920s. The term comes from standard English *sawbuck*, an X-shaped sawhorse; the X of the sawhorse is equated with the Roman numeral X, ten.

Twenty to a Hundred

The **double sawbuck**, **double saw** or **double sawski** appeared in America in the 1930s to mean a 20-year prison sentence, although in the 1970s it can also be found as a 25-year one. The modern Australianism **double-slagging** also runs for 20 years; it may be linked to slang's *slagging*, verbal criticism (which presumably refers to the judge's comments), or alternatively to *lagging*, a term for transportation (see page 305). An *izl* is an asterisk, and a sentence of **25 with an izl** is 25 years to life – the * notation next to the years of one's sentence denotes 'life'. Terms for 100 years, unlikely to be served in full but nevertheless regularly portioned out in America, return to money: a **C-note** appears in the 1970s as both $100 and a 100-year jail sentence, while **one hundred smackers** is the sentence in America but is more commonly found in Britain as £100.

Indeterminate Sentences

Alongside America's 1930s coinage of the **garter** (which stretches), the terms for an indeterminate sentence are both 20th-century Australian. The first is **the Oliver** or **oliver twist**, referring to the iconic scene in Dickens's book in which the hapless hero asks, 'Can I have some more?' The second will be familiar to those who have encountered the song 'Kathleen Mavourneen' and can recall its chorus: 'It may be for years, it may be forever'. **Kathleen mavourneen** (also found as a **kath**) has been an indeterminate sentence since the 1910s. It can also refer to the habitual criminal who is serving it.

A Long Sentence

Aside from the self-explanatory **big one** or **big 'un**, used in Australia and America since the 1960s, the long sentence has earned a number of nicknames. America's mid-20th-century term **chunk** and the contemporary British term a **big lump** are equally obvious, while America's 1970s coinage a **big hit** is an ironic use of standard English *big hit* (a success), and means at least three years inside. The pun in New Zealand's modern term **big huey** refers to Louisiana's notorious governor Huey P. Long (1893–1935). American coinages include the **top** (1950s to present) as the maximum sentence for one's crime, and the 21st-century term **alphabet**, which puns on the grammatical sentence – it is a 'sentence' so long that it requires the whole alphabet. Australia's modern **cricket score** reflects that country's sporting self-confidence, while Britain's 1940s **sticking-plaster** underpins the fact that the prisoner must 'stick' in jail.

A lengthy sentence is also a **packet** in contemporary America, a term that seems to be a back-reference to 20th-century slang's *cop a packet*, meaning to gain a great deal, possibly more than one bargained for, in this case a longer prison sentence than feared. The etymology is unresolved, although John Brophy and Eric Partridge, in *Songs and Slang of the British Soldier* (1930), suggest a link with the 'packet' of gauze and lint that comprised the First Field Dressing that would be applied to a wound.

A Life Sentence

At its baldest and briefest the penalty of a life in prison is quite simply **life**, an abbreviation of the standard *life sentence*. Coined in the mid-19th century it gave rise to **life off** and **life up**, meaning to imprison for life. America's 20th-century punning **lifeboat** and **life-saver** both mean a pardon or the commutation of a sentence, and during the same period, to do **life on the instalment plan** refers to the receiving of a succession of sentences which are served, with only brief periods of freedom, by a recidivist. A **lifer** has meant variously, from the mid-19th century onwards, one who has been transported for life, a life sentence and a prisoner serving a life sentence. In modern British use the **big L** is a life sentence, although in America it refers to Leavenworth Prison, Kansas. In the 21st century, America also sees a life sentence as an **L note**, while **L.W.O.P.**, pronounced 'el-wop', is life without parole.

Although a 'life' sentence is often far from the same as a lifetime in prison, the sense of spending one's entire future behind bars is reflected in a number of resigned usages, almost all American. Coined in the early 20th century, to **get it all** or **do it all** was to go to prison for life. As the century progressed, the sentence could be **all of it** or **all day**, with the extensions **all day and a night** (a life sentence without the opportunity of parole) and **all day from a quarter** (a sentence of 25 years to life, the *quarter* being a quarter-century). The sense of completeness is also found in the mid-20th century in America with **from now on**, in Australia with **the lot** and **a full hand**, and with the British **the rest of it**. One who is thus fated was **long-gone** in mid-19th-century England, **retired** in contemporary America, or **in the icebox** in the mid-20th-century United States.

To **throw the book at** (as well as its variations **chuck/toss the book at, drop the book on, hit with the book** and **shy the book**) all refer to a figurative 'book of rules' and in standard slang mean to discipline heavily or to reprimand severely. In criminal use from the early 20th century and primarily in America, they have meant to give out a life sentence, also known as a **bookful**. To **do the book** is to serve a life sentence, while to **do the book and cover** is to be imprisoned for the rest of one's natural life. There are many more terms, including Britain's mid-19th-century **breather**, which may refer to the image of the judge's words 'taking your breath away', and the mid-20th-century **strife**, which in general slang means trouble, disgrace or difficulties.

Initially baffling are a few British terms coined in the 1930s: **the knickers**, life imprisonment, **knickers and stockings**, any term of imprisonment, and to **get the knickers**, to get penal servitude. In all cases they have nothing to do with female underwear but are based on the original use of *knickers* as an abbreviation of *knicker-bockers*, specifically the knickerbocker suits once worn by convicts. Finally mid-20th-century America saw the term **do the rosary**, to serve a sentence of imprisonment for the rest of one's natural life. In religious contexts the rosary is made up of 'decades' of prayers; in prison use the decades are quite literal.

SENTENCING: HANGING

Geography

Capital punishment ceased in the UK in 1969; the law had claimed its final victim five years earlier. It had had thousands of others. Hanging, the mode of choice since at least the 14th century, was a regular public event until 1868, and London boasted two major execution sites. The first was *Tyburn*, near the village of *Paddington* (often found as a synonym), which lay near what is now Marble Arch. Tyburn was the principal site of public executions in London between 1388 and 1783; the final victim there was one John Austin, hanged for robbery with violence. After that, the gallows moved to the street outside Newgate prison, the site of today's Central Criminal Court – the Old Bailey.

The first Newgate prison was built in 1188 near the New Gate in the old City Wall. There was to be a prison on the site until in 1901; the last one was demolished to make way for the Old Bailey. The original version was rebuilt by the executors of Richard 'Dick' Whittington in 1422; this one in turn, having burned down during the Great Fire of 1666, was rebuilt again in 1672 (it included a statue of Whittington plus cat in its ornamentation). This, too, was demolished and rebuilt once more in 1770–1. This incarnation was destroyed during the Gordon Riots of 1780, and a final Newgate was erected in 1781. It took over public hangings from Tyburn in 1783 and they were performed in the adjacent street for the next 85 years, until complaints about the public's uproarious conduct during the executions had them taken indoors after 1868.

Both Tyburn and Newgate contributed heavily to the language of judicial death – of which there was a wealth, much of it grimly humorous – covering the wooden gallows itself, the noose, the criminal victim, the act of hanging and of course the hangman. What follows is perhaps half of what was coined.

The Gallows

The gallows loomed, both literally and metaphorically, over the criminal underworld. Its presence did not go unnoticed by language either, and it rejoiced in a wide range of synonyms, as well as a number of variations on the standard English word. However, it was the three corners of Tyburn's multi-gallows, plus the wood from which it was made, that inspired the most potent subset of terms.

The 16th century brought in the earliest: the **triple tree**, **fatal tree**, **sovereign tree**, **triple trestle** and **wooden tree**; or it could be simply **the tree** or **three trees**, since the early gallows was made of three vertical posts joined by a long horizontal bar. The 18th and 19th centuries added more in the same vein: the **three-cornered tree**, the **three-legged instrument**, the **crooked tree**, and the morbid image of the **tree that bears fruit all the year round**. The word *trine* meant threefold, and gave the **trining cheat**, in which cheat meant 'thing'. In addition there was the **turning-tree**, which 'turned off' the criminal (their corpse would also 'turn' as it hanged), the **leafless tree** and the **deadly nevergreen**. The image was still going strong in 1920s America, which used **tall timber**.

The hanged were seen as 'riding' the gallows, and thus the instrument might be the **three-** or **two-legged mare**, or the **three-legged stool**. Going back to equines, it could also be the **wooden horse** or **wooden-legged mare**.

Other names for the gallows drew on a variety of images. The 16th-century **chats**, from Anglo-Saxon *cheat*, a thing, represents a fearful euphemism; there was the late 18th-century **city scales**, on which the villain is 'weighed off'; and the **sheriff's picture frame** was another late 18th-century term – to **dangle in the sheriff's picture frame** was to be hanged. Meanwhile, asphyxiation underlines the **stifler**, the **squeezer** and the **crap** (from Dutch *krap*, cramp or clasp), which gave **knock down/up for the crap**, to sentence a prisoner to be hanged, and **crap-merchant**, the hangman. The gallows could also be the **ladder**, and to be hanged was to **go up the ladder to bed** or **to rest** (in the US in the 1930s it was simply **upstairs**). The mid-19th century's **government signpost** 'pointed the way' to the next world.

The Hangman

England's first hangman, Thomas de Warblynton, performed his grisly duties in the late 14th century, but it was the late 17th century's Jack Ketch who was probably the most notorious among the profession. Practice did not render Ketch, who performed the job from around 1663–86, perfect. He was inefficient and his cruelty to his victims earned him a grim fame. The link with the word *catch*, and the fact that after his death his name was given to the hangman in the puppet-play of *Punchinello* (recently arrived from Italy and the ancestor of Punch and Judy), guaranteed his immortality. His name became synonymous with that of any hangman and in time meant a prison sentence, via rhyming slang (*Jack Ketch* = a stretch).

The World of Jack Ketch

Jack Ketch's certificate a judicial flogging; it is 'given under his hand' (early 19th century)

Jack Ketch's frame the gallows (mid-19th century)

Jack Ketch's kitchen the room in Newgate prison where the hangman boiled the quarters of those dismembered for high treason (18th to 19th centuries)

Jack Ketch's necklace the hangman's noose (early 19th century)

Jack Ketch's pippin a candidate for the gallows (late 17th to 19th centuries)

Jack Ketch's warren the slum area in and around Turnmill Street, Clerkenwell, an area known both for its brothels and for its role as a breeding-ground of crime (19th century)

Pay and Hours

The 17th- to 19th-century hangman received a hangman's wages of 1s. 1½d. (approximately six pence), divided into one shilling for the execution and three halfpence for the rope. The wages were the equivalent of a Scots mark, the amount instituted as the executioner's fee by James VI and I (1566–1625), and the sum was also known as a *loonslate* or *loonslatt*, literally a 'fool's half-crown'.

The Neck
The man was often defined by his job description: the application of choking rope to criminal neck. Thus one finds the mid-19th-century *cramping-cull*, from *cramp*, to compress or cull. Execution day was *cramping-day*; *Cramp Abbey* denoted Newgate (and, later, any prison); and *cramp words* were a sentence of death (this may have been a play on standard English *cramp word*, a long, difficult or unusual word and that one perhaps 'choked on'). In the late 18th to mid-19th centuries, the hangman could also be a *scrag-boy* or *scraggier* – from *scrag*, meaning neck. Scrag offered additional linked terms: *scrag 'em fair* or *scrag-fair*, a hanging, and *scrag squeezer*, the gallows. From the 17th century until as late as the 1960s was the *stretcher*, who 'stretched' the neck, and in the mid-17th century came the *topman* and *topping cove*. He survived until Victorian times – later, in the 1920s, we find the *topper*. All refer to the 'top' of the body, as did *topping*, execution by hanging; *topping cheat* (literally 'hanging thing'), the gallows; and *topping shed*, a term in use from the mid-19th century until the 1950s to denote that part of a prison in which the gallows was kept.

The Noose

Although aristocrats might have demanded a silken rope, the average villain had no choice: it was invariably *hemp*, a plant that would earn some notoriety under its Latin name, *Cannabis sativa*, but which was synonymous with the hangman's noose from the 16th century onwards.

Thus one found the *hemp office*, the condemned cell; *hempseed* (from Elizabethan until Georgian times, and then briefly again in the 1940s), which meant both the hangman and the villain who is destined to hang; and the 17th-century warning *the hemp's grown* or *hemp-seed's sown for you*, implying that the person in question is bound to end on the gallows if they pursue their current lifestyle. The adjective *hempen*, i.e. made of hemp, offers many more compounds pertaining to hanging. The noose could be a *hempen cravat, . . . circle, . . . garment, . . . halter, . . . hood, . . . hornpipe, . . . knot, . . . necklace, . . . necktie, . . . noose, . . . ring, . . . snare, . . . string, . . . tackle, . . . twine,* or . . . *wings,* as well as a *hemp necktie, hemp tie* and *hemp neck-cloth.* It was also a *hempen caudle,* a pun on standard English *caudle,* a gruel spiced with wine or ale and given to the sick: the noose is an ironic a form of 'painkiller'. The *hempen habeas* punned on *habeas corpus,* literally 'thou shalt have the body'. To *frisk in a hempen cravat* or *look through a hempen window* was to be hanged; the *hempen fever* the act of hanging; the *hempen consummation* one's death; and the wife one left behind was the *hempen widow.*

A number of other terms refer to encirclement of the neck, but playing on less painful articles of dress. There is the *anodyne necklace*: such a necklace was originally a form of medicinal amulet peddled by charlatans and especially popular in the early 18th century; based on the original definition of *anodyne* as soothing pain, this too punned on 'painkiller'. The noose could also be a *tippet,* a *tight cravat,* a *halter,* a *neck-cloth, neckweed* or *necktie.* The late 16th-century *horse's nightcap* defined the cap that was pulled over the condemned man's head before his death.

To Be Hanged

A skilled hangman killed his victim by careful positioning of the rope, which effected a supposedly instantaneous snapping of the neck. Not all were skilful, however, and – especially prior to the late 18th-century introduction of the *drop* (the hinged boards beneath the victim's feet that dropped away at the moment of execution) – hanging, as often as not, meant slow strangulation. It was not unknown for friends to pull on a man's feet in order to hasten his asphyxiation. As the victim died the body writhed and kicked, and to the unkind the image was that of dancing.

This 'dance of death' coined the verbs *do the dance, dance on nothing* and *do the Newgate hornpipe,* and – later, in the 1920s

– the *dancehall*, the execution chamber. An 18th-century British sheriff's jurisdiction over the hanging gave *dance at the sheriff's ball and loll out one's tongue at the company*. Contemporary with that was *dance at Beilby's ball*, often extended with . . . *where the sheriff plays the music* or . . . *where the sheriff pays the fiddlers*. (One might also *shake* or *shiver one's trotters at Beilby's ball*.) The etymology of *Beilby's ball* is unknown and the identity of Mr Beilby remains a mystery, but theories do exist. The most obvious is that Beilby was a well-known sheriff; a second is that Beilby is a mispronunciation of Old Bailey, the court in which so many villains were sentenced to death. The third is that Beilby refers to the *bilbo*, a long iron bar that was furnished with sliding shackles to confine the ankles of prisoners and a lock by which to fix one end of the bar to the floor or ground. Bilbo comes from the Spanish town of Bilbao, where these fetters were invented.

The image of climbing provided further imagery, and the steps that led to the gallows went beyond that, it was hoped, to heaven. One could *climb* any of the words for gallows, for example the *leafless tree*, the *stalk* or the *ladder*, which could be the *six-foot ladder* (referring to the six-foot depth of a grave). One might *go up the ladder to bed* or *to rest*, or *walk up ladder Lane and down Hemp Street*. Alternatively, one might be seen to *jump* or *leap*, for example *leap at a daisy* (at Tyburn the gallows were surrounded by grass). One might also *take a leap in the dark*.

There seemed to be no end to the imagery or the imagination. A number of terms were based on choking: the 19th-century *nab the stifles*, from standard English *stifle*, choking; the earlier *cry cockles*, supposedly the sound made as one chokes; to *make a wry mouth*, playing on the rictus of suffocation and on the expression *make a wry mouth*; and the punning 19th-century *take a vegetable breakfast*, i.e. to have a 'hearty choke'.

Some were more complex. To *go off with* (or *at*) *the fall of the leaf* punned on the 'leaves' or hinged panels of the drop and the dead leaves that fall from a natural, rather than judicial, tree. Meanwhile, to *leave the world...* or *die with cotton in one's ears* was an early 19th-century reference to a Newgate chaplain, the Reverend Cotton, who would preach a last sermon to the condemned man. To *nap a winder* stole from prize-fighting jargon, where a *winder* was a blow 'that takes one's breath away'. The 18th-century to *piss when one cannot whistle* refers to the loss of bladder control that accompanies a hanging. A hanging was thus known as *wry mouth and a pissen pair of breeches*: the contorted mouth and breeches that bear evidence of a loosened bladder

The final journey from Newgate prison to Tyburn brought two popular phrases. One was to *walk* or *ride (backwards) up Holborn Hill*, used in the 17th and 18th centuries. The road ran along Holborn and criminals traditionally stood in the cart facing backwards, possibly to increase their ignominy but more likely to avoid seeing the approaching gallows until the last possible moment. It was traditional for the condemned to make two stops for refreshment on the way; the first was at the Bowl Inn in St Giles, the second at the Mason's Arms in Seymour Place. The second phrase, still in use (though less terminally), was to *go west*. This appears to combine the western direction of the journey plus the image of the setting sun – in this case on one's life.

SENTENCING: ELECTROCUTION, GAS AND LETHAL INJECTION

While the UK stayed consistently with the rope for the purpose of judicial executions, the US has been more inventive. Methods there have included electrocution, hanging, the firing squad, the gas chamber and beheading. The current preference is for lethal injection, otherwise known as the *big jab* or the *needle*. The mix of drugs – typically a barbiturate, a paralytic and a potassium solution – is known as *joy juice*. This form of execution is relatively new; others, particularly the gas chamber and the electric chair, have generated much more mordant slang.

The Gas Chamber

The chamber itself is known ironically as the **green room** or **house with green shutters**; the gas itself as **Arizona perfume**, from the one-time popularity of the death penalty in that state. To set the process in motion is to **drop the pill on** someone (the pill is the cyanide capsule dropped into a container of acid), and the condemned person has been **smoked** or **smogged**.

The Electric Chair

By far the most popular method of execution, certainly in Hollywood's renditions of the death house, has been the electric chair. First used in 1890 it became the execution of choice in 25 states, earning such grim nicknames as **Old Smokey** (New Jersey; a reference to the smoke that rises from the victim), **Old Sparky** (New York's Sing Sing prison), **Yellow Mama** (Alabama) and **Gruesome Gertie** (Louisiana). The apparatus had already earned its first, and obvious, nickname **the chair** by 1895 and other than hanging, it remained the greatest creator of terms of any agency of judicial death. The act of execution has attracted suitably grisly verbs, from the pre-war **cook**, **sizzle** and still-popular **fry** to the post-war **burn**, **roast**, **stew** and **nuke**. The executioner is sometimes known as **the chef**. As for his victims, they **get the juice**, **get toasted** or **ride the lightning**. In the graphic phrase of the 1910s and 1920s, they are **up salt creek**.

The Electric Chair

What follows is just a selection of the many terms that have been applied to the electric chair:

baker   1950s
fryer   1920s onwards
frying pan   1930s
hot chair, armchair, seat, squat or **stool**   1920s onwards
the heat   1940s
hot plate   1940s

humming bird   late 19th century to 1930s (electricity 'hums')
pew   1930s
sizzle seat   1940s–60s
smoky rocker or *seat*   1930s–60s
squat   1990s onwards (from the 1940s *squat hot*, to be executed in the electric chair)
squativoo   1930s (from the cod-French *squattez-vous*, sit down)
wires   1920s

SENTENCING: NON-CUSTODIAL PUNISHMENTS

Not all sentences ended in prison, nor indeed on the gallows. There were a number of non-custodial punishments which predated imprisonment and ran in parallel with hanging.

The *pillory*, a word that comes first from French and before that most likely from Latin, is first recorded in the 13th century but almost certainly pre-existed the written source. It was a means of public humiliation that took the form of a wooden framework mounted on a post, containing holes into which the victim's head and arms could be locked. He was condemned to stay there for a number of hours or even longer, during which time the public were at liberty to assault him both verbally and physically, sometimes even to the point of death. It was not inevitable, however, that the victim would be harmed; the crowd might sympathise, or its ring-leaders could be bribed.

The pillory was abolished as a form of punishment in Britain in 1837 but it earned a number of names from the 17th century onwards. Among them, the **wooden casement** or **wooden cravat**, the **stoop early**, which noted the position one had to adopt while thus confined, and the **nutcracker**. Despite – given the hurts that one might suffer – what might seem logical links to slang's *nut*, head, or *nuts*, testicles, this last term actually predates these slang usages; instead it appears that the word simply borrowed from standard English, on the basis that the framework resembled the kitchen utensil.

Considered to be less injurious than the pillory, and used on those convicted of lesser crimes, the stocks typically locked in only the feet, although some versions had holes into which the head and/ or arms could be inserted. The last recorded use of the stocks in Britain came in 1872. They generated a few terms from the 16th century, notably the **clogments**, based on the standard English *clog*, a heavy lump of wood attached to the leg or neck of a man or animal in order to restrict motion or escape; the **pigeonhole**, again from standard English and referring to a small hole or recess; and the **harmans**, which may have been linked to the 16th-century cant term *harman*, a parish constable or beadle, or to standard English *hard* plus the suffix *-mans* (found in a number of early cant terms), and thus meaning a 'hard state of being'.

More widespread as a punishment, and undoubtedly guaranteed to cause harm, was flogging: the application of a whip, whether one of single or multiple strands. One might be flogged at the pillory, which was often used as a proxy whipping post, but the action that underpinned several cant terms was that of being whipped at the cart's tail: the prisoner would be secured by the wrists to the end of a cart, horses would pull the vehicle slowly through the streets, and an official would apply the lash. This procedure offered a number of phrases, mostly 18th century and often blackly humorous, such as to **have/take air and exercise**, which could also apply to less public punishments in prison as well as simply standing unwhipped but otherwise assaulted in the pillory; and to **play the part of the strong man**, where the victim is seen to be 'pushing' the cart. Synonymous were to **shove the tumbler** or **nap the flog at the tumbler**; the tumbler could be expanded as the **flogging tumbler** or had previously been known as the **shove-tumbril**. Allied terms include to **cry carrots (and turnips)**, probably an ironic and ono-matopoeic reference to the usual carter's cries as well as those of the sufferer, or to be **fly-flapped** from the standard verb *fly-flap*, to beat, to whip (and originally to hit flies with a swatter).

Away from the cart in the 19th century, flogging inspired the **puzzling sticks**, a triangle to which a criminal was tied in order to receive a judicial whipping and on which the criminal was given an opportunity to 'puzzle' over their crimes while being punished. (On the other hand puzzle may be a misreading of standard English *posing*, which reflects the way the criminal would be lashed firmly to the triangle.) To **have claws for breakfast** was to receive any sort of a judicial whipping; the claws being, of course, those of the *cat*, first encountered in a non-feline form with its nine tails in the late 18th century, and still encountered among right-wingers in the old litany: 'bring back the cat'. Finally, in the 1930s, one finds **pop the bud**, meaning to administer a judicial whipping.

SENTENCING: TRANSPORTATION

Almost as soon as England began to establish an empire, first in the New World and later in Australia, the authorities appreciated the use of such distant lands as a dumping ground for the socially unpopular and criminal. Transportation to the Americas lasted from the 1610s until the American Revolution of the 1770s; it was quickly replaced by transportation to the mainly unknown land of Australia, usually called Botany Bay. The 'First Fleet' left England in 1787 and arrived on 26 January 1788. The penal colony that was founded was the first immigrant settlement of any sort in the country. It is not surprising that when the country's first dictionary was published in 1812, as an addendum to the memoirs of the recidivist transportee James Hardy Vaux (he made the voyage out three times), it was one of cant.

Lag

Transportation and the convict settlements it established helped to create a substantial and purpose-built subset of the canting vocabulary, all of which began with a single monosyllable: **lag**. Based on the 16th-century standard *lag*, to carry off, to steal, by the mid-18th century it meant to sentence to transportation for more than seven years. Further meanings, both in Australia and beyond, include: to arrest or apprehend; to cause trouble for; to lead to an arrest; to imprison;

to inform on; and finally, in 20th-century America, to imprison on trumped-up charges and faked evidence.

If there is any term synonymous with the image of a veteran convict it is the **old lag**. The phrase is recorded in Vaux's lists, but it is defined here as 'a man or woman who has been transported, and is so called on returning home'. Like the verb, the noun lag began life in Botany Bay, where it first described a term of transportation or penal servitude; it became a convict who has been transported or sentenced to penal servitude in the early 19th century, and then a convict who has finished his or her sentence, or has been released on parole. By the mid-19th century the term had acquired its lasting meaning and no longer had any link to a specific prison or country: it meant any convict, and offered such derivatives as **Lagland** and **old lagdom** for the criminal underworld. Lag moved on in the 20th century, primarily in Australia although also elsewhere, to mean a sentence of any length, and latterly one of three-months.

The basic term has developed a number of compounds, mostly in the 19th century. It was expanded to **lagger**, a convict, and thus a **long-lagger** was a convict serving a long sentence. (By the end of the century, a lagger could also be an informer, and to lag was to inform.) **Lag fever** was a spurious illness feigned in order to avoid transportation; those who failed to convince the doctor had to board the **lag ship**, the vessel used for the transportation of convicts to Australia – although it could also be a prison hulk moored in the Thames estuary (it was from one of these that Magwitch escaped in Dickens's *Great Expectations*). A **lag's farewell** is more usually known as a *soldier's farewell* and runs: 'Goodbye, good luck, and fuck you!' **Lagged** first appeared in the late 18th century to mean transported or imprisoned, especially, in 1930s America, with no hope of release. A **lagging** was a sentence of transportation; thus the **lagging matter** was any crime punishable by transportation, but this later meant any prison sentence and later still one of more than three years. **Lagging dues** also referred to transportation; usually in the phrase *lagging dues will be concerned* (i.e. this person is liable to be transported); such 'dues' also referred to a sentence of penal servitude. A **lagging station** was and remains a prison for long-term prisoners. The **leg** was a convict awaiting the boat; the term may have been a misspelling of lag, but it was also possibly a reference to the leg-irons that he might be wearing.

Euphemisms

The authorities made no attempt to disguise the process, but transportation still created a number of criminal euphemisms in the late 18th and 19th centuries. To be **abroad** was to be transported, giving **abroaded** for those transported to a penal colony; abroaded had a subsequent life in British society, where it meant living 'in exile' somewhere other than Britain (and back in Britain it meant imprisoned). Similar terms were to **go to foreign parts**, to **go out of the country**, to **travel** and thus to be a **traveller at Her Majesty's expense**; the Anglo-Irish to **go beyond** – that is, 'beyond' the world one knows – and the Irish to **go over**. The fact that both the last two also meant to die may have expressed the convicts' belief that it was very unlikely that they would survive the experience, whether during sea journey or after arrival on land.

The sea and its winds are found in one of the earliest terms from the late 17th century, the punning to **marinate** (and **marinated**, transported) as well as **bellowsed**. *Bellowsed* meant out of breath, and as such might refer to the sentence having 'taken one's breath away'; certainly the original use of the term was in prize-fighting, where a *bellowser* was a punch in the stomach or a 'blow in the wind'. A **bellowser** was thus a sentence of lifetime transportation, while the phrase **knap/nap a bellowser** meant to be transported for life. Wind imagery also underpins **winder**, a sentence of transportation for life; to **nap a winder, nap the winder, nap the winding post** and **knap a winder** were to suffer this punishment. Here, however, the wind is almost certainly the 'wind of life' (i.e. the breath) and gives an additional phrase **lagged for one's wind**, transported for one's natural life. To **settle** meant to sentence to penal transportation, while **settled** and **winded settled** meant transported. Finally a phrase that was more usually applied to not-so-young women who had failed to find a spouse: **on the shelf** was an ironic reference to the standard use meaning to put away for later.

Other Terms

Transportation generated a good deal more terms in the 19th century. Among its more arcane creations was the criminal phrase to **work under the armpits**, which was 'translated' as to confine one's criminality to such activities that would be classed as petty larceny, bringing a maximum sentence of seven years' transportation, rather than hanging; its converse was to **work above the armpits**, to commit crimes that could lead to one's execution. The armpits here refer to the limits of criminal safety: to work above them was to bring one into the realm of capital crimes and expose the neck to the noose; to stay below was at least to save one's life.

The sentence that destined one to a life 'abroad' was a **read of tripe**, which played on a standard term *read*, the stomach of an animal (from which comes tripe), and the 'tripe' that is read out in court. To **boat** was to transport a convict and to be **sent across the herring pond** or **cross the herring pond at the King's expense** was to be transported, although the use of *herring pond* to mean the sea had originally meant the Atlantic and is first recorded in the 17th century. To **lump the lighter** was to be transported; it was a figurative use of the standard words *lump*, to load, and *lighter*, a vessel used for loading/unloading ships.

Chapter 11

INCARCERATION

Dear Bill, this stone-jug, at which flats dare to rail
(From which till the next Central sittings I hail),
Is still the same snug, free-and-easy old hole,
Where Macheath met his blowens and Wild floor'd his bowl
In a ward with one's pals, not locked up in a cell
To an old hand like me it's a family hotel

'An Epistle from Toby Cracksman, in Newgate,
to Bill Sykes' in *Punch* (31 January 1857)

THE PRISON

Prison may 'work' for most civilians insofar as the idea of being
locked up definitely deters them from crime, but for the professional
villain it is just one more part of the job. 'If you can't do the time,
don't do the crime', runs the old adage, and the professional sees
regular spells behind bars as just part of the 'win some, lose some'
lottery. No wonder that cant offers such a rich and wide-ranging
terminology based on incarceration in the **queer ken** (literally 'bad
place', used in the 16th and 17th centuries for a prison).

General Terms

Stir
While the terms for a prison are numerous, some are more productive than others. **Stir**, from the Romany *sturiben*, a prison, and
staripen, to imprison, has been among the best-known terms since
the mid-19th century. Beyond the simple definition of a prison, stir

is probably most regularly found in the context of the emotional stress of serving time, especially in America. *Stir-crazy*, *stir-batty*, *stir-happy* and *stir-looney* all originate in 1930s America and are all used of a convict who has succumbed to prison-induced insanity; *stir-craziness*, psychosis induced by imprisonment, is a term that exists beyond the walls, meaning any breakdown resulting from some form of intolerable monotony. From the 1920s, a *stir-bug* or *stir-nut* is one who has gone mad due to the pressures of incarceration, and to be *stir-bugs*, *stir-nuts*, *stir-nutty*, *stir-psycho* or *stir-simple* is to be insane from too long a confinement. The 'bugs' are, of course, in the head. The attendant psychological or physical problems are *stir cramps* in the 1970s, while such cases may all too likely find their way to the *stir croaker* (1950s), a second-rate, barely qualified doctor assigned to prison work; his ministrations are more likely to *croak* or kill the patient than cure them. In the first half of the 20th century, stir has also produced *stir belly*, indigestion caused by tension or fear; *stirbum*, a jailbird; *stir hustler*, from slang's *hustler* (one who lives on their wits and thus here one who has mastered the 'art' of incarceration); and *stirwise*, well adjusted to prison life and capable of sustaining an existence in prison. The *big stir* is a federal prison, as opposed to a state one. Back to Britain in the late 19th century, to *crush the stir/stur* meant to break out of prison.

Stone Walls

Stone walls may or may not a prison make, but they provide a useful image for cant. The earliest such term, from the late 17th to 18th centuries, is the *stone doublet* (from standard English *doublet*, tight-fitting body armour), which was especially used of Newgate; the same imagery is found in America's late 18th-century *stone jacket*. The early 19th-century *stone tavern* might also refer specifically to Newgate prison, as might the *stone jug* or *stone pitcher*, although these were also generic for any prison establishment from the 17th century to the present, as were *stone john* and *stone kitchen*. Nor did the jug or pitcher have to be stone, just a container: since the early 19th century, *jug* by itself has meant a prison, while America's *jug-house* appeared in the 1930s to 1960s.

But to return to the imagery of stone, 20th-century America provides **stone crock** (from standard English *crock*, a jug) for a state prison (originally Sing Sing), as well as the **stone dump**, **stone mansion**, **stone house** and **stone college**. In the late 19th century, also in America, to have been **rocked in a stone cradle** was to have been born in prison, a phrase that summons up the pastiche 18th-century canting song 'Nix, My Doll, Pals, Fake Away' which was in fact created in 1834 for his novel *Rookwood* (the almost wholly spurious story of the highwayman Dick Turpin) by the bestselling 'Newgate novelist' Harrison Ainsworth. 'In a box of the stone jug I was born, / Of a hempen widow the kid forlorn.'

The **rockpile** or **pile** are American terms meaning the prison quarry from the late 19th century onwards, and later the prison itself. Any prison could also be the **rock** from the 1950s onwards, but **the Rock** was the supposedly escape-proof offshore prison island of Alcatraz in California, or Rikers Island prison in New York City, or (in mid-19th-century Britain) the prison at Gibraltar where felons were often transported. America also has the 20th-century **rock crusher** (also a prisoner in the 1960s) and **big rock** (1960s), while New Zealand uses **rock college** from the 1980s.

Hotels
One of the most recent of the stone/prison combinations is the **stone hotel**, appearing in 1970s America. The image of a prison as a 'hotel' is a widespread one, emerging in America in the early 19th century with – simply – **hotel**. This was soon embellished as a **spike hotel** (the metal spikes on the walls), a **teetotal hotel** (there is no liquor in prison, or not legally) and a **family hotel** (although this family was most likely the *Johnson Family*, the world of American crooks, rather than the yet to materialise Mafia). New Zealand's **Hotel de Garvey** of the 1900s recalls a governor of Wellington Jail. The 20th-century American terms **free hotel** and **free motel** depend on what might be seen as prison's single 'advantage': you don't pay for the accommodation. In 1920s Britain, a **country hotel** was a prison outside London. One returns to stones in the middle of the 20th century in America, with the **hard-rock**

hotel or *hard-rock city*, but whether these suggest the stones from which they are built or the rocks that prisoners are made to break is unknown. Current since the 1940s, the American term *cross-bar hotel/Hilton* refers to the metal strips that divide a cell window, while Britain's *crowbar hotel* is a variant, providing an extra reference to the need for a crowbar to escape. Finally, there is the contemporary *Windsor Group hotel*, which plays on Windsor, the surname of the Royal Family, and the legal phrase 'detained at Her Majesty's Pleasure'.

Shops and Colleges, Factories and Warehouses
Other forms of establishment have been used, starting with the late 17th-century coinage *shop*. Presumably, this was based on the prisoner's lack of status, like anything else that could be bought or sold. (It is echoed in *hock shop* from the 1950s, where it was prisoners rather than possessions who were 'pawned'.) From the late 18th century, *academy* appeared, however, it was rarely found by itself, and was more usual in compounds that paid respect to a given governor, such as *Adkins's academy*, or with *Campbell's academy*, a prison ship (or *floating academy*) that was named after the first director of such prison hulks. The *boarding house* is a jocular generality from the mid-19th century onwards, but initially it was used for New York City's Tombs prison, while the *home of rest* from the 1910s is all too ironically simple.

Among the most popular names for a prison was *college*, with its ironic reference to a 'university of crime'; it has been found on both sides of the Atlantic from the 17th century to the present day. Early on it specifically meant Newgate prison, and sometimes also the King's (or later Queen's) Bench or Fleet prisons. In the late 18th and early 19th centuries, the *city college* was Newgate prison (in the late 19th and early 20th centuries it was the Tombs Prison, New York City). To *go to college* was to go to prison, a *college chum* was a prisoner (coincidentally in American prisons in the 1960s a *college boy* was a fellow inmate), while the *college cove* was the turnkey of Newgate prison. The *grad* (for *graduate*) has meant an ex-convict since the late 19th century.

In America, still borrowing from other establishments, are the

20th-century *farm* and *factory*. The former is an abbreviation of
the standard term *work farm*; it gives *junk farm*, a federal re-
habilitation institution (*junk* being slang for narcotics) and *cherry
farm*, a prison that houses first-offenders (from slang's *cherry*, a
virgin or a novice). Factory is a 1910s term based on the prison's
architecture, which is not unlike that of contemporary factories
(a certain generation of British police stations have been similarly
named), and also on the 'manufacturing' therein of evidence. It is
sometimes modified as *behave factory* or *song factory*, a play
on the criminal *birds* within, and at the informers who 'sing' on
demand.

The last of these borrowings is the *booby-hatch*, which appeared
from the mid-19th century to the 1960s to mean a prison, and was
also found briefly as *hatch* or *hatch house*. The term is far more
frequently found as a politically incorrect term for the vast Victorian
barracks in which lunatics were shut away, but the sense of locking
up predates this. It probably comes from the nautical use, meaning
a small 'companion' or hood used to enclose staircases on merchant
ships, or alternatively it may refer to the *booby-hutch*, a small, clumsy
coach (with this spelling it came to mean a police station or lock-
up). *Booby*, from Spanish *bobo*, a fool (with a pun on the standard
English *booby*, a large, slow-flying bird), is much older, dating back
to the 17th century. The 20th-century *boob* was an abbreviation that
originated in Australia and was first used of a military prison. It
has provided a small lexicon of Antipodean compounds: *boob dot*,
a small blue dot tattooed beneath the eye, indicating a spell in borstal
or prison; *boob gear*, prison uniform; *boob talk*, prison jargon; *boob
tat*, a prison tattoo; *boob tea*, weak, prison-brewed tea; and
boob weed, prison-issue tobacco. The *boobhead* is an influential,
experienced prisoner, while the *boob rat* is his antithesis, often a
recidivist.

Crowded modern prisons are often condemned for 'warehousing'
the socially unacceptable; the *spring ankle warehouse* made no
attempt to hide the fact in the late 18th to early 19th centuries. The
phrase is based on standard English *spring*, to sprain (in this case
an ankle), and the inference is that once confined in such a place,
the inmates are unable easily to run off.

The Clink, Nick and Chokey

Other well-known terms include the clink, the nick and chokey. The Clink was originally an actual London prison, sited on the south bank of the Thames in Southwark. Originally used for the detention of religious heretics (the denomination of which changed according to whichever sect was currently performing the auto-da-fé), it functioned from 1151 until 1780, when it was burnt down during the Gordon Riots. Unlike other carceral victims of the riots the Clink was never rebuilt, however, **clink** lives on as a general term for a prison, used from the 16th century to the present day. While the term is popularly believed to be echoic of either dragging chains or shutting doors, it would more likely seem to have come from standard English *clinch*, to fasten securely, or from Dutch *klink* (or German and Danish *klinke*), a door-latch, a meaning that is also found in French *clinche*. It is thus cognate with another contemporaneous word for prison: **ferme**, from French *fermer*, to shut or close.

While the use of the **nick** as a police station, a lock-up or a prison is relatively late, appearing in the late 19th century, the use as a verb meaning to take, steal and – with the criminal as the object rather than subject – to arrest, is a century and a half older. (The ultimate standard English etymology suggests the making of a cut or notch.) Rhyming slang offers **shovel and pick**, usually found as **shovel**. **Chokey**, from Hindi *chauki*, is one of many words that returned to England with military veterans, first of the East India Company and latterly of the British Army. The original meaning is a four-sided building or a shed, especially a customs house or police station and thus a lock-up. Imported into Britain in the mid-19th century, it was used initially as a prison, specifically its punishment cells; two further meanings were added at the century's end: imprisonment in general and the prison punishment diet of bread and water (the **chokey merchant** is the one who is suffering such a punishment).

The Start and the Quod

Current as a general term for any prison in the mid-18th to 19th centuries, the **Start** or **Old Start** could also be Newgate prison in particular. Its origins are debatable. The standard English *start* means a shock or surprise, and might be seen as linked to the deracinating experiences of entering prison; alternatively it could mean a beginning, i.e. a new form of life (whether good or bad), an image that could also underlie the later use of the Start to mean the Old Bailey, where one received one's sentence. The same imagery could equally be linked to the start of the prisoner's final journey, as the cart took him west from Newgate to Tyburn.

From the late 17th century, the **quod** or **quad** also meant Newgate, and specifically its *quadrangle*, which housed debtors (it seems to have applied to the cells as well as the yards they surrounded), but the term became general and was still being used for any prison in the mid-20th century. Its first appearance is in B.E.'s *Dictionary of the Canting Crew* (*c*.1698): 'Quod, Newgate; also any Prison, tho' for Debt.' The **quod cove** and **quod cull** (*cove* and *cull* both meaning man) were either a prison governor or one of its turnkeys. In the 19th century, to be **quodded** was to be imprisoned and if *quodding dues are concerned* then the matter concerned would involve imprisonment.

London Prisons

Newgate
Of all London's prisons, none can rival Newgate. Its longevity is unsurpassed – in one form or another it lasted for over seven centuries – and its shadow extends over its successor on the same site, the Central Criminal Court (better known as the Old Bailey), the country's best-known theatre of the legal melodramas known as trials. It played host to many of the country's most notorious malefactors, and sent many of them on their way to Tyburn's gallows, later taking on the hanging itself. From a linguistic point of view, it certainly outperformed any rival prison in the range of its nick-names and the canting terms generated alongside them.

Its role as a site of execution produced many terms associated with hanging (see page 295), but this was only a small part, and a

relatively short-lived one, of Newgate's history and linguistic influence. The bulk of cant's references to the prison focused on its
custodial role, as an inevitable home for the criminal. In the 17th
century it spawned the term a *Newgate bird* for a prisoner, especially
a confidence trickster, even one held elsewhere. A *Newgate nightingale* was another caged bird, in this case a novice criminal in the
16th century. The *Newgate knocker* was a lock of hair shaped like
the figure 6 and twisted from the temple back towards the ear; for
a while in the mid- to late 19th century it was very fashionable,
especially apparently with the criminal classes. *Black/dark as
Newgate* or *Newgate's knocker* (the literal one) referred to a very
dark night in the late 19th century but gained a resurgence in the
1980s when it was recorded as meaning very dirty. When used of a
facial expression, black as Newgate meant frowning or glowering,
and of a garment, dirty. Less menacing, in fact rather mediocre, was
the *Newgate solicitor*, a second-rate lawyer found in the 18th and
19th centuries, who hung around prisons (including but not invariably Newgate) in the hope of picking up work.

Newgate offers one final specific term: the *abbey-croaker* of the
mid-19th century was the prison's 'ordinary' or chaplain; abbey is
used here as a generic for prison, and *croaker* refers to the clergyman's indistinct speech. While other chaplains may have been
despised figures, Newgate's Ordinary held a lucrative job. Among
his perks was that of publishing an account of the prisoners' last
dying speeches, known as *dies*, and the way that he or she might
have conducted themselves on the scaffold, along with stories of
their lives and crimes (however fantastical). Such stories were very
popular, predating the rash of villains' memoirs of subsequent years.
Over time some 400 editions of these accounts were published –
shortly following every hanging day – offering biographies for some
2,500 executed criminals.

Newgate itself was also used to mean any prison from the 16th
to the 19th centuries, while the actual prison gained a slew of
nicknames.

Names for Newgate Prison

Akerman's hotel   late 18th to mid-19th centuries
    (memorialising a celebrated jailer, *c*.1787)
Burrowdamp Museum   mid-19th-century (its burrowing
    rodents and damp cells)
Chequer Inn (in Newgate Street)   late 17th to mid-19th
    centuries
city college   late 18th to early 19th centuries
College, the   17th to 19th centuries
King's Head Inn (in Newgate Street)   late 17th to
    mid-19th centuries
Gate or **Gate-House**   19th century
**Newman's college, Newman's hotel, Newman's
    tea-gardens**   19th century
Old Start   mid-18th to 19th centuries
quad/quod   late 17th century
rumbo-ken   18th to mid-19th centuries (ironic blend of
    cant *rum*, i.e. good, plus *ken*, place)
Start, the   mid-18th to 19th centuries
stone doublet   late 17th to 18th centuries
stone tavern   early 19th century

Other London Prisons

Newgate was not unique; London boasted a number of prisons, just
as it does today. Most, however, have not survived. Coldbath Fields
Prison in Farringdon flourished from 1794 to 1877. It was known as
Bate's Farm, Bate's Garden or **Charley Bate's Farm/Garden**, after
the name of a well-known warder. The prison was also known for
its severity; and thus the phrase *feed the chickens on Charley Bate's
farm* meant to be sentenced to the treadmill. Coldbath Fields was
also known as **the Bastille**, drawing on the French *bastille*, a fortified
tower, but more specifically the main Paris prison, built in the 14th
century, the destruction of which in 1789 triggered the French

Revolution. (In America in the 1950s, San Quentin, the island prison near San Francisco, was named the **Bastille by the Bay**, coined by local columnist Herb Caen, whose better known creation was the word 'beatnik'.) The Bastille was often abbreviated as **the Steel**, and both in full and abbreviated it was used to describe any prison, while the Steel was also used of a treadmill, thus **on the steel** meant both imprisoned and 'working' on the treadmill.

The Fleet prison, the first example of which was opened in 1197 on the eastern bank of the Fleet River, which flowed down from Hampstead into the Thames, was almost as old as Newgate. Mainly used to house debtors and bankrupts, it suffered a succession of fires and was regularly rebuilt, but it was finally pulled down for good in 1846. The course of the Fleet River became what is now Farringdon Street, and among the prison's nicknames in the 18th and 19th centuries was the **Farringdon hotel**; others included the **man of war** (the image is of an anchored warship), the **never-wag (man of war)** (from slang's *wag*, to walk or leave), and **number 9** (from its official address at 9 Fleet Market). The inmates had a variety of privileges, not least of which was living outside the prison itself, in what was known as the 'liberty of the Fleet'. The prison and its immediate area were also the home to a thriving industry of 'Fleet marriages', irregular or clandestine ceremonies that sidestepped church regulations.

Among other London prisons was **the Horn** in the late 17th century, properly the Compter, although the site of this particular prison, since *compter* is a standard English generic, was not specified. It could have been the Poultry Compter or Counter, also known as the **rats' castle** in the early 18th century (although its population of vermin would not have been unique). **Burdon's hotel** was a mid-19th-century term for Whitecross Street prison, where a governor had been one Burdon; and the **mill doll** or **mill-dolly** (literally 'beat hemp') referred to the Bridewell in Bridge Street, Blackfriars, from the mid-18th to 19th centuries. **Bridewell** was itself a generic term for prison and one that, at least in Liverpool, is still used.

Nask or **naskin** (possibly linked to Romany *nasher*, to lose, to hang) could be used for any prison in the late 17th to 19th centuries, but was specifically used of Tothill Fields prison near modern Victoria (**Tuttle Nask**), City Bridewell prison (**Old Nask**) and the notoriously unpleasant Clerkenwell prison (*New Nask*).

South of the river in Southwark were the King's Bench and Horsemonger Lane establishments. The former was known as *the Spikes* in the early 19th century and boasted an unlikely 'attraction': the *brace tavern*, a room where prisoners could buy beer, originally administered by a pair of brothers named Brace. Horsemonger Lane prison was called *the Horse* or *Old Horse*. It had been erected in 1799 as a model prison and lasted until the 1880s; it was outside the Horse on 13 November 1847 that Charles Dickens witnessed the public hanging of the murderers Frederick and Maria Manning.

All these prisons have vanished. Pentonville Prison, in Caledonian Road, north London, has not. Opened in 1842 and known as *The Pent*, it was designed as a model prison on the 'separate system', continuous solitary confinement irrespective of one's crime (a method, pioneered in the Haviland Eastern Penitentiary in Philadelphia, which added a new refinement of cruelty to mere confinement). It was also known as *the Model*, and from the 1920s the *Ville* or *Vil*. Wormwood Scrubs, built in 1874 by an all-convict labour force, in West London, has always been the *Scrubs*.

American Prisons

The Standards
Penitentiary is, of course, a standard term, and is linked to the French *pénitentiaire*, a place of discipline or punishment; its ultimate etymology is the Latin *paenitentia* or *poenitentia*, penance. It is, perhaps, indicative of the religious strand that imbues American society that the term remains common there, specifically referring to large federal prisons in which convicted felons are imprisoned; as compared to a jail, which in Britain is simply a synonym for prison but in America refers to certain institutions that are often run on a local level, used for those with lighter sentences, or for those awaiting trial. Penitentiary is often found abbreviated as *pen*, although this is underpinned by the standard English *pen*, a small enclosure for animals, which may itself be from the German regional *pennen*, to bolt (a door). Both penitentiary and the other standard jailhouse have lent itself to a number of associated underworld terms.

Penitentiary and Jailhouse Favourites

All the following penitentiary compounds have been in use for much of the 20th century, and most were coined in the 1930s. The **penitentiary agent** and **penitentiary dispatcher** are both disparaging descriptions of the court-appointed public defender whose clients tend to end up convicted and who is seen more as working for the courts and police than providing a useful defence for the accused. **Penitentiary bait** is a synonym for the more widely used *jailbait*, an underage and thus illegal sexual partner; the **penitentiary punk** is a young prisoner who, at least while inside, is made the prey of older, tougher prison homosexuals; such victims are also known as **penitentiary turn-outs**, from the verb *turn out*, to initiate, in this case into same-sex prison intercourse. The **penitentiary highball** plays on the *highball*, a whiskey and soda (from the tall or 'high' glass and the *ball*, or shot of whiskey, it contains); it is a home-brewed prison alcohol based on strained shellac and milk. Finally the **penitentiary shot** or **pen shot** is an injection achieved by using a rudimentary 'needle', actually a pin and a medicine dropper: the pin is pushed into the vein and the dropper, filled with a solution of heroin and water, is pushed over it. Of course one does not need to be in prison to recourse to such substitute hypodermics.

Jailhouse terms tend to be more recent, with most coined in the mid- to late 20th century; an exception is **jailhouse lawyer** (also **jail lawyer**), used since the 1920s to mean a prison inmate who has taught themselves law, whether to pursue their own case, combat prison corruption or help fellow inmates. The **jailhouse bitch** is a wife or girlfriend who pays regular visits to her partner while he is in jail; the **jailhouse daddy** is a dominating male homosexual prisoner who exploits or protects his partner (who may well be a **jailhouse turnout**). A further synonym is **jailhouse pussy** or **jail tail** (both *pussy* and *tail* are more usually found referring to the female genitals but here mean the anus, and the effeminised man who has one).

The Joint, Calaboose and Hoosegow

Followers of hard-boiled fiction may have noticed the absence so far of a central term: the **joint**. This term is a venerable one in cant and slang usage. It has meant variously a penis, a man or woman, more recently a piece of music or song, as well as a range of drug-related terms. It has also meant a place: the first use of this sort was tied to the late 19th-century consumption of opium in America, and was a synonym for the more lurid and journalistic 'den'. From there its use (in the sense of an environment) progressed to mean a place in general but especially one of licit or illicit entertainment: a restaurant bar or club, a brothel or a gambling establishment. Meanwhile, and often accompanied by the definite article, it came to mean prison c.1920 and, given that the over-riding meaning is always that of 'a place', this canting use is therefore a euphemistic one.

Before large sections of America were American, they had been Spanish, and two of the best-known terms for prison have Iberian origins. Both are direct 'Englishings' (in linguistic jargon 'calques') of the synonymous Spanish word, and both will be well known to fans of Hollywood horse operas. The **calaboose** appears in the late 18th century and comes from *calabozo*, while the 20th-century **hoosegow** is from *juzgado*, a tribunal or court of justice; the latter can also mean any form of institution to which inmates are sent rather than volunteer for entrance and, perhaps not coincidentally, an outhouse or privy. Both are still common today.

The Big House and Others

It is to Hollywood as well that one owes the 20th-century classic **big house**. Its extension, the **big house up the river**, suggests that the term was originally used for Sing Sing, the New York state prison that is up the river at Ossining. The term was the title of one of the earliest Hollywood prison movies, a hit in 1930, which laid down the formula for all such movies that followed. Big house in turn gave the **big pasture**, as used by cowboys and other Westerners, the **big top** and the **big yard**, an extension of the *yard*, the exercise area of a prison. The warden, unsurprisingly, was the **big man**, although this was actually coined slightly earlier in the late 19th century; he could also be the **big fellow** and the **big honcho** (*honcho* was another calque, from the Japanese *han'cho*, group leader; it had been imported to the West by American forces in Korea).

Not all houses need be big. In the first half of the 20th century America saw the **hen house** for a women's prison, or women's section of a prison; the **house that Jack built** or **Jack's house** recalls Jack Ketch, both a real-life hangman and a generic name. The **house of many slammers** refers to slammed cell doors, and the **slammer**, coined in the 1940s, is still a popular term, as is its slightly later abbreviation **slam**. The contemporary black-American **house of pain** is self-evident. The **skookum house** or **skookum** combined the Chinook jargon *skookum*, meaning strong, with house.

The Can and Others

What prisons do is contain, and that's what the **can** does too, popular from the 1910s onwards. It can be found in similar terms: **cannery** and **pisscan**, which in turn leads to **crapper** in the 1920s (literally a lavatory, which itself can be a *can* in slang). To can someone is to imprison and to **crush the can** is to escape, as seen in the 1920s hobo song 'The Dealer Gets It All': 'Then Alton he got busy, and produced a fancy briar, / And we crushed the can at midnight, and decked an eastbound flyer.'

There are other containers, all coined in the first half of the 20th century: the **crate**, the **satchel**, the **match** (from matchbox) and the **keister**, which comes from the German *kiste*, a box or case, and which in German slang means the rump. The latter use is still found in prison slang's **keister-stash**, the concealment of an object in the rectum. The **sneezer** seems anomalous until one recalls its original cant use: a snuff-box. The **pokey** is usually small and local but it too confers a sense of containment since its etymology is most likely standard *poke*, a pocket (although being small it may also be 'poky' of itself). Its more immediate origins probably lie in the late 19th-century **pogey** (again from *poke*, i.e. something in which one is 'put away' although one may note the dialect *poghole*, a boggy hole, or French *poche*, a pocket). It was at first a workhouse, then a prison hospital and did not become the prison itself until the 1940s.

Other small or local American prisons, mostly 20th century, include the **county hotel**, the **little house** (which like can and hoosegow can double as a lavatory), the **bucket** (also found as **buck**) which is another container, as well as offering the rhyming slang **bucket and pail** (= jail) – and in dire straits a makeshift lavatory too; and a **bandbox**, from the standard English *bandbox*, a fragile structure or one in which space is restricted.

Alongside containment is the image of abandonment. **Dump** was used to mean a prison in the early 20th century, based on the standard English *dump*, a pile or heap of refuse or other matter 'dumped' or thrown down. In Australia and America in the same period, **slough** meant a prison (a true slough of despond), while as meaning to imprison, it has been used since the mid-19th century. Both are derived from the standard verb *slough*, to be swallowed up – ultimately a piece of soft, muddy ground. Cryogenesis has yet to reach the prison system, but prisons have been known as a **freezer** (1920s–1950s, also appearing in Australia), a **fridge** (1940s, purely in Australia) and a **deep freeze** (1950s).

Prisons are not monolithic. Some are seen as good, others less so. Since the 1950s, **Disneyland** or **Disneyworld** has been either, depending on the tone of sarcasm in the speaker's voice; in the 1920s a **playhouse**, which started life as a 17th-century brothel, was known for its liberal regime; so too were the mid-19th-century **Loafers' Hall** and **resthouse** of the 1920s–1930s. Both offered lax discipline and undemanding work. Quite the opposite is the **gladiator school** or **gladiator camp**, a maximum-security prison from the early 20th century, and from the 1990s one with a notably harsh regime and a violent atmosphere. The description also fits the 1920s–1930s **madhouse**, wherein any insanity is merely coincidental. The same era's **bughouse**, however, was geared towards holding psychologically unstable inmates, who will be held on **crazy alley** (1910s to present) or the **obs** or **obso** (1950s to present, America and Australia) – the observation wing. Finally the 20th-century **boot hill** is a prison cemetery, a name that was originated in Dodge City (famed as the quintessential lawless Western town), where the original Boot Hill was the cemetery set aside for those who died 'with their boots on', i.e. in a gunfight.

PRISON OFFICIALS

The Warden or Governor

Despite Elvis and 'Jailhouse Rock', the warden, however liberal, generally doesn't throw many parties in the county jail, nor in any other similar institution. He's much too busy running the show. Known in standard terms as the warden in Britain and the governor in America, in prison slang he tends to be big, or at least the job is. Thus, there are names such as the late 19th century's **big man**, **big fellow** and later **big honcho**, the 1940s **big head**, the 1910s **big finger** and thus the **second finger**, his deputy, who has also been the **big screw**. Big also gives the modern American **big six**, the prison riot squad (perhaps from the 'big' number six on a die), and thus **big six talk** which, while definitely aggressive, is ultimately just bluff. In 20th-century America the governor is undoubtedly the **boss** or **boss-man**, while Australia's modern **little boss** is a middle-level prison officer. Back in America the **whip boss** carried an actual whip; he was the chief officer on the prison farms of the 1940s and 1950s.

The Warder or Guard

The Key and the Screw
If Britain's prison officer or warder and America's prison guard have a single defining occupation it is turning keys. Recorded in standard English from the mid-17th century for a prison jailer, the word **turnkey** has been used in modern American prison slang for a guard who does the bare minimum required for their shift, i.e. no more than open and shut the doors. **Key** itself can stand, again in the 20th-century American system, for a guard; more recently it can also mean a pack of cigarettes, presumably from its role as a means of exchange – it figuratively 'opens doors'.

The longest lasting term also based on this primary image has to be the **screw**, which began as a late 18th-century term meaning skeleton key. There are many examples of this meaning, such as this from the anonymous *Leaves from the Diary of a Celebrated Burglar* (1865), in which the narrator regrets the current lack of the basic tools of his trade: 'No "darky" in hand now; no "jimmy" to pry a drawer open, or to "neddy" a "bloke," within our grasp; nor bunch of "screws" to open our way to what we wanted.' The first use of screw as a warder comes in 1812, in the sporting journalist Pierce Egan's chronicle of fisticuffs, *Boxiana*: 'Where flash has been pattered in all that native purity of style, and richness of eloquence, which would have startled a High Toby Gloque [i.e. a highwayman], and put a Jigger Screw [i.e. a prison warder] upon the alert.' *Jigger* is another word for key.

The screw can also be a **bull screw**, implying sternness of conduct, a **screwess**, an Australian wardress, and a **screwsman**, which among thieves who are still working also means a safecracker. Australia also uses **superscrew** for an over-officious warder and **screw on wheels** (i.e. his or her car) for a parole officer. To be **under the screw** was a 19th-century term for being in prison.

The Screw in Rhyming Slang

The 20th century has come up with a number of terms based on *screw* in rhyming slang:
flue
four by two
kangaroo
little boy blue (which also nods to his uniform)
scooby-doo (from the TV cartoon character)

However, screw was not the first term to be used based on the key. That was the 18th century's **dub-cull**. A century later he was the **dub-cove**, **dubsman** or **dubber**. The slang word *dub* had, again, started life meaning a key or a picklock in the late 17th century; the plural *dubs* was a bunch of keys. The dub was the opening of a door with a skeleton key or picklock, while the **dub-lay** was robbing a house by picking the lock and is supported by the phrase to **go on the dub**, to break into a house by this method. The 19th-century **black cove dubber** was a jailer or turnkey. As a verb, drawn from the dialect *dup*, to open (ultimately standard English *do up*), it had meant both to lock and to unlock, the latter being mainly in prison use. To **dub up** was and remains to lock up, whether in a cell or handcuffs; as wide-boy-turned-playwright Frank Norman wrote in his prison memoirs *Bang To Rights* (1958): 'Everybody in the nick had already been dubbed up for the night.'

Jigger (also spelt **jegger** or **gigger**) is probably linked to the Lancashire dialect term *jigger*, a narrow entry between houses, although the cant very likely preceded it. The ultimate connection is to slang's *gigger*, a door (itself, at least as suggested in Charles Ribton-Turner's *History of Vagrants* (1887), from the Welsh *gwddor*, a gate). Used in the 18th and 19th centuries, jigger has meant variously a door, a doorkeeper and a key and since the late 19th century a prison or cell. Hence the **jigger-dubber** or **gigger-dubber** has been a turnkey.

Twirl, another word that has also meant a key, especially a skeleton or duplicate one, was also used from the late 19th century for a prison officer and it remains in use as such. The **clicker** did his job in the 1920s, and in America the **lockup** and **spindle** were both found in the 1940s, while the **twister** is a contemporary American term.

Other Early Terms

Fittingly or otherwise the first recorded cant term for a turnkey was the 16th century's **adam**, perhaps punning on the Bible's supposed 'first man' and meaning a bailiff, and thus sergeant. In the absence of the modern prison system his responsibility would also include the local lockup. A **queer cove**, which in the 16th century had meant a villain, by the 18th had become his jailer, a job that at the time in Ireland was known as a **pinner** (from standard *pin down*). The 17th-century coinage *quod* or *quad* meant a prison, thus, in the 18th and 19th centuries, a **quod/quad cull** and **quod/quad cove** were both a turnkey and a warden.

The 19th century added the backslang **redraw** (warder), a **sneak**, an American term for the night guard, and a **Johnny**, who might also be a policeman. Journalist and sociologist Henry Mayhew notes this term in his *London Labour and the London Poor* (1861) in which a villain informs him: 'The "Johnnys" on the water are always on the look out, and if they sees any of us about, we has to cut our lucky.' Prisoners with no illusions as to their own status used the mid-19th-century term *cattle grazier*, while the *herder* is a 20th-century American term for the guard who works in the prison yard, controlling the prisoners.

20th-century Terms

The passage of time has not diminished the creation of terms for those *behind the ramp*, i.e. in authority (*ramp* stands for any form of desk). Coinages in the 20th century include a *skip*, originally a ship's captain (i.e. skipper) but recreated *c.*1920 as a jailer; a *pokey*, from its use as a small local prison or one of its cells; a *tube*, who makes a habit of listening for information from prison informers and takes his name from the speaking tube that was the predecessor of the telephone; and a *soaker*, which may be from *soak*, to hit. The modern American *new boot* is a new officer; the boot in question refers to the leggings worn by US naval recruits in training during the First World War and the coinage was originally military. Unsurprisingly, a number of contemporary terms for the guard or warder are simply derogatory, such as the *burglar* or the *coche*, used by America's Hispanic prisoners and which in Spanish means 'pig'. Contemporary Australian terms are also derogatory, including the female *bush pig* (more commonly used to brand an unattractive woman); the *baggy-arse*, defining the lowest rank of prison officer, and his fellow employee the *duck-arse*, who is either lazy or mediocre or both; the *hemorrhoid*, i.e. a 'pain in the arse', and the inexperienced *smurf* (from the animated children's TV characters the Smurfs).

But there are also those terms which refer to the guard's authority, and these often double as terms for the police. Among them are the *cop*, the *law*, the *blue boy* – from what was the choice of uniform colour in certain prisons (the term also gives *blue talk*, conversations held between prison officers) – the *blues* and the *uniform*. *Babylon*, coined by Rastafarians in the 1950s, refers as much to warders as it does to any area of the white power structure. The *roller*, usually seen in the context of policemen working from automobiles, is also found within prison walls, as are the **hawkeye** and the **April fool copper**, who can also be a small-town officer – the allusion presumably is that he is only playing at being a policeman. Australia has borrowed what is perhaps Britain's best-known term for the policeman: the **bobby**.

The **hack**, used in the United States and Canada (now with its 1990s variant **hacker**), dates from the 1930s. It had already meant a night watchman and a policeman and was probably linked to *hawk*, an 18th- to 19th-century term for a policeman. America offers two further crossover terms: the bull and the five-oh. **Bull** most likely originates from German *Bulle*, police officer, although one finds bailiffs defined as **napping bulls** (from slang's *nap*, to capture) in the *Canting Academy, or the Pedlar's-French Dictionary* of 1741. It was not heard again until the 1890s, and the term remains American thereafter, used to mean a prison warder in the 20th century. It is possible that there may be a further link, to **bulky**, which in 17th-century London meant self-important and was used for a policeman from the 1820s, and for a warder in the 1930s. **Five-oh**, coined by rappers in the 1980s, comes from the TV cop show *Hawaii Five-0*, first aired in the 1960s.

The Hard Man

If prison slang is to be believed there are no nice guards. *Porridge*'s kindly Mr Barraclough wouldn't survive a day in a real nick. Instead one finds the **footballer**, an Australianism of the 1910s (whose idea of discipline was kicking the prisoners); the 1960s American **ass-breaker**; the modern British **bash artist** or **basher**; and the modern American **bonecrusher**. All of them are dependent on physical force. Their aim is to **sort** or **bring around** a prisoner with treatment that is known, with black humour, as **counselling**. More honestly the phrase is to **break someone's guts**. The term **bitch's bastard** or **B.B.**, a British coinage of the 1950s, summed them all up. At least the **caser**, from *case*, to put on a disciplinary report, merely worked by the rules, however petty and illogical they may be.

The contemporary British warder is of course unarmed. Not so America's **trigger bull** or **gun bull**, who stands in a watch-tower, gazing down on the exercise yard with his shotgun or rifle at the ready. The gun also gives the **gun gang**, the chain gang or any gang of workers who are taken outside the prison and are supervised by armed guards; such men are **under the gun**. Finally, although he may not in fact recourse to violence, is the **zombie**, defined in standard English as 'a soulless corpse said to have been revived by witchcraft'. Such a guard looks permanently miserable and humourless. He is suffering, perhaps, from **convictitis**, the illusion, fostered by too long a career in the prison service, that every prisoner is about to attack them for no other reason than that they are a warder. They may be right, and he or one of his less restrained colleagues may be in line for a dose of **flying lessons**, the sardonic term for throwing them off the balcony of a cell tier.

The Corruptible

If there are no kindly guards, then there are undoubtedly those who, in return for money, are willing to **go bent** (from slang's *bent*, corrupt or criminal) and succumb to corruption. Such individuals, in the back-to-front logic of crime, are, from the late 19th century, **right screws** or **right twirls**, when *right* is (in respectable eyes) quite wrong.

THE PRISONER

The General Prisoner

In the criminal-turned-novelist (and actor, playing Mr Blue in Quentin Tarantino's film *Reservoir Dogs*) Edward Bunker's memoir *Mr Blue*, a fellow prisoner asks him 'Are you a convict?', and Bunker replies, 'I ain't no goddam *inmate*.' It is a difference possibly un-appreciated outside prison, but the inmate is the authorities' word and convict, even as standard English, the prisoners' choice. The former suggests acquiescence, the latter involuntary subjection to a disrespected but powerful authority.

To be more precise, prisoners prefer the term **con**, an abbreviation that has been in use since the late 19th century. It gives the **con boss** or **boss con**, an influential convict who runs a gang within a prison, and the idea of being **con-wise**, well adjusted to prison life, capable of sustaining one's existence in prison (it is also used of guards who are experienced). Like the *ex-con*, the **con-man** is a former prisoner. Those who are con-wise are experts in what since the 1970s has been known as *jailing*: the skill of accustoming oneself to life in jail and adapting one's lifestyle to make one's time there as tolerable as possible. Since then it has been used by rappers and their fans to describe wearing one's trousers in such a way that a few inches of underwear is visible; such a fashion was very popular among black youth and their white imitators from the 1990s onwards – the 'point' was that like prisoners, the youths had been deprived of their belts. Back in prison, one who has not learnt how to *jail* and is suffering through every day of their sentence is a *spider monkey*: they are 'climbing the walls'.

In American prisons since the 1930s, the *mainline* or *the line* is the prison convict population at large (excluding those who are detained in punishment cells); the *mainliner* is a part of that population. But ultimately, the larger group breaks down. Since the 1970s in America, the term for a small clique of powerful convicts has been the *car*, the image being of a few people riding or sitting together. A car might run money-making schemes, dominate other prisoners, and otherwise 'rule' the institution. In weaker and wider use it referred to any tight-knit group of friends, and since the 1990s it has been extended further to mean a group of prisoners who pool their supply of drugs. To be *in the car* is to be on good terms with the group, to be *out of the car* is to be on bad ones. To *drive the car*, again since the 1990s, has been for one member of the team to purchase the day's supply of marijuana, with each member of the group taking it in turns to provide for their fellows; those who are smoking the drugs but not purchasing that day are *hitch-hiking*. The most recent use of car is *bounce a car*, to borrow a fellow inmate's radio. The 'bouncing' may be linked to the vehicle known as a *lowrider*, which is fitted with hydraulic systems to adjust the height of the car while driving, making it appear to bounce.

In prison terminology at least, Britain has no cars: what it did have in the post-Second World War decades was the *carvie* or *carving china*, someone who helped to share or 'carve up' a ration of tobacco. A prisoner might take on a regular carvie for periods of his sentence and the term mutated into meaning a trusted friend. Not every prisoner wishes to team up. Some remain alone, and such an individual is known in America as a *cowboy*, and in Australia as the *one out*. The *square plug* is also an outsider; not a professional criminal, he is perhaps a middle-class murderer or embezzler. The term was originally used around 1920 for a 'civilian' who admires and mingles with criminals but lacks the courage or desire actually to commit a crime. South African prison gangs use the term *fransman*, literally a 'Frenchman' and thus 'foreigner' or outsider. The contemporary American *walkalone* is one who has to exercise alone, often through their own need to be saved from ill treatment.

Terms for different types of prisoner follow in the box below, but one last current general use is the *highbinder*. It appears to recall the name of an early 19th-century New York City gang, composed originally of butchers' boys and known as the Hide-binders.

Names for Convicts

cage-bird   late 17th century
con   late 19th century to present
cop   1920s (from *cop*, to take, in this case a sentence)
drag   19th century
geezo   1930s–40s, America (from *geezer*)
highbinder   1990s to present
mickey   1950s–60s, America
shut-in   1950s, America
slough   1910s, America
vic   1910s–50s, America (a self-styled 'victim' of justice)

Types of Prisoner

The New Prisoner
Life in a London prison, at least prior to the 19th-century reforms that saw the erection of such dismal Victorian 'factories' as Wandsworth or Wormwood Scrubs, depended like much else in the

country on class, or at least cash. Thus the phenomenon of **chummage**, described in 1785 by Captain Francis Grose as:

> money paid by the richer sort of prisoners in the Fleet and King's Bench, to the poorer for their share of a room; when prisons are very full, which is too often the case [. . .] two or three persons are obliged to sleep in a room. A prisoner who can pay for being alone, chuses two poor chums, who for a stipulated price, called chummage, give up their share of the room, and sleep on the stairs, or as the term is, ruff it.

(Incidentally, this rich-to-poor bribe to obtain better accommodation has also been recorded as taking place at mid-19th-century universities.) New prisoners might also face **chumming up**, the initiatory welcoming of a new prisoner, paid for by a mandatory fee of 2s 6d. If they refused to pay up, then their fellows would **walk the black dog** on them, inflicting some form of unspecified punishment, most likely physical. It was a precursor of the **clean shirt**, a 1940s practice whereby warders administered a beating to each new prisoner, doubtless to show them 'who's boss'. An alternative initiation was simply for a **ramper** (from slang's *ramp*, to rob with violence) to steal all one's possessions. The new arrival facing these practices might be a **new hand** or a **greeney** (i.e. naïve and 'green').

In American jails all new prisoners begin as **fish** or **new fish**. The term is first recorded around 1910 and had developed from the mid-19th-century **fresh fish**, with its attendant **fresh fish special**, the prison haircut given to a new inmate. In the early 20th century, to **skin** was to shave a prisoner's head and the new prisoner became known as a **skinner** or **short-hair** (1970s). He has also been a **lane**, either referring to a peasant (i.e. one who lives down a country lane and is as such stupid), or a variant pronunciation of *lame*, which also signifies stupidity. In contemporary Australia he is a **wood duck**, also suggesting a fool. The newly arrived fish brought to the prison on the **fish line**, the court-to-prison bus, is first processed through the **fish bowl** or **fish tank**, where he is allotted his **fish number**, the number issued to each prisoner by the US Department of Corrections (the Australian version being a **classo** or classification), gets **fogged**,

that is sprayed with a delousing agent, picks up a *fish roll*, a bundle
of clothing and other necessities issued to a new inmate, and will
initially be housed on *fish row* or the *fish gallery* before moving to
population. Once inside a cell the *fish line* takes on a new meaning;
it is a length of string that is used to pull items from one cell to
another.

The Veteran
If the new young prisoner of the mid-19th century was a fresh fish
then his veteran peer was a *stale fish*. Today, he can be an *old bird*
or *old head* and an *old cock* or *cocker*, which may be linked to the
Yiddish *alter kacker*, a foolish old man (literally an old shit). He
may be a *wrinkly* or a *limber dick*, literally a flaccid penis, but a
wannabe is not a veteran at all, merely a young prisoner who poses
as one.

The Popular Prisoner
In America, the popular prisoner can be a *right guy*, another use
of *right* meaning trustworthy in criminal terms, or a *real man* (both
used since the 1950s), or the contemporary *solid con*. He has been
ace-high with his peers from the 1930s onwards. Solid cons will also
warn their friends of a guard's approach, saying *man walking* or
phone's off the hook in contemporary America.

The Unpopular or Toadying Prisoner
Whether there are a larger percentage of unpopular than popular
prisoners, there are undoubtedly more terms to describe them. In
the majority of cases the disdain arises from a belief that the prisoner
in question is far too friendly with the authorities. The *jointman*
(from *joint*, a prison) was recorded in the 1920s and was followed
by the *stockholder* (who must have shares in the prison) and the
badgeman, the badge being that of the guards. The 1970s American
term *centerman* refers to the layout of many prisons, with wings
radiating from the centre, where the guards have some form of
'office'. Other modern toadies include New Zealand's *broken arse*
and Australia's *silvertail*, a term used since the late 19th century to
mean a real or self-imagined member of the upper classes, and thus

a social climber. Back in modern America a **rah-rah** is a female version, her image being that of a *rah-rah girl* or cheerleader for the guards, while the **walkie-talkie** is seen as walking with and talking to the guards far too enthusiastically. The **hobbit**, from Tolkien's mythology, is the most recent term, a 2000s British coinage.

Various modern terms for currying favour with the authorities are to **scab** in New Zealand, and America's to **stroke** and to be **hangin' on the leg**, with its image of an over-friendly dog; thus the **leg-hanger** is one who pursues such acquaintances.

But there are other reasons for unpopularity. In the fiercely segregated world of modern American prisons the **nigger rigger** is a white inmate who is seen as overly friendly to black ones. So too is the **spook juke** (literally one who has sex – jukes – with blacks – spooks). A black prisoner is a **rug** from the slang for hair. An inmate who has neither advantages nor respect is an **ass-out**, while in modern Australia a **crab** is an individual prisoner who acts in such a way as to provoke a collective punishment, and in Britain, a **Tilbury docker** is rhyming slang for a **knocker**, a prisoner who does not pay his debts. The Australian equivalent is a **wild duck**, i.e. a fuck. Still in modern Australia, a **camel** is likely to be unpopular, as he neglects personal hygiene. Meanwhile in modern America, to **grit**, i.e. one's teeth, is to stop talking to another inmate and to be **on bone** is to be out of favour among fellow prisoners after committing some form of mistake in terms of convict standards.

The Mad Prisoner

The contemporary **X-cat**, **J-Cat** or **Cat-J**, in all of which 'cat' stands for category, are all inmates in need of mental health care. So too is the 1930s coinage **ding-a-ling** (from the supposed ringing in the sufferer's head) but in his case it is the stress of confinement that has driven him mad. Also from the 1930s onwards, a **wing-ding** (from wing, an arm, i.e. the image of waving one's arms in a frenzy) is a fake fit 'thrown' by a prisoner in the hope of convincing authorities that he should be placed in the more comfortable surroundings of a mental ward.

PRISON LIFE

Smuggling and Contraband

The modern-day *keister* means the buttocks and thus the anus. In American prison use it gives a variety of compounds: the **keister bunny**, an inmate who places contraband items – tobacco, drugs – in his rectum; a **keister plant**, a cache of drugs hidden – usually in some form of hollow metal container – in the rectum; and a **keister stash**, any slim, hollow item (e.g. a biro tube) that can be placed in the anus and used to transport contraband. To **suitcase**, meaning to hide drugs or other contraband in the rectum, has similar imagery. The British equivalent is to **bottle**, based on the rhyming slang *bottle and glass* (= arse). The **joey** is any form of contraband smuggled into a prison.

To obtain contraband inevitably requires some form of collusion, usually through a corrupt (and well-paid) guard. In America, such a guard has been known as a **connection** in the mid-20th century, with exactly the same connotation as when the word is used for a drug supplier; the South African version is a **channel**. A connection is willing to smuggle contraband in and out of prison, an activity known in Ireland in the mid-20th century as **shopping in/out**. The crooked warder is, from the 1960s onward, either a **track** in Australia, or a **horse** in America, itself a variation on the more commonly used *mule*, who is best known in the context of transporting illegal drugs. To hand over contraband is to **cop and pass**. In British jails of the 1950s a favourite manoeuvre was the **twiddle**: the practice of letting a warder suspect one of holding contraband, only to reveal that one is holding something completely innocuous; once suspicions have been allayed, one can then reveal or pass on the actual contraband. Finally there is the modern American guard's least favourite task: the **potty watch**, the checking of a prisoner's body waste for contraband.

Not all consignments coming in from the outside world are contraband. **Relief**, a **score** and **boodle** all stand for anything sent in to a prisoner from friends or relatives outside the walls. And in Australia, a **buy-up** is a prisoner's weekly allowance and the purchases it allows them to make.

Transfers

For whatever reason, prisoners are often on the move, whether from cell to cell, wing to wing or from one prison to another. The use of diesel-powered vehicles to effect these transfers gives the term *diesel therapy* in the 2000s, meaning the continuing movement of an inmate between prisons – often so as to avoid enquiries from their lawyers or relatives. Such clandestine transfers have been widely known from the 1970s as *ghosting*: the late-night/early-hours transfer of prisoners from one prison to another with the intention of avoiding riots, frustrating external investigations and the like; such prisoners are 'spirited away'. The transfer is also known as the *ghost-train*.

Reputations and Reports

The *jacket*, i.e. the file in which the paperwork sits, is the police/prison file on a criminal, recording one's criminal record. It has meant such since the 1930s, but it has also been extended to mean one's reputation among one's peers. The quality of a such a reputation creates a number of compounds, usually with negative implications: the *fruit jacket*, a reputation as a homosexual; the *punk jacket*, a reputation for cowardice; and the *rat jacket* or *snitch jacket*, a reputation as an informer. For a policeman to *fit someone for a jacket* is to threaten them with an arrest and prison sentence. To *hang a jacket on* someone is for one inmate to accuse another of informing, while to *gee (up)* has meant to do the informing since the 1940s. The record can also be known in the 2000s as a *C file*, i.e. the central file of information held on each prisoner.

The 1930s *penman* was an inmate who writes letters to the authorities, presumably informing on his fellows. Today's *put one's pen to the wind* is a dismissive phrase used of a prisoner meaning to tell an officer to file a disciplinary report, or used of an officer, to tell a prisoner to file a grievance. To *pencil-whip* is for a guard to give a written reprimand and for a prisoner to file a lawsuit or a grievance (also known as to *paper-whip*). *Bad paper* is a negative report on a prisoner. A positive report is a *package*, from the package of papers on which it is written. To **pull someone's card** is to find out information about another inmate (although the file cards that underpin the expression have been replaced by computers), as is to **run someone's tags** (one reads their notional dogtags).

Tough Prisoners and Violent Acts

As the saying goes, 'you can fuck me but you can't make me like the baby', and while a prisoner may endure his punishment he need not necessarily enjoy it. And he may not allow others to 'enjoy' theirs either. The prison world, at least as recounted in the many available memoirs, is strictly Darwinian: class vanishes, intellectual attainments vanish, even the once-respected professional criminal hierarchy – bank robbers at the top, sneak thieves at the bottom (and only voluntary isolation is going to help the sex criminals) – doesn't matter much: what matters is physical toughness.

A tough, dominant prisoner can be an **atlas** in the 1980s, either from the mythical Atlas, who held up the earth in his hands, or the 20th-century American strongman Charles Atlas (1894–1972). In America, he can be a **chingoda**, from Spanish, literally meaning a fucker, from the 1990s; or, from the 1970s onwards, a **lowrider** (his figurative 'lowriding' in the area of morals and ethics) who intimidates other prisoners into paying protection money. Contemporary Britain has a **growler**, who prefers verbal to physical menaces, and Australia the **gaffer**, i.e. the boss.

It is not vital to be a tough guy oneself, but it is necessary to be tough. In contemporary American prisons, establishing that means passing the **heart check**, which tests the resilience (the 'heart') of an inmate, either by giving him an initiatory beating (also know as a **ho check**, from slang's *ho*, a whore and thus in prison terms one who will accept that role with its implications of femininity and subservience), or by giving a member of a prison gang a mission, such as a murder, to test his loyalty. The Australian equivalent is to **put someone on the poof** (from slang's *poof*, a gay man), i.e. to challenge, possibly physically, a fellow inmate's masculinity.

If one passes such tests, all well and good, although there will always be confrontations and 'heart' must be displayed on every occasion, but the rewards for failure are diverse and unpleasant. The *blanket party* may originally have meant sexual intercourse, but since the 1970s it has been the murder of a fellow prisoner by tossing a blanket over the head and then bludgeoning or stabbing them to death. Alternatively it is yet another 'check': an initiation rite whereby a new prisoner is forcibly smothered in a blanket, then beaten up or gang-raped by their fellows. The *coat party* takes the same format, with a coat thrown over a prisoner's head prior to beating him up. In 1930s America, to *hijack* was to violently rob a fellow prisoner; its abbreviation *jack* or *jack up* appeared in the 1970s, meaning to stun a fellow inmate with a blackjack before raping them, as did to *lug* or *open up*, which was to sexually assault or sodomise a victim. Also in America in the 1970s, *ride the broom* (wherein the assailant is equated with a witch) was to threaten or intimidate another inmate, while the 2000s term to *cut a knot* is to attack them. In contemporary Britain, *jerking* is a thrusting attack with a sharp object by one prisoner at another; it may come from *juking*, a Caribbean term for stabbing; while to *jug up* (in America no more than eating prison food) is to attack a fellow inmate with a jug of scalding water. To *PP9* is to cosh another prisoner with a sock, or similar container, loaded with PP9 batteries.

The weakling who suffers all this is known as a *lumps and bumps* in modern Australia – he is a convict who loses a lot of fights. Meanwhile American prisons from the 1970s onwards are home to the *cull* (from standard English *cull*, to select weak animals for killing) and the *maytag*, one who is abused by other inmates, forced to do their menial chores and possibly raped. The term comes from the Maytag brand of home appliances. As the rapper Grandmaster Flash put it in 'The Message' (1982): 'Now your manhood is took and you're a Maytag / Spend the next two years as an undercover fag.' Like the disdainful use of the word by whores, the *trick* describes a prisoner who can be easily exploited for money or presents in contemporary America.

Finally the ultimate in aggression: the prison riot. Terms have included the *kick-up*, first found in the late 19th century, the 1960s Australian *rally-up* and the contemporary American *rockin'*.

Death in Prison

In contemporary America, a **check-out** is a prisoner who commits suicide while in prison (from slang's *check out*, to die) and a **hung-up** is a prisoner who attempts the act via hanging. In Britain, one who succeeds is a **swinger**, i.e. at the end of whatever form of rope they have used. A **hunting license** in America is a commission to kill an inmate, often ordered by a gang leader. Whichever the method, the common aim is death, known in America since the 1920s as the **back-gate exit, back-gate commute, back-gate discharge** or **back-gate parole**, the **pine-box parole/release** and the **south gate discharge**. In all cases the reference is to the quiet removal of dead prisoners who are taken out through the back gate of the prison and buried without ceremony.

THE CELL

Names for a Cell

Cell is, of course, standard English, but certain uses are not. As a verb it was first applied to a monk in the 16th century; more recently to **cell** either means to share a cell with a fellow inmate or to live in a cell, thus the question: 'Where do you cell?' The **cell gangster** or **cell warrior** is a modern American use for one who poses as tough while in their cell but follows orders elsewhere. In Britain, in the 1940s–1950s, the **cell task** was a pin-up; the real cell task would be laid down by the authorities, the semi-clad young woman presumably redefined that 'task' as masturbation. Cell itself also has rhyming slang synonyms: **flowery dell**; this first appeared not as a rhyme, meaning a lodging in the mid-19th century, while the transfer to cell is first recorded in 1925; and the contemporary Australian **Alexander Graham Bell**, after the Scots-born American inventor of the telephone (1847–1922).

Peter is a word of many meanings, a subset of which all refer to some form of enclosure, be it a suitcase or a safe or, for these purposes, from the 1930s onwards – a cell. Two Australian terms extended this use: the contemporary **peter thief**, one who steals from a fellow prisoner's cell, and the 1950s coinage **black peter**, a cell for solitary confinement. One encounters the **tank** (from standard English *tank*, a storage receptacle) there too, as well as in America. Used since the late 19th century it has meant variously a cell, a prison or one of its wings, a holding cell and an isolation cell. Combined with a noun the tank can denote the type of prisoner it holds, e.g. the **drunk tank**, the **sissy tank** (homosexuals) and the **daddy tank** (effeminate homosexuals or lesbians). The **hype tank** (from slang's *hype*, a drug addict) and **junk tank** were for drug users; whether the inmates of the latter enjoyed the linguistic irony is unknown but *junk* had some previous: in the 19th century it had meant oakum (loose fibre, obtained by untwisting and picking old rope), the 'picking' of which provided the main cell task for prisoners at the time. Still looking at drugs, the 1940s prison also provided junkies with the **iron cure** or **steel and concrete cure**. In fact, it was the only one on offer: the prisoner was simply deprived of drugs and forced to undergo the pain of withdrawal behind the iron bars and within the steel and concrete of his cell.

Perhaps most frequently, the cell simply borrows from standard usage: in the 19th century it was a **black hole**, while from the early 20th century onwards America has seen such terms as the **cave**, the **hut**, the **monkey cage** and the **tent**. A **house** (usually accompanied by a possessive pronoun) leaves one in no doubt as to the role the cell has to play for one who is forced to occupy it. The concept is underlined in the 1950s phrase to **find a home**, meaning to become completely dependent on the prison system for stability. Back in Britain, the 20th-century **drum** was the least appealing sense of a slang word that might also mean a house, a brothel, a casino and many other 'rooms' beside.

Nor are many, in these days of widespread overcrowding, able to do their time alone. The original Victorian prisons, of which many still survive, assumed one man per cell but now the rule is multiple occupancy (as it is in America, where extra mattresses are often stuffed beneath lower level bunks, ready to be brought out at night for the cell's extra occupants). Thus one might be **two-ed up** or **three-ed up**, i.e. two or three to a cell; the Australian equivalent is **two-out**, etc.

The Yard

The American **yard** has been since the 1910s the open recreation area of a prison, the modern equivalent of the old quadrangles. To be **on the yard** is for a prisoner to be associating with the general population (rather than in solitary confinement or protective custody); a **yard patrol** can be both a group of convicts or of guards; a **yard rat** a prisoner who frequents the yard, socialising with friends; and a **yard queen** a prison homosexual. The **yardbird** is another word for prisoner, while the **yardbird lawyer** is one who has become a self-taught lawyer, either to pursue his own case, to combat prison corruption or to help fellow inmates.

The Cell Tier

In 1970s British prisons, the basic names for the various cell tiers, usually known as landings, consist in simply adding the letter 's' to the number, thus the **twos**, **threes** and so on. In contemporary use, the bottom floor, often used for association and recreation, is the **dungeon** in Britain or, in America, **Broadway**, the **flag** (from flagstone) or the **flats** (popular from the 1950s onwards). In Australia from the 1960s, the **chat's yard** was that area of a prison reserved for tramps and other derelicts (a *chat* is a flea). In 20th-century America a row of cells on any level is a **gallery** or **range**, and to **flash the range** or **flash the gallery**, to scan the area outside one's cell by using a hand mirror or similarly shiny object (a *gapper* or *eye*) to catch any reflections of approaching warders, inter-inmate fights and whatever else might be of interest. **Gallery 13** is the prison cemetery, from the traditional fear of the number 13.

The Condemned Cell

The first recorded condemned cell was that known in the early 19th century as the **salt box** (from its dimensions, or perhaps the salt tears shed within) that stood in London's Newgate prison. And around 1850, when England still pronounced death sentences, one might end up in *Cutler's Alms-house* (derived from slang's *cutlery*), which meant committing murder, presumably with some form of edged weapon. The remainder of the available terms are all from America, where the gallows, the electric chair, the gas chamber and the lethal injection are as widely used as ever.

The best-known term is *Death Row* or *the Row*, the line of cells in which men sentenced to death serve out what remains of their time, and used since the mid-19th century. It is also known in contemporary America as the *X-row*, a figurative use of x as 'name-less', or a play on the fact that the inmates are the *ex*-living, i.e. looking forward only to *ex*ecution.

In the 20th century, irrespective of the method used, the *death house* is the execution chamber. The abbreviation *C.C.*, 'condemned to capital punishment', has referred both to the cell and to the person who is living in it prior to execution since the 1950s. However, the cells of these death rows are not condemned cells as such. On the eve of execution the prisoner is moved to the *dancehall* or *birdcage*, both 20th-century terms describing a cell adjacent to the execution chamber, thus minimising the final walk to the execution chamber, which has been known since the 1930s as the *last mile* or *last waltz*. To go on that final journey was to *take a walk up back* in the 1920s and 30s.

The Isolation Cell

Solitary confinement is not always the 'reward' of those who refuse to acknowledge the prison rules; sometimes it is meted out, in the form of isolation cells, to those who cannot understand them: the insane. In the mid-20th century Britain used the *balmy* (from the general slang *barmy*, eccentric), the *peek* (which began life referring to a brothel peephole and thus refers to the spyhole used to survey the prisoner) and the *paddy*, which comes from its being a padded cell and from *paddy*, a tantrum (and ultimately from the stereotyped temperamental instability of the Irish). During the 20th century America has used the *shelf*; the *bug* or *bug-out cell* (from slang's *bug*, a mentally disturbed individual who has 'bugs in the head', thus the verb *bug*, to submit a prisoner to a psychiatric examination); the **screen** (from the mesh screen used to further contain psychotics); and **seg** or **seggie** (abbreviations of segregation). Ever-jokey, contemporary Australia prefers **Harry's hideaway**.

Behind Bars

Love may laugh at locksmiths; prisoners don't have that option. Instead they immortalise them, albeit somewhat masochistically: in the 1950s **chubb up** and **miln up** both meant to lock in a cell, referring to the firms of Chubb and Miln, the former of which is still going strong, both as a slang term and as a lock manufacturer. During the same period **carpy** (meaning to lock up for the night) lends a little learning, coming as it does from the Latin *carpe diem*, 'make the most of the day'. America is simpler: current uses include **rack** or **roll the bars/doors** and **slam the slats**. The *slats* are the steel mesh that covers the front of a prison cell. Slam, which also lies behind **slammer**, a prison or a cell door, gives **slam down**, to lock into one's cell as a punishment – no association with other prisoners is permitted. **Slam up** is to imprison, and **slammed** is to be locked into one's cell during a crisis, such as a prison strike.

The Cell Search

Prisoners are not to be trusted and guards are constantly subjecting them or their cells to searches. Terms from the 20th century still in use today are the **shakedown**, coined in the 1920s, a **turnover** from the 1950s and a **spin** from the 1970s. The verbs meaning to search a cell usually predate these, whether by a number of decades, such as **turn over** (late 19th century), or more immediately: **shake down** (20th century) and **spin** (1970s). The contemporary term is **hit a house**. A body search has been a **rubdown** since the 1930s, when the guard who performed the searches of new arrivals to the prison was a **rub-down dippy**.

Life in a Cell

In America, from the 1930s, to *lock* has meant to occupy a cell and to *lay in* to stay in one's cell when one might usually be out of it (a *lay-in* is a sick pass, permitting one to stay in the cell); this might be for a bit of peace or it might also be for communicating with a friend. The sending of such coded communication was known as *knuckletalk* around 1910, when prisoners would tap out messages by rapping their knuckles on their cell walls; a more recent version is the Australian *telephone*, in which the plumbing pipes that run from cell to cell are used as sound carriers. In the 20th century one's cell-mate was a *bunkie* or *bunky*; the contemporary Australian *mattressback* (which also means a sexually promiscuous woman) is a prisoner who spends a lot of time in their cell. In Britain, the modern *window warrior* likes to shout out of his cell window.

The cell might be seen as one's house but nothing lasts and prisoners are constantly on the move. From the 1980s in America, to *roll up/out* has meant to leave the prison, whether temporarily (for a court appearance) or permanently (after completing a sentence or moving to a new prison); it can also mean to move from one cell to another. Both come from the old practice of rolling up one's mattress on every occasion of leaving one's cell.

The cell may keep the prisoner in, but it does not automatically keep him safe, especially when bars, rather than a solid door, form one of its walls. Thus a *barbecue* or *burn out* and the verb to *torch* are all contemporary American terms meaning to murder a fellow-inmate by tossing a Molotov cocktail or petrol bomb into their cell. An inmate or guard who has been given *flying lessons* has been tossed from the balcony of a cell tier (hence the netting one sees between them in many prisons), while from the 1940s in America to *take a flier* is to kill oneself by leaping from an upper gallery. Britain's modern phrase *hang one up* is to make a 'dirty protest', i.e. to smear one's body and cell with one's excrement. (Contemporary Australian prisoners use *bronze up* for the same protest. The term comes from slang's *bronze* or *bronza*, meaning the anus or excrement; the underlying image is of the colour.) Alternatively one can *gas* a guard: this involves urinating into a cup and tossing the contents through the bars; the 'gas' in question is the standard American word for petrol. Also in contemporary America, to throw excrement or urine over another prisoner is to **sling trout**.

Finally in the late 18th century the British **flying pasty** was a packet of excrement wrapped in paper and flung over a neighbour's wall. In contemporary jail terms it is just the same: a package of human ordure wrapped in newspaper and tossed out of one's cell window. The idea of using what America's prisons have termed the **tin throne** since the 1930s, i.e. a cell latrine, did not seem to have entered the picture.

Solitary Confinement

The solitary confinement cell is a prison within prison. It's worse than prison: it's small and empty and there might be a hole for a toilet and food is even more dreadful than usual, and you're completely on your own. It is, and has been since the 16th century, the **hole**. The original *Hole* was found in the debtors' prison in Wood Street, London, where it was the nickname for the cell – a notably squalid one – in which the poorest prisoners were confined. The rich enjoyed the 'masters' side', while the middle classes went to the 'knights' side'; all were entered in the prison's Black Book.

Dark
The essence of the hole is that it is dark. Thus a number of terms, from the early 19th century onwards, are based on black. These include the **black hole**, which came from army use and could also mean a police cell or any room set aside for punishment, e.g. in a workhouse or orphanage. In addition are the **black lock** or **black lockup**, from the 1970s (which gives the phrase **behind the black lock(up)**, in solitary confinement), and the **black peter** (from *peter*, a cell). The **black annie** or **black betsy** can also mean a police van (a black maria) and, in the prison farms of the southern United States, a leather whip known as the *black aunty*, some three foot long and six inches wide, was used for doling out punishments.

Darkness was just as prominent in the mid-19th century, in which the *coal-scuttle*, the dark, the *dark cell* and the *darks* are all found. New Zealand's early 20th-century *dig-out* (and its extension *digger*) was originally a pit into which recalcitrant prisoners were placed for punishment; later the term encompassed the solitary confinement cell.

The Cage

If the ill-behaved prisoner is sometimes (and probably unfairly for the four-footed creatures) equated with an 'animal', then the solitary confinement cell is seen as his *cage*, a term particular to America from the 1930s onwards, and the mid-19th-century *doghouse* became a protective custody unit in the 1940s. In Australia, the solitary confinement cell has been the *pound* since the 1960s (or in rhyming slang, the *huckleberry hound*). In America, it has also been a *bullpen* since the 1920s and a *coop* since the 1940s.

The Box

Those who recall the book (and indeed movie) *Cool Hand Luke* (1965) will remember the regularly intoned command 'Night in the Box', which sends some unfortunate off to the tiny enclosure, perhaps not coincidentally reminiscent of an outside privy, which served as the chain gang's punishment cell. No such box necessarily exists within the usual prison but the shape and size of the punishment cell has taken 'box' as a recurring image. The first such evocation was the *sweat box*, dating from the mid-19th century; as explained to an American government committee in 1931:

> The original 'sweat box' used during the period following the (US) Civil War [. . .] was a cell in close proximity to a stove, in which a scorching fire was built and fed with old bones, pieces of rubber shoes etc, all to make great heat and offensive smells, until the sickened and perspiring inmate of the cell confessed in order to get released.

In the 1920s it was modified as *icebox*, a word that comes from the chilly conditions as well as *isolation*. Today's *box time* refers to the part of the greater sentence that is spent in solitary confinement.

Locked Away
The concept of being locked away from the larger prison population has added to the available terminology. In both Australia and America, the **lockup** can either be the state of solitary confinement or the cell in which the punishment is served. The primary modern term for solitary confinement is **lock-down**; this can also refer to a situation when the entire prison population is confined to their cells and deprived of exercise or association – usually brought about as a mass punishment or as a pre-emptive response to perceived escalating tensions. To **slam** is a 1970s coinage, rooted in *slammer*, both a prison and a door; an inmate who has been **red tagged** has been confined to their cell, while the order **behind your doors!** means get in your cells. Both terms can also be used in the context of the punishment cells.

There are also a number of verbs and phrases meaning to lock away in solitary confinement. To **bury** (used in New Zealand and America), to **button up** (America) and to **gaffle** (from the dialect *gaffle*, to encumber, to tease or incommode) are all synonyms that date from the 1930s and 1940s. Some inmates, typically those serving sentences for rape or child abuse, or corrupt policemen who have ended up in jail, all of whose well-being would be strictly limited if moving among the general prison population, volunteer for segregation. To do this, and move into protective solitary confinement, was known in American prisons between the 1940s and 50s as to **get oneself a banner** or **get oneself sloughed up**, which comes from standard English *slough*, to be swallowed up, and ultimately from a *slough*, a piece of soft, muddy ground. In Britain to **go on the numbers** is to do the same thing. The numbers (or **cucumbers** in rhyming slang) in question being rule number 43 (or now rule 45), which enables the segregation of vulnerable prisoners from the other prisoners for their own safety.

Proper Names
The **Klondike** was originally the site of the Alaskan gold rush in the late 19th century; miners worked alone and in darkness and the term was appropriated for the lower cells of American prisons in recent years. Not that such cells were always cold: thus the name

Florida, coined in the 1960s and still in use, which refers to the siting of such cells in the warmest areas of the prison, often underground. Equally warm are the *Bahamas*, a current term, and to *go to the Bahamas*, meaning to be put in solitary. Perhaps most apposite of all was *Siberia*, the traditional land of Russian exile: the name has not only meant the solitary confinement cells in America since the 1930s but also two of New York State's most notorious prisons: Sing Sing Penitentiary and Clinton Prison, Dannemora. Finally, around 1910, the *Pennsylvania diet* was the bread and water diet given to a prisoner in the punishment cell. With food in mind one also finds today's *judy* or *jupe ball*, a particularly unappealing item of food served to American prisoners in solitary confinement; the meal consists of a ground patty, approximately 10 × 10 × 8cm (4 × 4 × 3 inches), which is composed of the entire meal's ingredients put together through a blender; it is invariably burned on the outside and raw within. The etymology of this disgusting mess is unknown, perhaps all for the best.

Miscellaneous Terms

In theory, albeit somewhat undermined of late by global financial meltdowns, the *bank* is a symbol of security. Thus the borrowing since the 1930s of the term to mean a solitary cell, supposedly as tightly locked as a bank vault, and the phrase *bank off*, to place in solitary confinement. The 1930s also used the *cockpit* and the *bing*. The latter term has no obvious root, unless it holds the image of one being thrown into a cell and landing with a 'bing!' There is no mystery about America's wholly understandable *shitter*, which otherwise means the anus, and the *shitcan*, i.e. a figurative lavatory, both of which have been common since the 1960s. A *zoot suit* was prison clothing worn in the punishment cells of 1970s British prisons; the original zoot suits, with their draped jacket and exaggeratedly tapered trousers, had been worn by black Americans in the 1940s and 1950s. The wing that holds the punishment cells has since the 1930s been known as *the block*, an abbreviation of punishment block.

FOOD, DRINK AND DRUGS

Chow and Others

The word may come from a Chinese term for 'edible dog' and so may be an apt term for the unloved meals, but whatever the origin, the basic word for food in prison (and a number of other institutions) is *chow*. Chow was originally pidgin, used by English speakers in 19th-century India and China, and meant a mixture of any kind, e.g. mixed pickles or preserves, and thus undifferentiated food. It came in turn from China's *chow-chow*, which could either be a mixture or medley or a variety of dog raised for the table. It was adopted in the late 19th century as an American prison term, meaning variously the food and the meal at which it was consumed. *Chowtime* is meal time, the *chow cart* or *chow wagon* the trolley that carries food from cell to cell, the *chow hall* the mess hall, the *chow line* a queue for food and *chow hound* (or a *garbage hound*) a glutton, even for this basic level of cooking. To *chow down* is, of course, to eat.

Most other food-related prison terms have succeeded chow, but its earliest predecessor is the 17th century's *go to the basket*, to go to prison, which referred to the alms-basket on which poor prisoners in the public prisons were mainly dependent for food. The need to beg is also found in the 18th century's *angle for farthings*, to dangle a cap, box or other makeshift container from a prison window into the street below in the hope of picking up alms from kind-hearted passers-by. Since then one finds *thick shins* in the late 19th to early 20th centuries (perhaps a reference to cheap cuts of meat), *fuel* from the 1930s onwards, and the 1950s *depth charge* (any form of stodgy dish). In America, from the mid-18th century to the early 20th, food could be a *mess*, and in the 1950s *gooby* (from slang's *goo*, viscid slop). To *graze* is to eat prison food and to be *on the corn*, i.e. the hominy diet offered in many mid-20th-century American prisons, is to be imprisoned. *Muggins* was a name for food used by 1930s prisoners and hobos, while the modern South African *tand* probably uses the Dutch *tand*, a tooth, and thus the need to chew hard on the tough food. Most evocative is Australia's

chew 'n' spew or *chew it and spew it*: coined in the 1960s it refers
to prison food, especially any ready-cooked meal, such as hamburgers
or fish and chips, but also to a cheap restaurant.

The *beanery* was originally another form of downmarket caff,
but in the 1940s–1960s it was used for a prison mess hall. Still with
beans, *farts and cell partners* comprise a meal of beans and frankfurters: the beans make you fart while frankfurters are their 'partners'
in the tin.

Bread (and Water)

Traditional punishment rations in a prison are bread and water,
and as we know from many memoirs the former is probably teeming
with insect life while the latter is some murky facsimile of the real
thing. It has been known since the 1930s as *number one*, i.e. the
No.1 diet as laid down in prison regulations, and in America in the
early 20th century, ironically as *cake and wine*. To be put on bread
and water was, in the 19th century, to be *pannam-bound* and such
restriction made one *pannam-struck* (very hungry). *Pannam* takes
one back to the beginning of recorded slang, the cant of the 16th
century, when it was used for bread, rooted in the Latin *panis*,
bread. Bread could also be *chuck* from the mid-19th century (originally a lump or hunk and once used only of ship's biscuit), while
a sandwich in 1960s America was a *dukie*, from *duke*, the hand in
which it was held.

Meat

Before the menu reaches those dishes that contain meat one finds
a dish that is defined by its absence: the 19th-century *smiggins* or
smiggen was a poor-quality soup served up to convicts, especially
those imprisoned on the hulks moored out in the Thames estuary.
Its roots most likely lie in standard English *smidgen*, a very small
amount, in this case the almost invisible portions of appetising meat
or vegetables present in the broth. The 19th century also gave the
ball, a prison ration of 170g (6oz) of meat; the lump of flesh resembled the object (and was doubtless about as unappetising).

Modern American terms all reflect the prisoners' distaste for what appears on their plates: in the 1930s **canned cattle** was corned beef and **young horse**, roast beef; since the 1970s **red death** has been prison-cooked barbecue beef, and a **Gainesburger** a Salisbury steak – the 'gourmet' synonym for a hamburger (it plays on the proprietary brand name Gainesbury Puppy Chow, i.e. dog food); while the current **monkey nuts** (that is, testicles) are prison-cooked meatballs. The **grease patty** is a chicken-fried steak; the term appeared in the 1990s but a prison cook was a **grease pot** back in 1910. American prisoners refer to any kind of meat as either **pig** or **mountain goat** in the early 20th century. Sometimes one simply cannot tell, thus the 1940s **whodunit**, ostensibly a meat pie; the standard whodunit is a murder mystery and in this one the 'victim' is the prison cat. In America, the dubious-sounding 20th-century **mystery meat** is applied to meat loaf, stew or almost any meat concoction.

Fish

Since the 1910s, American prisoners have given the name **sewer trout** for any species of fish served at mealtimes. The contemporary **Hollywood stew** is creamed cod fish – one must assume that the Hollywood label ironically suggests some kind of luxury. No such euphemism accompanies the modern **pussy in a can**, canned sardines: the term brings up that very old stereotype, the supposed link between the smell of the vagina and that of less than wholly fresh fish.

À La Carte

Pasta, presumably cooked with the American prison's usual lack of care, has been **lead pipe** in the 1950s or **spa-gag-me** in current times (from *spaghetti* plus *gag*, to choke). There is only one term recorded for vegetables: the 1930s **steam engine** which means a potato pie or a cooked potato and refers to the steam that emanates from the hot potatoes. Puddings can be Britain's 20th-century **duffer** (from dough by way of *duff*, a pudding) or the casually racist **nigger heads** – prison-cooked prunes in 1950s America.

Coffee

Coffee, as will be expected, is invariably weak, as much as anything because the prison cooks steal it for private sales. It has been known in 20th-century America variously as **mouthwash**, **rain water** and **slop**, while **slops and slugs** are coffee and doughnuts (the slug is a metal one and points up the hardness of the doughnut). Perhaps most interesting is Britain's early 20th-century **skilly**, used for any weak beverage, whether coffee or tea. The word is an abbreviation of *skillagalee*, described by 'Bill Truck' in *The Man o' War's Man* (1821–6) as 'a vile oatmeal liquid in imitation of Scottish porridge'. The American writer Jack London, writing 80 years later, was more scientific: '"Skilly" is a fluid concoction of three quarts of oatmeal stirred into three buckets and a half of hot water.' Neither sound very appetising. Before its use as coffee it could mean gruel or gravy from the 19th century. **Skilly and toke**, meaning literally gruel and bread, was another way of describing anything mild or insipid in the late 19th century. A more recent name for prison-made coffee, the mid-20th-century **spow** (with its suggestion of slang's *spew*, to vomit), does not have one asking for another cup. **Sand** has meant sugar since the early 19th century, and is found in prisons and in the near-defunct jargon of short-order restaurants where an order of 'Joe with cow and sand' was a cup of coffee with milk and sugar.

The modern invention **stinger** is vital to prison cooking, at least at the cell level. This is essentially an improvised means of heating water that consists of wires with both ends exposed. One end is inserted into an electrical socket and the other is placed in the water to heat it.

Tea

It wouldn't be a cup of rosy if there wasn't any rhyming slang and Australia kindly provides the 20th-century **darrell lea**, honouring the chocolate makers Darrell Lea, the nation's self-styled 'Taste Place', who have been flogging chocs since 1927. Modern Australia also has the **boil-up**, making tea despite the rules forbidding it. The beverage has been known as **diesel** in contemporary Britain, **hop** in America (where optimistic early 20th-century convicts presumably were trying to pretend it had some intoxicating properties), and during the same period *nux*, an abbreviation of medical Latin's *nux vomica*, the fruit from which strychnine is produced. The phrase *smash the teapot*, used in English prisons around 1900, was for a prisoner to forfeit the privilege – gained for good behaviour – of substituting tea for the usual gruel. (In other contexts it was to abandon one's pledge of abstinence, taken earlier at the urging of the Salvation Army or a similar teetotalist body.) Cocoa, once a British prison staple, was known as *ki* in the mid-20th century, a term taken from earlier naval use (and which came supposedly from a dialect word *kyish*, muddy-looking, brown); the *English Dialect Dictionary* makes no mention of it, but Halliwell's *Dictionary of Archaic and Provincial Words* (1847) does.

Illicit Alcohol

The prison drink of choice, since the 1910s, is some form of illicit alcohol, homebrewed with whatever ingredient becomes available and will ferment, and stashed where the guards cannot find it. The usual 20th-century name for this is *pruno*, although prunes are far from mandatory. As explained in *The Other Side of the Wall: A Prisoner's Dictionary* (2000):

> Pruno: Homemade alcohol, fermented juice, the classic prison drink. It is made by putting fruit juice, fruit, fruit peelings in a plastic bag with bread and/or sugar. The yeast in the bread along with the sugar helps ferment the fruit juice, fruit, or peelings. The plastic bag is usually placed down the toilet and secured so that it is not detected.

The dictionary fails to mention certain downsides: the possibility of such a *brew* rendering the drinker blind, but as they say in jail: if you can't do the time, don't do the crime.

Apart from pruno, the other most well-known name, as much outside the walls as in, is *hooch* or *hootch*. The word comes from *hoochinoo*, an alcoholic liquor made by Alaskan Indians, the Hoochinoo people in particular. In the late 19th century it came to mean any inferior alcoholic drink (especially whisky) drunk in Alaska and the Canadian northwest, and the word was soon picked up by prisoners for their own illicitly distilled liquor.

Further names in America include *buck* (it 'bucks you up'), popular since the 1930s, and 2000s coinages *jump* and *julep*. This last takes its name, but probably not its ingredients, from the long-appreciated mint julep: 'a mixture of brandy, whisky, or other spirit, with sugar and ice and some flavouring, usually mint' (*Oxford English Dictionary*). The contemporary *shine* and the 20th-century term *mash* are reminiscent of the moonshiners who both make and sell contraband liquor, and the mash of ingredients from which they distil it. The use of potatoes or even their peelings has given *spud juice* and *potato jack*, both found from the 1970s. Modern Australian prisoners make a *brew-up* or some *funny stuff* (linked to the euphemistic 'feeling funny', i.e. tipsy).

Drugs

Drugs are available in prisons as never before and the war against them there has been no more successful than that outside. They are generally called by the same names as exist in the free world, although there are a few extras, all modern terms. Britain's *sausage* is a cannabis or cannabis/tobacco cigarette and America's *box-bag* is the amount of marijuana (the 'bag'), worth approximately ten dollars, that can be purchased in exchange for a carton of cigarettes (the 'box'). In Australia the *smoko* has been known since the mid-19th century as a break for smoking; modern prison use has extended this to mean marijuana. Rhyming slang adds New Zealand's *Miller's Point* (= a joint, i.e. a cannabis cigarette), which may ultimately be linked to Millers Point in Sydney, Australia. There are also a variety of medical drugs, usually major tranquillisers, that can be used to control those rebellious or 'difficult' prisoners who prove unamenable to other restraints. In Britain these are known as the *liquid cosh* or in the mid-20th century *bug juice* (as in *bug*, a crazy person). In America such treatments, which reduce a prisoner to catatonic immobility, are known as *attitude adjustment* in the 2000s; the term also applies to the physical subjugation of such a prisoner.

The contemporary American term *clavo* (from Calo *clavo*, a thief) is a prisoner who is in possession of something valuable, usually drugs. Such drugs will likely have been smuggled in, and if so are known as *cake* (from the 1950s), playing on the stereotyped smuggling of a file inside a cake. Perhaps the strangest term is the *cross* which in modern Australian prisons describes any spring-loaded device, such as a safety pin, held tight by a rubber band and swallowed; the gastric juices dissolve the rubber. The purpose of this self-wounding is to get into the hospital ward, as a means of either escaping harassment or obtaining pain-killing drugs.

Cigarettes

Cigarettes behind bars fall into two categories: the hand-rolled variety, made with prison-issued tobacco and papers, and the factory-made kind from the outside world, available under a variety of well-known brand-names.

The traditional British term, since the late 19th century, has been *snout*. It means tobacco rather than the cigarette rolled with it, and comes from the one-time prohibition of smoking within prison when the prisoner would mask his smoking by pretending to rub his nose. The word has created the *snout baron* (also *tobacco baron*), who exercises power and gains prison-level wealth by his control of the tobacco supply (a *baron* has been an influential criminal since the 1910s), and the *snout china*, from the rhyming *china plate* (= mate), who was an intimate friend, literally one with whom one shares tobacco; the snout china was the opposite of the *graft china*, someone with whom one works ('grafts') regularly. Current Australian rhyming slang also offers *johnny raper*, a cigarette paper, which has also been known as a *wrapper* in Australia and America throughout the 20th century. To *crank* a cigarette is to roll one in 1970s America. Terms for the home-made cigarettes themselves include the universal post-1950s usage the *roll-up*, America's early 20th-century coinages *rollie ready-made* (which is brought out pre-rolled) and South Africa's contemporary *private*. Sometimes the names seem to be wishful thinking, since *spliff* and *doobie* are also used for cigarettes that outside prison would usually be rolled with cannabis. Without context it is hard to tell whether the contemporary American terms *germ* and *fug* (which draws on standard English *fug*, a dense, smoky atmosphere) are hand-rolled or otherwise. Given that the Hispanic *fraho* otherwise means marijuana, one may assume that this contemporary prison cigarette is hand-rolled.

In mid-20th-century America, the *short* and the *clincher* were smokeable cigarette ends; the contemporary *swooper* is a prisoner who is constantly swooping down to pick them up. What prisoners really want, however, is what has been known since the 1920s as a *tailor* or *tailor-made* – a factory-made cigarette, whether prison-issue or commercially produced. Other terms have included the 1960s–1970s *grouse* (from Australian slang *grouse*, first-rate), the American *pearl handle*, an image of luxury present from the 1940s onwards, the 1970s American *free world*, the contemporary *real* and *flavor* from the United States, and Britain's *civvie*, i.e. civilian.

To smoke a cigarette, no matter its origin, is to *blow one up* in early 20th-century America or *cop a joint* later in the century (which otherwise means to fellate). In Australia, where *root* is the equivalent of *fuck*, to *monkey root* is to light one cigarette from the tip of another, while the cigarette lighter in a modern Canadian prison is a *block*.

ESCAPE

Over the Wall

If you're inside you want out. And that goes double for prison. Like a good deal of prison slang one needed the modern system to generate the vocabulary. The villain-turned-popular hero Jack Shepherd was celebrated for his ability – in all but the last time – to escape from the locks and chains that kept him in Newgate's death cell, but if his evasions earned him ballads, there was still no special terminology for describing them. The first recorded term seems to be the mid-18th-century coinage *give leg-bail (and land security)*; also as *tip leg-bail*. It was based on the standard English *bail*, the security given against the release of a prisoner pending their trial,

with the ironic addition of leg, as in the modern slang *leg it*. A pair
of 20th-century terms have retained the reference to the lower limb:
the 1930s *toey*, which in Australia has meant nervous or touchy (and
of horses keen to be off and running), and in the prison world liable
to attempt an escape; and to *toe it*, a British term from the 1950s,
meaning simply to run away.

Of the various stereotypes accorded the rabbit – notably an
insatiable appetite for copulation – that of running away is high on
the list. Since the late 19th century, American prisoners have had
rabbit, rabbit (in the) blood or *rabbit fever*, all defined as the desire
to escape. To *pull a rabbit* is to make an escape and a *rabbit foot*,
with its suggestion that in this at least he has been lucky, an escaped
convict. Since the 1970s, also in America, the *jackrabbit* (otherwise
meaning a mule, and as such an extension of *jack*) has been an
escapee, while the escape has been *jackrabbit parole*. The *fox* was
another American term for an escape, in the 1930s, while the
Australian rhyming slang *frog and toad*, originally the road, can be
used as a verb meaning to run off.

A contemporary American prisoner can *have go-go in one's eyes*,
i.e. wish to 'go', and the 1920s euphemism *go out* is still in use today.
The metaphorical hill gives the 20th-century *go over the hill*, which
ultimately refers to the ballad 'Over the hills and far away', recorded
as early as 1709 in Thomas D'Urfey's collection *Pills to Purge
Melancholy* and popularised in John Gay's *Beggar's Opera* (1728),
while one who is *over the hill* has made a successful escape.
Unsurprisingly, the high prison wall, over which one must climb,
plays its role. One can *go over the wall* (since the 1910s) and *hit the
wall* (since the 1950s) in which the 'hit' can, in Australia, describe
an unsuccessful escape as well; a *wallflower* is the contemporary
British equivalent of the rabbit: a prisoner obsessed with the possibility of getting out. To *make a hole* is another term from 1930s
America, although few prisoners have blown their way to freedom.
If not a wall then a fence: contemporary America has a *fence con*
for a prisoner planning an escape, and *fence parole* for an attempt
to make an escape by climbing the prison fence or wall; such efforts,
inevitably, lead to death, and to *sweat the fence* is to fantasise about
escape.

The early 20th-century coinage *lam* or *lam out* means to escape and is linked either to the early 19th-century cant *lammas*, to depart or leave, or may be a pun on *lam*, to hit, and thus a pun on the slang *beat it*. A *lamster* is the escapee, as are Australia's modern *coat-puller*, the Canadian *go-boy* and the late 19th-century British *scooter*.

Since the decision to escape is the prisoner's choice, many synonyms suggest a sense of 'taking' such an action. Thus from the late 19th century one finds *take a sneak* (also *do/make a sneak*), while America's 1920s coinages *take the air*, *cop a heel*, *take a mope* (also *cop a mope*) and *cop a moke* (literally 'grab a donkey') are still in use today, alongside *take a flier/flyer*. In the 1970s British phrase to *make one* 'one' is either an escape or the plan that lies behind one; it means to plan and effect an escape, and thus to *make one with*, to escape 'team-handed'. One *put it in the woods* or *put the long ones in*, which refers to the long strides of one who is running away; the first is 1970s American, the second contemporary Australian. Australia's verb from the late 19th century, to *bolt*, simply annexes a standard English word, and gives the rhyming slang *Harold Holt* (this had an added reference to the former Australian prime minister who, despite his reputation as a strong swimmer, vanished in the sea near Melbourne in 1967. No body was ever found and speculation attributed a suicide or a faked death in order to run off with a mistress). *Jake the rape* is another piece of Australian rhyming slang, meaning to escape.

Both the United States and Australia use the term *bush* for uncleared or untilled areas that are still in a state of nature. To *go bush* (Australia, 1950s) is to escape from prison and vanish; to *make bush* (contemporary America) is to do just the same. And America's 20th-century *bush parole* or *bush pass* is an escape. In 1920s America, the successful escapee reaches *Governor Green* or freedom, another reference to the countryside beyond the prison walls, as is to *do a cross country*, to run off. The energy and aggression that are required in an escape have given the 20th-century classic *bust out*; as well as other mostly American terms, *bust loose*, *cut loose*, *crash (out)*, *crush out* and *crush the can* (a pun on *can*, a prison).

Other terms that have emerged since the 1940s include to *raise* (i.e. one raises the body), to **split out** (from *split*, to leave), to **take off**, to **spring (out)** and to **duck (on)** (which is otherwise to avoid). Finally, for those who don't make it, is the British prison term **in patches**, explained by the inmate-author Neil 'Razor' Smith in his book *Raiders* (2007): 'We were both in "patches", which is the uniform that prison escapees have to wear, a bib-and-brace overall with a bright yellow stripe down its length.'

On the Run

Once over the wall or in the bushes a prisoner is on the run (or the **hot cross bun**, in rhyming slang), and he either keeps running or hides out. Such escapees can be a **runner**, giving the phrase **do a runner**, to abscond from the police or to be on the run, and the West Indian **hot stepper**, a fugitive who runs off 'as if his feet were on fire'. Other than the 17th-century **in lavender**, which recurred two centuries later, all the relevant phrases for being on the run are led by the preposition 'on'. The use of lavender is based on *lay up in lavender*, to put out of harm's way (i.e. to hide from the police), which comes ultimately from the standard English phrase meaning to put aside carefully for future use (lavender was then, as it is now, placed among linen to keep it 'sweet').

On the ...

Synonyms for *on the run* include, in chronological order, and starting in the late 19th century:

on the jump	**on the lam(m)**
on the lope	**on ice**
on the hop	**on the fade-out**
on the trot	**on one's toes**
on the dodge	

Wanted

One who manages to escape is wanted, and therefore he is 'hot': *hot as a two-/three-dollar pistol* or *ten-cent pistol* (the *hot as* can be substituted by *hotter than*). The modern Caribbean has **run hot**, while an American escapee might be said to be **running a temperature**. Other terms include the late 19th-century Australianism *poley*, which played on *poley*, a word used of one-horned cattle (and of a utensil's snapped-off handle). In convict context it meant that the man had lost his 'horns' (i.e. his hair); it could also mean wanted by the police. The era also gave **live shallow**, an antonym for *live high* and used of a villain who had decided that the most sensible way to steer clear of the police was to live quietly 'in retirement'.

PAROLE AND RELEASE

Parole

Escape is not mandatory. There is, at least in theory, the chance of parole, a supervised release that is the carrot that supposedly keeps prisoners in line. This is even more important in America where sentencing tends to a non-specific time (e.g. five to fifteen years), the actual end-point depending on one's good behaviour and the decision of a parole board. In the event, parole seems something of an illusion, at least for those prisoners who write their memoirs. The arbitrary stupidities of the prison rules, the kneejerk cruelties of the time-serving nonentities invariably appointed to parole boards, the efforts of one's fellow inmates to blot a copybook that is hard enough to keep unsullied on one's own: all this militates against these premature exits.

But it can be done. The American *copper*, which usually means a policeman, can also mean in the 20th century good behaviour during the sentence and, in the 1940s, parole. For the rhyming slangsters of Britain, parole is *jam roll*. If achieved in contemporary America, it is **outside time**, since one is still technically 'doing time' and as such faced by a wide range of petty rules, or the *tail* (i.e. of one's sentence).

To Get Parole

In contemporary America, to become an *early riser*, that is one who is released on parole, and to *get paid*, i.e. receive a favourable outcome at one's parole hearing, it is necessary to *make* by gaining the paper 'ticket-of-leave' that proves that one has been properly released. This document has been known since the 1910s as one's *pink slip*, a term also used of the paperwork that proves ownership of a car; to be *on paper* is to be on parole. Throughout the 20th century and beyond, the *get-up* has been the official date of one's release as given by a parole board. Returning to contemporary America, to leave the prison, whether as a fully free individual or on licence, is to *raise up* and *coffee-break parole* (so called because it is granted very quickly) is a nickname for a Special Circumstances release. Not strictly a parolee, but one who enjoys day release for study purposes, is a *bookrunner*; they and other ex-inmates may find themselves in an *outhouse*, a 'half-way house' or hostel in which newly released prisoners or parolees can learn to reacclimatise them-selves to the 'real' world. A pardon or discharge certificate given to a convict in mid-20th-century America was an *Annie Oakley*, named after the markswoman Annie Oakley (Phoebe Ann Mozee Butler, 1860–1926); the holes punched in such tickets supposedly resembled the aces out of which Ms Oakley would shoot the pips.

To Be Denied Parole

Despite the possibility of early release, the fact is that the denial of parole is somewhat more likely. The rejection itself has been a *flop* in America since the 1930s or, in modern Britain, a *knockback* or *k.b.* The most recent coinage is a *dump*. Two previous terms are the *blank* of the 1920s and *shoot down*, from 1960s America; most of the terms are used outside prison too. The traditional parole has been administered by a human agent; more recently he or she has been backed up by technology – the phrase *on tag* is used of a parolee wearing an electronic tag on their ankle as a condition of parole.

To Forfeit Parole

Hard to get, easy to lose, parole is often forfeited before it has been worked off. The primary term is **violate**, a 1950s coinage meaning to lose one's parole for a violation of the rules and to be returned to prison. The prisoner who first gains parole and then returns to the same prison after breaking the terms of that parole or committing a new crime is a **flip-flop** (from *flip-flop*, a somersault), and his revoked parole is a **brief**.

Release

A **chuck-up** in Britain since the late 19th century, in America a release has been a **gate** since the 1920s, although it is more usually found in its associated terms: to be **gatey**, or suffering from **gate fever**, is to be experiencing pre-release nerves (also known as **short-time pains**). **Gate money** was the small sum of money given to American prisoners on release, more recently known as a **pay-off**. An informal version of this was the late 19th-century **break**, a collection of cash taken among the friends of a British prisoner who was either awaiting trial or had been recently discharged.

One of the most popular terms for being released is the 20th-century verb to **spring**. The 'springing' may be done by the governor, but equally well may come from one's legal team or even a band of confederates who help one to escape. The 1920s use of **flag** suggests that the prison authorities are waving a white one, in effect surrendering the prisoner to their freedom. From the 1950s in America to be **on the pavement/bricks** has meant to be set free, although in other contexts it can mean working as a professional villain, especially an armed robber. Once released one is **buckshee**, a 1930s American word that plays on the term's usual meaning: free (of charge). It comes from the Persian *baksheesh*, a gift or present and thus a tip. **Killing one's number** is among the more recent terms. It refers to completing a sentence and requiring no further parole supervision; in this case one's prisoner number is 'dead'.

Freedom

Verbs meaning to release or to be released include:
cut loose   1950s to present, America
flag   1920s, America
get one's hat   1950s, America
give someone their hat   1950s, America
hit the pavement   1930s to present
raise   1970s, America
roll (someone) out   1990s to present, America
ship (someone) out   1920s to present
sing the hallelujah chorus   1990s to present, America
   (also means to die in prison)
spill   1920s, America
spring   20th century to present
street   1960s, America
unhook   1950s

Every sentence has what one might term its 'last rites'. Setting aside the nerves mentioned above, one gets one's **brekkie** or **brek**, the final breakfast that is one's last meal as a captive, used since the 1980s in Britain. In Canada the phrase is — **and a coffee** (as in 'sixteen days and a coffee left to serve'), the equivalent of America's — **and a wake-up**. These refer to the last half-day of one's sentence, when a prisoner has a final breakfast but is released before all other meals. It is then necessary to observe certain bureaucratic and administrative procedures before one can actually set foot back in the world: these are known in contemporary America as the **merry-go-round**. Equally unwanted and a good deal more painful was the late 19th-century **bashing-out**, the beating administered to a departing prisoner; they had already undergone a **bashing-in** on the day of their arrival.

Once on the street the modern American prisoner wants to **recoup**, which like the standard meaning refers to getting back something one has lost – in this case several years of one's life. Less positive, but perhaps more likely, is the contemporary Australian term **backdoor** (taken from the adulterous *back-door man*), which is for one prisoner – just released – to celebrate his freedom by cuckolding one who remains inside.

INDEX

bad dough 18
bad fall 262
bad paper 18, 336
bad-papered 19
bad rap 264
bad time 283
badge 238
badgeman 333
badger 98, 223
badger game 219
badger moll 219
badger-man 219
bag 141, 163
bag bride 164
bag-chasing 164
bag man 163
bag-swinger 197
bag-thief 100
bag up 164
baggage-man 71
bagger 100
baggy-arse 327
baghead 164
Bahamas 348
bail up 268
bail up! bale up! 120
bake 267
baker 302
balance 16
ball 350
baller 153
balloon 164
balmy 342
bananas 251
banco man 13
band 185
bandbox 323
bandera 155
bandog 242
bang 86
banger 153
banging 153
banging shop 211
bangle 266
bangtail 186
bank 86, 348
bank off 348
bankman 110
bankroll 36
baptist 58
bar 167

barbecue 344
barber 195
barfly 199
bark 258
barker 134
barking iron 134
Barnaby Rudge 278
barnacle 4
barnard's law 6
barrel house 209
base 166
bash artist 328
basher 200
bashing-out 363
Baskerville 257
baster 96
Bastille, the 317
Bastille by the Bay 318
bat 181, 286
bat carrier 254
bat-fowling 5
bat house 181
bat of Venus 181
Bate's Farm 317
bato loco 148
batter 200
battler 201
bawdy-house bottle 210
bawdy-ken 210
bawl 270
beak 278
beak-hunter 90
beak-runner 278
beaker-hauler 90
beaksman 278
beaky 278
beanery 350
beanie 142
bear 242
beard-jammer 225
bearer-up 223
beast 242
beast wagon 242
beastboy/beastman 242
beat 14, 86, 282
beat a trick 204
beat-basher 245
beat off 86
beat-pounder 245
beat the rap 264, 282
beater 14

beauman-prig 82
beaver palace 213
beavertail 142
bebop 149
bed-faggot 194
bed-house 209
bed-presser 194
Bedfordshire woman 194
beef 263
beef baby 263
beefer 261
beetle 238
beetle-crusher 245
beggar's lagging 287
behave factory 313
behind the ramp 327
belcher 260
belcher fogle 64
belcher wipe 65
belfa/bilfa 193
belfry 274
bellies in blue 237
bellowsed 307
bellswagger 222
belly-ache 274
belly gun 135
bend 87
bend over 271
bene faker 42
bene hooker boy 80
benfeaker of gybes 42
Bengal lancers 140
benny worker 63
bent copper 251
bernice/bernies 166
bessie 141
betty bangles 236
Betty Blue 236
BG 153
b'hoy 145
bice/byce 289
bid 284
biddy 240
big bag 163
big bird 165
big bit 285
big boy 132, 153
big cutor 277
big daddy 225
big fellow 322, 324
big finger 324

germ 356
German 162
Gestapo 150, 244
get a hard-on 139
get down 156
get it all 294
get jammed 156
get off 88
get off the gate 156
get one's hat 363
get one's head down 274
get paid 361
get real 156
get the glory 285
get the juice 302
get the knickers 294
get toasted 302
get-up 361
ghost-train 336
ghosting 336
ghoul 38
gig 254
gig shop 211
gigger 326
gilt-dubber 94
ginger 202, 238
ginger-cake 202
ginger girl 202
ginger-pop 240
girl of the town 193
girl shop 212
girlery 212
give up 253, 255
gladiator camp 323
glass 100
glazier 94
gleaner 83
gleep 89
glim-dropping 23
glom 86, 268
glue 81, 268
glueneck 195
gluepot 195
go bent 329
go beyond 307
go-boy 358
go bush 358
go commercial 199
go down the steps 273
go over 307
go to foreign parts 307

go wrong 254
goatmilker/goatsucker 190
gobble 86
going-over 267
gold-badge man 238
gold brick game 17
gold-dropping 22
goldfish 267
gone 156
gonnofing 84
gonsel/gonsil 258
gooby 349
good girl 193
good one 193
good time 283
goods, the 106
goofball 170
goose shearer 5
gooseberry 86
goosefoot 248
goosie 185
goosing ranch 211
gopher 110
Gophers 144
gorilla pimp 228
gouge game 11
government signpost 296
Governor Green 358
gow 158, 265
grab 246, 268
grab-and-flee 47
grabber 60
grad 312
graft 15, 88
graft china 355
grafter 15, 56
grafting 168
grande horizontale 199
granny 33
grass 160, 261
grass-eater 251
grasshopper 240
graze on the corn 349
grease patty 351
grease pit 159
grease pot 351
greasy fingers 61
greefo 160
Greek 7
green 33, 160
green-baggish 277

green bean 238
green goods game 21
green-goose fair 185
green hornet 238
green room 302
greeney 332
greenfly 238
griff 93
grift 15, 84
grind joint 210
grinding house 210
grip 268
grit 334
groaner 61
grouse 356
growler 337
Gruesome Gertie 302
grunter 189, 242
G-smack 244
G-ster 152
G-thang 152
gudgeon 8
guinea hen 185
gull-groper 5
gum 158
gumshoe 97, 250
gumshoe worker 97, 253
gun 57, 84, 86, 136, 181
gun bull 328
gun gang 328
gun moll 136
gun-up 156
guness 84
gunji 234
gunner 84
gunsel 258
gyp 11, 83, 89
gypsy 200
Gypsy Jokers 150

H 166
hack 247, 328
hacker 328
haircut 287
half/halfie 170
half-hitch 85
half-inch 85, 268
half-piece 169
half-quarter/h.q. 171
half-snacks 108